Real-Time Systems

Theory and Practice

Real-Time Systems
Theory and Practice

RAJIB MALL
Professor
Department of Computer Science and Engineering
Indian Institute of Technology Kharagpur
India

 Pearson

ISBN 978-81-317-0069-3

First Impression, 2006

Published by Pearson India Education Services Pvt. Ltd, CIN: U72200TN2005PTC057128.

Head Office: 1st Floor, Berger Tower, Plot No. C-001A/2, Sector 16B, Noida – 201 301, Uttar Pradesh, India

Registered Office: Featherlite, 'The Address' 5th Floor, Survey No 203/10B, 200 Ft MMRD Road, Zamin Pallavaram, Chennai - 600044
Phone: 044-66540100
Website: in.pearson.com, Email: companysecretary.india@pearson.com

Printer : Manipal Technologies Limited, Manipal

Contents

List of Figures

Preface

This book has taken shape while teaching real-time systems subject to the undergraduate and postgraduate students at IIT, Kharagpur, over the last decade. Each time I taught the subject, I acutely felt the necessity of a textbook that could be closely followed by the students and the teacher. In the absence of a textbook which I could follow, I had to do elaborate writing on the board and also give regular handouts to the students. This not only reduced the effectiveness of teaching, but the students were at a loss when they missed a class. I am sure my colleagues in other institutions in India and abroad would share my sentiments.

In a subject like real-time systems where there is no standard textbook, I had to dynamically evolve the contents of my teaching over the years based primarily on students' feedback, industry and technology trends, my increased understanding of the subject, and also on the new literature that became available every year.

Over my decade-long teaching of the subject, I have seen the student interest grow rapidly every year (as reflected by the number of course registrants)—driven primarily by its increased importance, and growth, and career opportunities that are available in this area.

The students intending to go through this book are expected to be familiar with first-level courses on operating systems, computer architecture, programming, computer communication, and database management systems. However, to reduce the hardship on the students who have lost touch with the first-level courses, I have tried to introduce concepts *ab initio* wherever possible, without unduly diluting the intended objective of this book. A few terms which could not be conveniently explained in the text have been explained in the glossary.

In the text, I have taken the liberty to use 'he'/'his' to actually mean both the genders. This has been done only to increase readability rather than with the intent of any bias.

I gratefully acknowledge the effort of several of my students who have contributed to this book in various ways—from raising thought-provoking questions in the class, to word processing some of the topics we discussed, proof reading several versions of the manuscript, and investigating some of the issues which were not addressed in the standard literature. The students who helped me in my effort to write this book are too numerous to be named individually. However, I must at least acknowledge Rakesh Tripathy, Ankur Jain, Chinmay Singh, Siddhartha Brahma, and Anshuman Jain. I must thank Thomas Mathew Rajesh, Editor, Pearson Education, for pestering me to complete the manuscript as early as possible and his invaluable help at all stages of publication.

Finally, I must thank my wife Prabina and daughter Mithi for all their encouragement to go ahead with this book. Without their constant encouragement and permission to spend extra hours at work, this book could never have been complete.

Typographical and other errors and comments should be reported to the author at rajib@cse.iitkgp.ernet.in or prof_r_mall@yahoo.com

RAJIB MALL

1 Introduction

Commercial usage of computer dates back to a little over 50 years. This brief period can be roughly divided into mainframe, PC, and post-PC eras of computing. The mainframe era was marked by expensive computers that were quite unaffordable by individuals, and each computer served a large number of users. The PC era saw the emergence of affordable desktops that could be used by individual users. The post-PC era is seeing the emergence of small and portable computers, and computers embedded in everyday applications, making an individual interact with several computers everyday.

In the first two computing eras, real-time and embedded computing applications were rather rare and restricted to a few specialized applications such as space and defence. In the post-PC era of computing, the use of computer systems based on real-time and embedded technologies has already touched every facet of our life and is still growing at an unprecedented pace. While embedded processing and Internet-enabled devices have now captured everyone's imagination, they are just a small fraction of applications that have been made possible by real-time systems. If we casually look around us, we can discover several of them—they are often camouflaged inside simple looking devices. If we observe carefully, we can notice that several gadgets and applications which have today become indispensable to our every day life, are in fact based on embedded real-time systems. For example, we have ubiquitous consumer products such as digital cameras, cell phones, microwave ovens, camcorders, video game sets; telecommunication domain products and applications such as set-top boxes, cable modems, voice over IP (VoIP), and video conferencing applications; office products such as fax machines, laser printers, and security systems. Besides, we encounter real-time systems in hospitals in the form of medical instrumentation equipments and imaging systems. There are also a large number of equipments and gadgets based on real-time systems which though we normally do not use directly, but are nevertheless still important to our daily life. A few examples of such systems are Internet routers, base stations in cellular systems, industrial plant automation systems, and industrial robots.

It can be easily inferred from the above discussion that in recent times real-time computers have become ubiquitous and have permeated a large number of application areas. At present, the computers used in real-time applications vastly outnumber the computers that are being used in conventional applications. According to an estimate [22], 70% of all processors manufactured worldwide are deployed in real-time embedded applications. While it is already true that an overwhelming majority of all processors being manufactured are getting deployed in real-time applications, what is more remarkable is the unmistakable trend of steady rise in the fraction of all processors manufactured worldwide finding their way to real-time applications.

Some of the reasons attributable to the phenomenal growth in the use of real-time systems in the recent years are the manifold reductions in the size and the cost of the computers, coupled with the magical improvements to their performance. The availability of computers at rapidly falling prices, reduced weight, shrinking sizes, and increasing processing power have together contributed to the present scenario. Applications which not too far back were considered prohibitively expensive to automate, can now be affordably automated. For instance, when the cost of microprocessors ran into lakhs, they were considered too expensive to be put inside a washing machine; but when they cost only a few hundred rupees, their use makes commercial sense.

The rapid growth of applications deploying real-time technologies has been matched by the evolutionary growth of the underlying technologies supporting the development of real-time systems. In this book, we discuss some of the core technologies used in developing real-time systems. However, we restrict ourselves to software issues and keep hardware discussions to bare minimum. The software issues that we address are quite expansive—we discuss the operating system and program development issues, as well as networking and database issues.

In this chapter, we restrict ourselves to some introductory and fundamental issues. In the next three chapters, we discuss some core theories underlying the development of practical real-time and embedded systems. In the subsequent chapter, we discuss some important features of commercial real-time operating systems. After that, we shift our attention to real-time communication technologies and databases.

1.1 WHAT IS REAL TIME?

Real time is a quantitative notion of time and is measured using a physical (real) clock. Whenever we quantify time using a physical clock, we deal with real time. An example use of this quantitative notion of time can be observed in a description of an automated chemical plant. Consider this: When the temperature of the chemical reaction chamber attains a certain predetermined temperature, say 250°C, the system automatically switches off the heater within a predetermined time interval, say within 30 mSec. In this description of a part of the behaviour of a chemical plant, the time value that was referred to denotes the readings of some physical clock present in the plant automation system.

In contrast to real time, **logical time** (also known as virtual time) deals with a qualitative notion of time and is expressed using event ordering relations such as before, after, sometimes, eventually, precedes, succeeds, etc. While dealing with logical time, time readings from a physical clock are not necessary for ordering the events. As an example, consider the following part of the behaviour of a library automation software used to automate the bookkeeping activities of a college library: "After a *query book* command is given by the user, details of all matching books are displayed by the software." In this example, the events "issue of query book command" and "display of results" are logically ordered in terms of which events follow the other. But, no quantitative expression of time was required. Clearly, this example behaviour is devoid of any real-time considerations. We are now in a position to define what is a real-time system:

> A system is called a **real-time system**, when we need quantitative expression of time (i.e., real time) to describe the behaviour of the system.

Remember that in this definition of a real-time system, it is implicit that all quantitative time measurements are carried out using a physical clock. A chemical plant, whose part behaviour description is—when temperature of the reaction chamber attains certain predetermined temperature value, say 250°C, the system automatically switches off the heater within say 30 mSec—is clearly a real-time system. It should, however, be remembered that both the computer system and the controlled system (environment) use the same time scale. So far our examples were restricted to the description of partial behaviour of systems. The complete behaviour of a system can be described by listing its response to various external stimuli. It may be noted that all the clauses in the description of the behaviour of a real-time system need not involve quantitative measures of time. That is, large parts of a description of the behaviour of a system may not have any quantitative expressions of time at all, and still qualify as a real-time system. Any system whose behaviour can completely be described without using any quantitative expression of time is not a real-time system.

1.2 APPLICATIONS OF REAL-TIME SYSTEMS

Real-time systems have of late, found applications in wide-ranging areas. In the following, we list some of the prominent areas of application of real-time systems and in each identified case, we discuss a few example applications in some detail. The list would become very vast if we try to exhaustively list all areas of applications of real-time systems. We have, therefore, restricted our list to only a handful of areas, and out of these we have explained only a few selected applications. We have pointed out the quantitative notions of time used in the discussed applications. The examples we present are important to our subsequent discussions and would be referred to in the later chapters whenever required.

Industrial Applications: Industrial applications constitute a major usage area of real-time systems. A few examples of industrial applications of real-time systems are: process control systems, industrial automation systems, SCADA applications, test and measurement equipment, and robotic equipment.

Example 1: Chemical Plant Control

Chemical plant control systems are essentially a type of process control application. In an automated chemical plant, a real-time computer periodically monitors plant conditions. The plant conditions are determined based on current readings of pressure, temperature, and chemical concentration of the reaction chamber. These parameters are sampled periodically. Based on the values sampled at any time, the automation system decides on the corrective actions necessary at that instant to maintain the chemical reaction at a certain rate. Each time the plant conditions are sampled, the automation system should decide on the exact instantaneous corrective actions required such as changing the pressure, temperature, or chemical concentration and carry out these actions within certain predefined time bounds. Typically, the time bounds in such a chemical plant control application range from a few microseconds to several milliseconds.

Example 2: Automated Car Assembly Plant

An automated car assembly plant is an example of a plant automation system. In an automated car assembly plant, the work product (partially assembled car) moves on a conveyor belt (see Fig. 1.1). Alongside the conveyor belt, several workstations are placed. Each workstation performs some specific work on the product such as fitting engine, fitting door, fitting wheel, and spray painting the car, etc. as it moves on the conveyor belt. An empty chassis is introduced near the first workstation on the conveyor belt. A fully assembled car comes out after the work

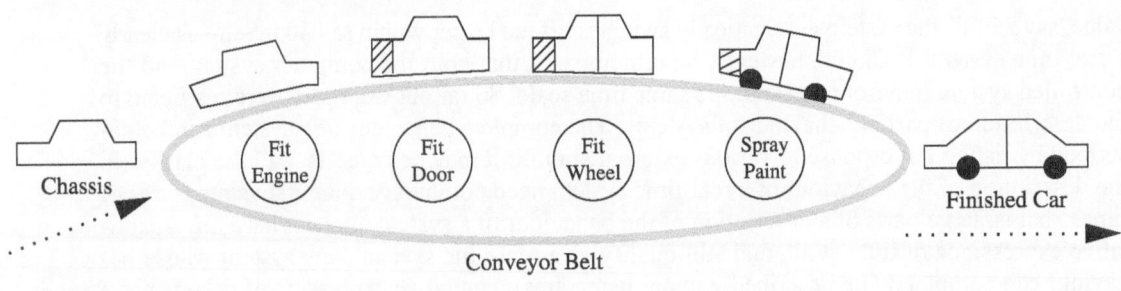

▲ **FIGURE 1.1**

Schematic Representation of an Automated Car Assembly Plant

product goes past all the workstations. At each workstation, a sensor senses the arrival of the next partially assembled product. As soon as the partially assembled product is sensed, the workstation begins to perform its work on the work product. The time constraint imposed on the workstation computer is that the workstation must complete its work before the work product moves away to the next workstation. The time bounds involved here are typically of the order of a few hundreds of milliseconds.

Example 3: Supervisory Control and Data Acquisition (SCADA)

SCADA are a category of distributed control systems being used in many industries. A SCADA system helps monitor and control a large number of distributed events of interest. In SCADA systems, sensors are scattered at various geographic locations to collect raw data (called events of interest). These data are then processed and stored in a real-time database. The database models (or reflects) the current state of the environment and is updated frequently to make it a realistic model of the up-to-date state of the environment. An example of a SCADA application is an Energy Management System (EMS). An EMS helps to carry out load balancing in an electrical energy distribution network. It senses the energy consumption at the distribution points and computes the load across different phases of power supply. It also helps dynamically balance the load. Another example of a SCADA system is a system that monitors and controls traffic in a computer network. Depending on the sensed load in different segments of the network, the SCADA system makes the router change its traffic routing policy dynamically. The time constraint in such a SCADA application is that the sensors must sense the system state at regular intervals (say, every few milliseconds) and the same must be processed before the next state is sensed.

Medical: A few examples of medical applications of real-time systems are: robots, MRI scanners, radiation therapy equipment, bedside monitors, and Computerized Axial Tomography (CAT).

Example 4: Robot Used in Recovery of Displaced Radioactive Material

Robots have become very popular nowadays and are being used in a wide variety of medical applications. An application that we discuss here is a robot used in retrieving displaced radioactive materials. Radioactive materials such as cobalt and radium are used for treatment of cancer. At times during treatment, the radioactive cobalt (or radium) gets dislocated and falls. Since human beings can not come near a radioactive material, a robot is used to restore the radioactive material to its proper position. The robot walks into the room containing the radioactive material, picks it up, and restores it to its proper position. The robot has to sense its environment frequently and based on this information, plan its path. The real-time constraint on the path planning task of the robot is that unless it plans the path fast enough after an obstacle is detected, it may collide with it. The time constraints involved here are of the order of a few milliseconds.

Peripheral Equipment: A few examples of peripheral equipment that contain embedded real-time systems are: laser printers, digital copiers, fax machines, digital cameras, and scanners.

Example 5: Laser Printer

Most laser printers have powerful microprocessors embedded in them to control different activities associated with printing. The important activities that a microprocessor embedded in a laser printer performs include: getting data from the communication port(s), typesetting fonts, sensing paper jams, noticing when the printer runs out of paper, sensing when the user presses a button on the control panel, and displaying various messages to the user. The most complex activity that the microprocessor performs is driving the laser engine. The basic command that a laser engine supports is to put a black dot on the paper. However, the laser engine has no idea about the exact shapes of different fonts, font sizes, italic, underlining, boldface, etc. that it may be asked to print. The embedded microprocessor receives print commands on its input port and determines how the dots can be composed to achieve the desired document and manages printing the exact shapes through a series of dot commands issued to the laser engine. The time constraints involved here are of the order of a few milliseconds.

Automotive and Transportation: A few examples of automotive and transportation applications of real-time systems are: automotive engine control systems, road traffic signal control, air-traffic control, high-speed train control, car navigation systems, and MPFI engine control systems.

Example 6: Multi-Point Fuel Injection (MPFI) System

An MPFI system is an automotive engine control system. A conceptual diagram of a car embedding an MPFI system is shown in Fig. 1.2. An MPFI is a real-time system that controls the rate of fuel injection and allows the engine to operate at its optimal efficiency. In older models of cars, a mechanical device called the carburettor was used to control the fuel

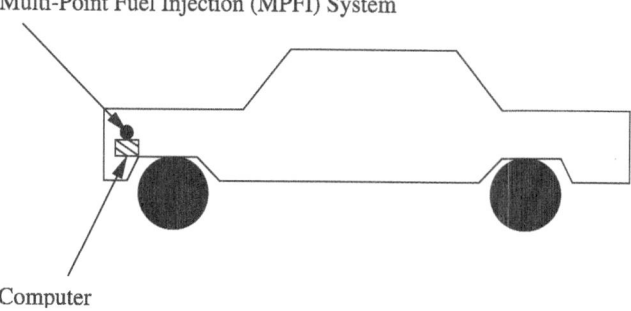

Multi-Point Fuel Injection (MPFI) System

Computer

▲ **FIGURE 1.2**

A Real-Time System Embedded in an MPFI Car

injection rate to the engine. It was the responsibility of the carburettor to vary the fuel injection rate depending on the current speed of the vehicle and the desired acceleration. Careful experiments have suggested that for optimal energy output, the required fuel injection rate is highly nonlinear with respect to the vehicle speed and acceleration. Also, experimental results show that the precise fuel injection through multiple points is more effective than single point injection. In MPFI engines, the precise fuel injection rate at each injection point is determined by a computer. An MPFI system injects fuel into individual cylinders resulting in better 'power balance' among the cylinders as well as higher output from each one along with faster throttle response. The processor primarily controls the ignition timing and the quantity of fuel to be injected. The latter is achieved by controlling the duration for which the injector valve is open—popularly known as *pulse width*. The actions of the processor are determined by the data gleaned from sensors located all over the engine. These sensors constantly monitor the ambient temperature, the engine coolant temperature, exhaust temperature, emission gas contents, engine rpm (speed), vehicle road speed, crankshaft position, camshaft position, etc. An MPFI engine with even an 8-bit computer does a much better job of determining an accurate fuel injection rate for given values of speed and acceleration compared to a carburettor-based system. An MPFI system not only makes a vehicle more fuel efficient, it also minimizes pollution by reducing partial combustion.

Telecommunication Applications: A few example uses of real-time systems in telecommunication applications are: cellular systems, video conferencing, and cable modems.

Example 7: A Cellular System
Cellular systems have become a very popular means of mobile communication. A cellular system usually maps a city into cells. In each cell, a base station monitors the mobile handsets present in the cell. Besides, the base station performs several tasks such as locating a user, sending and receiving control messages to a handset, keeping track of call details for billing purposes, and hand-off of calls as the mobile moves. Call hand-off is required when a mobile moves away from a base station. As a mobile moves away, its Received Signal Strength (RSS) falls at the base station. The base station monitors this and as soon as the RSS falls below a certain threshold value, it hands-off the details of the ongoing call of the mobile to the base station of the cell to which the mobile has moved. The hand-off must be completed within a sufficiently small predefined time interval so that the user does not feel any temporary disruption of service during the hand-off. Typically, call hand-off is required to be achieved within a few milliseconds.

Aerospace: A few important uses of real-time systems in aerospace applications are: avionics, flight simulation, airline cabin management systems, satellite tracking systems, and computer on-board an aircraft.

Example 8: Computer On-Board an Aircraft
In many modern aircraft, the pilot can select an "auto pilot" option. As soon as the pilot switches to the "auto pilot" mode, an on-board computer takes over all controls of the aircraft including navigation, take-off, and landing of the aircraft. In the "auto pilot" mode, the computer periodically samples velocity and acceleration of the aircraft. From the sampled data, the on-board computer computes X, Y, and Z co-ordinates of the current aircraft position and compares them with the prespecified track data. Before the next sample values are obtained, it computes the deviation from the specified track values and takes any corrective actions that may be necessary. In this case, the sampling of the various parameters, and their processing need to be completed within a few microseconds.

Internet and Multimedia Applications: Important uses of real-time systems in multimedia and Internet applications include: video conferencing and multimedia multicast, Internet routers and switches.

Example 9: Video Conferencing

In a video conferencing application, video and audio signals are generated by cameras and microphones, respectively. The data are sampled at a certain prespecified frame rate. These are then compressed and sent as packets to the receiver over a network. At the receiver-end, packets are ordered, decompressed, and then played. The time constraint at the receiver-end is that the receiver must process and play the received frames at a predetermined constant rate. Thus, if 30 frames are to be shown every minute, once a frame play-out is complete, the next frame must be played within 2 sec.

Consumer Electronics: Consumer electronics area is replete with numerous applications of real-time systems. A few sample applications of real-time systems in consumer electronics are: set-top boxes, audio equipment, Internet telephony, microwave ovens, intelligent washing machines, home security systems, air conditioning and refrigeration, toys, and cell phones.

Example 10: Cell Phones

Cell phones are possibly the fastest growing segment of consumer electronics. A cell phone at any point of time carries out a number of tasks simultaneously. These include: converting input voice to digital signals by deploying Digital Signal Processing (DSP) techniques, converting electrical signals generated by the microphone to output voice signals, and sampling incoming base station signals in the control channel. A cell phone responds to the communications received from the base station within certain specified time bounds. For example, a base station might command a cell phone to switch the ongoing communication to a specific frequency. The cell phone must comply with such commands from the base station within a few milliseconds.

Defence Applications: Typical defence applications of real-time systems include: missile guidance systems, anti-missile systems, satellite-based surveillance systems.

Example 11: Missile Guidance System

A guided missile is one that is capable of sensing the target and homes onto it. Homing becomes easy when the target emits either electrical or thermal radiation. In a missile guidance system, missile guidance is achieved by a computer mounted on the missile. The mounted computer computes the deviation from the required trajectory and effects track changes of the missile to guide it onto the target. The time constraint on the computer-based guidance system is that the sensing and the track correction tasks must be activated frequently enough to keep the missile from straying from the target. The target sensing and track correction tasks are typically required to be completed within a few hundreds of microseconds or even lesser time depending on the speed of the missile and the type of the target.

Miscellaneous Applications: Besides the areas of applications already discussed, real-time systems have found numerous other applications in our every day life. An example of such an application is a railway reservation system.

Example 12: Railway Reservation System

In a railway reservation system, a central repository maintains up-to-date data on the booking status of various trains. Ticket booking counters are distributed across different geographic locations. Customers queue up at different booking counters and submit their reservation requests. After a reservation request is made at a counter, it normally takes only a few seconds for the system to confirm the reservation and print the ticket. A real-time constraint in this application is that once a request is made to the computer, it must print the ticket or display the seat unavailability message before the average human response time (about 20 sec) expires, so that the customers do not notice any delay and get a feeling of having obtained instant results. However, as we discuss a little later (in Section 1.6), this application is an example of a category of applications that is in some aspects different from the other discussed applications. For example, even if the results are produced just after 20 sec, nothing untoward is going to happen—this may not be the case with the other discussed applications.

1.3 A BASIC MODEL OF A REAL-TIME SYSTEM

We have already pointed out that this book confines itself to the software issues in real-time systems. However, in order to be able to see the software issues in a proper perspective, we need to have a basic conceptual understanding of the underlying hardware. Therefore, in this section we try to develop a broad understanding of the high-level issues of the underlying hardware in a real-time system. For a more detailed study of the underlying hardware issues, we refer the reader to [8]. Figure 1.3 shows a simple model of a real-time system in terms of its important functional blocks. Unless otherwise mentioned, all our subsequent discussions would implicitly assume such a model. Observe that in Fig. 1.3, the sensors are interfaced with the input conditioning block, which, in turn, is connected to the input interface. The output interface, output conditioning, and the actuator are interfaced in a complementary manner. In the following, we briefly describe the roles of the different functional blocks of a real-time system:

Sensor.   A sensor converts some physical characteristic of its environment into electrical signals. An example of a sensor is a photo-voltaic cell which converts light energy into electrical energy. A wide variety of temperature and pressure sensors are also used. Typically, a temperature sensor operates on the principle of a **thermocouple**. Temperature sensors based on

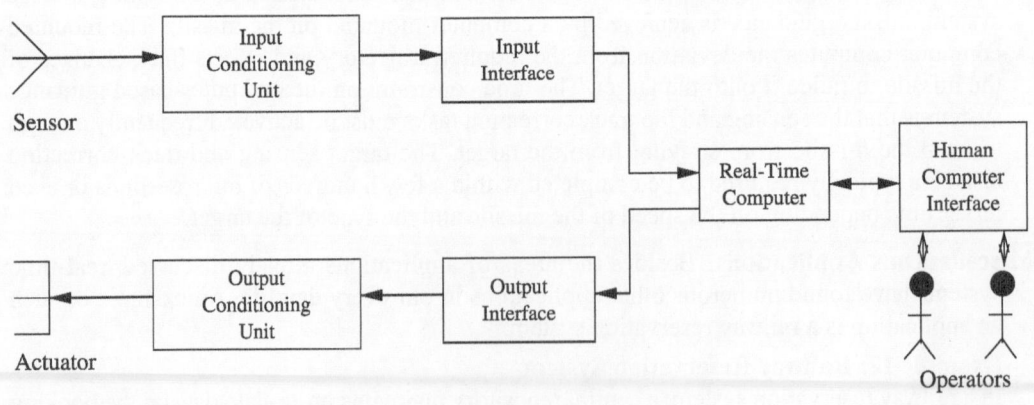

▲ **FIGURE 1.3**

A Model of a Real-Time System

many other physical principles also exist. For example, one type of temperature sensor employs the principle of variation of electrical resistance with temperature (called a *varistor*). A pressure sensor typically operates on the *piezoelectricity* principle. Pressure sensors based on other physical principles also exist.

Actuator.   An actuator is any device that takes its inputs from the output interface of a computer and converts these electrical signals into some physical actions on its environment. The physical actions may be in the form of motion, change of thermal, electrical, pneumatic, or physical characteristics of some objects. A popular actuator is a motor. Heaters are also very commonly used. Besides, several hydraulic and pneumatic actuators are also popular.

Signal Conditioning Units.   The electrical signals produced by a computer can rarely be used to directly drive an actuator. The computer signals usually need conditioning before they can be used by the actuator. This is termed *output conditioning*. Similarly, input conditioning is required to be carried out on sensor signals before they can be accepted by the computer. For example, analog signals generated by a photo-voltaic cell are normally in the millivolts range and need to be conditioned before they can be processed by a computer. The following are some important types of conditioning carried out on raw signals generated by sensors and digital signals generated by computers:

1. **Voltage Amplification:** Voltage amplification is normally required to be carried out to match the full-scale sensor voltage output with the full-scale voltage input to the interface of a computer. For example, a sensor might produce voltage in the millivolts range, whereas the input interface of a computer may require the input signal level to be of the order of a volt.

2. **Voltage Level Shifting:** Voltage level shifting is often required to align the voltage level generated by a sensor with that acceptable to the computer. For example, a sensor may produce voltage in the range -0.5 to $+0.5$ volt, whereas the input interface of the computer may accept voltage only in the range of 0 to 1 volt. In this case, the sensor voltage must undergo level shifting before it can be used by the computer.

3. **Frequency Range Shifting and Filtering:** Frequency range shifting is often used to reduce the noise components in a signal. Various types of noise occur in narrow bands and the signal must be shifted from the noise bands so that noise can be filtered out.

4. **Signal Mode Conversion:** A type of signal mode conversion that is frequently carried out during signal conditioning involves changing direct current into alternating current and vice versa. Another type of signal mode conversion frequently used is conversion of analog signals to a constant amplitude pulse train such that the pulse rate or pulse width is proportional to the voltage level. Conversion of analog signals to a pulse train is often necessary for input to systems such as **transformer coupled circuits** that do not pass direct current.

Interface Unit.   Normally, commands from the CPU are delivered to the actuator through an output interface. An output interface converts the stored voltage into analog form and then outputs this to the actuator circuitry. This would require the value generated to be written on a register (see Fig. 1.4). In order to produce an analog output, in an output interface, the CPU selects a data register of the output interface and writes the necessary data to it. The two main functional blocks of an output interface are shown in Fig. 1.4. The interface takes care of the

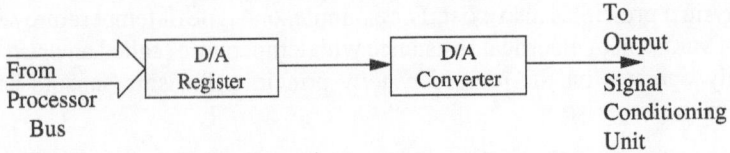

▲ **FIGURE 1.4**

An Output Interface

buffering and the handshake control aspects. Analog to digital conversion is frequently deployed in an input interface. Similarly, digital to analog conversion is frequently used in an output interface.

In the following, we discuss the important steps of Analog to Digital Signal Conversion (ADC).

Analog to Digital Conversion.   Digital computers can not process analog signals. Therefore, analog signals need to be converted to digital form using a circuitry whose block diagram is shown in Fig. 1.7. Using that block diagram, analog signals are normally converted to digital form through the following two main steps:

- Sample the analog signal (shown in Fig. 1.5) at regular intervals. This sampling can be done by a capacitor circuitry that stores the voltage levels. The stored voltage level can be discretized. After sampling the analog signal (shown in Fig. 1.5), a step waveform as shown in Fig. 1.6 is obtained.

- Convert the stored value to a binary number by using an ADC as shown in Fig. 1.7, and store the digital value in a register.

Digital to analog conversion can be carried out through a complementary set of operations. We leave it as an exercise to the reader to figure out the details of the circuitry that can perform the Digital to Analog Conversion (DAC).

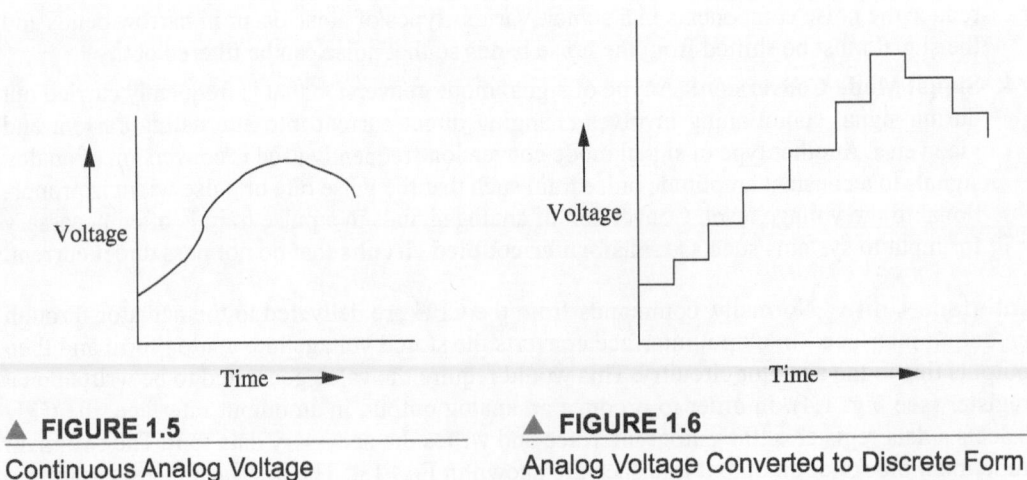

▲ **FIGURE 1.5**

Continuous Analog Voltage

▲ **FIGURE 1.6**

Analog Voltage Converted to Discrete Form

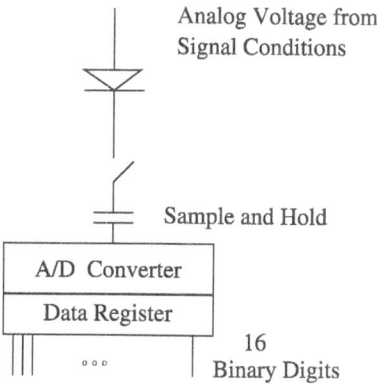

Analog Voltage from
Signal Conditions

Sample and Hold

A/D Converter

Data Register

16
Binary Digits

▲ **FIGURE 1.7**

Conversion of an Analog Signal to a 16-bit Binary Number

1.4 CHARACTERISTICS OF REAL-TIME SYSTEMS

We now discuss a few key characteristics of real-time systems that distinguish it from non-real-time systems. However, the reader may note that all the discussed characteristics may not be applicable to every real-time system. Real-time systems cover such an enormous range of applications and products that a generalization of the characteristics into a set that is applicable to each and every system is difficult. Different categories of real-time systems may exhibit the characteristics that we identify to different extents or may not even exhibit some of the characteristics at all.

1. **Time Constraints:** Every real-time task is associated with some time constraints. One very common form of time constraints is deadlines associated with tasks. A task deadline specifies the time before which the task must complete and produce the results. Other types of timing constraints are delay and duration (see Section 1.7). It is the responsibility of the Real-Time Operating System (RTOS) to ensure that all tasks meet their respective time constraints. In later chapters we shall examine how an RTOS can ensure that tasks meet their respective timing constraints through appropriate task scheduling strategies.

2. **New Correctness Criterion:** The notion of correctness in real-time systems is different from that used in the context of traditional systems. In real-time systems, correctness implies not only logical correctness of the results, but the time at which the results are produced is important. A logically correct result produced after the deadline would be considered an incorrect result.

3. **Embedded:** A vast majority of real-time systems are embedded in nature [22]. An embedded computer system is physically "embedded" in its environment and often controls it. Figure 1.8 shows a schematic representation of an embedded system. As shown in Fig. 1.8, the sensors of the real-time computer collect data from the environment, pass them on to the real-time computer for processing. The computer, in turn, passes information (processed data) to the actuators to carry out the necessary work on the environment, which

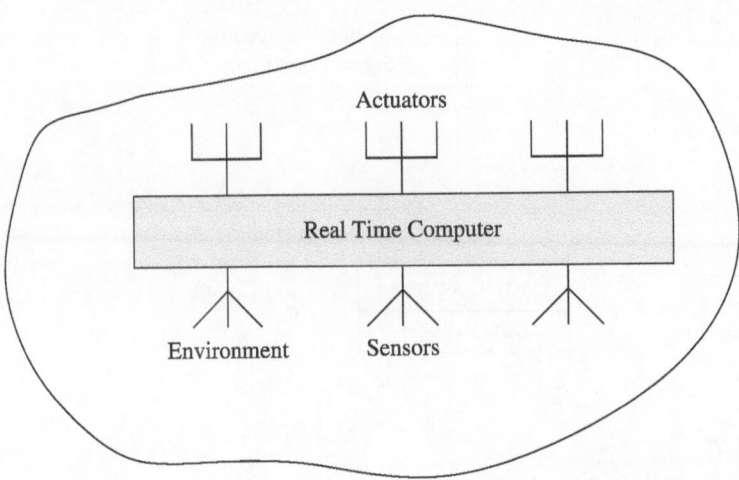

▲ FIGURE 1.8

A Schematic Representation of an Embedded Real-Time System

results in controlling some characteristics of the environment. Several examples of embedded systems were discussed in Section 1.2. An example of an embedded system that we would often refer is the Multi-Point Fuel Injection (MPFI) system discussed in Example 6 of Section 1.2.

4. **Safety-Criticality:** For traditional non-real-time systems safety and reliability are independent issues. However, in many real-time systems these two issues are intricately bound together making them *safety-critical*. Note that a **safe** system is one that does not cause any damage even when it fails. A **reliable** system, on the other hand, is one that can operate for long durations of time without exhibiting any failures. A safety-critical system is required to be highly reliable since any failure of the system can cause extensive damages. We elaborate this issue in Section 1.5.

5. **Concurrency:** A real-time system usually needs to respond to several independent events within very short and strict time bounds. For instance, consider a chemical plant automation system (see Example 1 of Section 1.2), which monitors the progress of a chemical reaction and controls the rate of reaction by changing the different parameters of reaction such as pressure, temperature, and chemical concentration. These parameters are sensed using sensors fixed in the chemical reaction chamber. These sensors may generate data asynchronously at different rates. Therefore, the real-time system must process data from all the sensors concurrently, otherwise signals may be lost and the system may malfunction. These systems can be considered non-deterministic, since the behaviour of the system depends on the exact timing of its inputs. A non-deterministic computation is one in which two runs using the same set of input data can produce two distinct sets of output data in the two runs.

6. **Distributed and Feedback Structure:** In many real-time systems, the different components of the system are naturally distributed across widely spread geographic locations. In such systems, the different events of interest arise at the geographically separate locations.

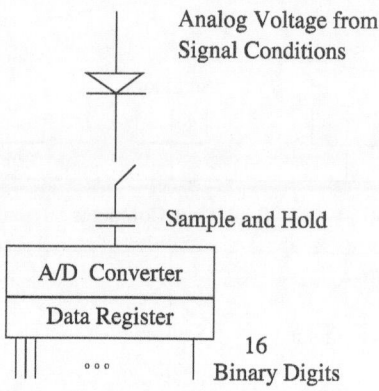

▲ FIGURE 1.7

Conversion of an Analog Signal to a 16-bit Binary Number

1.4 CHARACTERISTICS OF REAL-TIME SYSTEMS

We now discuss a few key characteristics of real-time systems that distinguish it from non-real-time systems. However, the reader may note that all the discussed characteristics may not be applicable to every real-time system. Real-time systems cover such an enormous range of applications and products that a generalization of the characteristics into a set that is applicable to each and every system is difficult. Different categories of real-time systems may exhibit the characteristics that we identify to different extents or may not even exhibit some of the characteristics at all.

1. **Time Constraints:** Every real-time task is associated with some time constraints. One very common form of time constraints is deadlines associated with tasks. A task deadline specifies the time before which the task must complete and produce the results. Other types of timing constraints are delay and duration (see Section 1.7). It is the responsibility of the Real-Time Operating System (RTOS) to ensure that all tasks meet their respective time constraints. In later chapters we shall examine how an RTOS can ensure that tasks meet their respective timing constraints through appropriate task scheduling strategies.

2. **New Correctness Criterion:** The notion of correctness in real-time systems is different from that used in the context of traditional systems. In real-time systems, correctness implies not only logical correctness of the results, but the time at which the results are produced is important. A logically correct result produced after the deadline would be considered an incorrect result.

3. **Embedded:** A vast majority of real-time systems are embedded in nature [22]. An embedded computer system is physically "embedded" in its environment and often controls it. Figure 1.8 shows a schematic representation of an embedded system. As shown in Fig. 1.8, the sensors of the real-time computer collect data from the environment, pass them on to the real-time computer for processing. The computer, in turn, passes information (processed data) to the actuators to carry out the necessary work on the environment, which

can only be ensured through increased reliability. It should now be clear why safety-critical systems need to be highly reliable.

Just to give an example of the level of reliability required of safety-critical systems, consider the following. For any fly-by-wire aircraft, most of its vital parts are controlled by a computer. Any failure of the controlling computer is clearly not acceptable. The standard reliability requirement for such aircraft is at most 1 failure per 10^9 flying hours (that is, a million years of continuous flying!). In the next section, we examine how a highly reliable system can be developed.

1.5.1 How to Achieve High Reliability?

If you are asked by your organization to develop a software which should be highly reliable, how would you proceed to achieve it? Highly reliable software can be developed by adopting all the following three important techniques:

- **Error Avoidance.** For achieving high reliability, every possibility of occurrence of errors should be minimized during product development as much as possible. This can be achieved by adopting a variety of means: using well-founded software engineering practices and sound design methodologies, adopting suitable CASE tools, and so on.

- **Error Detection and Removal.** In spite of using the best available error avoidance techniques, many errors still manage to creep into the code. These errors need to be detected and removed. This can be achieved to a large extent by conducting thorough reviews and testing. Once errors are detected, they can be easily fixed.

- **Fault-Tolerance.** No matter how meticulously error avoidance and error detection techniques are used, it is virtually impossible to make a practical software system entirely error free. Few errors still persist even after carrying out thorough reviews and testing. Errors cause failures, that is, failures are manifestation of the errors latent in the system. Therefore, to achieve high reliability, even in situations where errors are present, the system should be able to tolerate the faults and compute the correct results. This is called fault-tolerance. Fault-tolerance can be achieved by carefully incorporating redundancy.

It is relatively simple to design a hardware equipment to be fault-tolerant. The following are two methods that are popularly used to achieve hardware fault-tolerance:

- **Built-in Self Test (BIST).** In BIST, the system periodically performs self tests of its components. Upon detection of a failure, the system automatically reconfigures itself by switching out the faulty component and switching in one of the redundant good components.

- **Triple Modular Redundancy (TMR).** In TMR, as the name suggests, three redundant copies of all critical components are made to run concurrently (see Fig. 1.11). Observe that in Fig. 1.11, C1, C2, and C3 are the redundant copies of the same critical component. The system performs voting of the results produced by the redundant components to select the majority result. TMR can help tolerate occurrence of only a single failure at any time. (Can you answer why a TMR scheme can effectively tolerate a single component failure only?) An assumption that is implicit in the TMR technique is that at any time only one of the three redundant components can produce erroneous results. The majority result after voting would be erroneous if two or more components can fail simultaneously (more precisely, before a repair can be carried out). In situations where two or more components are likely to fail (or produce erroneous results), then greater amounts of redundancies would be

1.5 SAFETY AND RELIABILITY

In traditional systems, safety and reliability are normally considered to be independent issues. It is, therefore, possible to identify a traditional system that is safe and unreliable and systems that are reliable but unsafe. Consider the following two examples. A word processing software may not be very reliable but is safe. A failure of the software does not usually cause any significant damage or financial loss. It is, therefore, an example of an unreliable but safe system. On the other hand, a hand gun can be unsafe but is reliable. A hand gun rarely fails. A hand gun is an unsafe system because if it fails for some reason, it can misfire or even explode and cause significant damage. It is an example of an unsafe but reliable system. These two examples show that for traditional systems, safety and reliability are independent concerns—it is, therefore, possible to increase the safety of a system without affecting its reliability and vice versa.

In real-time systems, on the other hand, safety and reliability are coupled together. Before analyzing why safety and reliability are no longer independent issues in real-time systems, we need to first understand what exactly is meant by a **fail-safe state**.

> A fail-safe state of a system is one which if entered when the system fails, no damage would result.

For example, the fail-safe state of a word processing program is one where the document being processed has been saved onto the disk. All traditional non-real-time systems do have one or more fail-safe states which help separate the issues of safety and reliability—even if a system is known to be unreliable, it can always be made to fail in a fail-safe state, and still considered a safe system.

If no damage can result if a system enters a fail-safe state just before it fails, then through careful transition to a fail-safe state upon a failure, it is possible to turn an extremely unreliable and unsafe system into a safe system. In many traditional systems this technique is in fact frequently adopted to turn an unreliable system into a safe system. For example, consider a traffic light controller that controls the flow of traffic at a road intersection. Suppose the traffic light controller fails frequently and is known to be highly unreliable. Though unreliable, it can still be considered safe if whenever a traffic light controller fails, it enters a fail-safe state where all the traffic lights are orange and blinking. This is a **fail-safe state**, since the motorists on seeing blinking orange traffic light become aware that the traffic light controller is not working and proceed with caution. Of course, a fail-safe state may not be to make all lights green, in which case severe accidents could occur. Similarly, all lights turned red is also not a fail-safe state—it may not cause accidents, but would bring all traffic to a standstill leading to traffic jams. However, in many real-time systems there are no fail-safe states. Therefore, any failure of the system can cause severe damages. Such systems are said to be **safety-critical systems**.

> A safety-critical system is one whose failure can cause severe damages.

An example of a safety-critical system is a navigation system on-board an aircraft. An on-board navigation system has no fail-safe states. When the computer on-board an aircraft fails, a fail-safe state may not be one where the engine is switched-off! In a safety-critical system, the absence of fail-safe states implies that safety can only be ensured through increased reliability. Thus, for safety-critical systems the issues of safety and reliability become interrelated—safety

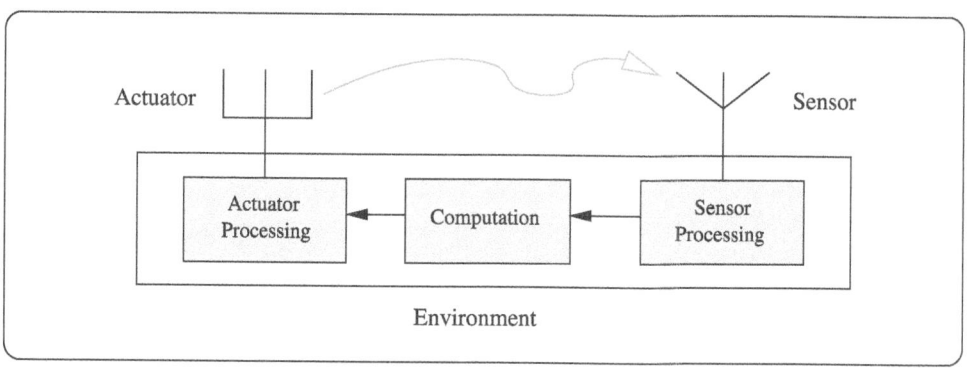

▲ FIGURE 1.9

Feedback Structure of Real-Time Systems

Therefore, these events may often have to be handled locally and responses produced to them to prevent overloading of the underlying communication network. Therefore, the sensors and the actuators may be located at places where the events are generated. An example of such a system is a petroleum refinery plant distributed over a large geographic area. At each data source, it makes good design sense to locally process the data before being passed on to a central processor.

Many distributed as well as centralized real-time systems have a feedback structure as shown in Fig. 1.9. In these systems, the sensors usually sense the environment periodically. The sensed data about the environment is processed to determine the necessary corrective actions. The results of the processing are used to carry out the necessary corrective actions on the environment through the actuators, which, in turn, again cause a change to the required characteristics of the controlled environment, and so on.

7. **Task Criticality:** Task criticality is a measure of the cost of failure of a task. Task criticality is determined by examining how critical are the results produced by the task to the proper functioning of the system. A real-time system may have tasks of very different criticalities. It is, therefore, natural to expect that the criticalities of the different tasks must be taken into consideration while designing for fault-tolerance. The higher the criticality of a task, the more reliable it should be made. Further, in the event of a failure of a highly critical task, immediate failure detection and recovery are important. However, it should be realized that task priority is a different concept and task criticality does not solely determine the task priority or the order in which various tasks are to be executed (these issues shall be elaborated in the later chapters).

8. **Custom Hardware:** A real-time system is often implemented on custom hardware that is specifically designed and developed for the purpose. For example, a cell phone does not use traditional microprocessors. Cell phones use processors which are tiny, supporting only those processing capabilities that are really necessary for cell phone operation and specifically designed to be power-efficient to conserve battery life. The capabilities of the processor used in a cell phone are substantially different from that of a general purpose processor. Another example is the embedded processor in an MPFI car. In this case, the processor

used need not be a powerful general purpose processor such as a Pentium or an Athlon processor. Some of the most powerful computers used in MPFI engines are 16- or 32-bit processors running at approximately 40 MHz. However, unlike the conventional PCs, a processor used in these car engines do not deal with processing frills such as screen-savers or a dozen of different applications running at the same time. All that the processor in an MPFI system needs to do is to compute the required fuel injection rate that is most efficient for a given speed and acceleration.

9. **Reactive:** Real-time systems are often *reactive*. A reactive system is one in which an on-going interaction between the computer and the environment is maintained. Ordinary systems compute functions on the input data to generate the output data (see Fig. 1.10 (a)). In other words, traditional systems compute the output data as some function ϕ of the input data. That is, output data can be mathematically expressed as: *output data = ϕ(input data)*. For example, if some data I_1 is given as the input, the system computes O_1 as the result $O_1 = \phi(I_1)$. To elaborate this concept, consider an example involving a library automation software. In a library automation software, when the query book function is invoked and "Real-Time Systems" is entered as the input book name, then the software displays "Author name: R. Mall, Rack Number: 001, Number of Copies: 1."

    In contrast to the traditional computation of the output as a simple function of the input data, real-time systems do not produce any output data but enter into an ongoing interaction with their environment. In each interaction step, the results computed are used to carry out some actions on the environment. The reaction of the environment is sampled and is fed back to the system. Therefore, the computations in a real-time system can be considered non-terminating. This reactive nature of real-time systems is schematically shown in Fig. 1.10 (b).

10. **Stability:** Under overload conditions, real-time systems need to continue to meet the deadlines of the most critical tasks, though the deadlines of non-critical tasks may not be met. This is in contrast to the requirement of *fairness* for traditional systems even under overload conditions.

11. **Exception Handling:** Many real-time systems work round-the-clock and often operate without human operators. For example, consider a small automated chemical plant that is set up to work non-stop. When there are no human operators, taking corrective actions on a failure becomes difficult. Even if no corrective actions can be immediately taken, it is desirable that a failure does not result in catastrophic situations. A failure should be detected and the system should continue to operate in a gracefully degraded mode rather than shutting off abruptly.

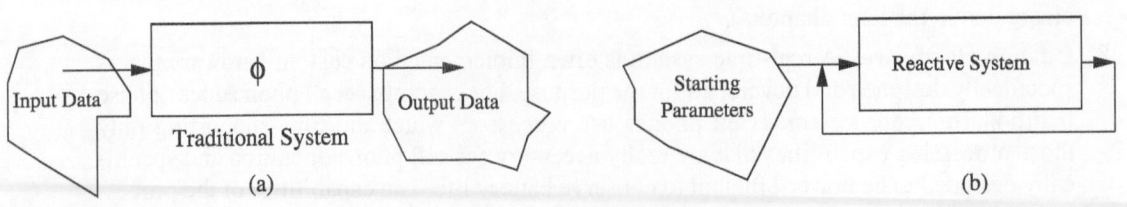

(a)   (b)

▲ **FIGURE 1.10**

Traditional versus Reactive Systems

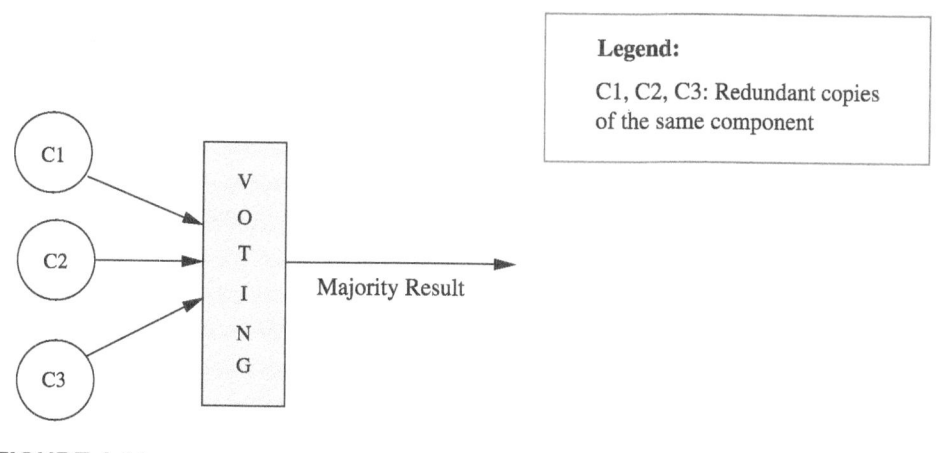

Legend:

C1, C2, C3: Redundant copies
of the same component

Majority Result

▲ **FIGURE 1.11**

Schematic Representation of TMR

required to be incorporated. A little thinking can show that at least $2n + 1$ redundant components are required to tolerate simultaneous failures of n component.

As compared to hardware, software fault-tolerance is much harder to achieve. To investigate the reason behind this, let us first discuss the techniques currently being used to achieve software fault-tolerance.

1.5.2 Software Fault-Tolerance Techniques

Two methods are now popularly being used to achieve software fault-tolerance: N-version programming and recovery block techniques. These two techniques are simple adaptations of the basic techniques used to provide hardware fault-tolerance.

N-Version Programming: This technique is an adaptation of the TMR technique for hardware fault-tolerance. In the N-version programming technique, independent teams develop N different versions (value of N depends on the degree of fault-tolerance required) of a software component (module). The redundant modules are run concurrently (possibly on redundant hardware). The results produced by the different versions of the module are subjected to voting at run time and the result on which majority of the components agree is accepted. The central idea behind this scheme is that independent teams would commit different types of mistakes, which would be eliminated when the results produced by them are subjected to voting. However, this scheme is not very successful in achieving fault-tolerance, and the problem can be attributed to *statistical correlation of failures*. Statistical correlation of failures means that even though individual teams worked in isolation to develop the different versions of a software component, even then the different versions fail for identical reasons. In other words, the different versions of a component show similar failure patterns. This does mean that the different modules developed by independent programmers, after all, contain identical errors. The reason for this is not far to seek, programmers commit errors in those parts of a problem which they perceive to be difficult—and what is difficult to one team is usually difficult to all teams. So, identical errors remain in the most complex and least understood parts of a software component.

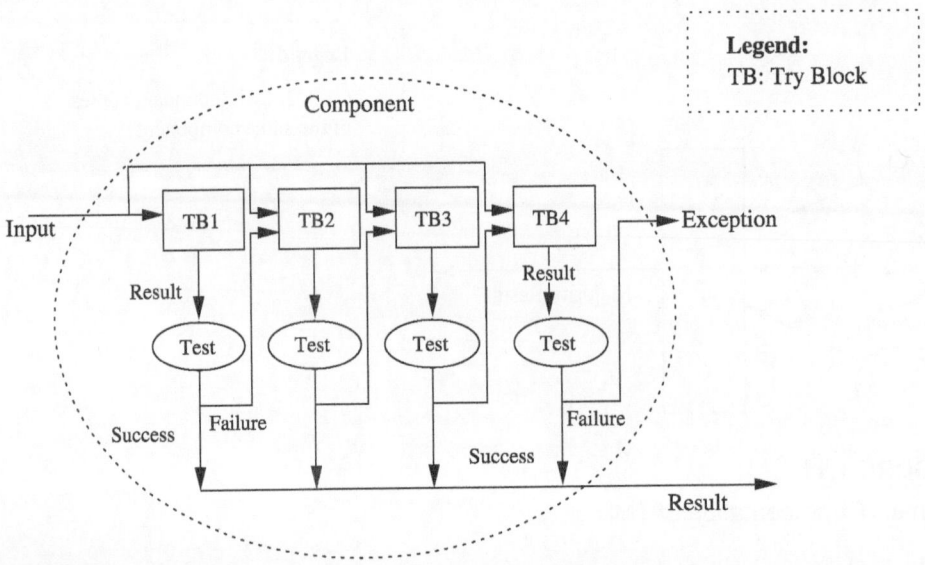

▲ **FIGURE 1.12**

A Software Fault-Tolerance Scheme Using Recovery Blocks

Recovery Blocks: In the recovery block scheme, the redundant components are called *try blocks*. Each try block computes the same end result as the others but is intentionally written using a different algorithm compared to the other try blocks. In N-version programming, the different versions of a component are written by different teams of programmers, whereas in recovery block different algorithms are used in different try blocks. Also, in contrast to the N-version programming approach where the redundant copies are run concurrently, in the recovery block approach they are (as shown in Fig. 1.12) run one after another. The results produced by a try block are subjected to an acceptance test (see Fig. 1.12). If the test fails, then the next try block is tried. This is repeated in a sequence until the result produced by a try block successfully passes the acceptance test. Note that in Fig. 1.12 we have shown acceptance tests separately for different try blocks to help understand that the tests are applied to the try blocks one after the other, though it may be the case that the same test is applied to each try block.

As was the case with N-version programming, the recovery blocks approach also does not achieve much success in providing effective fault-tolerance. The reason is again statistical correlation of failures. Different try blocks fail for identical reasons as was explained in the case of N-version programming approach. Besides, this approach suffers from a further limitation: it can only be used if the task deadlines are much larger than the task computation times (i.e., tasks have large laxity), since the different try blocks are put to execution one after the other when failures occur. The recovery block approach poses special difficulty when used with real-time tasks with very short slack time (i.e., short deadline and considerable execution time), as the try blocks are tried out one after the other deadlines may be missed. Therefore, in such cases the later try blocks usually contain only skeletal code.

Of course, it is possible that the later try blocks containing only skeletal code, produce only approximate results and, therefore, take much less time for computation than the first try block.

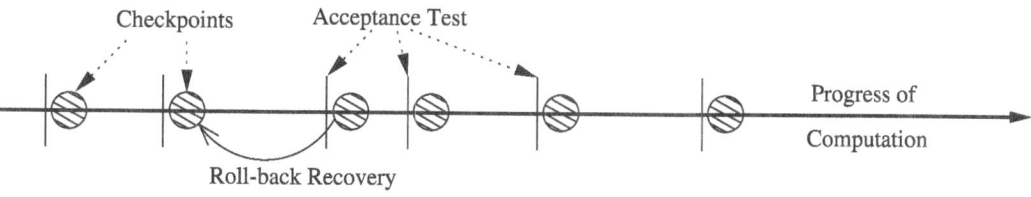

▲ FIGURE 1.13

Checkpointing and Roll-back Recovery

Checkpointing and Roll-Back Recovery: Checkpointing and roll-back recovery is another popular technique to achieve fault-tolerance. In this technique as the computation proceeds, the system state is tested each time after some meaningful progress in computation is made. Immediately after a state-check test succeeds, the state of the system is backed up on a stable storage (see Fig. 1.13). In case the next test does not succeed, the system can be made to roll back to the last checkpointed state. After a roll back, from a checkpointed state a fresh computation can be initiated. This technique is especially useful, if there is a chance that the system state may be corrupted as the computation proceeds, such as data corruption or processor failure.

1.6   TYPES OF REAL-TIME TASKS

We have already seen that a real-time task is one for which quantitative expressions of time are needed to describe its behaviour. This quantitative expression of time usually appears in the form of a constraint on the time at which the task produces results. The most frequently occurring timing constraint is a deadline constraint which is used to express that a task is required to compute its results within some deadline. We, therefore, implicitly assume only deadline type of timing constraints on tasks in this section, though other types of constraints (as explained in Section 1.7) may occur in practice. Real-time tasks can be classified into the following three broad categories:

> A real-time task can be classified into either hard, soft, or firm real-time task depending on the consequences of a task missing its deadline.

It is not necessary that all tasks of a real-time application belong to the same category. It is possible that different tasks of a real-time system can belong to different categories. We now elaborate these three types of real-time tasks.

Hard Real-Time Tasks: A hard real-time task is one that is constrained to produce its results within certain predefined time bounds. The system is considered to have failed whenever any of its hard real-time tasks does not produce its required results before the specified time bound.

An example of a system having hard real-time tasks is a robot. The robot cyclically carries out a number of activities including communication with the host system, logging all completed activities, sensing the environment to detect any obstacles present, tracking the objects of interest, path planning, effecting next move, etc. Now, consider that the robot suddenly encounters an obstacle. The robot must detect it and as soon as possible try to escape colliding with it. If it fails to respond to it quickly (i.e., the concerned tasks are not completed before the required time bound) then it would collide with the obstacle and the robot would be considered to have failed. Therefore, detecting obstacles and reacting to it are hard real-time tasks.

Another application having hard real-time tasks is an anti-missile system that has to perform these critical activities (tasks): it must first detect all incoming missiles, properly position the anti-missile gun, and then fire to destroy the incoming missile before the incoming missile can do any damage. All these tasks are hard real-time in nature and the anti-missile system would be considered to have failed, if any of its tasks fails to complete before the corresponding deadlines.

Applications having hard real-time tasks are typically safety-critical (Can you think an example of a hard real-time system that is not safety-critical?).[1] This means that any failure of a real-time task, including its failure to meet the associated deadlines, would result in severe consequences. This makes hard real-time tasks extremely critical. Criticality of a task can range from extremely critical to not so critical. Task criticality, therefore, is a different dimension than hard or soft characterization of a task. Criticality of a task is a measure of the cost of a failure—the higher the cost of failure, the more critical the task.

For hard real-time tasks in practical systems, the time bounds usually range from several microseconds to a few milliseconds. It may be noted that a hard real-time task does not need to be completed within the shortest time possible, but it is merely required that the task must complete within the specified time bound. In other words, there is no reward in completing a hard real-time task much ahead of its deadline. This is an important observation and this would take a central part in our discussions on task scheduling in the next two chapters.

Firm Real-Time Tasks: Every firm real-time task is associated with some predefined deadline before which it is required to produce its results. However, unlike a hard real-time task, even when a firm real-time task does not complete within its deadline, the system does not fail. The late results are merely discarded. In other words, the utility of the results computed by a firm real-time task becomes zero after the deadline. Figure 1.14 schematically shows the utility of the results produced by a firm real-time task as a function of time. In Fig. 1.14 it can be seen that if the response time of a task exceeds the specified deadline, then the utility of the results becomes zero and the results are discarded.

Firm real-time tasks typically abound in multimedia applications. The following are two examples of firm real-time tasks:

- **Video Conferencing.** In a video conferencing application, video frames and the accompanying audio are converted into packets and transmitted to the receiver over a network. However, some frames may get delayed at different nodes during transit on a packet-switched network due to congestion at different nodes. This may result in varying queuing delays experienced by packets travelling along different routes. Even when packets traverse the same route, some packets can take much more time than the other packets due to the specific transmission strategy used at the nodes. (This issue is discussed in greater detail in Chapter 7). When a certain frame is being played, if some preceding frame arrives at the receiver, then this frame is of no use and is discarded. Due to this reason, when a frame is delayed by more than, say, 1 sec, it is simply discarded at the receiver end without carrying out any processing on it.

---

[1]Some computer games have hard real-time tasks, these are not safety-critical though. Whenever a timing constraint is not met, the game may fail, but the failure may at best be a mild irritant to the user.

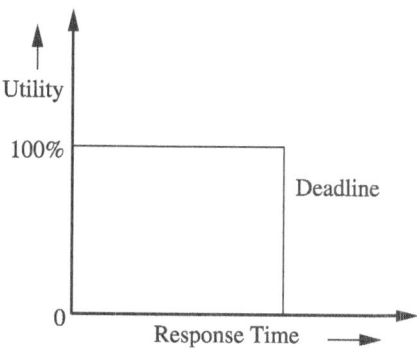

▲ **FIGURE 1.14**

Utility of Result of a Firm Real-Time Task with Time

- **Satellite-Based Tracking of Enemy Movements.** Consider a satellite that takes pictures of an enemy territory and beams it to a ground station computer frame by frame. The ground computer processes each frame to find the positional difference of various objects of interest with respect to their position in the previous frame to determine the movements of the enemy. When the ground computer is overloaded, a new image may be received even before an older image is taken up for processing. In this case, the older image is not of much use. Hence, the older images may be discarded and the recently received image could be processed.

For firm real-time tasks, the associated time bounds typically range from a few milliseconds to several hundreds of milliseconds.

Soft Real-Time Tasks: Soft real-time tasks also have time bounds associated with them. However, unlike hard and firm real-time tasks, the timing constraints on soft real-time tasks are not expressed as absolute values. Instead, the constraints are expressed in terms of the average response times required.

An example of a soft real-time task is web browsing. Normally, after an Uniform Resource Locater (URL) is clicked, the corresponding web page is fetched and displayed within a couple of seconds on an average. However, when it takes several minutes to display a requested page, we still do not consider the system to have failed, but merely express that the performance of the system has degraded.

Another example of a soft real-time task is a task handling a request for a seat reservation in a railway reservation application. Once a request for reservation is made, the response should occur within 20 sec on an average. The response may either be in the form of a printed ticket or an apology message on account of unavailability of seats. Alternatively, we might state the constraint on the ticketing task as: At least in case of 95% of reservation requests, the ticket should be processed and printed in less than 20 sec.

Let us take the example of a railway reservation task to analyze the impact of the failure of a soft real-time task to meet its deadline. If the ticket is printed in about 20 sec, we feel that the system is working fine and get a feel of having obtained instant results. As already stated, missed deadlines of soft real-time tasks do not result in system failures. However, the utility of the results produced by a soft real-time task falls continuously with time after the expiry of the deadline as shown in Fig. 1.15. In Fig. 1.15, the utility of the results produced are 100% if

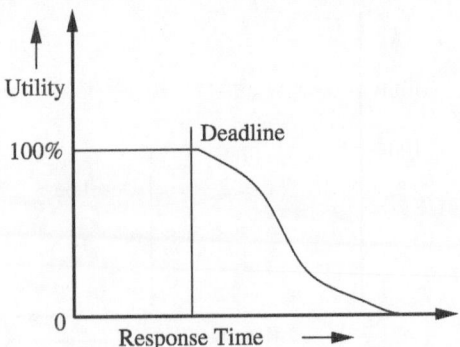

▲ FIGURE 1.15

Utility of the Results Produced by a Soft Real-Time Task as a Function of Time

produced before the deadline, and after the deadline is passed the utility of the results slowly falls off with time. For soft real-time tasks that typically occur in practical applications, the time bounds usually range from a fraction of a second to a few seconds.

Non-Real-Time Tasks: A non-real-time task is not associated with any time bounds. Can you think of any example of a non-real-time task? Most of the interactive computations you perform nowadays are handled by soft real-time tasks. However, about three decades ago, when computers were not interactive almost all tasks were non-real-time. A few examples of non-real-time tasks are: batch processing jobs, e-mail, and background tasks such as event loggers. You may, however, argue that even these tasks, in the strict sense of the term, do have certain time bounds. For example, an e-mail is expected to reach its destination at least within a couple of hours of being sent. Similar is the case with a batch processing job such as pay-slip printing. What then really is the difference between a non-real-time task and a soft real-time task? For non-real-time tasks, the associated time bounds are typically of the order of a few minutes, hours or even days. In contrast, the time bounds associated with soft real-time tasks are at most of the order of a few seconds.

1.7 TIMING CONSTRAINTS

We have seen that the correctness of real-time tasks depend both on the logical correctness of the result as well as on the satisfaction of the corresponding timing constraints that apply to certain events in a system. These events may be generated by the tasks themselves or the environment of the system. An example of such an event is the activation of a motor. Remember, the results may be generated at different times and it may not be in the form of a single one time result. We must first properly characterise the events in a system, to understand the timing behaviour of real-time systems.

1.7.1 Events in a Real-Time System

An event may be generated either by the system or its environment. Based on this consideration, events can be classified into the following two types:

Stimulus Events: Stimulus events are generated by the environment and act on the system. These events can be produced asynchronously (i.e., aperiodically). For example, a user pressing a button on a telephone set generates a stimulus event to act on the telephone system. Stimulus events can also be generated periodically. As an instance, consider the periodic sensing of the temperature of the reactor in a nuclear plant.

Response Events: Response events act on the environment and are usually produced by the system in response to some stimulus events. For example, consider a chemical plant where as soon as the temperature exceeds 100°C, the system responds by switching off the heater. Here, the event of temperature exceeding 100°C is the stimulus and switching off of the heater is the response. Response events can either be periodic or aperiodic.

An event may either be instantaneous or may have certain duration. For example, a button press event is described by the duration for which the button was kept pressed. Some authors argue that durational events are really not a basic type of event, but can be expressed using other events. In fact, it is possible to consider a duration event as a combination of two events: a start event and an end event. For example, the button press event can be described by a combination of 'start button press' and 'end button press' events. However, it is often convenient to retain the notion of a durational event. In this text, we consider durational events as a special class of events. Using the preliminary notions about events discussed in this subsection, we classify various types of timing constraints in Section 1.7.2.

1.7.2 Classification of Timing Constraints

A classification of the different types of timing constraints is important. Not only would it give us an insight into the different types of timing constraints that can exist in a system, but it can also help us quickly identify the different timing constraints that can exist from a casual examination of a problem. That is, in addition to better understanding of the behaviour of a system, it can also let us work out the specification of a real-time system accurately.

Different timing constraints associated with a real-time system can broadly be classified into performance and behavioural constraints.

> Performance constraints are the constraints that are imposed on the response of the system. Behavioural constraints are the constraints that are imposed on the stimuli generated by the environment.

Behavioural constraints ensure that the environment of a system is well behaved, whereas performance constraints ensure that the computer system performs satisfactorily.

Each of the *performance* and *behavioural* constraints can further be classified into the following three types:

- Delay Constraint
- Deadline Constraint
- Duration Constraint

Delay: A delay constraint captures the *minimum* time (delay) that must elapse between the occurrence of two arbitrary events e_1 and e_2. After e_1 occurs, if e_2 occurs earlier than the

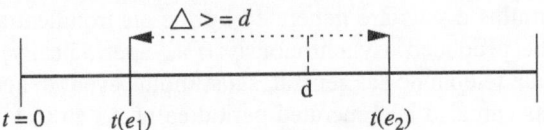

▲ FIGURE 1.16

Delay Constraint Between Two Events e_1 and e_2

minimum delay, then a delay violation is said to occur. A delay constraint on the event e_2 can be expressed more formally as follows:

$$t(e_2) - t(e_1) \geq d$$

Where $t(e_2)$ and $t(e_1)$ are the time stamps on the events e_2 and e_1, respectively, and d is the *minimum delay* specified from e_2. A delay constraint on the events e_2 with respect to the event e_1 is shown in Fig. 1.16. In Fig. 1.16, Δ denotes the actual separation in time between the occurrence of the two events e_1 and e_2 and d is the required minimum separation between the two events (delay). It is easy to see that e_2 must occur after at least d time units have elapsed since the occurrence of e_1, otherwise we shall have a delay violation.

Deadline: A deadline constraint captures the permissible *maximum* separation between any two arbitrary events e_1 and e_2. In other words, the second event (i.e., e_2) must follow the first event (i.e., e_1) within the permissible maximum separation time. Consider that $t(e_1)$ and $t(e_2)$ are the time stamps on the occurrence of the events e_1 and e_2, respectively, and d is the *deadline* as shown in Fig. 1.17. In Fig. 1.17, Δ denotes the actual separation between the time of occurrence of the two events e_1 and e_2, and d is the deadline. A deadline constraint implies that e_2 must occur within d time units of e_1's occurrence. We can alternatively state that $t(e_1)$ and $t(e_2)$ must satisfy the constraint:

$$t(e_2) - t(e_1) \leq d$$

The deadline and delay constraints can further be classified into two types, each based on whether the constraint is imposed on the stimulus or on the response event. This has been explained with some examples in Section 1.7.3.

Duration: A duration constraint on an event specifies the time period over which the event acts. A duration constraint can either be minimum type or maximum type. The minimum type

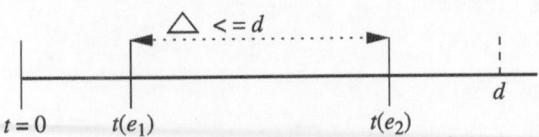

▲ FIGURE 1.17

Deadline Constraint Between Two Events e_1 and e_2

duration constraint requires that once the event starts, the event must not end before a certain minimum duration; whereas a maximum type duration constraint requires that once the event starts, the event must end before a certain maximum duration elapses.

1.7.3 Examples of Different Types of Timing Constraints

We illustrate the different classes of timing constraints by using the examples from a telephone system discussed in [4]. A schematic diagram of a telephone system is given in Fig. 1.18. Note that I have intentionally drawn an old styled telephone, because its operation is easier to understand! Here, the telephone handset and the Public Switched Telephone Network (PSTN) are considered as constituting the computer system and the users as forming the environment. In the following, we give a few simple example operations of the telephone system to illustrate the different types of timing constraints.

Deadline Constraints: In the following, we discuss four different types of deadline constraints that may be identified in a real-time system depending on whether the two events involved in a deadline constraint are stimulus type or response type.

Stimulus–Stimulus (SS): In this case, the deadline is defined between two stimuli. This is a behavioural constraint, since the constraint is imposed on the second event which is a stimulus. An example of an SS type of deadline constraint is the following:

```
Once a user completes dialling a digit, he must dial the next digit
within the next 5 sec. Otherwise, an idle tone is produced.
```

In this example, dialling two consecutive digits represents the two stimuli to the telephone system.

Stimulus–Response (SR): In this case, the deadline is defined on the response event, measured from the occurrence of the corresponding stimulus event. This is a performance constraint,

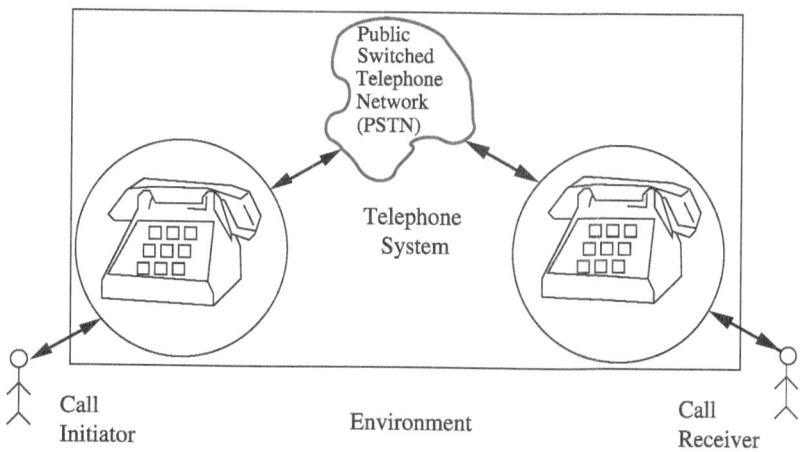

▲ **FIGURE 1.18**

Schematic Representation of a Telephone System

since the constraint is imposed on a response event. An example of an SR type of deadline constraint is the following:

```
Once the receiver of the handset is lifted, the dial tone must be pro-
duced by the system within 2 sec, otherwise a beeping sound is produced
until the handset is replaced.
```

In this example, the lifting of the receiver handset represents a stimulus to the telephone system and production of the dial tone is the response.

Response–Stimulus (RS): Here the deadline is on the production of response counted from the corresponding stimulus. This is a behavioral constraint, since the constraint is imposed on the stimulus event. An example of an RS type of deadline constraint is the following:

```
Once the dial tone appears, the first digit must be dialled within 30
sec, otherwise the system enters an idle state and an idle tone is pro-
duced.
```

Response–Response (RR): An RR type of deadline constraint is defined on two response events. In this case, once the first response event occurs, the second response event must occur before a certain deadline. This is a performance constraint, since the timing constraint has been defined on a response event. An example of an RR type of deadline constraint is the following:

```
Once the ring tone is given to the callee, the corresponding ring back
tone must be given to the caller within 2 sec, otherwise the call is
terminated.
```

Here the ring back tone and the corresponding ring tone are the two response events.

Delay Constraint: We can identify only one type of delay constraint (SS type) in the telephone system example that we are considering. However, in other problems it may be possible to identify different types of delay constraints. An SS type of a delay constraint is a behavioural constraint. An example of an SS type of delay constraint is the following:

```
Once a digit is dialled, the next digit should be dialled after at least
1 sec. Otherwise, a beeping sound is produced until the call initiator
replaces the handset.
```

Here the delay constraint is defined on the event of dialling of the next digit (stimulus) after a digit is dialled (also a stimulus).

Duration: A duration constraint on an event specifies the time interval over which the event acts. An example of a duration constraint is the following:

```
If you press the button of the handset for less than 15 sec, it con-
nects to the local operator. If you press the button for any duration
lasting between 15 to 30 sec, it connects to the international opera-
tor. If you keep the button pressed for more than 30 sec, then on re-
leasing it would produce the dial tone.
```

A classification of the different types of timing constraints that we discussed in this section is shown in Fig. 1.19. Note that a performance constraint can either be delay, deadline, or durational type. The delay or deadline constraints on performance can either be RR or RS type. Similarly, the behavioural constraints can either be delay, deadline, or durational type. The delay or deadline constraints on the behaviour of environment can either be RS or SS type.

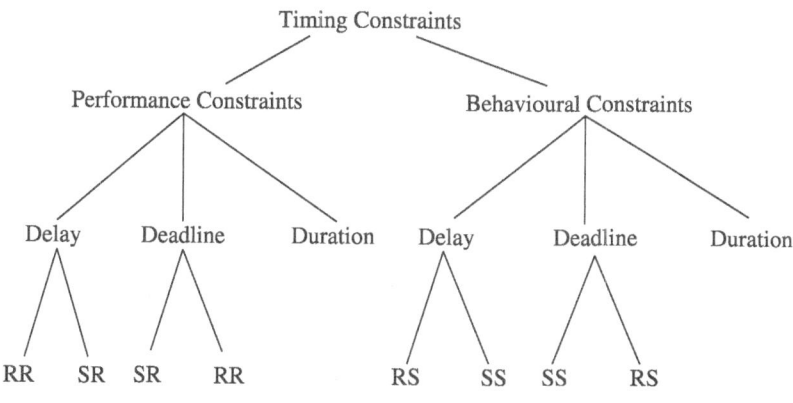

▲ FIGURE 1.19

Classification of Timing Constraints

1.8 MODELLING TIMING CONSTRAINTS

In this section we describe how the timing constraints identified in Section 1.7.3 can be modelled. Modelling time constraints is very important since once a model of the time constraints in a system is constructed, it can serve as a formal specification of the system. Further, if all the timing constraints in a system are modelled accurately, then it may even be used to automatically generate code from it. Besides serving as a specification, modelling time constraints can help to verify and understand a real-time system.

The modelling approach we discuss here is based on *Finite State Machines* (FSMs). An FSM is a powerful tool which has long been used to model traditional systems. In an FSM, a state is defined in terms of the values assumed by some attributes. For example, the states of an elevator may be denoted in terms of its directions of motion. Here direction is the attribute, based on which the states up, down, and stationery are defined.

In an FSM model, at any point of time a system can be in any one of a (possibly infinite) number of states. A state is represented by a circle. The system changes state due to events that change the values of, or relations among the state variables. A state change is also called a state transition. A transition causing event may either be an interface event that are transmitted between the environment and the computer system or it could also be an internal event that is generated and consumed solely within the system. A transition from one state to another is represented by drawing a directed arc from the source to the destination (see Fig. 1.20). The event causing a transition is annotated on the arc. We keep our discussions of FSM to the bare minimum since we assume that the reader is familiar with basic FSM modelling of traditional systems.

We use an *Extended Finite State Machine* (EFSM) to model time constraints. EFSM extends the traditional FSM by incorporating the action of setting a timer and the expiry event of a timer. The notations we use for construction of EFSMs are simple and straightforward. Therefore rather than introducing them formally, we have illustrated them through an example in Fig. 1.20, that describes that if an event e_1 occurs when the current state of the system is s_1, then an action will be taken by setting a timer to expire in the next 20 mSec and the system transits to state s^2.

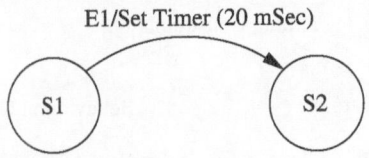

▲ FIGURE 1.20

Conventions Used in Drawing an EFSM

We have already discussed that events can be of two types: stimulus events and response events. We had also discussed different types of timing constraints in Section 1.7.3. Now we explain how these constraints can be modelled by using EFSMs.

Stimulus–Stimulus (SS) Constraints: Let us consider the example of an SS type of deadline constraint we had discussed in Section 1.7.3:

    Once the first digit has been dialled on the telephone handset, the next
    digit must be dialled within the next 5 mSec.

This has been modelled in Fig. 1.21. In Fig. 1.21 observe that as soon as the first digit is dialled, the system enters the "Await Second Digit" state and the timer is set to 20 mSec. If the next digit does not appear within 20 mSec, then the timer alarm expires and the system enters the "Await Caller On-hook" state and a beeping sound is produced. If the second digit occurs before 20 mSec, then the system transits to the "Await Next Digit" state.

Response–Stimulus (RS) Constraint: In Section 1.7.3, we had considered the following example of an RS type of deadline constraint:

    Once the dial tone appears, the first digit must be dialled within 30 sec,
    otherwise the system enters an idle state and an idle tone is produced.

The EFSM model for this constraint is shown in Fig. 1.22. In Fig. 1.22, as soon as dial tone appears, a timer is set to expire in 30 sec and the system transits to the "Await First Digit" state. If the timer expires before the first digit arrives, then the system transits to an idle state where an idle tone is produced. Otherwise, if the digit appears first, then the system transits to the "Await Second Digit" state.

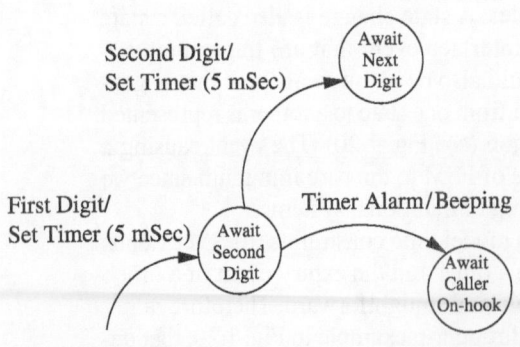

▲ FIGURE 1.21

Model of an SS Type of Deadline Constraint

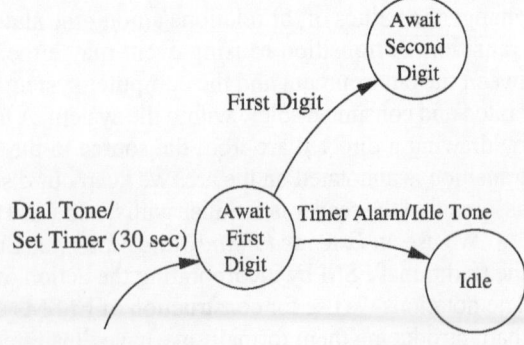

▲ FIGURE 1.22

Model of an RS Type of Deadline Constraint

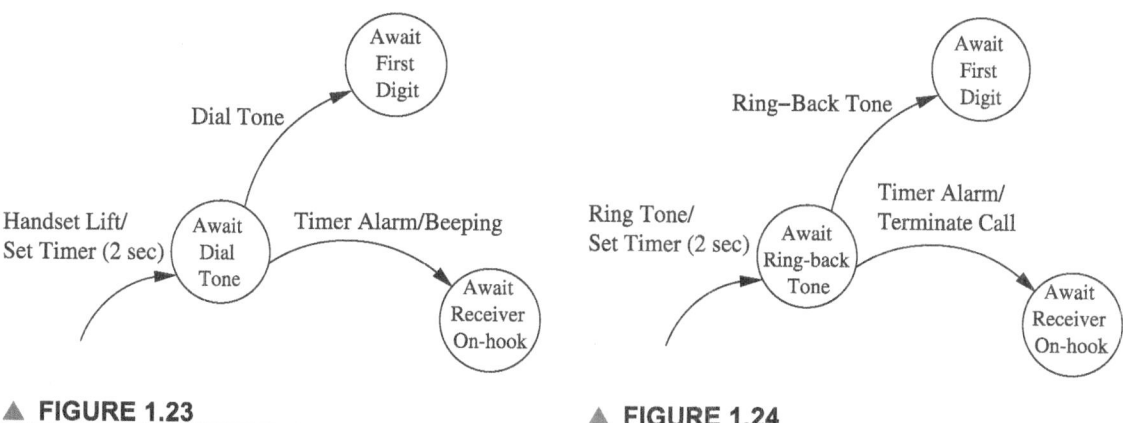

▲ FIGURE 1.23

Model of an SR Type of Deadline Constraint

▲ FIGURE 1.24

Model of an RR Type of Deadline Constraint

Stimulus–Response (SR):   In Section 1.7.3, we had considered the following example of an SR type of deadline constraint:

```
Once the receiver of the handset is lifted, the dial tone must be pro-
duced by the system within 20 sec, otherwise a beeping sound is produced
until the handset is replaced.
```

The EFSM model for this constraint is shown in Fig. 1.23. As soon as the handset is lifted, a timer is set to expire after 2 sec and the system transits to "Await Dial Tone" state. If the dial tone appears first, then the system transits to "Await First Digit" state. Otherwise, it transits to "Await Receiver On-hook" state.

Response–Response (RR):   In Section 1.7.3, we had considered the following example of an RR type of constraint:

```
Once the ring tone is given to the callee, the corresponding ring back tone
must be given to the caller within 2 sec, otherwise the call is terminated.
```

The EFSM model for this constraint is shown in Fig. 1.24. In Fig. 1.24, as soon as the ring tone is produced, the system transits to await "Ring-Back Tone State" and a timer is set to expire in 2 sec. If the ring-back tone appears first, the system transits to "Await First Digit" state, else it enters "Await Receiver On-hook" state, and the call is terminated.

Delay Constraint: A delay constraint between two events is one where after an event occurs, a minimum time must elapse before the other event can occur. We had considered the following example of delay constraint in Section 1.7.3:

```
After a digit is dialled, the next digit should be dialled no sooner
than 10 milliseconds.
```

The EFSM model for it is shown in Fig. 1.25. In Fig. 1.25, if the next digit appears before the alarm, then the beeping sound is produced and the system transits to "Await Caller On-Hook" state.

Durational Constraint: In case of a durational constraint, an event is required to occur for a specific duration. The example of a durational constraint we had considered in Section 1.7.3 is the following:

```
If you press the button of the handset for less than 15 sec it connects
to the local operator. If you press the button for any duration lasting
```

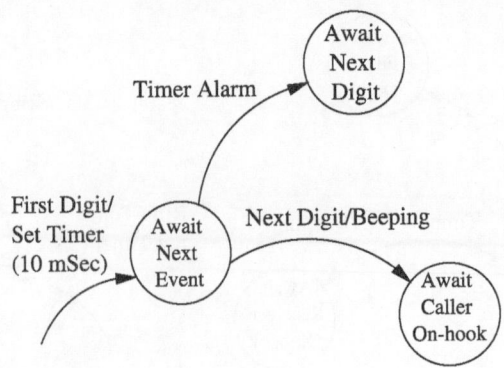

▲ **FIGURE 1.25**

Model of an SS Type of Delay Constraint

```
between 15 to 30 sec, it connects to the international operator. If you
keep the button pressed for more than 30 sec, then on releasing it would
produce the dial tone.
```

The EFSM model for this example is shown in Fig. 1.26. Note that we have introduced two intermediate states "Await Event"and "Await Event 2" to model a durational constraint.

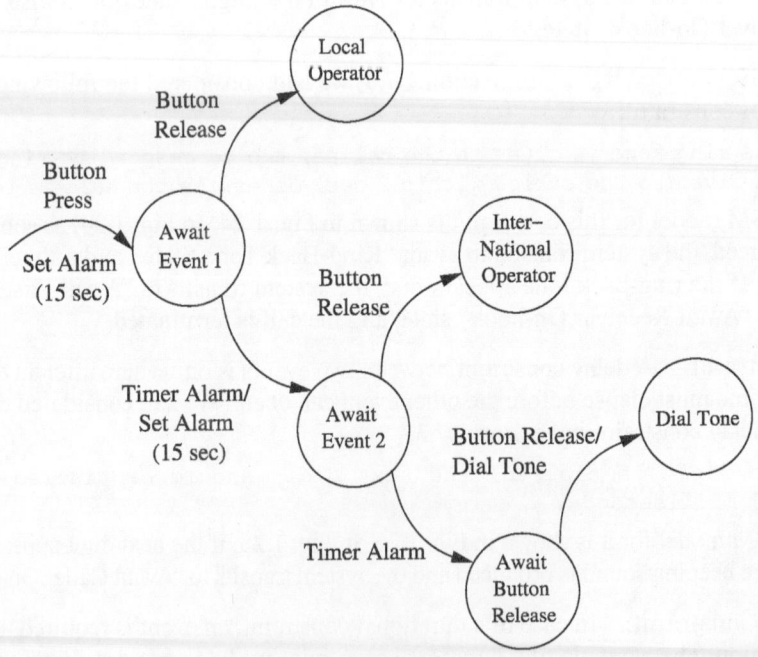

▲ **FIGURE 1.26**

A Model of a Durational Constraint

SUMMARY

- The main aim of this chapter was to introduce you to some very basic concepts and terminologies associated with real-time systems that would be used throughout this book.

- A system is said to be *real-time* when quantitative expressions of time are necessary to describe the behaviour of the system.

- A real-time task is one that is associated with some time constraints.

- A real-time task is classified into either hard, firm, or soft real-time type depending on the consequences of a task failing to meet its timing constraints.

- A safety-critical system is one which does not have a fail-safe state and any failure of the system can cause severe damage. Many hard real-time systems are safety-critical in nature.

- The characteristic features of a hard real-time system include embedded, feedback and distributed structure, and safety-criticality. It is possible though that some hard real-time systems may not have these features.

- There are two main categories of time constraints in embedded hard real-time systems: performance constraints and behavioural constraints. Performance constraints are timing constraints imposed on the response of the controlling computer system, whereas behavioural constraints are timing constraints imposed on the behaviour of the environment. The performance constraints may not be guaranteed if the behavioural constraints are not satisfied.

- We discussed how to model the performance and behavioural types of constraints using an Extended Finite State Machine (EFSM) that extends the traditional FSM with the concepts of setting a timer and the corresponding generation of a timer alarm event. Such a model in addition to serving as a specification technique, can also help in verification and automatic code generation.

EXERCISES

1. State whether you consider the following statements to be TRUE or FALSE. Justify your answer in each case.
    (a) A hard real-time application is made up of only hard real-time tasks.
    (b) Every safety-critical real-time system has a fail-safe state.
    (c) A deadline constraint between two stimuli can be considered to be a behaviorial constraint on the environment of the system.
    (d) Hardware fault-tolerance techniques can easily be adapted to provide software fault-tolerance.
    (e) A good algorithm for scheduling hard real-time tasks must try to complete each task in the shortest time possible.
    (f) All hard real-time systems are safety-critical in nature.
    (g) Performance constraints on a real-time system ensure that the environment of the system is well-behaved.
    (h) Soft real-time tasks are those which do not have any time bounds associated with them.
    (i) Minimization of average task response times is the objective of any good hard real-time task-scheduling algorithm.
    (j) It should be the goal of any good real-time operating system to complete every hard real-time task as ahead of its deadline as possible.

2. What do you understand by the term "real-time?" How is the concept of real-time different from the traditional notion of time? Explain your answer using a suitable example.

3. What does the term "real" in a real-time system signify? Explain what do you mean by a real-time system.

4. Using a block diagram show the important hardware components of a real-time system and their interactions. Explain the roles of the different components.

5. In a real-time system, raw sensor signals need to be preprocessed before they can be used by a computer. Why is it necessary to preprocess the raw sensor signals before they can be used by a computer? Explain the different types of preprocessing that are normally carried out on sensor signals to make them suitable to be used directly by a computer.

6. Identify the key differences between hard real-time, soft real-time, and firm real-time systems. Give at least one example of real-time tasks corresponding to these three categories. Identify the timing constraints in your tasks and justify why the tasks should be categorized into the categories you have indicated.

7. Explain the key differences between the characteristics of a soft real-time task such as web browsing and a non-real-time task such as e-mail delivery.

8. Give an example of a soft real-time task and a non-real-time task. Explain the key difference between the characteristics of these two types of tasks.

9. Name any two important sensor devices and two actuator devices used in real-time applications and explain the physical principles behind their working.

10. Draw a schematic model showing the important components of a typical hard real-time system. Explain the working of the output interface using a suitable schematic diagram. Using a suitable circuit diagram explain how Digital to Analog Conversion (DAC) can be achieved in an output interface.

11. Draw a schematic model showing the important components of a typical hard real-time system. Explain the working of the input interface using a suitable schematic diagram. Using a suitable circuit diagram explain how Analog to Digital Conversion (ADC) is achieved in an input interface.

12. In a hard real-time system, is it necessary that every task in the system be of hard real-time type? Explain your answer using a suitable example.

13. In the context of providing system-level fault-tolerance, why are hardware failures more predictable and easier to handle compared to software failures? Explain the N-version scheme to provide software fault-tolerance. What are the shortcomings of this scheme? How does the recovery block technique attempt to overcome it? Does it succeed? Explain.

14. Explain the checkpointing and rollback recovery scheme to provide fault-tolerant real-time computing. Explain the types of faults it can help tolerate and the faults it can not tolerate. Explain the situations in which this technique is useful.

15. Answer the following questions concerning fault-tolerance of real-time systems.

    (a) Explain why hardware fault-tolerance is easier to achieve compared to software fault-tolerance.

    (b) Explain the main techniques available to achieve hardware fault tolerance.

    (c) What are the main techniques available to achieve software fault-tolerance? What are the shortcomings of these techniques?

16. Briefly explain how hardware failures (e.g., processor failures) can be tolerated in safety-critical hard real-time applications. Consider the fact that hard real-time tasks have stringent deadlines which must be met under all circumstances.

17. What do you understand by the "fail-safe" state of a system? Safety-critical real-time systems do not have a fail-safe state. What is the implication of this?

18. Explain why safety and reliability are not independent issues in safety-critical hard real-time systems. Explain the basic techniques you would adopt to develop a software product that is required to be highly reliable.

19. Is it possible to have an extremely safe but unreliable system? If your answer is affirmative, then give an example of such a system. If you answer in the negative, then justify why it is not possible for such a system to exist.

20. What is a safety-critical system? Give a few practical examples safety-critical hard real-time systems. Are all hard real-time systems safety-critical? If not, give at least one example of a hard real-time system that is not safety-critical.

21. Explain with the help of a schematic diagram how the recovery block scheme can be used to achieve fault-tolerance of real-time tasks. What are the shortcomings of this scheme? Explain situations where it can be used satisfactorily and situations where it can not be used.

22. Identify and represent the timing constraints in the following air-defence system by means of an extended state machine diagram. Classify each constraint into either performance or behavioural constraint.

    Every incoming missile must be detected within 0.2 sec of its entering the radar coverage area. The intercept missile should be engaged within 5 sec of detection of the target missile. The intercept missile should be fired after 0.1 sec of its engagement but no later than 1 sec.

23. Represent a washing machine having the following specification by means of an extended state machine diagram.

    The washing machine waits for the start switch to be pressed. After the user presses the start switch, the machine fills the wash tub with either hot or cold water depending upon the setting of the HotWash switch. The water filling continues until the high level is sensed. The machine starts the agitation motor and continues agitating the wash tub until either the preset timer expires or the user presses the stop switch. After the agitation stops, the machine waits for the user to press the start Drying switch. After the user presses the startDrying switch, the machine starts the hot air blower and continues blowing hot air into the drying chamber until either the user presses the stop switch or the preset timer expires.

24. In a real-time system what is the difference between a performance constraint and a behaviourial constraint? Give practical examples of each type of constraint.

25. Represent the timing constraints in a collision avoidance task in an air surveillance system as an Extended Finite State Machine (EFSM) diagram. The collision avoidance task consists of the following activities.

    • The first subtask named radar signal processor processes the radar signal on a signal processor to generate the track record in terms of the target's location and velocity within 100 mSec of receipt of the signal.

    • The track record is transmitted to the data processor within 1 mSec after the track record is determined.

    • A subtask on the data processor correlates the received track record with the track records of other targets that come close to detect potential collision that might occur within the next 500 mSec.

    • If a collision is anticipated, then the corrective action is determined within 10 mSec by another subtask running on the data processor.

    • The corrective action is transmitted to the track correction task within 25 mSec.

26. Consider the following (partial) specification of a real-time system:

    The velocity of a space craft must be sampled by a computer on-board the space craft at least once every second (the sampling event is denoted by second). After sampling the velocity, the current position is computed (denoted by event C) within 100 mSec, parallelly the expected position of the space craft is retrieved from the database within 200 mSec (denoted by event R). Using these data, the deviation from the normal course of the space craft must be determined within 100 mSec (denoted by event D) and corrective velocity adjustments must be carried out before a new velocity value is sampled in (the velocity adjustment event is denoted by A). Calculated positions must be transmitted to the earth station at least once every minute (position transmission event is denoted by the event T).

Identify the different timing constraints in the system. Classify these into either performance or behavioural constraints. Construct an EFSM to model the system.

27. Construct the EFSM model of a telephone system whose (partial) behaviour is described below:

After lifting the receiver handset, the dial tone should appear within 20 sec. If a dial tone can not be given within 20 sec, then an idle tone is produced. After the dial tone appears, the first digit should to be dialled within 10 sec and the subsequent five digits within 5 sec of each other. If the dialling of any of the digits is delayed, then an idle tone is produced. The idle tone continues until the receiver handset is replaced.

28. What are the different types of timing constraints that can occur in a system? Give examples of each.

2 Real-Time Task Scheduling

In the last chapter we defined a real-time task as one that has some constraints associated with it. Out of the three broad classes of time constraints we discussed, deadline constraint on tasks is the most common. In all subsequent discussions we, therefore, implicitly assume only deadline constraints on real-time tasks, unless we mention otherwise.

Real-time tasks get generated in response to some events that may either be external or internal to the system. For example, a task might get generated due to an internal event such as a clock interrupt occurring every few milliseconds to periodically poll the temperature of a chemical plant. Another task might get generated due to an external event such as the user pressing a switch. When a task gets generated, it is said to have *arrived* or *got released*. Every real-time system usually consists of a number of real-time tasks. The time bounds on different tasks may be different. We had already pointed out that the consequences of a task missing its time bounds may also vary from task to task. This is often expressed as the criticality of a task.

In the last chapter we had pointed out that the appropriate scheduling of tasks is the basic mechanism adopted by a real-time operating system to meet the time constraints of a task. Therefore, selection of an appropriate task scheduling algorithm is central to the proper functioning of a real-time system. In this chapter we discuss some fundamental task-scheduling techniques that are available. An understanding of these techniques would help us to not only satisfactorily design a real-time application, but also understand and appreciate the features of modern commercial real-time operating systems discussed in later chapters.

This chapter is organized as follows. We first introduce some basic concepts and terminologies associated with task scheduling. Subsequently, we discuss two major classes of task schedulers: clock-driven and event-driven. Finally, we explain some important issues that must be considered while developing practical applications.

2.1 SOME IMPORTANT CONCEPTS

In this section we introduce a few important concepts and terminologies which would be useful in understanding the rest of this chapter.

Task Instance: Each time an event occurs, it triggers the task that handles this event to run. In other words, a task is generated when some specific event occurs. Real-time tasks, therefore, normally recur a large number of times at different instants of time depending on the event occurrence times. It is possible that real-time tasks recur at random instants. However, most real-time tasks recur with certain fixed periods. For example, a temperature sensing task in a chemical plant might recur indefinitely with a certain period because the temperature is sampled

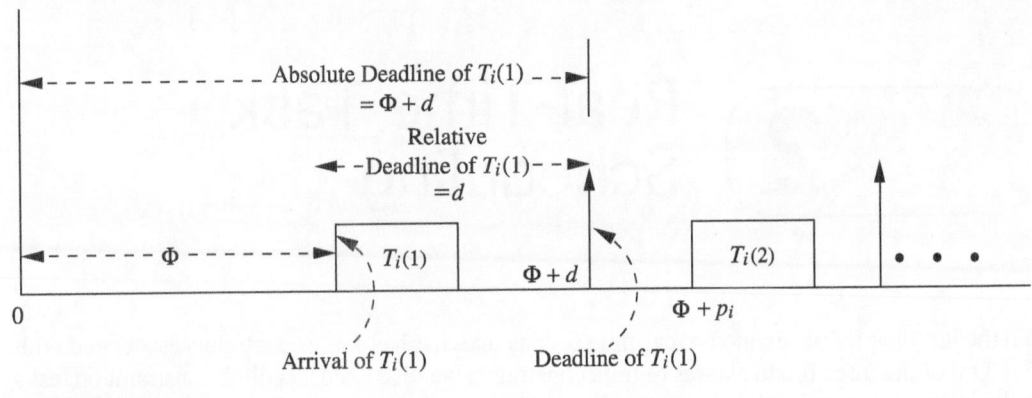

▲ **FIGURE 2.1**

Relative and Absolute Deadlines of a Task

periodically, whereas a task handling a device interrupt might recur at random instants. Each time a task recurs, it is called an *instance* of the task. The first time a task occurs, it is called the first instance of the task. The next occurrence of the task is called its second instance, and so on. The jth instance of a task T_i would be denoted as $T_i(j)$. Each instance of a real-time task is associated with a deadline by which it needs to complete and produce results. We shall at times refer to task instances as processes and use these two terms interchangeably when no confusion arises.

Relative Deadline versus Absolute Deadline: The absolute deadline of a task is the absolute time value (counted from time 0) by which the results from the task are expected. Thus, absolute deadline is equal to the interval of time between the time 0 and the actual instant at which the deadline occurs as measured by some physical clock. Relative deadline is the time interval between the start of the task and the instant at which the deadline occurs. In other words, relative deadline is the time interval between the arrival of a task and the corresponding deadline. The difference between relative and absolute deadlines is illustrated in Fig. 2.1. It can be observed from Fig. 2.1 that the relative deadline of the task $T_i(1)$ is d, whereas its absolute deadline is $\phi + d$.

Response Time: The response time of a task is the time it takes (as measured from the task arrival time) for the task to produce its results. As already remarked, task instances get generated due to occurrence of events. These events may be internal to the system, such as clock interrupts, or external to the system such as a robot encountering an obstacle.

> The response time is the time duration from the occurrence of the event generating the task to the time the task produces its results.

For hard real-time tasks, as long as all their deadlines are met, there is no special advantage of completing the tasks early. However, for soft real-time tasks, average response time of tasks is an important metric to measure the performance of a scheduler. A scheduler for soft real-time tasks should try to execute the tasks in an order that minimizes the average response time of tasks.

Task Precedence: A task is said to precede another task, if the first task must complete before the second task can start. When a task T_i precedes another task T_j, then each instance of T_i precedes the corresponding instance of T_j. That is, if T_1 precedes T_2, then $T_1(1)$ precedes $T_2(1)$, $T_1(2)$ precedes $T_2(2)$, and so on. A precedence order defines a partial order among tasks. Recollect from a first course on discrete mathematics that a partial order relation is reflexive, anti-symmetric, and transitive. An example of partial ordering among tasks is shown in Fig. 2.2. Here T_1 precedes T_2, but we cannot relate T_1 with either T_3 or T_4. We shall later use task precedence relation to develop appropriate task scheduling algorithms.

Data Sharing: Tasks often need to share their results among each other when one task needs to share the results produced by another task; clearly, the second task must precede the first task. In fact, precedence relation between two tasks sometimes implies data sharing between the two tasks (e.g., first task passing some results to the second task). However, this is not always true. A task may be required to precede another even when there is no data sharing. For example, in a chemical plant it may be required that the reaction chamber must be filled with water before chemicals are introduced. In this case, the task handling filling up the reaction chamber with water must complete, before the task handling introduction of the chemicals is activated. It is, therefore, not appropriate to represent data sharing using precedence relation. Further, data sharing may occur not only when one task precedes the other, but might occur among truly concurrent tasks, and overlapping tasks. In other words, data sharing among tasks does not necessarily impose any particular ordering among tasks. Therefore, data sharing relation among tasks needs to be represented using a different symbol. We shall represent data sharing among two tasks using a dashed arrow. In the example of data sharing among tasks represented in Fig. 2.2, T_2 uses the results of T_3, but T_2 and T_3 may execute concurrently. T_2 may even start executing first, after sometimes it may receive some data from T_3, and continue its execution, and so on.

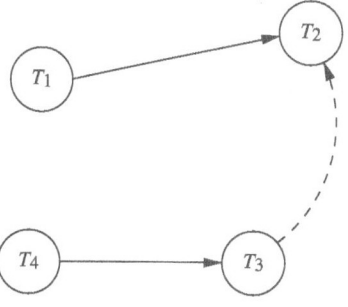

▲ **FIGURE 2.2**

Precedence Relation Among Tasks

2.2 TYPES OF REAL-TIME TASKS AND THEIR CHARACTERISTICS

Based on the way real-time tasks recur over a period of time, it is possible to classify them into three main categories: periodic, sporadic, and aperiodic tasks. In the following, we discuss the important characteristics of these three major categories of real-time tasks.

Periodic Tasks: A periodic task is one that repeats after a certain fixed time interval. The precise time instants at which periodic tasks recur are usually demarcated by clock interrupts. For this reason, periodic tasks are sometimes referred to as clock-driven tasks. The fixed time interval after which a task repeats is called the *period* of the task. If T_i is a periodic task, then the time from 0 till the occurrence of the first instance of T_i (i.e., $T_i(1)$) is denoted by ϕ_i; and is called the phase of the task. The second instance (i.e., $T_i(2)$) occurs at $\phi_i + p_i$. The third instance (i.e., $T_i(3)$) occurs at $\phi_i + 2 * p_i$ and so on. Formally, a periodic task T_i can be represented by a four tuple (ϕ_i, p_i, e_i, d_i) where p_i is the period of task, e_i is the worst case execution time of the task, and d_i is the relative deadline of the task. We shall use this notation extensively in the remainder of this book.

To illustrate the above notation to represent real-time periodic tasks, let us consider the track correction task typically found in a rocket control software. Assume the following characteristics of the track correction task. The track correction task starts 2000 mSec after the launch of the rocket, and it periodically recurs every 50 mSec then on. Each instance of the task requires a processing time of 8 mSec, and its relative deadline is 50 mSec. Recall that the phase of a task is defined by the occurrence time of the first instance of the task. Therefore, the phase of this task is 2000 mSec. This task can formally be represented as (2000 mSec, 50 mSec, 8 mSec, 50 mSec). This task is shown in Fig. 2.3. When the deadline of a task equals its period (i.e., $p_i = d_i$), we can omit the fourth tuple. In this case, we can represent the task as $T_i = $ (2000 mSec, 50 mSec, 8 mSec). This would automatically mean $p_i = d_i = 50$ mSec. Similarly, when $\phi_i = 0$, it can be omitted when no confusion arises. So, $T_i = $ (20 mSec, 100 mSec) would indicate a task with $\phi_i = 0, p_i = 100$ mSec, $e_i = 20$ mSec, and $d_i = 100$ mSec. Whenever there

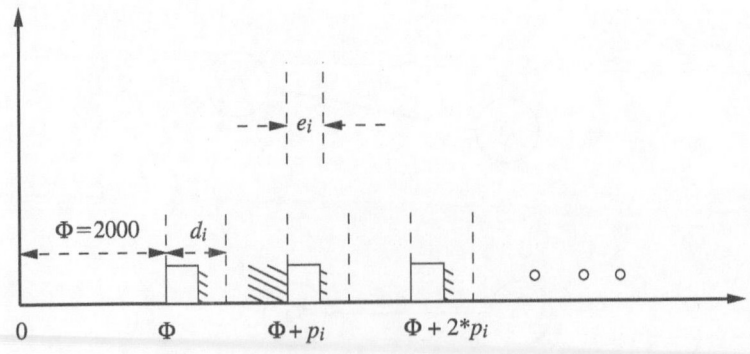

▲ **FIGURE 2.3**

Track Correction Task (2000 mSec, p_i, e_i, d_i) of a Rocket is any scope for confusion, we shall explicitly write out the parameters $T_i = (p_i = 50$ mSec, $e_i = 8$ mSec, $d_i = 40$ mSec), etc.

A vast majority of the tasks present in a typical real-time system are periodic. The reason being many activities carried out by real-time systems are periodic in nature, for example, monitoring certain conditions, polling information from sensors at regular intervals to carry out certain action at regular intervals (such as drive some actuators). We shall consider examples of such tasks found in a typical chemical plant. In a chemical plant several temperature monitors, pressure monitors, and chemical concentration monitors periodically sample the current temperature, pressure, and chemical concentration values which are then communicated to the plant controller. The instances of the temperature, pressure, and chemical concentration monitoring tasks are normally generated through the interrupts received from a periodic timer. These inputs are used to compute corrective actions required to maintain the chemical reaction at a certain rate. The corrective actions are then carried out through actuators.

The periodic task in the above example exists from the time of system initialization. However, periodic tasks can also come into existence dynamically. The computation that occurs in air traffic monitors, once a flight is detected by the radar till the radar exits the radar signal zone is an example of a dynamically created periodic task.

Sporadic Task: A sporadic task is one that recurs at random instants. A sporadic task T_i can be is represented by a three tuple:

$$T_i = (e_i, g_i, d_i)$$

where e_i is the worst case execution time of an instance of the task, g_i denotes the minimum separation between two consecutive instances of the task, d_i is the relative deadline. The minimum separation g_i between two consecutive instances of the task implies that once an instance of a sporadic task occurs, the next instance cannot occur before (g_i) time units have elapsed. That is, g_i restricts the rate at which sporadic tasks can arise. As done for periodic tasks, we shall use the convention that the first instance of a sporadic task T_i is denoted by $T_i(1)$ and the successive instances by $T_i(2)$, $T_i(3)$, etc.

Many sporadic tasks such as emergency message arrivals are highly critical in nature. For example, in a robot a task that gets generated to handle an obstacle that suddenly appears is a sporadic task. In a factory, the task that handles fire conditions is a sporadic task. The time of occurrence of these tasks can not be predicted.

The criticality of sporadic tasks varies from highly critical to moderately critical. For example, an I/O device interrupt, or a DMA interrupt is moderately critical. However, a task handling the reporting of fire conditions is highly critical.

Aperiodic Task: An aperiodic task is in many ways similar to a sporadic task. An aperiodic task can arise at random instants. However, in case of an aperiodic task, the minimum separation g_i between two consecutive instances can be 0. That is, two or more instances of an aperiodic task might occur at the same time instant. Also, the deadline for an aperiodic tasks is expressed as either an average value or is expressed statistically. Aperiodic tasks are generally soft real-time tasks.

It is easy to realize why aperiodic tasks need to be soft real-time tasks. Aperiodic tasks can recur in quick succession. It, therefore, becomes very difficult to meet the deadlines of all instances of an aperiodic task. When several aperiodic tasks recur in quick succession, there is a bunching of the task instances and it might lead to a few deadline misses. As already discussed, soft real-time tasks can tolerate a few deadline misses. An example of an aperiodic task is a logging task in a distributed system. The logging task can be started by different tasks running on different nodes. The logging requests from different tasks may arrive at the logger almost at the same time, or the requests may be spaced out in time. Other examples of aperiodic tasks include operator requests, keyboard presses, mouse movements, etc. In fact, all interactive commands issued by users are handled by aperiodic tasks.

2.3   TASK SCHEDULING

Real-time task scheduling essentially refers to determining the order in which the various tasks are to be taken up for execution by the operating system. Every operating system relies on one or more task schedulers to prepare the schedule of execution of various tasks it needs to run. Each task scheduler is characterized by the scheduling algorithm it employs. A large number of algorithms for scheduling real-time tasks have so far been developed. Real-time task scheduling on uniprocessors is a mature discipline now with most of the important results having been worked out in the early 1970s. The research results available in the literature are very extensive and it would indeed be gruelling to study them exhaustively. In this text, we, therefore, classify the available scheduling algorithms into a few broad classes and study the characteristics of a few important ones in each class.

2.3.1 A Few Basic Concepts and Terminologies

Before focussing on the different classes of schedulers more closely, let us first introduce a few important concepts and terminologies which would be used in our later discussions.

Valid Schedule: A valid schedule for a set of tasks is one where at most one task is assigned to a processor at a time, no task is scheduled before its arrival time, and the precedence and resource constraints of all tasks are satisfied.

Feasible Schedule: A valid schedule is called a feasible schedule, only if all tasks meet their respective time constraints in the schedule.

Proficient Scheduler: A task scheduler sch. 1 is said to be *more proficient* than another scheduler sch. 2, if sch. 1 can feasibly schedule all task sets that sch. 2 can feasibly schedule, but not vice versa. That is, sch. 1 can feasibly schedule all task sets that sch. 2 can, but there exists at least one task set that sch. 2 can not feasibly schedule, whereas sch. 1 can. If sch. 1 can feasibly schedule all task sets that sch. 2 can feasibly schedule and vice versa, then sch. 1 and sch. 2 are called *equally proficient schedulers*.

Optimal Scheduler: A real-time task scheduler is called *optimal*, if it can feasibly schedule any task set that can be feasibly scheduled by any other scheduler. In other words, it would not be possible to find a more proficient scheduling algorithm than an optimal scheduler. If an optimal scheduler can not schedule some task set, then no other scheduler should be able to produce a feasible schedule for that task set.

Scheduling Points: The scheduling points of a scheduler are the points on time line at which the scheduler makes decisions regarding which task is to be run next. It is important to note that a task scheduler does not need to run continuously, it is activated by the operating system only at the scheduling points to make the scheduling decision as to which task to be run next. In a clock-driven scheduler, the scheduling points are defined at the time instants marked by interrupts generated by a periodic timer. The scheduling points in an event-driven scheduler are determined by occurrence of certain events. This topic is discussed more elaborately in Section 2.6.

Preemptive Scheduler: A preemptive scheduler is one which when a higher priority task arrives, suspends any lower priority task that may be executing and takes up the higher priority task for execution. Thus, in a preemptive scheduler, it can not be the case that a higher priority task is ready and waiting for execution, and the lower priority task is executing. A preempted lower priority task can resume its execution only when no higher priority task is ready.

Utilization: The processor utilization (or simply utilization) of a task is the average time for which it executes per unit time interval. In notations: for a periodic task T_i, the utilization $u_i = \frac{e_i}{p_i}$, where e_i is the execution time and p_i is the period of T_i. For a set of periodic tasks $\{T_i\}$: the total utilization due to all tasks $U = \sum_{i=1}^{n} \frac{e_i}{p_i}$. It is the objective of any good scheduling algorithm to feasibly schedule even those task sets that have very high utilization, i.e., utilization approaching 1. Of course, on a uniprocessor it is not possible to schedule task sets having utilization more than 1.

Jitter: Jitter is the deviation of a periodic task from its strict periodic behaviour. The arrival time jitter is the deviation of the task from arriving at the precise periodic time of arrival. It may be caused by imprecise clocks, or other factors such as network congestions. Similarly, completion time jitter is the deviation of the completion of a task from precise periodic points. The completion time jitter may be caused by the specific scheduling algorithm employed which takes up a task for scheduling as per convenience and the load at an instant, rather than scheduling at some strict time instants. Jitters are undesirable for some applications. More discussions on this later.

2.3.2 Classification of Real-Time Task Scheduling Algorithms

Several schemes of classification of real-time task scheduling algorithms exist. A popular scheme classifies the real-time task scheduling algorithms based on how the scheduling points are defined. According to this classification scheme, the three main types of schedulers are: clock-driven, event-driven, and hybrid.

> The clock-driven schedulers are those in which the scheduling points are determined by the interrupts received from a clock. In the event-driven ones, the scheduling points are defined by certain events which precludes clock interrupts. The hybrid ones use both clock interrupts as well as event occurrences to define their scheduling points.

A few important members of each of these three broad classes of scheduling algorithms are the following:

1. Clock Driven:
   - Table-driven
   - Cyclic

2. Event Driven:
   • Simple priority-based
   • Rate Monotonic Analysis (RMA)
   • Earliest Deadline First (EDF)

3. Hybrid:
   • Round-robin

Important members of clock-driven schedulers that we discuss in this text are table-driven and cyclic schedulers. Clock-driven schedulers are simple and efficient. Therefore, these are frequently used in embedded applications. We investigate these two schedulers in some detail in Section 2.4.

Important examples of event-driven schedulers are Earliest Deadline First (EDF) and Rate Monotonic Analysis (RMA). Event-driven schedulers are more sophisticated and usually more proficient and flexible than clock-driven schedulers. These are more proficient because they can feasibly schedule some task sets which clock-driven schedulers can not. These are more flexible because they can feasibly schedule sporadic and aperiodic tasks in addition to periodic tasks, whereas clock-driven schedulers can satisfactorily handle only periodic tasks. Event-driven scheduling of real-time tasks in a uniprocessor environment was a subject of intense research during early 1970s, leading to the publication of a large number of research results, of which the following two popular algorithms are the essence of all EDF and RMA. If we understand these two schedulers well, we would get a good grip on real-time task scheduling on uniprocessors. Several variations to these two basic algorithms exist.

Another classification of real-time task scheduling algorithms can be made based upon the type of task acceptance test that a scheduler carries out before it takes up a task for scheduling. The acceptance test is used to decide whether a newly arrived task would at all be taken up for scheduling or be rejected. Based on the task acceptance test used, there are two broad categories of task schedulers:

• Planning-based
• Best effort

In planning-based schedulers, when a task arrives the scheduler first determines whether the task can meet its deadlines, if it is taken up for execution. If not, it is rejected. If the task can meet its deadline and does not cause other already scheduled tasks to miss their respective deadlines, then the task is accepted for scheduling. Otherwise, it is rejected. In best effort schedulers, no acceptance test is applied. All tasks that arrive are taken up for scheduling and best effort is made to meet its deadlines. But, no guarantee is given as to whether a task's deadline would be met.

A third type of classification of real-time tasks is based on the target platform on which the tasks are to be run. According to this scheme, the different classes of scheduling algorithms are:

• Uniprocessor
• Multiprocessor
• Distributed

Uniprocessor scheduling algorithms are possibly the simplest of the three classes of algorithms. In contrast to uniprocessor algorithms, in multiprocessor and distributed scheduling algorithms first a decision has to be made regarding which task needs to run on which processor and then these tasks are scheduled. In contrast to multiprocessors, the processors in a distributed system do not possess shared memory. Also, in contrast to multiprocessors, there is no global up-to-date state information available in distributed systems. This makes uniprocessor scheduling algorithms that assume a central state information of all tasks and processors to exist unsuitable for use in distributed systems. Further in distributed systems, the communication among tasks is through message passing which is costly. This means that a good distributed scheduling algorithm should not incur too much communication overhead. So, carefully designed distributed algorithms are normally considered suitable for use in a distributed system. We study multiprocessor and distributed scheduling algorithms in Chapter 4.

In the following sections, we study the different classes of schedulers in more detail.

2.4 CLOCK-DRIVEN SCHEDULING

Clock-driven schedulers make their scheduling decisions regarding which task to run next only at the clock interrupt points. Clock-driven schedulers are those for which the scheduling points are determined by timer interrupts. They are also called off-line schedulers because these schedulers fix the schedule before the system starts to run. That is, the scheduler pre-determines which task will run when. Therefore, these schedulers incur very little run time overhead. However, a prominent shortcoming of this class of schedulers is that they can not satisfactorily handle aperiodic and sporadic tasks since the exact time of occurrence of these tasks can not be predicted. For this reason, this type of schedulers are also called a static scheduler.

In this section, we study the basic features of two important clock-driven schedulers: table-driven and cyclic schedulers.

2.4.1 Table-Driven Scheduling

Table-driven schedulers usually precompute which task would run when and store this schedule in a table at the time the system is designed or configured. Rather than automatic computation of the schedule by the scheduler, the application programmer can be given the freedom to select his own schedule for the set of tasks in the application and store the schedule in a table (called *schedule table*) to be used by the scheduler at run time.

An example of a schedule table is shown in Table 2.1. Table 2.1 shows that task T_1 would be taken up for execution at time instant 0, T_2 would start execution 3 mSec afterwards, and so on. An important question that needs to be addressed at this point is what would be the size of the schedule table that would be required for some given set of periodic real-time tasks to be run on a system? An answer to this question can be given as follows: if a set ST = $\{T_i\}$ of n tasks is to be scheduled, then the entries in the table will replicate themselves after LCM($p_1, p_2, \ldots, p_n$) time units, where $p_1, p_2, \ldots, p_n$ are the periods of $T_1, T_2, \ldots$ For example, if we have the following three tasks: (e_1 = 5 mSec, p_1 = 20 mSec), (e_2 = 20 mSec, p_2 = 100 mSec), (e_3 = 30 mSec, p_3 = 250 mSec). Then, the schedule will repeat after every 500 mSec. So, for any given task set it is sufficient to store entries only for LCM($p_1, p_2, \ldots, p_n$) duration in the schedule table. LCM($p_1, p_2, \ldots, p_n$) is called the *major cycle* of the set of tasks ST.

TABLE 2.1   An Example of a Table-Driven Schedule

Task	Start Time in milliseconds
T_1	0
T_2	3
T_3	10
T_4	12
T_5	17

A major cycle of a set of tasks is an interval of time on the time line such that in each major cycle, the different tasks recur identically.

In the above reasoning for the computation of the size of a schedule table, one assumption that we implicitly made is that $\phi_i = 0$ That is, all tasks are in phase.

However, tasks often do have non-zero phase. It would be interesting to determine what would be the major cycle when tasks have non-zero phase. The results of an investigation into this issue has been given as Theorem 2.1.

THEOREM 2.1   *The major cycle of a set of tasks $ST = \{T_1, T_2, \ldots, T_n\}$ is $LCM(\{p_1, p_2, \ldots, p_n\})$ even when the tasks have arbitrary phasings.*

PROOF   As per our definition of a major cycle, even when tasks have non-zero phasings, task instances would repeat the same way in each major cycle. Let us consider an example in which the occurrences of a task T_i in a major cycle be as shown in Fig. 2.4. In Fig. 2.4, there are $k - 1$ occurrences of the task T_i during a major cycle. The first occurrence of T_i starts ϕ time units from the start of the major cycle. The major cycle ends x time units after the last (i.e., $(k - 1)$th) occurrence of the task T_i in the major cycle. Of course, this must be the same in each major cycle.

Assume that the size of each major cycle is M. Then, from an inspection of Fig. 2.4, for the task to repeat identically in each major cycle.

$$M = (k - 1)p_i + \phi + x \tag{2.1}$$

Now, for the task T_i to have identical occurrence times in each major cycle, $\phi + x$ must equal to p_i (see Fig. 2.4).

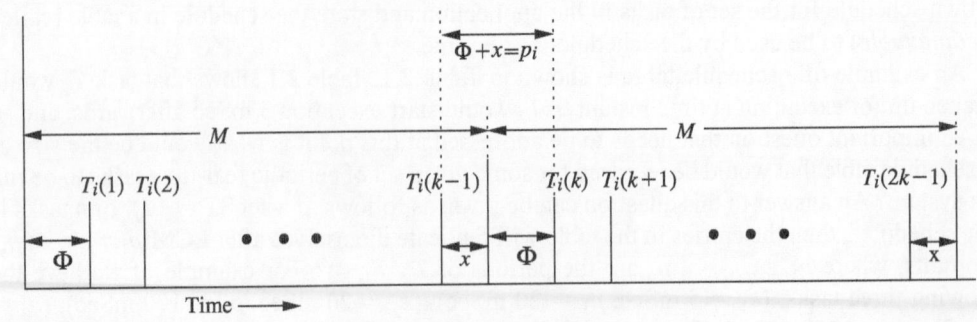

▲ **FIGURE 2.4**

Major Cycle When a Task T_i has Non-Zero Phasing

Substituting this in Expr. 2.1 we get, $M = (k - 1) * p_i + p_i = k * p_i$

So, the major cycle M contains an integral multiple of p_i. This argument holds for each task in the task set irrespective of its phase. Therefore, $M = \text{LCM}(\{p_1, p_2, \ldots, p_n\})$.

2.4.2 Cyclic Schedulers

Cyclic schedulers are very popular and are being extensively used in the industry. A large majority of all small embedded applications being manufactured presently are based on cyclic schedulers that are simple, efficient, and are easy to program. An example application where a cyclic scheduler is normally used is a temperature controller. A temperature controller periodically samples the temperature of a room and maintains it at a preset value. Such temperature controllers are embedded in typical computer-controlled air conditioners.

A cyclic scheduler repeats a precomputed schedule. The precomputed schedule needs to be stored only for one *major cycle* as discussed in Section 2.4.1. Each task in the task set to be scheduled repeats identically in every major cycle. The major cycle is divided into one or more minor cycles (see Fig. 2.6). Each minor cycle is also called a *frame*. In the example shown in Fig. 2.6, the major cycle has been divided into four minor cycles (frames). The scheduling points of a cyclic scheduler occur at frame boundaries. This means that a task can start executing only at the beginning of a frame.

The frame boundaries are defined through the interrupts generated by a periodic timer. Each task is assigned to run in one or more frames. The assignment of tasks to frames is stored in a *schedule table*. An example schedule table is shown in Fig. 2.5.

The size of the frame to be used by the scheduler is an important design parameter and needs to be chosen very carefully. A selected frame size should satisfy the following three constraints.

1. Minimum Context Switching: This constraint is imposed to minimize the number of context switches occurring during task execution. The simplest interpretation of this constraint is that a task instance must complete running within its assigned frame. Unless a task completes within its allocated frame, the task might have to be suspended and restarted in a later frame. This would require a context switch involving some processing overhead. To avoid unnecessary context switches, the selected frame size should be larger than the execution time of each task, so that when a task starts at a frame boundary it should be able to complete within the same

Task Number	Frame Number
T_3	F_1
T_1	F_2
T_3	F_3
T_4	F_2

▲ FIGURE 2.5

An Example Schedule Table for a Cyclic Scheduler

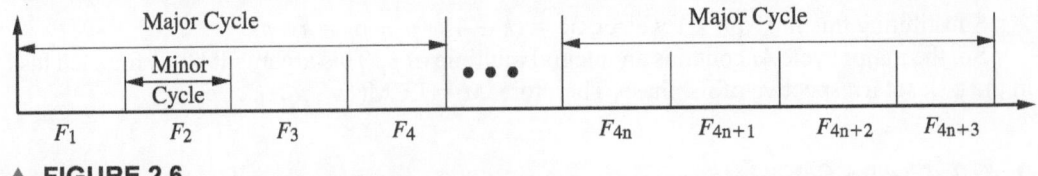

▲ FIGURE 2.6

Major and Minor Cycles in a Cyclic Scheduler

frame. Formally, we can state this constraint as: $\max(\{e_i\}) \leq F$ where e_i is the execution times of the of task T_i, and F is the frame size. Note that this constraint imposes a lower-bound on frame size, i.e., the frame size F must not be smaller than $\max(\{e_i\})$.

2. Minimization of Table Size: This constraint requires that the number of entries in the schedule table should be minimum in order to minimize the storage requirement of the schedule table. Remember that cyclic schedulers are used in small embedded applications with very small storage capacity. So, this constraint is important to the commercial success of a product. Minimization of the number of entries to be stored in the schedule table can be achieved when the minor cycle squarely divides the major cycle. When the minor cycle squarely divides the major cycle, the major cycle contains an integral number of minor cycles (no fractional minor cycles). Unless the minor cycle squarely divides the major cycle, storing the schedule for one major cycle would not be sufficient, as the schedules in the major cycle would not repeat and this would make the size of the schedule table large. We can formulate this constraint as:

$$\left\lfloor \frac{M}{F} \right\rfloor = \frac{M}{F}$$

In other words, if the floor of M/F equals M/F, then the major cycle would contain an integral number of frames.

3. Satisfaction of Task Deadline: This third constraint on frame size is necessary to meet the task deadlines. This constraint imposes that between the arrival of a task and its deadline, there must exist at least one full frame. This constraint is necessary since a task should not miss its deadline, because by the time it could be taken up for scheduling, the deadline was imminent. Consider this: A task can only be taken up for scheduling at the start of a frame. If between the arrival and completion of a task not even one frame exists, a situation as shown in Fig. 2.7 might arise. In this case, the task arrives a little after the kth frame has started. Obviously, it can not be taken up for scheduling in the kth frame and can only be taken up in the $(k+1)$th frame. But, then it may be too late to meet its deadline since the execution time of a task can be up to the size of a full frame. This might result in the task missing its deadline since the task might complete only at the end of $(k+1)$th frame much after the deadline d has passed. We, therefore, need a full frame to exist between the arrival of a task and its deadline as shown in Fig. 2.8, so that task deadlines could be met.

More formally, this constraint can be formulated as follows: Suppose a task arises after Δt time units have passed since the last frame (see Fig. 2.8). Then, assuming that a single frame is sufficient to complete the task, the task can complete before its deadline if $2F - \Delta t$ or, $\leq d_i$. or, $2F \leq d_i + \Delta t$. Remember that the value of Δt might vary from one instance of the task to another. The worst case scenario (where the task is likely to miss its deadline) occurs for the task instance having the minimum value of Δt, such that $\Delta t > 0$. This is the worst case scenario, since under this the task would have to wait the longest before its execution can start.

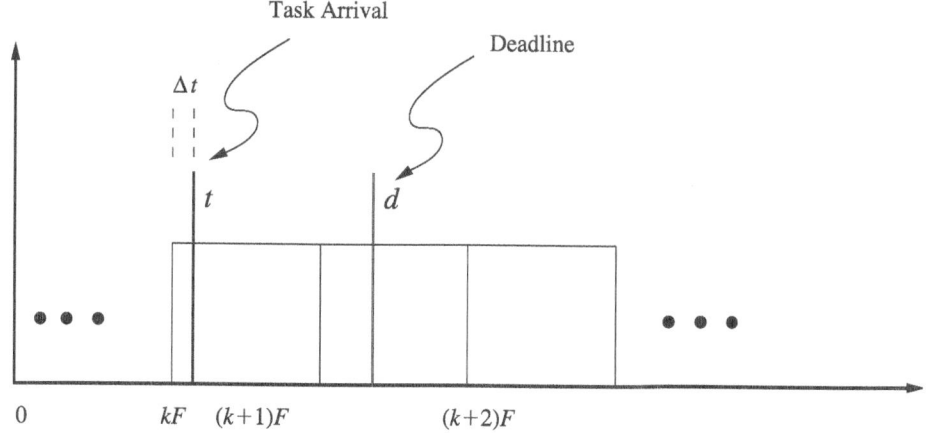

▲ FIGURE 2.7

Satisfaction of a Task Deadline

It should be clear that if a task arrives just after a frame has started, then the task would have to wait for the full duration of the current frame before it can be taken up for execution. If a task at all misses its deadline, then certainly it would be under such situations. In other words, the worst case scenario for a task to meet its deadline occurs for its instance that has the minimum separation from the start of a frame. The determination of the minimum separation value (i.e., $\min(\Delta t)$) for a task among all instances of the task would help in determining a feasible frame size. We show by Theorem 2.2 that $\min(\Delta t)$ is equal to $\mathrm{GCD}(F, p_i)$ Consequently, this constraint can be written as: for every T_i:

$$2F - \mathrm{GCD}(F, p_i) \le d_i \tag{2.5}$$

Note that this constraint defines an upper-bound on frame size for a task T_i. That is, if the frame size is any larger than the defined upper-bound, then tasks might miss their deadlines. Expr. 2.5 defines the frame size, from the consideration of only one task. Now considering all tasks, the frame size must be smaller than $\max(\mathrm{GCD}(F, p_i) + d_i)/2$.

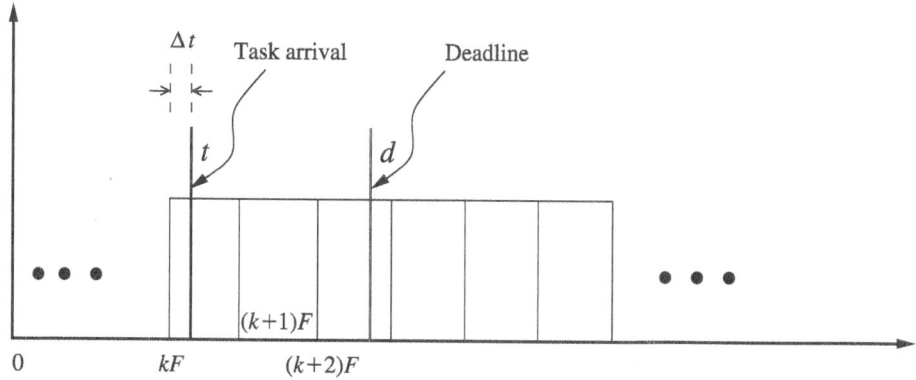

▲ FIGURE 2.8

A Full Frame Exists between the Arrival and Deadline of a Task

THEOREM 2.2   *The minimum separation of the task arrival from the corresponding frame start time ($min(\Delta t)$) considering all instances of a task T_i is equal to $GCD(F, p_i)$.*

PROOF   Let $g = GCD(F, p_i)$, where GCD is the function determining the greatest common divisor of its arguments. It follows from the definition of GCD that g must squarely divide each of F and p_i. Let T_i be a task with zero phasing. Now, assume that this Theorem is violated for certain integers m and n, such that the $T_i(n)$ occurs in the mth frame and the difference between the start time of the mth frame and the arrival time of the nth task is less than g. That is, $0 < (m * F - n * p_i) < g$. Dividing this expression throughout by g, we get:

$$0 < (m * F/g - n * p_i/g) < 1 \tag{2.6}$$

However, F/g and p_i/g are both integers because g is $GCD(p_i, F)$. Therefore, we can write $F/g = I_1$ and $P_i/g = I_2$; for some integral values I_1 and I_2. Substituting this in Expr. 2.6, we get $0 < m * I_1 - n * I_2 < 1$. Since $m * I_1$ and $n * I_2$ are both integers, their difference cannot be a fractional value lying between 0 and 1. Therefore, this expression can never be satisfied.

It can, therefore, be concluded that the minimum time between a frame boundary and the arrival of the corresponding instance of T_i can not be less than $GCD(F, p_i)$.

For a given task set it is possible that more than one frame size satisfies all the three constraints. In such cases, it is better to choose the shortest frame size. This is, because of the fact that the schedulability of a task set increases as more number of frames become available over a major cycle.

It should, however, be remembered that the mere fact that a suitable frame size can be determined does not mean that a feasible schedule would be found. It may so happen that there are not enough number of frames available in a major cycle to be assigned to all the task instances.

Through a few examples we now illustrate how an appropriate frame size can be selected for cyclic schedulers.

Even though for Example 2.1 we could successfully find a suitable frame size that satisfies all the three constraints, it is quite probable that a suitable frame size may not exist for many

Example 2.1

A cyclic scheduler is to be used to run the following set of periodic tasks on a uniprocessor: $T_1 = (e_1 = 1, p_1 = 4)$, $T_2 = (e_2 = 1, p_2 = 5)$, $T_3 = (e_3 = 1, p_3 = 20)$, $T_4 = (e_4 = 2, p_4 = 20)$. Select an appropriate frame size.

Solution.   For the given task set, an appropriate frame size is the one that satisfies all the three required constraints. In the following, we determine a suitable frame size F which satisfies all the three required constraints.

Constraint 1. Let F be an appropriate frame size, then max $\{e_i\} \leq F$. From this constraint, we get $F \geq 1.5$.

Constraint 2. The major cycle M for the given task set is given by $M = LCM(4, 5, 20) = 20$. M should be an integral multiple of the frame size F, i.e., $M \bmod F = 0$. This consideration implies that F can take on the values 2, 4, 5, 10, 20. Frame size of 1 has been ruled out since it would violate the constraint 1.

Constraint 3. To satisfy this constraint, we need to check whether a selected frame size F satisfies the inequality: $2F - \text{GCD}\,(F, p_i) \leq di$ for each p_i.

Let us first try frame size 2.
For $F = 2$ and task T_1:

$$2 * 2 - \text{GCD}\,(2, 4) \leq 4 \equiv 4 - 2 \leq 4$$

Therefore, for p_1 the inequality is satisfied.
Let us try for $F = 2$ and task T_2:

$$2 * 2 - \text{GCD}\,(2, 5) \leq 4 \equiv 4 - 1 \leq 5$$

Therefore, for p_2 the inequality is satisfied.
Let us try for $F = 2$ and task T_3:

$$2 * 2 - \text{GCD}\,(2, 20) \leq 4 \equiv 4 - 2 \leq 20$$

For p_3 the inequality is satisfied.
Therefore, for $F = 2$ and task T_4:

$$2 * 2 - \text{GCD}\,(2, 20) \leq 4 \equiv 4 - 2 \leq 20$$

For p_4 the inequality is satisfied.
Thus, constraint 3 is satisfied by all tasks for frame size 2.
So, frame size 2 satisfies all the three constraints. Hence, 2 is a feasible frame size.

Let us try frame size 4.
For $F = 4$ and task (T_1):

$$2 * 4 - \text{GCD}\,(4, 4) \leq 4 \equiv 8 - 4 \leq 4$$

Therefore, for p_1 the inequality is satisfied.
Let us try for $F = 4$ and task T_2:

$$2 * 4 - \text{GCD}\,(4, 5) \leq 5 \equiv 8 - 1 \leq 5$$

For p_2 the inequality is not satisfied. We need not, therefore, look any further. Clearly, $F = 4$ is not a suitable frame size.

Let us now try frame size 5, to check if that is also feasible.
For $F = 5$ and task T_1, we have

$$2 * 5 - \text{GCD}\,(5, 4) \leq 4 \equiv 10 = 1 \leq 4$$

The inequality is not satisfied for T_1. We need not look any further. Clearly, $F = 5$ is not a suitable frame size

Let us now try frame size 10.
For $F = 10$ and task T_1, we have

$$2 * 10 - \text{GCD}\,(10, 4) \leq 4 \equiv 20 - 2 \leq 4$$

The inequality is not satisfied for T_1. We need not look any further. Clearly, $F = 10$ is not a suitable frame size

Let us try if 20 is a feasible frame size.
For $F = 20$ and task T_1, we have

$$2 * 20 - \text{GCD}\,(20, 4) \leq 4 \equiv 40 - 4 \leq 4$$

Therefore, $F = 20$ is also not suitable.
So, only the frame size 2 is suitable for scheduling.

Example 2.2

Consider the following set of periodic real-time tasks to be scheduled by a cyclic scheduler: $T_1 = (e_1 = 1, p_1 = 4)$, $T_2 = (e_2 = 2, p_2 = 5)$, $T_3 = (e_3 = 5, p_3 = 20)$. Determine a suitable frame size for the task set.

Solution.   Using the first constraint, we have $F \geq 5$.

Using the second constraint, we have the major cycle $M = \text{LCM}(4, 5, 20) = 20$. So, the permissible values of F are 5, 10 and 20. Checking for a frame size that satisfies the third constraint, we can find that no value of F is suitable. To overcome this problem, we need to split the task that is making the task set unschedulable. It is easy to observe that the task T_3 has the largest execution time and consequently, due to the constraint 1 makes the feasible frame sizes quite large.

We try splitting T_3 into two or three tasks. After splitting T_3 into three tasks, we have: $T_{3.1} = (20, 1, 20)$, $T_{3.2} = (20, 2, 20)$, $T_{3.3} = (20, 2, 20)$.

Now the possible values of F are 2 and 4. We can check that after splitting the tasks, $F = 2$ and $F = 4$ become feasible frame sizes.

problems. In such cases, to find a feasible frame size we might have to split the task (or a few tasks) that is (are) causing violation of the constraints into smaller sub-tasks that can be scheduled in different frames.

It is very difficult to come up with a clear set of guidelines to identify the exact task that is to be split, and the parts into which it needs to be split. This, therefore, needs to be done by trial and error. Further, as the number of tasks to be scheduled increases, this method of trial and error becomes impractical since each task needs to be checked separately. However, when the task set consists of only a few tasks we can easily apply this technique to find a feasible frame size for a set of tasks otherwise unschedulable by a cyclic scheduler.

2.4.3 A Generalized Task Scheduler

We have already stated that cyclic schedulers are overwhelmingly popular in low-cost real-time applications. However, our discussion on cyclic schedulers was so far restricted to scheduling periodic real-time tasks. On the other hand, many practical applications typically consist of a mixture of several periodic, aperiodic, and sporadic tasks. In this section, we discuss how aperiodic and sporadic tasks can be accommodated by cyclic schedulers.

Recall that the arrival times of aperiodic and sporadic tasks are expressed statistically. Therefore, there is no way to assign aperiodic and sporadic tasks to frames without significantly lowering the overall achievable utilization of the system. In a generalized scheduler, initially a schedule (assignment of tasks to frames) for only periodic tasks is prepared. The sporadic and aperiodic tasks are scheduled in the slack times that may be available in the frames. Slack time in a frame is the time left in the frame after a periodic task allocated to the frame completes its execution. Non-zero slack time in a frame can exist only when the execution time of the task allocated to it is smaller than the frame size.

A sporadic task is taken up for scheduling only if enough slack time is available for the arriving sporadic task to complete before its deadline. Therefore, a sporadic task on its arrival is subjected to an acceptance test. The acceptance test checks whether the task is likely to be completed within its deadline when executed in the available slack times. If it is not possible to meet the task's deadline, then the scheduler rejects it and the corresponding recovery routines for the task are run. Since aperiodic tasks do not have strict deadlines, they can be taken up for scheduling without any acceptance test and best effort can be made to schedule them in the available slack times. Though for aperiodic tasks no acceptance test is done, but no guarantee is given for a task's completion time and best effort is made to complete the task as early as possible.

An efficient implementation of this scheme is that the slack times are stored in a table and during acceptance test this table is used to check the schedulability of the arriving tasks.

Another popular alternative is that the aperiodic and sporadic tasks are accepted without any acceptance test, and best effort is made to meet their respective deadlines.

Pseudo-code for a Generalized Scheduler.   The following is the pseudo-code for a generalized cyclic scheduler we discussed which schedules periodic, aperiodic, and sporadic tasks. It is assumed that the precomputed schedule for periodic tasks is stored in a schedule table, and, if required, the sporadic tasks have already been subjected to an acceptance test and only those which have passed the test are available for scheduling.

```
cyclic-scheduler() {
current-task T = Schedule-Table [ k] ;
k = k + 1;
k = k mod N;                      //N is the total number of tasks
                                  //in the schedule table
dispatch-current-Task(T);
schedule-sporadic-tasks();        //Current task T completed early,
                                  //sporadic tasks can be taken up.
schedule-aperiodic-tasks();       //At the end of the frame, the running
                                  //task is preempted, if not complete.
idle(),                           //No task to run, idle.
}
```

The cyclic scheduler routine cyclic-scheduler() is activated at the end of every frame by a periodic timer. If the current task is not complete by the end of the frame, then it is suspended and the task to be run in the next frame is dispatched by invoking the routine cyclic-scheduler(). If the task scheduled in a frame completes early, then any existing sporadic or aperiodic task is taken up for execution.

2.4.4 Comparison of Cyclic with Table-Driven Scheduling

Both table-driven and cyclic schedulers are important clock-driven schedulers. A cyclic scheduler needs to set a periodic timer only once at the application initialization time. This timer continues to give an interrupt exactly at every frame boundary. But in table-driven scheduling, a timer has to be set every time a task starts to run. The execution time of a typical real-time task is usually of the order of a few milliseconds. Therefore, a call to a timer is made every few milliseconds. This represents a significant overhead and results in degraded system performance. Therefore, a cyclic scheduler is more efficient than a table-driven scheduler. This probably is a reason why cyclic schedulers are so overwhelmingly popular especially in embedded applications. However, if the overhead of setting a timer can be ignored, a table-driven scheduler is more proficient than a cyclic scheduler because the size of the frame that needs to be chosen should be at least as long as the size of the largest execution time of a task in the task set. This is a source of inefficiency, since this results in processor time being wasted in case of those tasks whose execution times are smaller than the chosen frame size.

2.5 HYBRID SCHEDULERS

We had seen that for clock-driven schedulers, the scheduling points are defined through clock interrupts and in case of event-driven schedulers these are defined by events such as arrival and completion of tasks. In hybrid schedulers, the scheduling points are defined both through the clock interrupts and the event occurrences. In the following, we discuss time-sliced round-robin scheduling—a popular hybrid scheduler.

Time-Sliced Round-Robin Scheduling: Time-sliced round-robin schedulers are very commonly used in the traditional operating systems, and are profusely discussed in the standard operating systems books and in the available literature. We, therefore, keep our discussion on time-sliced round-robin scheduling to the minimum. Time-sliced round-robin scheduling is a preemptive scheduling method. In round-robin scheduling, the ready tasks are held in a circular queue. The tasks are taken up one after the other in a sequence from the queue. Once a task is taken up, it runs for a certain fixed interval of time called its time slice. If a task does not complete within its allocated time slice, it is inserted back into the circular queue. A time-sliced round-robin scheduler is less proficient than table-driven or cyclic scheduler for scheduling real-time tasks. It is rather easy to see why this is so. A time-sliced round-robin scheduler treats all tasks equally, and all tasks are assigned identical time slices irrespective of their priority, criticality, or closeness of deadline. So, tasks with short deadlines might fail to complete on time.

However, it is possible to consider task priorities in the time-sliced round-robin schedulers through a minor extension to the basic round-robin scheme. The scheduler can assign larger time slices to higher priority tasks. In fact, the number of slices allocated to a task can be made proportional to the priority of the task. Even with this modification, time-sliced round-robin scheduling is far from satisfactory for real-time task scheduling (Can you identify the reasons?). In this case, the higher priority tasks are made to complete as early as possible. However, proficient real-time schedulers should try to meet the deadlines of as many tasks as possible, rather than completing the higher priority tasks in the shortest time.

2.6 EVENT-DRIVEN SCHEDULING

Cyclic schedulers are very efficient. However, a prominent shortcoming of the cyclic schedulers is that it becomes very complex to determine a suitable frame size as well as a feasible schedule when the number of tasks increases. Further, in almost every frame some processing time is wasted (as the frame size is larger than all task execution times) resulting in sub-optimal schedules. Event-driven schedulers overcome these shortcomings. Further, event-driven schedulers can handle aperiodic and sporadic tasks more proficiently. On the flip side, event-driven schedulers are less efficient as they deploy more complex scheduling algorithms. Therefore, event-driven schedulers are less suitable for embedded applications as these are required to be of small size, low cost, and consume minimal amount of power.

It should now be clear why event-driven schedulers are invariably used in all moderate and large-sized applications having many tasks, whereas cyclic schedulers are predominantly used in small applications. In event-driven scheduling, the scheduling points are defined by task completion and task arrival events. This class of schedulers are normally preemptive. That is, a higher priority task when ready, preempts any lower priority task that may be running. We discuss three important examples of event-driven schedulers. The simplest of these is the foreground-background scheduler, which we discuss next. In Section 2.7 we discuss EDF and in Section 2.8 we discuss RMA.

Foreground-Background Scheduler: A foreground-background scheduler is possibly the simplest priority-driven preemptive scheduler. In foreground-background scheduling, the real-time tasks in an application are run as foreground tasks. The sporadic, aperiodic, and non-real-time tasks are run as background tasks. Among the foreground tasks, at every scheduling point the highest priority task is taken up for scheduling. A background task can run when none of the foreground tasks is ready. In other words, the background tasks run at the lowest priority.

Let us assume that in a certain real-time system, there are n foreground tasks which are denoted as: $T_1, T_2, \ldots, T_n$. As already mentioned, the foreground tasks are all periodic. Let T_B be the only background task. Let e_B be the processing time requirement of T_B. In this case, the completion time (ct_B) for the background task is given by:

$$ct_B = \frac{e_B}{1 - \sum_{i=1}^{n} \frac{e_i}{p_i}} \tag{2.7}$$

This expression is easy to interpret. When any foreground task is executing, the background task waits. The average CPU utilization due to the foreground task T_i is e_i/p_i, since e_i amount of processing time is required over every p_i period. It follows that all foreground tasks together would result in CPU utilization of $\sum_{i=1}^{n} \frac{e_i}{p_i}$. Therefore, the average time available for execution of the background tasks in every unit of time is $1 - \sum_{i=1}^{n} \frac{e_i}{p_i}$. From this, Expr. 2.7 follows easily. We now illustrate the applicability of Expr. 2.7 through the following three simple examples.

Now using Expr. 2.7, we get the time required by the background task to complete:

$$\frac{1000}{1 - \frac{52}{100}} = 2083.4 \text{ mSec}$$

Example 2.3

Consider a real-time system in which tasks are scheduled using foreground-background scheduling. There is only one periodic foreground task T_f: ($\phi_f = 0, p_f = 50$ mSec, $e_f = 100$ mSec, $d_f = 100$ mSec) and the background task be $T_B = (e_B = 1000$ mSec). Compute the completion time for background task.

Solution. By using the expression (2.7) to compute the task completion time, we have

$$ct_B = \frac{1000}{1 - \frac{50}{100}} \text{ mSec} = 2000 \text{ mSec}$$

So, the background task T_B would take 2000 mSec to complete.

Example 2.4

In a simple priority-driven preemptive scheduler, two periodic tasks T_1 and T_2 and a background task are scheduled. The periodic task T_1 has the highest priority and executes once every 20 mSec and requires 10 mSec of execution time each time. T_2 requires 20 mSec of processing every 50 mSec. T_3 is a background task and requires 100 mSec to complete. Assuming that all the tasks start at time 0, determine the time at which T_3 will complete.

Solution. The total utilization due to the foreground tasks: $\Sigma_{i=1}^{2} \frac{e_i}{p_i} = \frac{10}{20} + \frac{20}{50} = \frac{90}{100}$. This implies that the fraction of time remaining for the background task to execute is given by $\Sigma_{i=1}^{2} \frac{e_i}{p_i} = \frac{10}{100}$. Therefore, the background task gets 1 mSec every 10 mSec. Thus, the background task would take $100 * (10/1) = 1000$ mSec to complete.

Example 2.5

Suppose in Example 2.3, an overhead of 1 mSec on account of every context switch is to be taken into account. Compute the completion time of T_B.

Solution. The very first time the foreground task runs (at time 0), it incurs a context switching overhead of 1 mSec. This has been shown as a shaded rectangle in Fig. 2.9. Subsequently, each time the foreground task runs, it preempts the background task and incurs one context switch. On completion of each instance of the foreground task, the background task runs and incurs another context switch. With this observation, to simplify our computation of the actual completion time of T_B, we can imagine that the execution time of every foreground task is increased by two context switch times (one due to itself and the other due to the background task running after each time it completes). Thus, the net effect of context switches can be imagined to be causing the execution time of the foreground task to increase by two context switch times, i.e., to 52 mSec from 50 mSec. This has been shown in Fig. 2.9.

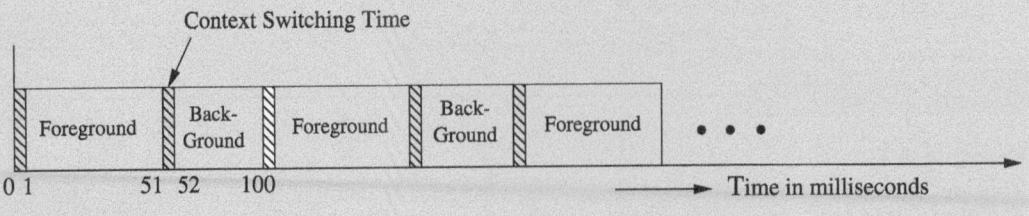

▲ **FIGURE 2.9**
Task Schedule for Example 2.3

In the following two sections, we examine two important event-driven schedulers: Earliest Deadline First (EDF) and Rate Monotonic Algorithm (RMA). EDF is the optimal dynamic priority real-time task scheduling algorithm and RMA is the optimal static priority real-time task scheduling algorithm.

2.7 EARLIEST DEADLINE FIRST (EDF) SCHEDULING

In Earliest Deadline First (EDF) scheduling, at every scheduling point the task having the shortest deadline is taken up for scheduling. The basic principle of this algorithm is very intuitive and simple to understand. The schedulability test for EDF is also simple. A task set is schedulable under EDF, if and only if it satisfies the condition that the total processor utilization due to the task set is less than 1. For a set of periodic real-time tasks $\{T_1, T_2, \ldots, T_n\}$, EDF schedulability criterion can be expressed as:

$$\sum_{i=1}^{n} \frac{e_i}{p_i} = \sum_{i=1}^{n} u_i \leq 1 \tag{2.8}$$

where u_i is average utilization due to the task T_i and n is the total number of tasks in the task set. Expression 2.8 is both a necessary and a sufficient condition for a set of tasks to be EDF schedulable.

EDF has been proven to be an optimal uniprocessor scheduling algorithm [12]. This means that if a set of tasks is unschedulable under EDF, then no other scheduling algorithm can feasibly schedule this task set. In the simple schedulability test for EDF (Expr. 2.8), we assumed that the period of each task is the same as its deadline. However, in practical problems the period of a task may at times be diffcrent from its deadline. In such cases, the schedulability test needs to be changed. If $p_i > d_i$, then each task needs e_i amount of computing time every min (p_i, d_i) duration of time. Therefore, we can rewrite Expr. 2.8 as:

$$\sum_{i=1}^{n} \frac{e_i}{\min(p_i, d_i)} \leq 1 \tag{2.9}$$

However, if $p_i < d_i$, it is possible that a set of tasks is EDF schedulable, even when the task set fails to meet the Expr. 2.9. Therefore, Expr. 2.9 is conservative when, $p_i < d_i$ and is not a necessary condition, but only a sufficient condition for a given task set to be EDF schedulable.

A variant of EDF scheduling is Minimum Laxity First (MLF) scheduling. In MLF, at every scheduling point, a laxity value is computed for every task in the system, and the task having the minimum laxity is executed first. Laxity of a task measures the amount of time that would remain if the task is taken up for execution next. Essentially, laxity is a measure of the flexibility available for scheduling a task. The main difference between MLF and EDF is that unlike EDF, MLF takes into consideration the execution time of a task.

Though EDF is a simple as well as an optimal algorithm, it has a few shortcomings which render it almost unusable in practical applications. The main problems with EDF are discussed in Section 2.7.3. Next, we discuss the concept of task priority in EDF and how it can be practically implemented.

Example 2.6
Consider the following three periodic real-time tasks to be scheduled using EDF on a uniprocessor: $T_1 = (e_1 = 10, p_1 = 20)$, $T_2 = (e_2 = 5, p_2 = 50)$, $T_3 = (e_3 = 10, p_3 = 35)$. Determine whether the task set is schedulable.

Solution.   The total utilization due to the three tasks is given by: $\sum_{i=1}^{3} \frac{e_i}{p_i} = \frac{10}{20} + \frac{5}{50} = \frac{10}{35}$ $= 0.89$. This is less than 1. Therefore, the task set is EDF schedulable.

2.7.1 Is EDF Really a Dynamic Priority Scheduling Algorithm?

We stated in Section 2.6 that EDF is a dynamic priority-scheduling algorithm. Was it after all correct on our part to assert that EDF is a dynamic priority task-scheduling algorithm? If EDF were to be considered a dynamic priority-scheduling algorithm, we should be able determine the precise priority value of a task at any point of time and also be able to show how it changes with time. If we reflect on our discussions of EDF in this section, EDF scheduling does not require any priority value to be computed for any task at any time. In fact, EDF has no notion of a priority value for a task. Tasks are scheduled solely on the proximity to their deadline. However, the longer a task waits in a ready queue, the higher is the chance (probability) of being taken up for scheduling. So, we can imagine that a virtual priority value associated with a task keeps increasing with time until the task is taken up for scheduling. However, it is important to understand that in EDF the tasks neither have any priority value associated with them, nor does the scheduler perform any priority computations to determine the schedulability of a task at either run time or compile time.

2.7.2 Implementation of EDF

A naive implementation of EDF would be to maintain all tasks that are ready for execution in a queue. Any freshly arriving task would be inserted at the end of the queue. Every node in the queue would contain the absolute deadline of the task. At every preemption point, the entire queue would be scanned from the beginning to determine the task having the shortest deadline. However, this implementation would be very inefficient. Let us analyze the complexity of this scheme. Each task insertion will be achieved in O (1) or constant time, but task selection (to run next) and its deletion would require O(n) time, where n is the number of tasks in the queue.

A more efficient implementation of EDF would be as follows. EDF can be implemented by maintaining all ready tasks in a sorted priority queue that can efficiently be implemented by using a heap data structure. In the priority queue, the tasks are always kept sorted according to the proximity of their deadline. When a task arrives, a record for it can be inserted into the heap in O($log_2 n$) time where n is the total number of tasks in the priority queue. At every scheduling point, the next task to be run can be found at the top of the heap. When a task is taken up for scheduling, it needs to be removed from the priority queue. This can be achieved in O(1) time.

A still more efficient implementation of the EDF can be achieved under the assumption that the number of distinct deadlines that tasks in an application can have are restricted. In this approach, whenever a task arrives, its absolute deadline is computed from its release time and its relative deadline. A separate first in first out (FIFO) queue is maintained for each distinct relative deadline that tasks can have. The scheduler inserts a newly arrived task at the end of the corresponding relative deadline queue. Clearly, tasks in each queue are ordered according to their absolute deadlines.

To find a task with the earliest absolute deadline, the scheduler only needs to search among the threads of all FIFO queues. If the number of priority queues maintained by the scheduler is Q, then the order of searching would be O(1). The time to insert a task would also be O(1).

2.7.3 Shortcomings of EDF

In this subsection, we highlight some of the important shortcomings of EDF when used for scheduling real-time tasks in practical applications.

Transient Overload Problem: Transient overload denotes the overload of a system for a very short time. Transient overload occurs when some task takes more time to complete than what was originally planned during the design time. A task may take longer to complete due to several reasons. For example, it might enter an infinite loop or encounter an unusual condition and enter a rarely used branch due to some abnormal input values. When EDF is used to schedule a set of periodic real-time tasks, a task overshooting its completion time can cause some other task(s) to miss their deadlines. It is usually very difficult to predict during program design which task might miss its deadline when a transient overload occurs in the system due to a low priority task overshooting its deadline. The only prediction that can be made is that the task (tasks) that would run immediately after the task causing the transient overload would get delayed and might miss its (their) respective deadline(s). However, at different times a task might be followed by different tasks in execution. However, this lead does not help us to find which task might miss its deadline. Even the most critical task might miss its deadline due to a very low priority task overshooting its planned completion time. So, it should be clear that under EDF any amount of careful design will not guarantee that the most critical task would not miss its deadline under transient overload. This is a serious drawback of the EDF scheduling algorithm.

Resource Sharing Problem: When EDF is used to schedule a set of real-time tasks, unacceptably high overheads might have to be incurred to support resource sharing among the tasks without making tasks to miss their respective deadlines. We examine this issue in some detail in the next chapter.

Efficient Implementation Problem: The efficient implementation that we discussed in Section 2.7.2 is often not feasible as it is difficult to restrict the number of tasks with distinct deadlines to a reasonable number. The efficient implementation that achieves O(1) overhead assumes that the number of relative deadlines is restricted. This may be unacceptable in some situations. For a more flexible EDF algorithm, we need to keep the tasks ordered in terms of their deadlines using a priority queue. Whenever a task arrives, it is inserted into the priority queue.

The complexity of insertion of an element into a priority queue is of the order $\log_2 n$, where n is the number of tasks to be scheduled. This represents a high run time overhead, since most real-time tasks are periodic with small periods and strict deadlines.

2.8 RATE MONOTONIC ALGORITHM (RMA)

We had already pointed out that RMA is an important event-driven scheduling algorithm. This is a static priority algorithm and is extensively used in practical applications. RMA assigns priorities to tasks based on their rates of occurrence. The lower the occurrence rate of a task, the lower is the priority assigned to it. A task having the highest occurrence rate (lowest period) is accorded the highest priority. RMA has been proved to be the optimal static priority real-time task scheduling algorithm. The interested reader may see [12] for a proof.

In RMA, the priority of a task is directly proportional to its rate (or, inversely proportional to its period). That is, the priority of any task T_i is computed as: $priority = \frac{k}{p_i}$, where p_i is the period of the task T_i and k is a constant. Using this simple expression, plots of priority values of tasks under RMA for tasks of different periods can be easily obtained. These plots have been shown in Fig. 2.10(a) and Fig. 2.10(b) where you can observe that the priority of a task increases linearly with the arrival rate of the task and inversely with its period.

Schedulability Test for RMA: An important problem that is addressed during the design of a uniprocessor-based real-time system is to check whether a set of periodic real-time tasks can feasibly be scheduled under RMA. Schedulability of a task set under RMA can be determined from a knowledge of the worst-case execution times and periods of the tasks. A pertinent question at this point is how can a system developer determine the worst-case execution time of a task even before the system is developed. The worst-case execution times are usually determined experimentally or through simulation studies.

The following are some important criteria that can be used to check the schedulability of a set of tasks set under RMA.

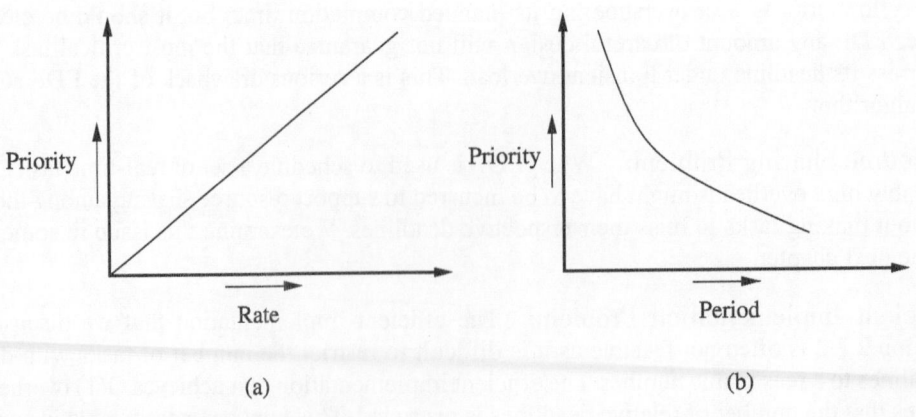

(a)   (b)

▲ **FIGURE 2.10**

Priority Assignment to Tasks in RMA

1. Necessary Condition: A set of periodic real-time tasks would not be RMA schedulable unless they satisfy the following necessary condition:

$$\sum_{i=1}^{n} \frac{e_i}{p_i} = \sum_{i=1}^{n} u_i \leq 1$$

where e_i is the worst case execution time and p_i is the period of the task T_i, n is the number of tasks to be scheduled, and u_i is the CPU utilization due to the task T_i. This test simply expresses the fact that the total CPU utilization due to all the tasks in the task set should be less than 1.

2. Sufficient Condition: The derivation of the sufficiency condition for RMA schedulability is an important result and was obtained by Liu and Layland in 1973 [18]. A formal derivation of the Liu and Layland's results from first principles is beyond the scope of this book. The interested reader is referred to [12] for a formal treatment of this important result. We would subsequently refer to the sufficiency as the Liu and Layland's condition. A set of n real-time periodic tasks are schedulable under RMA, if

$$\sum_{i=1}^{n} u_i \leq n(2^{\frac{1}{n}} - 1) \tag{2.10}$$

where u_i is the utilization due to task T_i. Let us now examine the implications of this result. If a set of tasks satisfies the sufficient condition, then it is guaranteed that the set of tasks would be RMA schedulable.

Consider the case where there is only one task in the system, i.e., $n = 1$. Substituting $n = 1$ in Expr. (2.10), we get

$$\sum_{i=1}^{1} u_i \leq 1(2^{\frac{1}{1}} - 1), \text{ or } \sum_{i=1}^{1} u_i \leq 1$$

Similarly, for $n = 2$ we get

$$\sum_{i=1}^{2} u_i \leq 2(2^{\frac{1}{2}} - 1), \text{ or } \sum_{i=1}^{2} u_i \leq 0.824$$

For $n = 3$ we get

$$\sum_{i=1}^{3} u_i \leq 3(2^{\frac{1}{3}} - 1), \text{ or } \sum_{i=1}^{3} u_i \leq 0.78$$

When $n \to \infty$ we get

$$\sum_{i=1}^{\infty} u_i \leq \infty(2^{\frac{1}{\infty}} - 1), \text{ or } \sum_{i=1}^{\infty} u_i \leq \infty.0$$

Evaluation of Expr. 2.10 when $n \to \infty$. involves an indeterminate expression of the type $\infty.0$. By applying L' Hospital's rule we can verify that the right hand side of the expression evaluates to $log_e 2 = 0.692$. From the above computations, it is clear that the maximum CPU utilization that can be achieved under RMA is 1. This is achieved when there is only a single task in the system. As the number of tasks increases, the achievable CPU utilization falls and as $n \to \infty$ the achievable

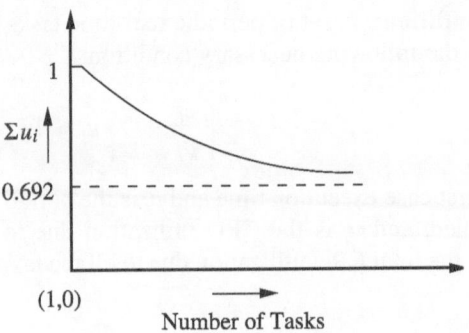

▲ **FIGURE 2.11**

Achievable Utilization with the Number of Tasks under RMA

utilization stabilizes at $log_e 2$, which is approximately 0.692. This is shown in Fig. 2.11. We now illustrate the applicability of the RMA schedulability criteria through a few examples.

The Liu and Layland test (Expr. 2.10) is pessimistic in the following sense.

> If a task set passes the Liu and Layland test, then it is guaranteed to be RMA schedulable. On the other hand, even if a task set fails the Liu and Layland test, it may still be RMA schedulable.

Example 2.7

Check whether the following set of periodic real-time tasks is schedulable under RMA on a uniprocessor: $T_1 = (e_1 = 20, p_1 = 100)$, $T_2 = (e_2 = 30, p_2 = 150)$, $T_3 = (e_3 = 60, p_3 = 200)$.

Solution.   Let us first compute the total CPU utilization achieved due to the three given tasks.

$$\sum_{i=1}^{3} u_i = \frac{20}{100} + \frac{30}{150} + \frac{60}{200} = 0.7$$

This is less than 1, therefore, the necessary condition for schedulability of the tasks is satisfied. Now checking for the sufficiency condition, the task set is schedulable under RMA if Liu and Layland's condition given by Expr. 2.10 is satisfied. Checking for satisfaction of Expr. 2.10, the maximum achievable utilization is given by: $3(2^{\frac{1}{3}} - 1) = 0.78$. The total utilization has already been found to be 0.7. Now substituting these in the Liu and Layland's criterion: $\sum_{i=1}^{3} u_i \leq 3(2^{\frac{1}{3}} - 1)$, we get $0.7 < 0.78$. Expr. 2.10 which is a sufficient condition for RMA schedulability is satisfied. Therefore, the task set is RMA schedulable.

Example 2.8

Check whether the following set of three periodic real-time tasks is schedulable under RMA on a uniprocessor: $T_1 = (e_1 = 20, p_1 = 100)$, $T_2 = (e_2 = 30, p_2 = 150)$, $T_3 = (e_3 = 90, p_3 = 200)$.

Solution. Let us first compute the total CPU utilization due to the given task set:

$$\sum_{i=1}^{3} u_i = \frac{20}{100} + \frac{30}{150} + \frac{90}{200} = 0.85$$

Now checking for Liu and Layland's criterion: $\sum_{i=1}^{3} u_i \nleq 0.78$; since $0.85 \nleq 0.78$, the task set is not RMA schedulable.

It follows from this that even when a task set fails Liu and Layland's test, we should not conclude that it is not schedulable under RMA. We need to test further to check if the task set is RMA schedulable. A test that can be performed to check whether a task set is RMA schedulable when it fails the Liu and Layland test is the Lehoczky's test [17].

Lehoczky test has been expressed as Theorem 2.3.

THEOREM 2.3   *A set of periodic real-time tasks is RMA schedulable under any task phasing, if all the tasks meet their respective first deadlines under zero phasing.*

A formal proof of this Theorem is beyond the scope of this book. However, we provide an intuitive reasoning as to why Theorem 2.3 must be true. For a formal proof of the Lehoczky' results the reader is referred to [17]. Intuitively, we can understand this result from the following reasonings.

First, let us try to understand the following fact.

> The worst case response time for a task occurs when it is in phase with its higher priority tasks.

To see why this statement must be true, consider the following. Under RMA whenever a higher priority task is ready, the lower priority tasks can not execute and have to wait. This implies that a lower priority task will have to wait for the entire duration of execution of each higher priority task that arises during the execution of the lower priority task. More number of instances of a higher priority task will occur during an execution of a lower priority task, when the higher priority task is in phase with it rather than out of phase with it. This has been illustrated through a simple example in Fig. 2.12. In Fig. 2.12(a), a higher priority task $T_1 = (10, 30)$ is in phase with a lower priority task $T_2 = (60, 120)$, the response time of T_2 is 90 mSec. However, in Fig. 2.12 (b), when T_1 has a 20 mSec phase, the response time of T_2 becomes 80. Therefore, if a task meets its first deadline under zero phasing, then it will meet all its deadlines.

Let us now try to derive a formal expression for this important result of Lehoczky. Let $\{T_1, T_2, \ldots, T_i\}$ be the set of tasks to be scheduled. Let us also assume that the tasks have been ordered in descending order of their priority. That is, task priorities are related as: pri $(T_1) >$

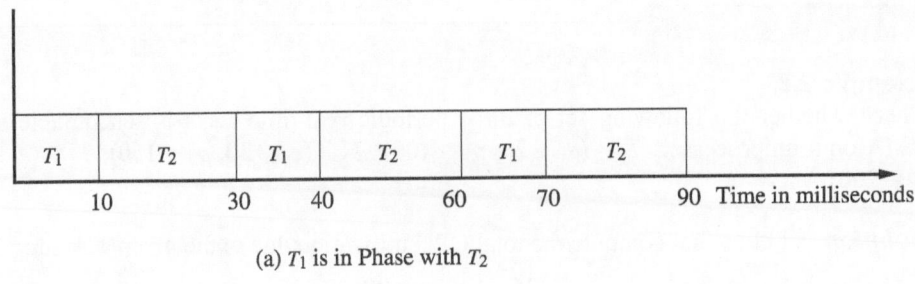

(a) T_1 is in Phase with T_2

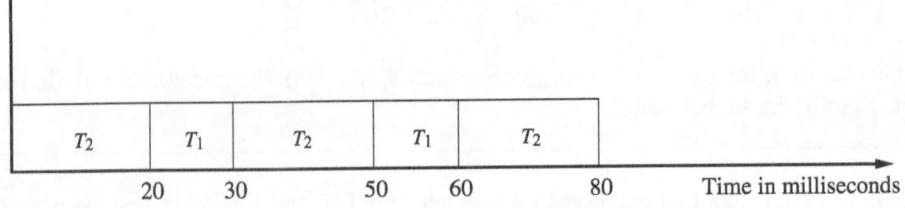

(b) T_1 has a 20 mSec Phase with respect to T_2

▲ **FIGURE 2.12**

Worst Case Response Time for a Task Occurs When it is in Phase with its Higher Priority Tasks

Example 2.9

Check whether the task set of Example 2.8 is actually schedulable under RMA.

Solution.   Though the results of Liu and Layland's test were negative, as per the results of Example 2.8 we can apply the Lehoczky test and observe the following:

For the task T_1: $e_1 < p_1$ holds since 20 mSec < 100 mSec. Therefore, it would meet its first deadline (it does not have any tasks that have higher priority).

For the task T_2: T_1 is its higher priority task and considering 0 phasing, it would occur once before the deadline of T_2. Therefore, $(e_1 + e_2) < p_2$ holds since 20 + 30 = 50 mSec < 150 mSec. Therefore, T_2 meets its first deadline.

For the task T_3: $(2e_1 + 2e_2 + e_3) < p_3$ holds, since 2 * 20 + 2 * 30 + 90 = 190 mSec < 200 mSec. We have considered 2 * e_1 and 2 * e_2 since T_1 and T_2 occur twice within the first deadline of T_3. Therefore, T_3 meets its first deadline. So, the given task set is schedulable under RMA. The schedulability test for T_3 has been shown in Fig. 2.13. Since all the tasks meet their first deadlines under zero phasing, they are RMA schedulable according to Lehoczky's results.

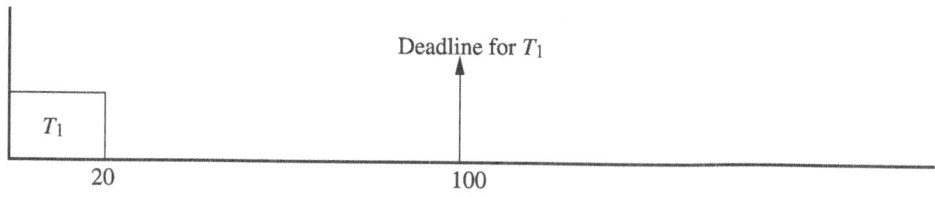

(a) T_1 Meets its First Deadline

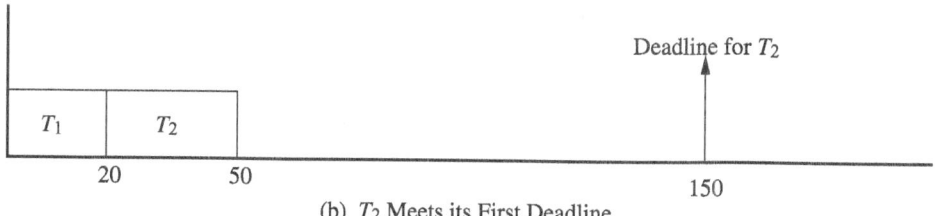

(b) T_2 Meets its First Deadline

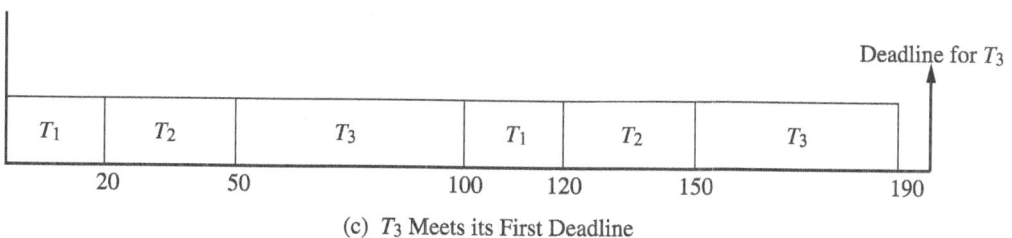

(c) T_3 Meets its First Deadline

▲ **FIGURE 2.13**

Checking Lehoczky's Criterion for Tasks of Example 2.9

pri $(T_2) > \ldots >$ pri (T_i), where pri(T_i) denotes the priority of the task T_i. Observe that the task T_1 has the highest priority and task T_i has the least priority. This priority ordering can be assumed without any loss of generality since the required priority ordering among an arbitrary collection of tasks can always be achieved by a simple renaming of the tasks. Consider that the task T_i arrives at the time instant 0 in the example shown in Fig. 2.14. During the first instance of the task T_i, three instances of the task T_1 have occurred. Each time T_1 occurs, T_i has to wait since T_1 has higher priority than T_i.

Let us now determine the exact number of times that T_1 occurs within a single instance of T_i. This is given by $\left\lceil \frac{p_i}{p_1} \right\rceil$. Since T_1's execution time is e_1, then the total execution time required due to task T_1 before the deadline of T_i is $\left\lceil \frac{p_i}{p_1} \right\rceil \times e_1$. This expression can easily be generalized to consider the execution times all tasks having higher priority than T_i (i.e., $T_1, T_2, \ldots, T_{i-1}$). Therefore, the time for which T_i will have to wait due to all its higher priority tasks can be expressed as:

$$\sum_{k=1}^{i-1} \left\lceil \frac{p_i}{p_k} \right\rceil \times e_k \qquad (2.11)$$

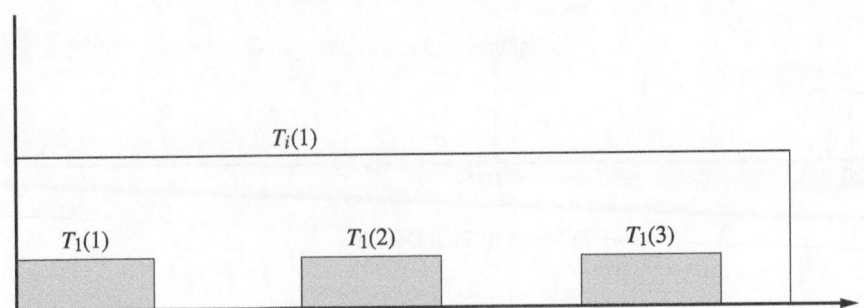

▲ **FIGURE 2.14**

Instances of T_1 over a Single Instance of T_i

Expression 2.11 gives the total time required to execute T_i's higher priority tasks for which T_i would have to wait.

So, the task T_i would meet its first deadline, if

$$e_i + \sum_{k=1}^{i-1} \left\lceil \frac{p_i}{p_k} \right\rceil \times e_k \leq p_i \qquad (2.12)$$

That is, if the sum of the execution times of all higher priority tasks occurring before T_i's first deadline, and the execution time of the task itself is less than its period p_i, then T_i would complete before its first deadline. Note that in Expr. 2.12 we have implicitly assumed that the task periods equal their respective deadlines, i.e., $p_i = d_i$. If $p_i < d_i$, then the Expr. 2.12 would need the following modifications.

$$e_i + \sum_{k=1}^{i-1} \left\lceil \frac{d_i}{p_k} \right\rceil \times e_k \leq d_i \qquad (2.13)$$

Note that even if Expr. 2.13 is not satisfied, there is some possibility that the task set may still be schedulable. This might happen because in Expr. 2.13 we have considered zero phasing among all the tasks, which is the worst case. In a given problem, some tasks may have non-zero phasing. Therefore, even when a task set narrowly fails to meet Expr 2.13, there is some chance that it may in fact be schedulable under RMA. To understand why this is so, consider a task set where one particular task T_i fails Expr. 2.13, making the task set unschedulable. The task misses its deadline when it is in phase with all its higher priority task. However, when the task has non-zero phasing with at least some of its higher priority tasks, the task might actually meet its first deadline contrary to any negative results of Expression 2.13.

Let us now consider two examples to illustrate the applicability of the Lehoczky's results.

As a consequence of the results of Example 2.11, by observing that the lowest priority task of a given task set meets its first deadline, we can not conclude that the entire task set is RMA schedulable. On the contrary, it is necessary to check each task individually as to whether it meets its first deadline under zero phasing. If one finds that the lowest priority task meets its deadline, and concludes from this that the entire task set would be feasibly scheduled under RMA is likely to be flawed.

Example 2.10

Consider the following set of three periodic real-time tasks: $T_1 = (10, 20)$, $T_2 = (15, 60)$, $T_3 = (20, 120)$ to be run on a uniprocessor. Determine whether the task set is schedulable under RMA.

Solution. First, let us try the sufficiency test for RMA schedulability. By Expr. 2.10 (Liu and Layland test), the task set is schedulable if $\sum u_i \leq 0.78$. $\sum u_i = 10/20 + 15/60 + 20/120 = 0.91$. This is greater than 0.78. Therefore, the given task set fails Liu and Layland test. Since Expr. 2.10 is a pessimistic test, we need to test further.

Let us now try Lehoczky's test. All the tasks T_1, T_2, T_3 are already ordered in decreasing order of their priorities.

Testing for task T_1: Since $e_1 = 10$ mSec is less than $d_1 = 20$ mSec. Therefore, T_1 would meet its first deadline.

Testing for task T_2: $10 + \left\lceil \frac{60}{20} \right\rceil \times 10 \leq 60$ or, $20 + 30 = 50 \leq 60$

This is satisfied. Therefore, T_2 would meet its first deadline.

Testing for Task T_3: $20 + \left\lceil \frac{120}{20} \right\rceil \times 10 + \left\lceil \frac{120}{60} \right\rceil \times 15 = 20 + 60 + 30 = 110$ mSec

This is less than T_3's deadline of 120. Therefore, T_3 would meet its first deadline. Since all the three tasks meet their respective first deadlines, the task set is RMA schedulable according to Lehoczky's results.

Example 2.11

RMA is used to schedule a set of periodic hard real-time tasks in a system. Is it possible in this system that a higher priority task misses its deadline, whereas a lower priority task meets its deadlines? If your answer is negative, prove your assertion. If your answer is affirmative, give an example involving two or three tasks scheduled using RMA where the lower priority task meets all its deadlines whereas the higher priority task misses its deadline.

Solution. Yes. It is possible that under RMA a higher priority task misses its deadline where as a lower priority task meets its deadline. We show this by constructing an example. Consider the following task set: $T_1 = (e_1 = 15$ mSec, $p_1 = 20$ mSec$)$, $T_2 = (e_2 = 6$ mSec, $p_2 = 35$ mSec$)$, $T_3 = (e_3 = 3$ mSec, $p_3 = 100$ mSec$)$. For the given task set, it is easy to observe that $\text{pri}(T_1) > \text{pri}(T_2) > \text{pri}(T_3)$. That is, T_1, T_2, T_3 are ordered in decreasing order of their priorities.

For this task set, T_3 meets its deadline according to Lehoczky's test since $e_3 + \left(\left\lceil \frac{p_3}{p_2} \right\rceil \times e_2 \right) + \left(\left\lceil \frac{p_3}{p_1} \right\rceil \times e_1 \right) = 3 + 3 * 6 + 5 * 15 = 96 \leq 100$. But, T_2 does not meet its deadline since, $e_2 + \left(\left\lceil \frac{p_2}{p_1} \right\rceil \times e_1 \right) = 6 + 2 * 15 = 36$, which is greater than the deadline of T_2.

2.8.1 Can the Achievable CPU Utilization Be Any Better Than What was Predicted?

Liu and Layland's results (Expr. 2.10) bounded the CPU utilization below which a task set would be schedulable. It is clear from Expr. 2.10 and Fig. 2.11 that the Liu and Layland schedulability criterion is conservative and restricts the maximum achievable utilization due to any task set which can be feasibly scheduled under RMA to 0.69 when the number of tasks in the task set is large. However, (as you might have already guessed) this is a pessimistic figure. In fact, it has been found experimentally that for a large collection of tasks with independent periods, the maximum utilization below which a task set can feasibly be scheduled is on an average close to 88%.

For harmonic tasks, the maximum achievable utilization (for a task set to have a feasible schedule) can still be higher. In fact, if all the task periods are harmonically related, then even a task set having 100% utilization can be feasibly scheduled. Let us first understand when the periods of a task set are said to be harmonically related. The task periods in a task set are said to be harmonically related, if for any two arbitrary tasks T_i and T_k in the task set, whenever $p_i > p_k$, it should imply that p_i is an integral multiple of p_k. That is, whenever $p_i > p_k$, it should be possible to express p_i as $n \times p_k$ for some integer $n > 1$. In other words, p_k should squarely divide p_i. An example of a harmonically related task set is the following: $T_1 = (5 \text{ mSec}, 30 \text{ mSec})$, $T_2 = (8 \text{ mSec}, 120 \text{ mSec})$, $T_3 = (12 \text{ mSec}, 60 \text{ mSec})$.

It is easy to prove that a harmonically related task set with even 100% utilization can feasibly be scheduled.

THEOREM 2.4 *For a set of harmonically related tasks $HS = \{T_i\}$, the RMA schedulability criterion is given by $\Sigma_{i=1}^n u_i \leq 1$.*

PROOF Let us assume that $T_1, T_2, \ldots, T_n$ be the tasks in the given task set. Let us further assume that the tasks in the task set $\{T_1, T_2, \ldots, T_n\}$ have been arranged in increasing order of their periods. That is, for any i and j, $p_i < p_j$ whenever $i < j$. If this relationship is not satisfied, then a simple renaming of the tasks can achieve this. Now according to Expr. 2.14, a task T_i meets its deadline, if

$$e_i + \Sigma_{k=1}^{i-1} \left\lceil \frac{p_i}{p_k} \right\rceil * e_k \leq p_i \tag{2.14}$$

However, since the task set is harmonically related, p_i can be written as $m * p_k$ for some m. Using this, $\left\lceil \frac{p_i}{p_k} \right\rceil = \frac{p_i}{p_k}$ Now, Expr. 2.12 can be written as: $e_i + \Sigma_{k=1}^{i-1} \frac{p_i}{p_k} * e_k \leq p_i$. For $T_i = T_n$, we can write, $e_n + \Sigma_{k=1}^n \frac{p_n}{p_k} = *e_k \leq p_n$. Dividing both sides of this expression by p_n we get the required result, the task set would be schedulable if $\Sigma_{k=1}^n \frac{e_k}{p_k} \leq 1$, or $\Sigma_{i=1}^n u_i \leq 1$.

2.9   SOME ISSUES ASSOCIATED WITH RMA

In this section, we address some miscellaneous issues associated with RMA scheduling of tasks. We first discuss the advantages and disadvantages of using RMA for scheduling real-time tasks and then discuss why RMA is not optimal when task deadlines differ from the corresponding task periods.

2.9.1 Advantages and Disadvantages of RMA

In this section we first discuss the important advantages of RMA over EDF and then look at some disadvantages of using RMA. As we had pointed out earlier, RMA is very commonly used for scheduling real-time tasks in practical applications. Basic support is available in almost all commercial real-time operating systems for developing applications using RMA. RMA is simple and efficient and is also the optimal static priority task scheduling algorithm. Unlike EDF, it requires very few special data structures. Most commercial real-time operating systems support real-time (static) priority levels for tasks. Tasks having real-time priority levels are arranged in multilevel feedback queues (see Fig. 2.15). Among the tasks in a single level, these commercial real-time operating systems generally provide an option of either time slicing and round-robin scheduling or FIFO scheduling. We discuss in the next chapter why this choice of scheduling among equal priority tasks has an important bearing on the resource sharing protocols.

RMA Transient Overload Handling: RMA possesses good transient overload handling capability. Good transient overload handling capability essentially means that when a lower priority task does not complete within its planned completion time, it can not make any higher priority task to miss its deadline. Let us now examine how transient overload would affect a set of tasks scheduled under RMA. Will a delay in completion by a lower priority task affect a higher priority task? The answer is: "No." A lower priority task even when it exceeds its planned execution time, cannot make a higher priority task wait according to the basic principles of RMA—whenever a higher priority task is ready, it preempts any executing lower priority task. Thus, RMA is stable under transient overload and a lower priority task overshooting its completion time can not make a higher priority task miss its deadline.

The disadvantages of RMA include the following: It is very difficult to support scheduling of aperiodic and sporadic tasks under RMA. Further, RMA is not optimal when task periods and deadlines differ.

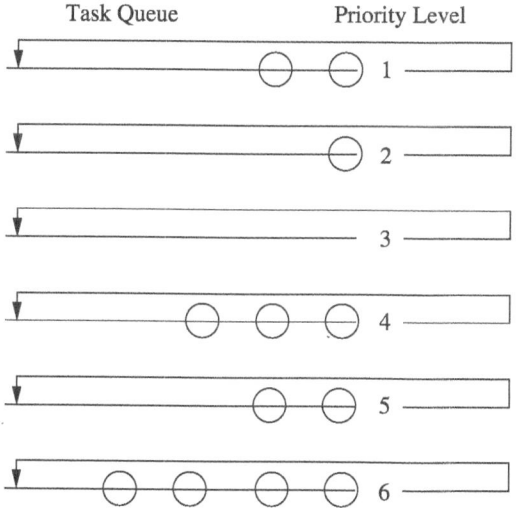

▲ **FIGURE 2.15**

Multi-Level Feedback Queue

2.9.2 Deadline Monotonic Algorithm (DMA)

RMA no longer remains an optimal scheduling algorithm for periodic real-time tasks, when task deadlines and periods differ (i.e., $d_i \neq p_i$) for some tasks in the task set to be scheduled. For such task sets, Deadline Monotonic Algorithm (DMA) turns out to be more proficient than RMA. DMA is essentially a variant of RMA and assigns priorities to tasks based on their deadlines, rather than assigning priorities based on task periods as done in RMA. DMA assigns higher priorities to tasks with shorter deadlines. When the relative deadline of every task is proportional to its period, RMA and DMA produce identical solutions. When the relative deadlines are arbitrary, DMA is more proficient than RMA in the sense that it can sometimes produce a feasible schedule when RMA fails. On the other hand, RMA always fails when DMA fails. We now illustrate our discussions using an example task set that is DMA schedulable but not RMA schedulable.

Example 2.12

Is the following task set schedulable by DMA? Also, check whether it is schedulable using RMA. $T_1 = (e_1 = 10$ mSec, $p_1 = 50$ mSec, $d_1 = 35$ mSec), $T_2 = (e_2 = 15$ mSec, $p_2 = 100$ mSec, $d_2 = 20$ mSec), $T_3 = (e_3 = 20$ mSec, $p_3 = 200$ mSec, $d_3 = 200$ mSec).

Solution. First, let us check RMA schedulability of the given set of tasks, by checking the Lehoczky's criterion. The tasks are already ordered in descending order of their priorities. Checking for T_1: 10 mSec < 35 mSec. Therefore, T_1 would meet its first deadline. Checking for T_2: $10 + 15 \nleq 20$. Therefore, T_2 will miss its first deadline. Hence, the given task set can not be feasibly scheduled under RMA.

Now let us check the schedulability using DMA:
Under DMA, the priority ordering of the tasks is as follows: $Pr(T_2) > Pr(T_1) > Pr(T_3)$
Checking for T_2: 10 mSec < 35 mSec. Hence, T_2 will meet its first deadline.
Checking for T_1: $(15 + 20)$ mSec ≤ 20 mSec, Hence, T_1 will meet its first deadline.
Checking for T_3: $(70 + 30 + 20)$ mSec < 200 mSec. Therefore, T_3 will meet its deadline.

Therefore, the given task set is schedulable under DMA but not under RMA.

2.9.3 Context Switching Overhead

So far, while determining schedulability of a task set, we had ignored the overheads incurred on account of context switching. Let us now investigate the effect of context switching overhead on schedulability of tasks under RMA.

It is easy to realize that under RMA, whenever a task arrives, at most it preempts one task—the task that is currently running. From this observation, it can be concluded that in the worst case, each task incurs at most two context switches under RMA: one, when it runs possibly preempting the currently running task, and the other when it completes. Of course, a task may incur just one context switching overhead, if it does not preempt any task. For example, it arrives when the processor is idle or when a higher priority task was running. However, we need

Example 2.13

Check whether the following set of periodic real-time tasks is schedulable under RMA on a uniprocessor: $T_1 = (e_1 = 20 \text{ mSec}, p_1 = 100 \text{ mSec})$, $T_2 = (e_2 = 30 \text{ mSec}, p_2 = 150 \text{ mSec})$, $T_3 = (e_3 = 90 \text{ mSec}, p_3 = 200 \text{ mSec})$. Assume that context switching overhead does not exceed 1 mSec and is to be taken into account in schedulability computations.

Solution. The net effect of context switches is to increase the execution time of each task by two context switching times. Therefore, the utilization due to the task set is:

$$\sum_{i=1}^{3} u_i = \frac{22}{100} + \frac{32}{150} + \frac{92}{200} = 0.893$$

Since $\Sigma_{i=1}^{3} u_i > 0.78$, the task set is not RMA schedulable according to the Liu and Layland test. Let us try Lehoczky's test: The tasks are already ordered in descending order of their priorities.

Checking for task T_1: $22 < 100$. This is satisfied, therefore, T_1 meets its first deadline.
Checking for task T_2: $22 * 2 + 32 < 150$. This is satisfied, therefore, T_2 meets its first deadline.
Checking for task T_3: $22 * 2 + 32 * 2 + 90 < 200$. This is satisfied, therefore, T_3 meets its first deadline.

Therefore, the task set can be feasibly scheduled under RMA even when context switching overhead is taken into consideration.

to consider two context switches for every task, if we try to determine the worst-case context switching overhead.

For simplicity we can assume that context switching time is constant, and equals c milliseconds where c is a constant. From this, it follows that the net effect of context switches is to increase the execution time e_i of each task T_i to at most $e_i + 2 * c$. It is, therefore, clear that in order to take context switching time into consideration, in all schedulability computations, we need to replace e_i by $e_i + 2c$ for each T_i.

2.9.4 Self Suspension

A task might cause its self suspension, when it performs its input/output operations or when it waits for some events/conditions to occur. When a task self suspends itself, the operating system removes it from the ready queue, places it in the blocked queue, and takes up the next eligible task for scheduling. Thus, self suspension introduces an additional scheduling point, which we did not consider in Section 2.3.1. We, therefore, need to augment our definition of a scheduling point given in Section 2.3.1 accordingly.

In event-driven scheduling, the scheduling points are defined by task completion, task arrival, and self-suspension events.

Let us now determine the effect of self suspension on the schedulability of a task set. Let us consider a set of periodic real-time tasks $\{T_1, T_2, \ldots, T_n\}$, which have been arranged in the increasing order of their priorities (or decreasing order of their periods). Let the worst case self suspension time of a task T_i be b_i. Let the delay that the task T_i might incur due to its own self suspension and the self suspension of all higher priority tasks be bt_i. Then, bt_i can be expressed as:

$$bt_i = b_i + \sum_{k=1}^{i-1} \min(e_k, b_k) \tag{2.15}$$

Self suspension of a higher priority task T_k may affect the response time of a lower priority task T_i by as much as its execution time e_k if $e_k < b_k$. This worst case delay might occur when the higher priority task after self suspension starts its execution exactly at the time instant the lower priority task would have otherwise executed. That is, after self suspension, the execution of the higher priority task overlaps with the lower priority task, with which it would otherwise not have overlapped. However, if $e_k > b_k$, then the self suspension of a higher priority task can delay a lower priority task by at most b_k, since the maximum overlap period of the execution of a higher priority task due to self suspension is restricted to b_k.

Note that in a system where some of the tasks are non-preemptable, the effect of self suspension is much more severe than that computed by Expr. 2.15. The reason for this is that every time a processor self suspends itself, it loses the processor. It may be blocked by a non-preemptive lower priority task after the completion of self suspension. Thus, in a non-preemptable scenario, a task incurs delays due to self-suspension of itself and its higher priority tasks and the delay caused due to non-preemptable lower priority tasks. Obviously, a task can not get delayed due to the self suspension of a lower priority non-preemptable task.

The RMA task schedulability condition of Liu and Layland (Expr. 2.10) needs to change when we consider the effect of self suspension of tasks. To consider the effect of self suspensions in Expr. 2.10, we need to substitute e_i by $(e_i + bt_i)$. If we consider the effect of self suspension on task completion time, the Lehoczky criterion (Expr. 2.12) would also have to be generalized:

$$e_i + bt_i + \sum_{k=1}^{i-1} \left\lceil \frac{p_i}{p_k} \right\rceil * (e_k \leq p_i) \tag{2.16}$$

Example 2.14

Consider the following set of periodic real-time tasks: $T_1 = (e_1 = 10 \text{ mSec}, p_1 = 50 \text{ mSec})$, $T_2 = (e_2 = 25 \text{ mSec}, p_2 = 150 \text{ mSec})$. $T_3 = (e_3 = 50 \text{ mSec}, p_3 = 200 \text{ mSec})$. Assume that the self suspension times of T_1, T_2, and T_3 are 3 mSec, 3 mSec, and 5 mSec, respectively. Determine whether the tasks would meet their respective deadlines, if scheduled using RMA.

Solution. The tasks are already ordered in descending order of their priorities. By using the generalized Lehoczky's condition given by Expr. 2.16 we get:
For T_1 to be schedulable: $(10 + 3)$ mSec < 50 mSec. Therefore, T_1 would meet its first deadline. For T_2 to be schedulable: $(25 + 6 + 10 * 3)$ mSec < 150 mSec. Therefore, T_2 meets its first deadline. For T_3 to be schedulable: $(50 + 11 + (10 * 4 + 25 * 2))$ mSec < 200 mSec. This inequality is also satisfied. Therefore, T_3 would also meet its first deadline.

We have so far implicitly assumed that a task undergoes at most a single self suspension. However, if a task undergoes multiple self suspensions, then the Expr. 2.16 we derived above would have to be changed. We leave this as an exercise for the reader.

It can, therefore, be concluded that the given task set is schedulable under RMA even when self suspension of tasks is considered.

2.9.5 Self Suspension with Context Switching Overhead

Let us examine the effect of context switches on the generalized Lehoczky's test (Expr. 2.16) for schedulability of a task set that takes self suspension by tasks into account. In a fixed priority preemptable system, each task preempts at most one other task if there is no self suspension. Therefore, each task suffers at most two context switches—one context switch when it starts and another when it completes. It is easy to realize that any time when a task self-suspends, it causes at most two additional context switches. Using a similar reasoning, we can determine that when each task is allowed to self-suspend twice, additional four context switching overheads are incurred. Let us denote the maximum context switch time as c. The effect of a single self-suspension of tasks is to effectively increase the execution time of each task T_i in the worst case from e_i to $e_i + 4 * c$. Thus, context switching overhead in the presence of a single self-suspension of tasks can be taken care of by replacing the execution time of a task T_i by $(e_i + 4 * c)$ in Expr. 2.16. We can easily extend this argument to consider two, three, or more self suspensions.

2.10 ISSUES IN USING RMA IN PRACTICAL SITUATIONS

While applying RMA to practical problems, a few interesting issues come up. The first issue that we discuss arises due to the fact that RMA does not consider task criticalities. The other issues that we discuss are coping with limited number of priority levels that commercial operating systems support, and handling of aperiodic and sporadic tasks.

2.10.1 Handling Critical Tasks with Long Periods

A situation that real-time system designers often have to deal with while developing practical applications, is handling applications for which the task criticalities are different from task priorities. Consider the situation where a very critical task has a higher period than some task having a lower criticality. In this case, the highly critical task would be assigned lower priority than a low criticality task. As a result, the critical task might at times miss its deadline due to a simple transient overload of a low critical (but high priority) task. If we simply raised the priority of a critical task to high levels, then the RMA schedulability results would not hold and determining the schedulability of a set of tasks would become extremely difficult.

A solution to this problem was proposed by Sha and Raj Kumar [23] and is called the period transformation technique. In this technique, a critical task is logically divided into many small subtasks. Let T_i be a critical task that is split into k subtasks. Let each of these subtasks have period $\frac{p_i}{k}$. Similarly, the deadline and worst case execution times of these subtasks will be $\frac{d_i}{k}$ and $\frac{e_i}{k}$, respectively. The net effect when a task T_i is split into k subtasks: $\{Ti_1, \ldots, Ti_k\}$ is to effectively raise the priority of T_i.

Each subtask of the critical task T_i would be represented by $T_{ij} = <\frac{e_i}{k}, \frac{p_i}{k}, \frac{d_i}{k}>$. Though we talked of a critical task being split up into k parts, this is done virtually at a conceptual level, rather than making any changes physically to the task itself. The period transformation technique effectively raises the priority of a critical task to higher values without making the RMA analysis results totally invalid. However, due to the raising of the priority of the critical task, RMA schedulability results do not hold accurately. The culprit is the fact that the utilization due to all the higher priority tasks is in fact $k * (e_i/k)/(p_i/k) = k * e_i/p_i$, whereas their actual utilization is e_i/p_i. Therefore, even when tasks appear to be unschedulable after task splitting as indicated by the RMA schedulability analysis results, they may actually be schedulable.

2.10.2 Handling Aperiodic and Sporadic Tasks

Under RMA it is difficult to assign high priority values to sporadic tasks, since a burst of sporadic task arrivals would overload the system and cause many tasks to miss their deadlines. Also, RMA schedulability analysis results that we discussed in this chapter are no longer applicable when aperiodic and sporadic tasks are assigned high priority values. Therefore, aperiodic and sporadic tasks are usually assigned very low priority values. However, in many practical situations tasks such as handling emergency conditions are time bound and critical and may require high priority value to be assigned to a sporadic task. In such situations, the following aperiodic server technique can be used.

Aperiodic Server: An aperiodic server handles aperiodic and sporadic tasks as they arise, selects them at appropriate times, and passes them to an RMA scheduler. It makes it otherwise difficult to analyze aperiodic and sporadic tasks suitable for schedulability analysis. The server deposits a "ticket" which is replenished at the expiration of a certain replenishment period. When an aperiodic event occurs, the server checks to see whether any ticket is available. If it is, the system immediately passes on the arriving task to the scheduler. It then creates another ticket based on the specific ticket creation policy it uses. An aperiodic server makes aperiodic tasks more predictable, and hence makes them suitable for analysis with RMA. Based on the ticket creation policies, there are essentially two types of aperiodic servers: *deferrable* and *sporadic*. Of these, the sporadic server results in higher schedulable utilization and lends itself more easily to analysis. However, it is more complex to implement.

In a deferrable server, tickets are replenished at regular intervals, completely independent of the actual ticket usage. If an aperiodic task arrives, the system will process it immediately if it has enough tickets, and wait till the tickets are replenished if it does not. Thus, there can be bursts of tasks sent to the scheduler and tickets are accumulated when no task is sent over a duration. While a deferrable server is simpler to implement compared to a sporadic server, it deviates from the RMA strict periodic execution model, which leads to conservative system design and low processor utilization.

In a sporadic server, the replenishment time depends on exact ticket usage time. As soon as a ticket is used, the system sets a timer that replaces any used tickets when it goes off. A sporadic server, therefore, guarantees a minimum separation between two instances of a task. Thus, it helps us to consider a sporadic or aperiodic task as a periodic task during schedulability analysis and assign a suitable priority to it. Of course, in some periods the aperiodic or sporadic task may not arise. This leads to some unavoidable CPU idling.

In effect, an aperiodic server helps overcome the non-deterministic nature of aperiodic and sporadic tasks and help consider them to a fast approximation as periodic tasks with period equal to the token generation time.

2.10.3 Coping with Limited Priority Levels

While developing a real-time system, sometimes engineers face a situation where the number of real-time tasks in the application exceed the number of distinct priority levels supported by the underlying operating system. This situation often occurs while developing small embedded applications, where the embedded computers have severe limitations on memory size. Even otherwise, real-time operating systems normally do not support too many priority levels (why?). Also, often out of the total number of priority levels supported by an operating system, only a few are earmarked as real-time levels. The number of priority values typically varies from 8 to 256 in commercial operating systems. As the number of priority levels increases, the number of feedback queues to be maintained by the operating system (see Fig. 2.15) also increases. This not only increases the memory requirement, but also increases the processing overhead at every scheduling point. At every scheduling point, the operating system selects the highest priority task by scanning all the priority queues. Scanning a large number of queues would incur considerable computational overhead. To reduce the operating system overload and to improve the task response times, real-time operating systems support only a restricted number of priority levels.

When there are more real-time tasks in an application than the number of priority levels available from the operating system, more than one task would have to be made to share a single priority value among themselves. This, of course, would result in lower achievable processor utilization than what was predicted by the RMA schedulability expressions. This would be apparent from the following analysis.

Let us now analyze the effect of sharing a single priority level among a set of tasks. First, let us investigate how the Lehoczky's test (Expr. 2.12) would change when priority sharing among tasks is considered. Let $SP(T_i)$ be the set of all tasks sharing a single priority value with the task T_i. Then, for a set of tasks to be schedulable,

$$e_i + b_{it} + \sum_{Tk \in SP(T_i)} e_k + \sum_{k=1}^{i-1} \left[\frac{p_i}{p_k}\right] * e_k \leq p_i \qquad (2.17)$$

The term $\sum_{Tk \in SP(T_i)} e_k$ is necessary since a round first come first served (FCFS) scheduling policy is assumed among equal priority tasks. In this case, the task T_k can be blocked by an equal priority task only once unlike the higher priority tasks (third term in the expression) which block T_k at their every arrival during the execution of T_k. An equal priority task unlike higher priority tasks can block a task only once.

To understand why a task may get blocked by an equal priority task at most once, let us consider the following example. Suppose T_i and T_j share the same priority level, but T_j has a much shorter period compared T_i. A task instance T_i can get blocked by an equal priority task T_j only once (for the duration of task T_j) even though task T_j might have a shorter period compared to T_i. This is because once T_j completed its execution, T_i would get to execute; T_i would execute to completion since T_j instances that may arrive during the execution can not preempt T_i. A task instance T_i can get blocked by an equal priority task T_j only once (for the duration of task T_j).

Priority Assignment to Tasks: It is clear that when there are more real-time tasks tasks with distinct relative deadlines than the number of priority levels supported by the operating system being used, some tasks would have to share the same priority value. However, the exact method of assigning priorities to tasks can significantly affect the achievable processor utilization.

Assigning priority to tasks: It is not difficult to reason that randomly selecting tasks for sharing priority levels would severely lower the achievable schedulable utilization. Therefore, systematic ways of selecting which tasks need to share a priority value are required.

A large number of schemes are available for assigning priority values to tasks when the number of real-time tasks to be scheduled exceeds the distinct real-time priority levels supported by the underlying operating system. Some of the important schemes that are being used are the following:

- Uniform Scheme
- Arithmetic Scheme
- Geometric Scheme
- Logarithmic Scheme

We now discuss these schemes in some detail.

Uniform Scheme: In this scheme, all the tasks in the application are uniformly divided among the available priority levels. Uniform division of tasks among the available priority levels can easily be achieved when the number of priority levels squarely divides the number of tasks to be scheduled. If uniform division is not possible, then more tasks should be made to share the lower priority levels (i.e., higher priority values are shared by lesser number of tasks) for better schedulability. Accordingly, if there are N number of tasks and n priority levels, then–number

Example 2.15

In a certain application being developed, there are 10 periodic real-time tasks $T_1, T_2, \ldots,$ T_{10} whose periods are: 5, 6, . . . , 14 mSec, respectively. These tasks are to be scheduled using RMA. However, only four priority levels are supported by the underlying operating system. In this operating system, the lower the priority value, the higher is the priority of the task. Assign suitable priority levels to tasks using the uniform assignment scheme for scheduling the tasks using RMA.

Solution.   Since the number of priority levels does not squarely divide the number of tasks to be scheduled, some priority values have to be assigned more tasks than the others. The tasks are already sorted in ascending order of their periods (i.e., in decreasing order of their priorities). First, let us uniformly divide the tasks among the priority levels, each level is assigned two tasks each. The rest of the tasks can now be distributed among the lower priority levels. A possibility is that the two lower priority levels are assigned three tasks each. From this, the following is a suitable task assignment scheme:

Priority Level 1: T_1, T_2
Priority Level 2: T_3, T_4
Priority Level 3: T_5, T_6, T_7
Priority Level 4: T_8, T_9, T_{10}

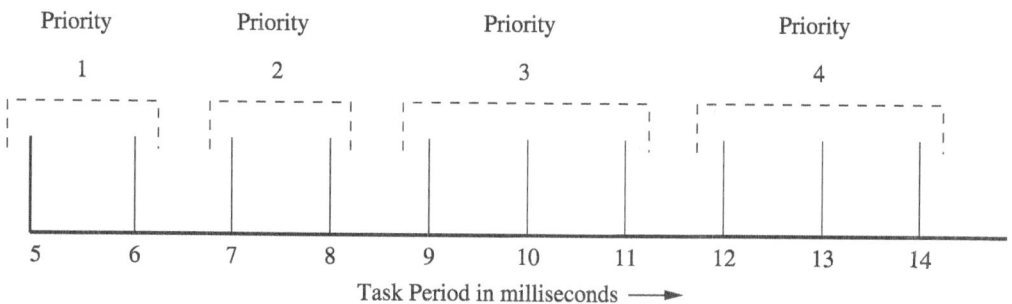

▲ FIGURE 2.16

Uniform Priority Assignment to Tasks of Example 2.15

of tasks are assigned to each level and the rest of the tasks are distributed among the lower priority levels. The uniform priority assignment scheme has been illustrated through the following example.

This priority assignment scheme has been shown in Fig. 2.16.

Arithmetic Scheme: In this scheme, the number of tasks assigned to different priority levels form an arithmetic progression. A possibility is that "r" tasks having the shortest periods are assigned to the highest priority level, $2r$ tasks are assigned the next highest priority level, and so on. Let N be the total number of tasks. Then, $N = r + 2r + 3r + 4r + \ldots nr$, where n is the total number of priority levels.

Geometric Scheme: In this scheme, the number of tasks assigned to different priority levels form a geometric progression. This means that if r tasks having the shortest periods are assigned the highest priority, then the next kr^2 tasks are assigned the immediately lower priority, and so on. Therefore, if N is the total number of tasks, and n is the total number of priority levels then $N = r + kr^2 + kr^3 + kr^4 + \ldots kr^n$.

Logarithmic Scheme: The logarithmic scheme is also popularly known as the *logarithmic grid assignment scheme*. The basic idea behind the logarithmic grid assignment scheme is that the shorter period (higher priority) tasks should be allotted distinct priority levels as much as possible. Many lower priority tasks, on the other hand, can be clubbed together at the same priority levels without causing any problem to the schedulability of the high priority tasks.

To achieve logarithmic grid assignment, the tasks are first arranged in increasing order of their periods. For priority allocation, the range of task periods are divided into a sequence of logarithmic intervals. The tasks can then be assigned to priority levels based on the logarithmic interval they belong to. In this scheme, if p_{max} is the maximum period among the tasks and p_{min} is the minimum period among the tasks, then r is calculated as $r = \left(\frac{p_{max}}{p_{min}}\right)^{1/n}$, where n is the total number of priority levels. Tasks with periods up to r are assigned to the highest priority, tasks with periods in the range r to r^2 are assigned to next highest priority level (assuming $k = 1$ for simplicity), tasks with periods in the range of r^2 to r^3 are assigned to the next highest level, and so on. Simulation experiments have shown that the logarithmic priority assignment works very well for practical problems.

Note that logarithmic task assignment works well only when the task periods are uniformly distributed over an interval. However, if most of the task periods are clustered over a small part of the interval, and the other tasks are sparsely distributed in the rest of the interval, then the logarithmic scheme may yield poor results.

The logarithmic grid assignment scheme has been illustrated in the following example.

Example 2.16

Consider an operating system supporting only four priority levels. An application with 10 periodic real-time tasks are to be scheduled on this operating system using RMA. It is also known that of the given tasks, the largest period is 10,000 mSec and the shortest period is 1 mSec. Other task periods are distributed uniformly over this interval. Assign the tasks to priority levels using the logarithmic grid assignment scheme.

Solution. $r = \left(\frac{10000}{1}\right)^{1/4} = 10$

Accordingly, tasks with periods in the range of 1 mSec and 10 mSec would be assigned to the highest priority level. Tasks with periods in the range of 11 to 100 mSec would be assigned to the the next lower priority level, and so on.

2.10.4 Dealing with Task Jitter

We have already defined task jitter as the magnitude of variation in the arrival or completion times of a periodic task. That is, the arrival time jitter is given by the latest arrival time minus the earliest arrival time among all instances of the task. Similarly, the completion time jitter is given by the latest completion time minus the earliest completion time of the task. Presence of small amounts of arrival time jitter is normally unavoidable as all physical clocks show some amount of skew. Completion time jitters are caused by the basic nature of RMA scheduling which schedules a task at the earliest opportunity at which it can run. Thus, the response time of a task depends on how many higher priority tasks arrive (or were waiting) during the execution of the task. Small amounts of jitter normally do not cause much problems as long as the arrival and completion times of tasks all stay within certain tolerance bounds. However, certain applications might require that the jitter be minimized as much as possible.

Real-time programmers commonly handle tasks with tight completion time jitter requirements using any one of the following two techniques:

- If only one or two actions (tasks) have tight jitter requirements, these actions are assigned very high priority. This method works well only when there are a very small number of actions (tasks). When it is used in an application in which the tasks are barely schedulable, it may result in some tasks missing their respective deadlines.

- If jitter must be minimized for an application that is barely schedulable, each task needs to be split into two: one which computes the output but does not pass it on, and one which passes the output on. This method involves setting the second task's priority to very high values and its period to be the same as that of the first task. An action scheduled with this approach will run one cycle behind schedule, but the tasks will have tight completion time jitter.

SUMMARY

- Scheduling of real-time tasks on a uniprocessor was an area of intense research in the 1970s and the underlying theory is now well-developed.

- Uniprocessor real-time task scheduling algorithms can be broadly classified into clock-driven, event-driven, and hybrid algorithms.

- In clock-driven schedulers, the scheduling points are defined by the interrupts generated by the system clock. Important clock-driven schedulers are table-based and cyclic. Cyclic schedulers are being predominantly used in small embedded applications due to their simplicity and low run time overhead.

- Among the large number of results that are available in event-driven scheduling of real-time tasks on a uniprocessor, two algorithms are most significant:
  Earliest Deadline First (EDF): This is an optimal dynamic priority scheduling algorithm.
  Rate Monotonic Analysis (RMA): This is an optimal static priority scheduling algorithm.

- Though EDF is an optimal real-time task scheduling algorithm on a uniprocessor, it suffers from a few shortcomings. It cannot guarantee that the critical tasks meet their respective deadlines under transient overload. Besides, implementation of resource sharing among real-time tasks is extremely difficult. Therefore, EDF-based algorithms are rarely used in practice and RMA-based scheduling algorithms have become popular.

- We discussed the main results concerning how to determine the schedulability of a set of tasks under EDF and RMA.

- We also discussed how to overcome some problems that arise while developing a practical real-time system. In particular, we discussed how to handle situations such as when task priorities differ from task criticalities, and assigning priorities to tasks for RMA scheduling when the priority levels supported by the operating system is less than the number of tasks to be scheduled.

EXERCISES

1. State whether the following assertions are True or False. Write one or two sentences to justify your choice in each case.

   (a) Average response time is an important performance metric for real-time operating systems handling running of hard real-time tasks.

   (b) Unlike table-driven schedulers, cyclic schedulers do not require to store a precomputed schedule.

   (c) When RMA is used for scheduling a set of hard real-time periodic tasks, the upper bound on achievable utilization improves as the number in tasks in the system being developed increases.

   (d) If a set of periodic real-time tasks fails Lehoczky's test, then it can safely be concluded that this task set can not be feasibly scheduled under RMA.

   (e) A time-sliced round-robin scheduler uses preemptive scheduling.

   (f) The minimum period for which a table-driven scheduler scheduling n periodic tasks needs to pre-store the schedule is given by max $\{p_1, p_2, \ldots p_n\}$, where p_i is the period of the task T_i.

   (g) RMA is an optimal static priority scheduling algorithm to schedule a set of periodic real-time tasks on a non-preemptive operating system.

   (h) A cyclic scheduler is more proficient than a pure table-driven scheduler for scheduling a set of hard real-time tasks.

(i)   RMA is an optimal static priority scheduler in the general case where the task periods and deadlines of a set of hard real-time periodic tasks may differ.

(j)   Self suspension of tasks impacts the worst case response times of the individual tasks much more adversely when preemption of tasks is supported by the operating system compared to the case when preemption is not supported.

(k)   A suitable figure of merit to compare the performance of different hard real-time task scheduling algorithms can be the average task response times resulting from each algorithm.

(l)   When a set of periodic real-time tasks is being scheduled using RMA, it can not be the case that a lower priority task meets its deadline, whereas some higher priority task does not.

(m)   EDF (Earliest Deadline First) algorithm possesses good transient overload handling capability.

(n)   A time-sliced round-robin scheduler is an example of a non-preemptive scheduler.

(o)   RMA (Rate Monotonic Analysis) is an optimal algorithm for scheduling static priority non-preemptive periodic real-time tasks having hard deadlines.

(p)   EDF algorithm is an optimal algorithm for scheduling hard real-time tasks on a uniprocessor when the task set is a mixture of periodic and aperiodic tasks.

(q)   Suppose we have a set of real-time independent tasks to be run on a uniprocessor under RMA scheduling. We observe that a task of period 10 mSec has met its deadline. From this observation, it would be safe to conclude that a task having period of 5 mSec would definitely have met its deadlines.

(r)   Cyclic schedulers are more proficient than table-driven schedulers.

(s)   In a non-preemptable operating system employing RMA scheduling of a set of real-time periodic tasks, self suspension of a higher priority task (due to I/O etc.) may increase the response time of a lower priority task.

(t)   The worst-case response time for a task occurs when it is out of phase with its higher priority tasks.

(u)   A sporadic server used to handle aperiodic and sporadic tasks for RMA scheduling achieves higher schedulable utilization compared to a deferrable server.

(v)   While using a cyclic scheduler to schedule a set of real-time tasks on a uniprocessor, when a suitable frame size satisfying all the three required constraints has been found, it is guaranteed that the task set would be feasibly scheduled by the cyclic scheduler.

(w)   When more than one frame satisfies all the constraints on frame size while scheduling a set of hard real-time periodic tasks using a cyclic scheduler, the largest of these frame sizes should be chosen.

(x)   Good real-time task scheduling algorithms ensure fairness to real-time tasks while scheduling.

2.   State whether the following assertions are True or False. Write one or two sentences to justify your choice in each case.

(a)   In table-driven scheduling of three periodic tasks T_1, T_2, T_3, the scheduling table must have schedules for all tasks drawn up to the time interval $[0, \max(p_1, p_2, p_3)]$, where p_i is the period of the task T_i.

(b)   When a set of hard real-time periodic tasks are being scheduled using a cyclic scheduler, if a certain frame size is found to be unsuitable, then any frame size smaller than this would also not be suitable for scheduling the tasks.

(c)   When a set of hard real-time periodic tasks are being scheduled using a cyclic scheduler, if a candidate frame size exceeds the execution time of every task and squarely divides the major cycle, then it would be a suitable frame size to schedule the given set of tasks.

(d) Finding an optimal schedule for a set of independent periodic hard real-time tasks without any resource-sharing constraints under static priority conditions is an NP-complete problem.

(e) The EDF algorithm is optimal for scheduling real-time tasks in a uniprocessor in a non-preemptive environment.

(f) When RMA is used to schedule a set of hard real-time periodic tasks in a uniprocessor environment, if the processor becomes overloaded any time during system execution due to overrun by the lowest priority task, it would be very difficult to predict which task would miss its deadline.

(g) While scheduling a set of real-time periodic tasks whose task periods are harmonically related, the upper bound on the achievable CPU utilization is the same for both EDF and RMA algorithms

(h) In a non-preemptive event-driven task scheduler, scheduling decisions are made only at the arrival and completion of tasks.

(i) The following is the correct arrangement of the three major classes of real-time scheduling algorithms in ascending order of their run-time overheads.
   • static priority preemptive scheduling algorithms
   • table-driven algorithms
   • dynamic priority algorithms

(j) The EDF scheduling algorithm needs to frequently examine the ready queue of the tasks at regular intervals to determine which task should start running next.

(k) In RMA scheduling, if you observe the sequence in which a set of periodic real-time tasks $\{T_1, T_2, \ldots, T_n\}$ are taken up for execution, the task execution pattern would repeat every LCM $(p_1, p_2, \ldots, p_n)$ interval, where p_i is the period of the task T_i.

(l) While scheduling a set of independent hard real-time periodic tasks on a uniprocessor, RMA can be as proficient as EDF under some constraints on the task set.

(m) For scheduling real-time tasks in practical uniprocessor-based real-time systems, sub-optimal heuristic scheduling algorithms are normally used as optimal scheduling algorithms are computationally intractable.

(n) The RMA schedulability of a set of periodic real-time tasks would be higher if their periods are harmonically related compared to the case where their periods are not related.

(o) RMA should be preferred over the time-sliced round-robin algorithm for scheduling a set of soft real-time tasks on a uniprocessor.

(p) Under RMA, the achievable utilization of a set of hard real-time periodic tasks would drop when task periods are multiples of each other compared to the case when they are not.

(q) RMA scheduling of a set of real-time periodic tasks using the Liu and Layland criterion might produce infeasible schedules when the task periods are different from the task deadlines.

(r) Assume that a task set can be scheduled under RMA and every task meets its corresponding deadline when no task self suspends. In this system, a task might miss its deadline when a higher priority task self suspends for some finite duration.

(s) In a non-preemptive scheduler, scheduling decisions are made only at the arrival and completion of tasks.

(t) A time sliced round-robin scheduler uses preemptive scheduling.

(u) It is not possible to have a system that is safe and at the same time is unreliable.

(v) Precedence ordering among a set of tasks is essentially determined by the data dependency among them.

(w) When a set of periodic real-time tasks are being scheduled on a uniprocessor using RMA scheduling, all tasks would show similar completion time jitter.

3. What do you understand by *scheduling point* of a task scheduling algorithm? How are the scheduling points determined in (i) clock-driven, (ii) event-driven, (iii) hybrid schedulers? How will your definition of scheduling points for the three classes of schedulers change when (a) self-suspension of tasks, and (b) context switching overheads of tasks are taken into account.

4. Identify the constraints that a set of periodic real-time tasks need to satisfy for RMA to be an optimal scheduler for the set of tasks?

5. Real-time tasks are normally classified into periodic, aperiodic, and sporadic real-time task.

    (a) What are the basic criteria on which a real-time task can be determined to belong to one of the three categories?

    (b) Identify some characteristics that are unique to each of the three categories of tasks.

    (c) Give examples of tasks in practical systems which belong to each of the three categories.

6. What do you understand by an optimal scheduling algorithm? Is it true that the time complexity of an optimal scheduling algorithm for scheduling a set of real-time tasks in a uniprocessor is prohibitively expensive to be of any practical use? Explain your answer.

7. What do you understand by jitter associated with a periodic task? How are these jitters caused? How can they be overcome?

8. Suppose a set of three periodic tasks is to be scheduled using a cyclic scheduler on a uniprocessor. Assume that the CPU utilization due to the three tasks is less than 1. Also, assume that for each of the three tasks, the deadlines equals the respective periods. Suppose that we are able to find an appropriate frame size (without having to split any of the tasks) that satisfies the three constraints of minimization of context switches, minimization of schedule table size, and satisfaction of deadlines. Does this imply that it is possible to assert that we can feasibly schedule the three tasks using the cyclic scheduler? If you answer affirmatively, then prove your answer. If you answer negatively, then show an example involving three tasks that disproves the assertion.

9. Classify the existing algorithms for scheduling real-time tasks into a few broad classes. Explain the important features of these broad classes of task scheduling algorithms.

10. Consider a real-time system which consists of three tasks T_1, T_2, and T_3, which have been characterized in the following table.

Task	Phase (mSec)	Execution Time (mSec)	Relative Deadline (mSec)	Period (mSec)
T_1	20	10	20	20
T_2	40	10	50	50
T_2	70	20	80	80

If the tasks are to be scheduled using a table-driven scheduler, what is the length of time for which the schedules have to be stored in the precomputed schedule table of the scheduler.

11. Is EDF algorithm used for scheduling real-time tasks a dynamic priority-scheduling algorithm? Does EDF compute any priority value of tasks any time? If you answer affirmatively, then explain when and how the priority is computed. If you answer negatively, explain the concept of priority in EDF.

12. What is the sufficient condition for EDF schedulability of a set of periodic tasks whose period and deadline are different? Construct an example involving a set of three periodic tasks whose period differ from their respective deadlines such that the task set fails the sufficient condition and yet is EDF schedulable. Verify your answer. Show all your intermediate steps.

13. A preemptive static priority real-time task scheduler is used to schedule two periodic tasks T_1 and T_2 with the following characteristics:

Task	Phase (mSec)	Execution time (mSec)	Relative Deadline (mSec)	Period (mSec)
T_1	0	10	20	20
T_2	0	20	50	50

Assume that T_1 has higher priority than T_2. A background task arrives at time 0 and would require 1000 mSec to complete. Compute the completion time of the background task assuming that context switching takes no more than 0.5 mSec.

14. Assume that a preemptive priority-based system consists of two periodic foreground tasks T_1, T_2, and T_3 with the following characteristics:

Task	Phase (mSec)	Execution time (mSec)	Relative Deadline (mSec)	Period (mSec)
T_1	0	20	100	100
T_2	0	30	150	150
T_3	0	30	300	300

T_1 has higher priority than T_2 and T_2 has higher priority than T_3. A background task Tb arrives at time 0 and would require 2000 mSec to complete. Compute the completion time of the background task Tb assuming that context switching time takes no more than 1 mSec.

15. A cyclic real-time scheduler is to be used to schedule three periodic tasks T_1, T_2, and T_3 with the following characteristics:

Task	Phase (mSec)	Execution Time (mSec)	Relative Deadline (mSec)	Period (mSec)
T_1	0	20	100	100
T_2	0	20	80	80
T_2	0	30	150	150

Suggest a suitable frame size that can be used. Show all intermediate steps in your calculations.

16. Consider the following set of three independent real-time periodic tasks.

Task	Phase (mSec)	Execution Time (mSec)	Relative Deadline (mSec)	Period (mSec)
T_1	20	25	150	100
T_2	40	10	50	30
T_3	60	50	200	150

Suppose a cyclic scheduler is to be used to schedule the task set. What is the major cycle of the task set? Suggest a suitable frame size and provide a feasible schedule (task to frame assignment for a major cycle) for the task set.

17. Consider the following set of four independent real-time periodic tasks.

Task	Start-Time (mSec)	Processing-Time (mSec)	Period (mSec)
T_1	20	25	150
T_2	40	10	50
T_3	20	15	50
T_4	60	50	200

Assume that task T_3 is more critical than task T_2. Check whether the task set can be feasibly scheduled using RMA.

18. What is the worst case response time of the background task of a system in which the background task requires 1000 mSec to complete. There are two foreground tasks. The higher priority foreground task executes once every 100 mSec and each time requires 25 mSec to complete. The lower priority foreground task executes once every 50 mSec and requires 15 mSec to complete. Context switching requires no more than 1 mSec.

19. Construct an example involving more than one hard real-time periodic task whose aggregate processor utilization is 1, and yet schedulable under RMA.

20. Explain the difference between clock-driven, event-driven, and hybrid schedulers for real-time tasks. Which type of scheduler would be preferred for scheduling three periodic tasks in an embedded application. Justify your answer.

21. Determine whether the following set of periodic tasks is schedulable on a uniprocessor using DMA (Deadline Monotonic Algorithm). Show all intermediate steps in your computation.

Task	Start-Time (mSec)	Processing-Time (mSec)	Period (mSec)	Deadline (mSec)
T_1	20	25	150	140
T_2	60	10	60	40
T_3	40	20	200	120
T_4	25	10	80	25

22. Consider the following set of three independent real-time periodic tasks.

Task	Start-Time (mSec)	Processing-Time (mSec)	Period (mSec)	Deadline (mSec)
T_1	20	25	150	100
T_2	40	10	50	30
T_3	60	50	200	150

Determine whether the task set is schedulable on a uniprocessor using EDF. Show all intermediate steps in your computation.

23. Determine whether the following set of periodic real-time tasks is schedulable on a uniprocessor using RMA. Show the intermediate steps in your computation. Is RMA optimal when the task deadlines differ from the task periods?

Task	Start-Time (mSec)	Processing-Time (mSec)	Period (mSec)	Deadline (mSec)
T_1	20	25	150	100
T_2	40	7	40	40
T_3	60	10	60	50
T_4	25	10	30	20

24. Construct an example involving two periodic real-time tasks of which one can be feasibly scheduled by both RMA and EDF, but the schedule generated by RMA differs from that generated by EDF. Draw the two schedules on a time line and highlight how the two schedules differ. Consider the two tasks such that for each task:

(a) the period is the same as the deadline

(b) period is different from the deadline

25. Briefly explain while scheduling a set of hard real-time periodic tasks, why RMA can not achieve 100% processor utilization without missing task deadlines.

26. Can multiprocessor real-time task scheduling algorithms be used satisfactorily in distributed systems. Explain the basic difference between the characteristics of a real-time task scheduling algorithm for multiprocessors and a real-time task scheduling algorithm for applications running on distributed systems.

27. Construct an example involving three arbitrary real-time periodic tasks to be scheduled on a uniprocessor, for whom the task schedules worked out by EDF and RMA would be different.

28. Construct an example involving three periodic real-time tasks (for each task, task period should be equal to its deadline) which would be schedulable under EDF but unschedulable under RMA. Justify why your example is correct.

29. Construct an example involving a set of hard real-time periodic tasks that are not schedulable under RMA but could be feasibly scheduled by DMA. Verify your answer showing all the intermediate steps.

30. Three hard real-time periodic tasks T_1 = (50 mSec, 100 mSec, 100 mSec), T_2 = (70 mSec, 200 mSec, 200 mSec), and T_3 = (60 mSec, 400 mSec, 400 mSec) are to be scheduled on a uniprocessor using RMA. Can the task set be feasibly be scheduled? Suppose context switch overhead of 1 mSec is to be taken into account, determine the schedulability.

31. Consider the following three real-time periodic tasks.

Task	Start-Time (mSec)	Processing-Time (mSec)	Period (mSec)	Deadline (mSec)
T_1	20	25	150	150
T_2	40	10	50	50
T_3	60	50	200	200

(a) Check whether the three given tasks are schedulable under RMA. Show all intermediate steps in your computation.

(b) Assuming that each context switch incurs an overhead of 1 mSec, determine whether the tasks are schedulable under RMA. Also, determine the average context switching overhead per unit of task execution.

(c) Assume that T_1, T_2, and T_3 self suspend for 10 mSec, 20 mSec, and 15 mSec, respectively. Determine whether the task set remains schedulable under RMA. The context switching overhead of 1 mSec should be considered in your result. You can assume that each task undergoes self suspension only once during each of its execution.

(d) Assuming that T_1 and T_2 are assigned the same priority value, determine the additional delay in response time that T_2 would incur compared to the case when they are assigned distinct priorities. Ignore the self suspension times and the context switch overhead for this part of the question.

(e) Assume that T_1, T_2, and T_3, each require certain critical section C during their computation. Would it be correct to assert that T_1 and T_3 would not undergo any priority inversion due to T_2? Justify your answer. Ignore the self suspension times and the context switch overheads for this part of the question.

(f) Assume that T_3 is known to be the most critical of the three tasks. Explain a suitable scheme by which it may be possible to ensure that T_3 does not miss its deadlines under transient overload conditions when the task set is scheduled using RMA.

(g) Assume that you have been asked to implement an EDF task scheduler for an application where the efficiency of the scheduling algorithm is a very important concern:

    i. Explain the data structure you would use to maintain the ready list. What would be the complexity of inserting and removing tasks from the ready list.

    ii. Identify the events which would trigger your scheduler.

(h) Explain how an EDF (Earliest Deadline First) scheduler for scheduling a set of real-time tasks can be implemented most efficiently. What is the complexity of handling a task arrival in your implementation? Explain your answer.

(i) Assume that T_2 and T_3, each require certain critical resource CR1 during their computation. T_2 needs CR1 for 10 mSec and T_3 needs CR1 for 20 mSec. Also, tasks T_1 and T_2, each require critical resource CR2 during their computation. T_1 needs CR1 for 15 mSec and T_2 needs CR2 for 5 mSec. Assume that each task instance tries to get all its required resources before starting to use any of the resources. Also, a task instance returns a resource as soon as it completes computing it. Once a task instance returns a resource, it does not try to acquire it again. If PCP (priority ceiling protocol) is used for resource arbitration, determine if the task set is schedulable when the context switching overhead of 1 mSec is considered (assume no self suspension of tasks).

(j) Typically, what is the number of priority levels supported by any commercial real-time operating system that you are aware of? What is the minimum number of priority levels required by RT-POSIX? Why do operating systems restrict the number of priority levels they support?

Handling Resource Sharing and Dependencies Among Real-Time Tasks

3

The different task scheduling algorithms that we discussed in the last chapter were all based on the premise that the different tasks in a system are all independent. However, that is rarely the case in real-life applications. Tasks often have explicit dependencies specified among themselves, however implicit dependencies are more common. Tasks might become inter dependent for several reasons. A common form of dependency arises when one task needs the results of another task to proceed with its computations. For example, the positional error computation task of a fly-by-wire aircraft may need the results of a task computing the current position of the aircraft from the sampled velocity and acceleration values. Thus, the positional error computation task can meaningfully run only after the "current position determination" task completes. Further, even when no explicit data exchanges are involved, tasks might be required to run in a certain order. For example, the system initialization task may need to run first, before other tasks can run.

Dependency among tasks severely restricts the applicability of the results on task scheduling we developed in the last chapter. The reason is that EDF and RMA schedulers impose no constraints on the order in which various tasks execute. Schedules produced by EDF or RMA might violate the constraints imposed due to task dependencies. We, therefore, need to extend the results of the last chapter in order to be able to cope up with inter-task dependencies.

Further, the CPU scheduling techniques that we studied in the last chapter cannot be satisfactorily used to schedule access of a set of real-time tasks to shared critical resources. We had assumed in the last chapter that tasks can be started and preempted at any time without making any difference to the correctness of the final computed results. However a task using a critical resource can not be preempted at any time from resource usage without risking the correctness of the computed results. Non-preemptability is a violation of one of the basic premises with which we had developed the scheduling results of the last chapter. So, the results of the last chapter are clearly inapplicable to scheduling the access of several real-time tasks to some critical resources and new methods to schedule critical resources among tasks are required.

In this chapter we first discuss how critical resources may be shared (scheduled) among a set of real-time tasks. We investigate the problems that may arise if the traditional resource sharing mechanisms are deployed in real-time applications. Subsequently, we discuss a few important protocols for effective sharing of critical resources among real-time tasks. Finally, we discuss how the scheduling methods of the last chapter can be augmented to make them applicable to tasks with dependencies.

3.1 RESOURCE SHARING AMONG REAL-TIME TASKS

In many applications, real-time tasks need to share some resources among themselves. Often these shared resources need to be used by the individual tasks in exclusive mode. This means that a task that is using a resource, can not immediately hand over the resource to another task that requests the resource at any arbitrary point in time; but it can do so only after it completes its use of the resource. If a task is preempted from using a resource before it completes using the resource, then the resource can become corrupted. Examples of such resources are files, devices, and certain data structures. These resources are also called non-preemptable resources, or critical resources. Some authors loosely refer to non-preemptable resources as *critical sections*, though the standard operating system literature uses this term to refer to sections of code in which some non-preemptable resources are used in exclusive mode.

Sharing of critical resources among tasks requires a different set of rules, compared to the rules used for sharing resources such as a CPU among tasks. We have in the last chapter discussed how resources such as CPU can be shared among tasks with cyclic scheduling, EDF, and RMA being the popular methodologies. We must understand that CPU is an example of a *serially reusable resource*. But, what exactly is a serially reusable resource and how does it differ from a critical resource? Once a task gains access to a serially reusable resource such as CPU, it uses it exclusively. That is, two different tasks can not run on one CPU at the same time. Another important feature of a serially reusable resource is that a task executing on a CPU can be preempted and restarted at a later time without any problem. A serially reusable resource is one which is used in exclusive mode, but a task using it may at any time be preempted from using it, and then allowed to use it at some later time without affecting the correctness of the computed results. A non-preemptable resource is also used in the exclusive mode. However, a task using a non-preemptable resource can not be preempted from the resource usage, otherwise the resource would become inconsistent and can lead to system failure. Therefore, when a lower priority task has already gained access to a non-preemptable resource and is using it, even a higher priority task would have to wait until the lower priority task using the resource completes. For this reason, algorithms such as EDF and RMA that are popularly used for sharing a set of serially reusable resources (e.g., CPU) can not satisfactorily be used to share non-preemptable resources among a set of real-time tasks.

We now discuss the problems that would arise when traditional techniques of resource sharing such as semaphores and locks are used to share critical resources among a set of real-time tasks.

3.2 PRIORITY INVERSION

In traditional systems, the mechanisms popularly employed to achieve mutually exclusive use of data and resources among a set of tasks include semaphores, locks, and monitors. However, these traditional operating system techniques prove inadequate for use in real-time applications. The reason being that if these techniques are used for resource sharing in a real-time application, not only simple *priority inversions* but also more serious *unbounded priority inversions* can occur. Unbounded priority inversions are severe problems that may lead to a real-time task to miss its deadline and cause system failure.

To explain the concept of a simple priority inversion, consider the following. When a lower priority task is already holding a resource, a higher priority task needing the same resource has to wait and can not make progress with its computations. The higher priority task would remain blocked until the lower priority task releases the required non-preemptable resource. In this situation, the higher priority task is said to undergo simple priority inversion on account of the lower priority task for the duration it waits while the lower priority task keeps holding the resource.

It should be obvious that simple priority inversions are often unavoidable when two or more tasks share a non-preemptable resource. Fortunately, a single simple priority inversion is not really that difficult to cope with. The duration for which a simple priority inversion can occur is bounded by the longest duration for which a lower priority task might need a critical resource in an exclusive mode. While even a simple priority inversion does delay a higher priority task by some time, the duration for which a task blocks due to a simple priority inversion can be made very small if all tasks are made to restrict themselves to very brief periods of critical section usage. Therefore, a simple priority inversion can easily be tolerated through careful programming. However, a more serious problem that arises during sharing of critical resource among tasks is unbounded priority inversion.

Unbounded priority inversion is a troublesome problem that programmers of real-time and embedded systems often encounter. Unbounded priority inversions can upset all calculations of a programmer regarding the worst case response time of a real-time task and cause it to miss its deadline.

> Unbounded priority inversion occurs when a higher priority task waits for a lower priority task to release a resource it needs, and meanwhile intermediate priority tasks preempt the lower priority task from CPU usage repeatedly. As a result, the lower priority task can not complete its usage of the critical resource and the higher priority task waits indefinitely for its required resource to be released.

Let us now examine more closely what is meant by unbounded priority inversion and how it arises through a simple example. Consider a real-time application having a high priority task T_H and a low priority task T_L. Assume that T_H and T_L need to share a critical resource R. Besides T_H and T_L, assume that there are several tasks T_{I1}, T_{I2}, T_{I3}, ... that have priorities intermediate between T_H and T_L, and do not need the resource R in their computations. These tasks have schematically been shown in Fig. 3.1. Assume that the low priority task (T_L) starts executing at some instant and locks the non-preemptable resource as shown in Fig. 3.1. Suppose soon afterwards, the high priority task (T_H) becomes ready, preempts T_L and starts executing. Also assume that it needs the same non-preemptable resource. It is clear that T_H would block for the resource as it is already being held by T_L and T_L would continue its execution. But, the low priority task T_L may be preempted (from CPU usage) by other intermediate priority tasks (T_{I1}, T_{I2}, ...) which become ready and do not require R. In this case, the high priority task (T_H) would have to wait not only for the low priority task (T_L) to complete its use of the resource, but also all intermediate priority tasks (T_{I1}, T_{I2}, ...) preempting the low priority task to complete their computations. This might result in the high priority task having to wait for the required resource for a considerable period of time. In the worst case, the high priority task might have to wait indefinitely for a low priority task to complete its use of the resource in the face of repeated preemptions of the low priority tasks by the intermediate priority tasks not needing the resource. In such a scenario, the high priority task is said to undergo *unbounded priority inversion*.

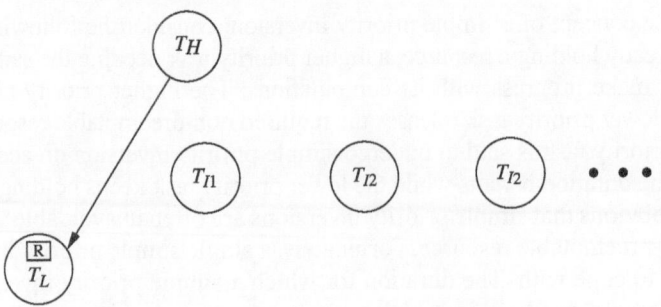

▲ **FIGURE 3.1**

Unbounded Priority Inversion

Unbounded priority inversion is an important problem that real-time system developers face. We, therefore, illustrate this problem using another example and this time showing the actions of the different tasks on a time line. Consider the example shown in Fig. 3.2. In this example, there are five tasks: $T_1 \ldots T_5$. T_5 is a low priority task and T_1 is a high priority task. Tasks T_2, T_3, T_4 have priorities higher than T_5 but lower than T_1 (called intermediate priority tasks). At time t_0, the low priority task T_5 is executing and is using a non-preemptable resource (CR). After a while (at time instant t_1) the higher priority task T_1 arrives, preempts T_5 and starts to execute. Task T_1 requests to use the resource CR at t_2 and blocks since the resource is being held by T_5. Since T_1 blocks, T_5 resumes its execution at t_2. However, the task T_4 which does not require the non-preemptable resource CR preempts T_5 from CPU usage and starts to execute at time t_3. T_4 is in turn preempted by T_3 and so on. As a result, T_1 suffers multiple priority inversions and may even have to wait indefinitely for T_5 to get a chance to execute and complete its usage of the critical resource CR and release it. It should be clear that when a high priority task undergoes unbounded priority inversion, it is very likely to miss its deadline.

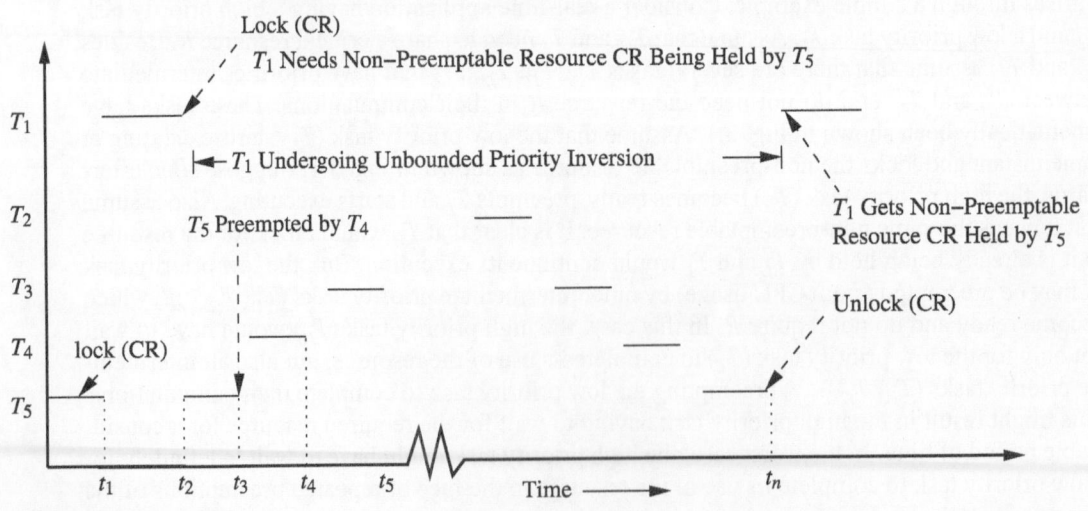

▲ **FIGURE 3.2**

Explanation of Unbounded Priority Inversion Using a Timing Diagram

It is important to note that unbounded priority inversions arise when traditional techniques for sharing non-preemptable resources such as semaphores or monitors are deployed in real-time applications. Possibly the simplest way to avoid priority inversions is to prevent preemption (from CPU usage) of the low priority task holding a critical resource by intermediate priority tasks. This can be achieved by raising the priority level of the low priority task to be equal to that of the waiting high priority task. In other words, the low priority task is made to inherit the priority of the waiting high priority task. This basic mechanism of a low priority task inheriting the priority of a high priority task forms the central idea behind the *priority inheritance protocol (PIP)*. This simple protocol serves as the basic real-time resource sharing mechanism, based on which more sophisticated protocols have been designed.

In the following sections we first discuss the basic priority inheritance protocol (PIP) in some detail. Subsequently, we discuss highest locker protocol (HLP) and priority ceiling protocol (PCP) that have been developed by extending the simple priority inheritance idea further.

3.3 PRIORITY INHERITANCE PROTOCOL (PIP)

The basic priority inheritance protocol (PIP) is a simple technique to share critical resources among tasks without incurring unbounded priority inversions. As it turns out, real-time operating system designers do not find it very difficult to support the basic priority inheritance mechanism. In fact, as we discuss in Chapter 5, most of the real-time operating systems that are commercially available at present do support this protocol.

The basic PIP was proposed by Sha and Rajkumar [24]. The essence of this protocol is that whenever a task suffers priority inversion, the priority of the lower priority task holding the resource is raised through a priority inheritance mechanism. This enables it to complete its usage of the critical resource as early as possible without having to suffer preemptions from the intermediate priority tasks. When several tasks are waiting for a resource, the task holding the resource inherits the highest priority of all tasks waiting for the resource (if this priority is greater than its own priority). Since the priority of the low priority task holding the resource is raised to equal the highest priority of all tasks waiting for the resource being held by it, intermediate priority tasks can not preempt it and unbounded priority inversion is avoided. As soon as a task that had inherited the priority of a waiting higher priority task (because of holding a resource), releases the resource it gets back its original priority value if it is holding no other critical resources. In case it is holding other critical resources, it would inherit the priority of the highest priority task waiting for the resources being held by it.

```
if the required resource is free then
        grant it.
if the required resource is being held by a higher priority task then
        wait for the resource
if the required resource is held by a lower priority task then
{
        wait for the resource
        the low priority task holding the
        resource acquires the highest priority of
        tasks waiting for the resource.
}
```

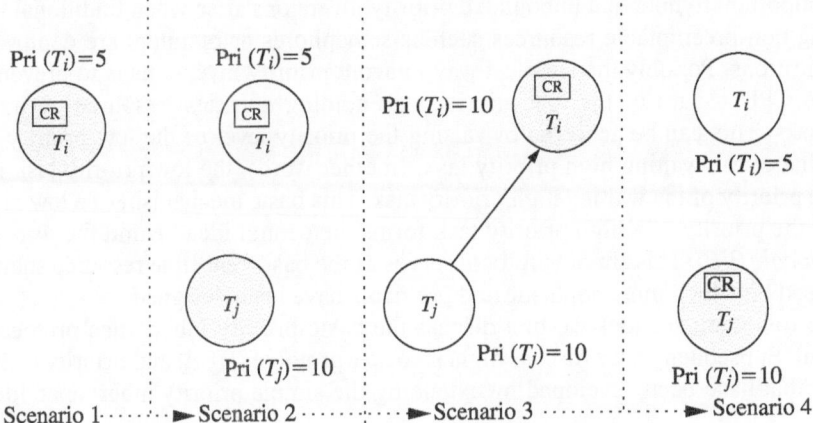

▲ FIGURE 3.3

Snapshots Showing Working of Priority Inheritance Protocol

The priority changes that a task holding a resource undergoes has been illustrated through an example as shown in the Figs. 3.3 and 3.4. In Fig. 3.3 four consecutive scenarios in the execution of a system deploying PIP are shown. In each scenario, the executing task is shown shaded, and the blocked task are shown unshaded. In this figure, how the priority of the two tasks T_i and T_j change due to priority inheritance in the course of execution of the system is shown. T_i is a low priority task with priority 5 and T_j is a higher priority task with priority 10. In scenario 1, T_i is executing and has acquired a critical resource CR. In scenario 2, T_j has became ready and being of higher priority is executing. In scenario 3, T_j is blocking after requesting for the resource R and T_i inherits T_j's priority. In scenario 4, T_i has unlocked the resource and has got back its original priority and T_j is executing with the resource.

In Fig. 3.4 the priority changes of tasks are captured on a time line. The task T_3 initially locks the resource CR. After some time it is preempted by T_2. The task T_2 requests the resource CR at t_2. Since, T_3 already holds the resource, T_2 blocks and T_3 inherits the priority of T_2. This has been shown by drawing T_2 and T_3 at the same priority levels. Before T_3 could complete use of resource CR, it is preempted by a higher priority task T_1. T_1 requests for CR_1 at time t_3 and T_1 blocks as CR_1 is still being held by T_3. So, at this point there are two tasks (T_2 and T_1) waiting for the resource. T_3 inherits the priority of the highest priority waiting task (that is, T_1). T_3 completes its usage of the resource at t_4 and as soon as it releases the resource, it gets back its original priority. It should be noted that a lower priority task retains the inherited priority, until it holds the resource required by the waiting higher priority task. Whenever more than one higher priority task are waiting for the same resource, the task holding the resource inherits the maximum of the priorities of all waiting high priority tasks.

It is clear that PIP can let real-time tasks share critical resources without letting them incur unbounded priority inversions. However, it suffers from two important problems: deadlock and chain blocking.

PIP is susceptible to chain blocking and it does nothing to prevent deadlocks.

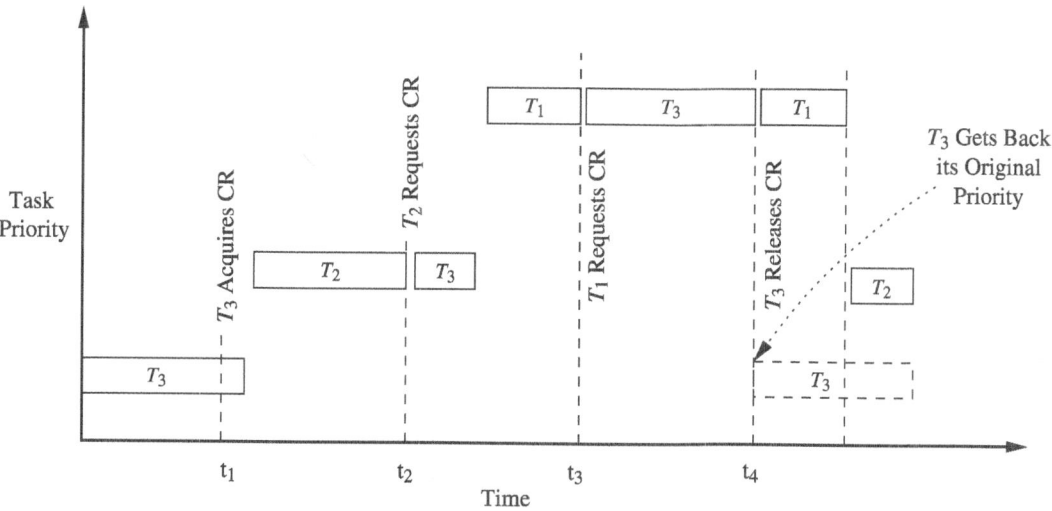

Priority Changes Under Priority Inheritance Protocol

Deadlock: The basic priority inheritance protocol (PIP) leaves open the possibility of deadlocks. In the following we illustrate how deadlocks can occur in PIP. Consider the following sequence of actions by two tasks T_1 and T_2 which need access to two shared critical resources CR_1 and CR_2.

T_1: Lock CR_1, Lock CR_2, Unlock CR_2, Unlock CR_1

T_2: Lock CR_2, Lock CR_1, Unlock CR_1, Unlock CR_2

Assume that T_1 has higher priority than T_2. T_2 starts running first and locks critical resource CR_2 (T_1 was not ready at that time). After some time, T_1 arrives, preempts T_2, and starts executing. After some time, T_1 locks CR_1 and then tries to lock CR_2 which is being held by T_2. As a consequence T_1 blocks and T_2 inherits T_1's priority according to the priority inheritance protocol. T_2 resumes its execution and after some time needs to lock the resource CR_1 being held by T_1. Now, T_1 and T_2 are both deadlocked.

Chain Blocking: A task is said to undergo chain blocking, if each time it needs a resource, it undergoes priority inversion. Thus, if a task needs n resources for its computations, it might have to undergo priority inversions n times to acquire all its resources. Let us now explain how chain blocking can occur using the example shown in Fig. 3.5. Assume that a task T_1 needs several resources. In the first snapshot (shown in Fig. 3.5), a low priority task T_2 is holding two resources CR_1 and CR_2, and a high priority task T_1 arrives and requests to lock CR_1. It undergoes priority inversion and causes T_2 to inherit its priority. In the second snapshot, as soon as T_2 releases CR_1 its priority reduces to its original priority and T_1 is able to lock CR_1. In the third snapshot, after executing for some time, T_1 requests to lock CR_2. This time it again undergoes priority inversion since T_2 is holding CR_2. T_1 waits until T_2 releases CR_2. From this example, we can see that chain blocking occurs when a task undergoes multiple priority inversions to lock its required resources.

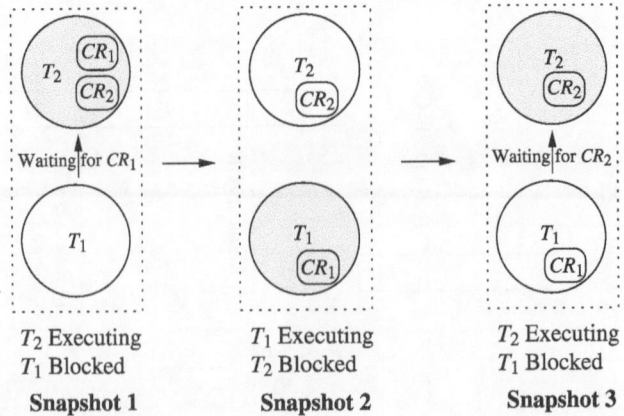

T_2 Executing	T_1 Executing	T_2 Executing
T_1 Blocked	T_2 Blocked	T_1 Blocked
Snapshot 1	**Snapshot 2**	**Snapshot 3**

▲ **FIGURE 3.5**

Chain Blocking in Priority Inheritance Protocol

3.4   HIGHEST LOCKER PROTOCOL (HLP)

HLP is an extension of PIP and overcomes some of the shortcomings of PIP. In HLP every critical resource is assigned a *ceiling priority* value. The ceiling priority of a critical resource CR is informally defined as the maximum of the priorities of all those tasks which may request to use this resource. Under HLP, as soon as a task acquires a resource, its priority is set equal to the ceiling priority of the resource. If a task holds multiple resources, then it inherits the highest ceiling priority of all its locked resources. An assumption that is implicitly made while using HLP is that the resource requirements of every task is known before compile time.

Though we informally defined the ceiling priority of a resource as the maximum of the priorities of all those tasks which may request to use this resource, the rule for computing the ceiling priority is slightly different for the schedulers that follow FCFS (first come first served) policy among equal priority ready tasks and the schedulers that follow a time-sliced round-robin scheduling among equal priority ready task. In the FCFS policy, a task runs to completion while (any ready) equal priority tasks wait. On the other hand, in time-sliced round-robin scheduling, the equal priority tasks execute for one time slice at a time in a round-robin fashion.

Let us first consider a scheduler that follows FCFS scheduling policy among equal priority tasks. Let the ceiling priority of a resource R_i be denoted by Ceil (R_i) and the priority of a task T_j be denoted as pri(T_j). Then, Ceil (R_i) can be defined as follows:

$$\text{Ceil } (R_i) \;=\; \max \left(\{\text{pri } (T_j)/T_j \text{ needs } R_i\}\right) \tag{3.1}$$

That is, the ceiling priority of a critical resource R_i is the maximum of the priority of all tasks that may use R_i. This expression holds only when higher priority values indicate higher priority (as in Windows operating system). If higher priority values indicate lower priorities (as in Unix), then the ceiling priority would be the minimum priority of all tasks needing the resource. That is,

$$\text{Ceil } (R_i) \;=\; \min \left(\{\text{pri } (T_j)/T_j \text{ needs } R_i\}\right) \tag{3.2}$$

For operating systems supporting time-slicedround-robin scheduling among equal priority tasks and larger priority value indicates higher priority, the rule for computing the ceiling priority is:

$$\text{Ceil } (R_i) = \max (\{\text{pri } (T_j)/T_j \text{ needs } R_i\}) + 1 \qquad (3.3)$$

For the case where larger priority value indicates lower priority (and time-sliced round-robin scheduling among equal priority tasks), we have to take the minimum of the task priorities. That is:

$$\text{Ceil } (R_i) = \min (\{\text{pri } (T_j)/T_j \text{ needs } R_i\}) + 1 \qquad (3.4)$$

In the rest of this chapter we shall assume FCFS scheduling among equal priority tasks and also that increasing priority values indicate increasing priority of tasks. To illustrate how priority ceilings of resources are computed, consider the following example system with FCFS scheduling among equal priority tasks. In this system, a resource CR_1 is shared by the tasks T_1, T_5, and T_7 and CR_2 is shared by T_5, and T_7. Let us assume that the priority of $T_1 = 10$, that of $T_2 = 5$, priority of $T_7 = 2$. Then, the priority of CR_1 will be the maximum of the priorities of T_1, T_5, and T_7. Then, the celling priority of CR_1 is Ceil $(CR_1) = \max (\{10, 5, 2\}) = 10$. Therefore, as soon as either of T_1, T_5, or T_7 acquires CR_1, its priority will be raised to 10. The rule of inheritance of priority is that any task that acquires the resource inherits the corresponding ceiling priority. If a task is holding more than one resource, its priority will become maximum of the celling priorities of all the resources it is holding. For example, Ceil $(CR_2) = \max (\{5, 2\} = 5$. A task holding both CR_1 and CR_2 would inherit the larger of the two ceiling priorities, i.e., 10.

Under HLP, soon after acquiring a resource operates a task at the ceiling priority.

A little thinking can convince you that this helps eliminate the problems of unbounded priority inversions, deadlock, and chain blocking. However, it creates new problems. We formally analyze this point a little later in this section.

HLP solves the problems of unbounded priority inversion, chain blocking, and deadlock. Recollect that the basic PIP was susceptible to these problems. The following theorem and its corollaries substantiate these features of HLP.

THEOREM 3.1 *When HLP is used for resource sharing, once a task gets a resource required by it, it is not blocked any further.*

PROOF Let us consider two tasks T_1 and T_2 that need to share two critical resources CR_1 and CR_2. Let us assume that a task T_1 acquires CR_1. Then, T_1's priority becomes Ceil (CR_1) by HLP. Assume that subsequently it also requires a resource CR_2. Suppose T_2 is already holding CR_2. If T_2 is holding CR_2, T_2's priority should have been raised to Ceil (CR_2) by HLP rule. Obviously, Ceil (CR_2) must be greater than pri(T_1), because Ceil (CR_2) is one more than the maximum of the priority of all tasks using the resource (that includes T_1). Therefore, T_2 being of higher priority should have been executing, and T_1 should not have got a chance to execute. This is a contradiction to the assumption that T_1 is executing while T_2 is holding the resource CR_2. Therefore, T_2 could not be holding a resource requested by T_1 when T_1 is executing. Using a similar reasoning, we can show that when T_1 acquires one resource, all resources required by it must be free. From this we can conclude that a task blocks at best once for all its resource requirements for any set of tasks and resource requirements.

It follows from Theorem 3.1 that under HLP tasks are blocked at most once for all their resource requirements. That is, tasks are *single blocking*. However, we should remember that once a task after getting a resource may be preempted (from CPU usage) by a higher priority task which does not share any resources with the task. But, the "single blocking" we discussed, is blocking on account of resource sharing.

Another point which we must remember is that the deadlock and chain blocking results of HLP (as well as that of PCP discussed in the next section) are valid only under the assumption that once a task releases a resource, it does not acquire any further resources. That is, the request and release of resources by a task can be divided into two clear phases: it first acquires all resources it needs and then releases the resources.

The following are two important corollaries which easily follow from Theorem 3.1.

Corollary 1. *Under HLP, before a task can acquire one resource, all the resources that might be required by it must be free.*

Corollary 2. *A task can not undergo chain blocking in HLP.*

An interesting observation regarding HLP is the following. In PIP whenever several tasks request a critical resource that is already in use, they are maintained in a queue in the order in which they requested the resource. When a resource becomes free, the longest waiting task in the queue is granted the resource. Thus, every critical resource is associated with a queue of waiting tasks. However, in HLP no such queue is needed. The reason is that whenever a task acquires a resource, it executes at the ceiling priority of the resource, and other tasks that may need this resource do not even a get chance to execute and request for the resource.

HLP prevents deadlocks from occurring because when a task gets a single resource, all other resources required by it must be free (by Corollary 2).

Shortcomings of HLP: Though HLP solves the problems of unbounded priority inversion, deadlock, and chain blocking, it opens up the possibility for inheritance-related inversion. Inheritance-related inversion occurs when the priority value of a low priority task holding a resource is raised to a high value by the ceiling rule, the intermediate priority tasks not needing the resource can not execute and are said to undergo inheritance-related priority inversion.

We now illustrate inheritance-related inversion through an example. Consider a system consisting of five tasks: T_1, T_2, T_3, T_4, and T_5, and their priority values be 1, 2, 3, 4, and 5, respectively. Also, assume that the higher the priority value, the higher is the priority of the task. That is, 5 is the highest and 1 is the lowest priority value. Let T_1, T_2, *and* T_3 need the resource CR1 and T_1, T_4, and T_5 need the resource CR_2. Then, Ceil (CR_1) is max (1, 2, 3) = 3, and Ceil (CR_2) is max (1, 4, 5) = 5. When T_1 acquires the resource CR_2 its priority would become 5. After T_1 acquires CR_2, T_2 and T_3 would not be able to execute even though they may be ready, since their priority is less than the inherited priority of T_1. In this situation, T_2 and T_3 are said to be undergoing inheritance-related inversion.

HLP is rarely used in real-life applications as the problem of inheritance-related inversion often become so severe as to make the protocol unusable. This arises because the priority of even very low priority tasks might be raised to very high values when it acquires any resource. As a result, several intermediate priority tasks not needing any resource might undergo inheritance-related inversion and miss their respective deadlines. In spite of this major handicap of HLP, we study this protocol in this text as the foundation for understanding the *priority ceiling protocol* that is very popular and is being used extensively in real-time application developments.

3.5 PRIORITY CEILING PROTOCOL (PCP)

Priority Ceiling Protocol (PCP) extends the ideas of PIP and HLP to solve the problems of unbounded priority inversion, chain blocking, and deadlocks, while at the same time minimizing inheritance-related inversions. A fundamental difference between PIP and PCP is that the former is a greedy approach whereas the latter is not. In PIP whenever a request for a resource is made, the resource will be allocated to the requesting task if it is free. However, in PCP a resource may not be granted to a requesting task even if the resource is free.

Just as HLP does, PCP associates a ceiling value Ceil (CR$_i$) with every resource CR$_i$, that is the maximum of the priority values of all tasks that might use CR$_i$. An operating system variable called CSC (Current System Ceiling) is used to keep track of the maximum ceiling value of all the resources that are in use at any instant of time. Thus, at any time CSC = max ({Ceil (CR$_i$)/CR$_i$ is currently in use}). At system start, CSC is initialized to 0 (lower priority than the least priority task in the system).

Resource sharing among tasks under PCP is regulated using two rules for handling resource requests: resource grant and resource release.

Resource Grant Rule: Resource grant rule consists of two clauses. These two clauses are applied when a task T_i requests to lock a resource.

1. **Resource request clause:**

   (a) If the task T_i is holding a resource whose ceiling priority equals CSC, then the task is granted access to the resource.

   (b) Otherwise, T_i will not be granted CR$_j$, unless its priority is greater than CSC (i.e., pri $(T_i) >$ CSC). In both (a) and (b), if T_i is granted access to the resource CR$_j$, and, if CSC $<$ Ceil (CR$_j$), then CSC is set to Ceil (CR$_j$)

2. **Inheritance clause:**   When a task is prevented from locking a resource by failing to meet the resource grant clause, it blocks and the task holding the resource inherits the priority of the blocked task if the priority of the task holding the resource is less than that of the blocked task.

Resource Release Rule: If a task releases a critical resource it was holding and if the ceiling priority of this resource equals CSC, then CSC is made equal to the maximum of the ceiling value of all other resources in use; else CSC remains unchanged. The task releasing the resource either gets back its original priority or the highest priority of all tasks waiting for any resources which it might still be holding, whichever is higher.

PCP is very similar to HLP except that in PCP a task when granted a resource does not immediately acquire the ceiling priority of the resource. In fact, under PCP the priority of a task does not change upon acquiring a resource, only the value of a system variable CSC changes. The priority of a task changes by the inheritance clause of PCP only when one or more tasks wait for a resource it is holding. Tasks requesting a resource block almost under identical situations under PCP and HLP. The only difference with PCP is that a task T_i can also be blocked from entering a critical section, if there exists any resource currently held by some other task whose priority ceiling is greater or equal to that of T_i. A little thought would show that this arrangement prevents the unnecessary inheritance blockings that could be caused due to the priority of a task acquiring a resource being raised to very high values (ceiling priority) at the instant it acquires a resource. In PCP, instead of actually raising the priority of the task acquiring a resource, only the value of a system variable (CSC) is raised to the ceiling value. By comparing the value of CSC against the priority of a task requesting a resource, the possibility of deadlocks is avoided. If no comparison with CSC would have been made (as in PIP), a higher priority task may later lock some resource required by this task leading to a potential deadlock situation where each task holds a part of the resources required by the other task.

We now explain the working of PCP through an example.

Example 3.1

Consider a system consisting of four real-time tasks T_1, T_2, T_3, T_4. These four tasks share two non-preemptable resources CR_1 and CR_2. Assume CR_1 is used by T_1, T_2, and T_3, and CR_2 is used by T_1 and T_4. Assume that the priority values of T_1, T_2, T_3, and T_4 are 10, 12, 15, and 20, respectively. Assume FCFS scheduling among equal priority tasks, and that higher priority values indicate higher priorities.

From the given data, the ceiling priority of the two resources can be easily computed.

Ceil (CR_1) = max (pri (T_1), pri (T_2), pri (T_3)) = 15.

Ceil (CR_2) = max (pri (T_1), Pri (T_4)) = 20.

Let us consider an instant in the execution of the system in which T_1 is executing after acquiring the resource CR_1.

When T_1 acquires CR_1, CSC is set to Ceil (CR_1) = 15.

Now consider the following two alternate situations that might arise in the course of execution of the tasks.

Situation 1

Assume that T_4 becomes ready. Being of higher priority T_4, preempts T_1 and starts to execute. After some time, T_4 requests the resource CR_2. Since the priority value of T_4 (given to be 20) is greater than CSC (which is 15); T_4 is granted the resource CR_2 (by the resource request clause) and CSC is set to 20. When T_4 completes its execution, T_1 will get a chance to execute.

Situation 2

Assume that T_3 becomes ready. Being of higher priority, T_3 preempts T_1 and starts to execute. After some time, T_3 requests for the resource CR_1. As the priority of T_3 (given to be 15) is not greater than CSC (which is 15); T_3 will not be granted CR_1. T_3 would block, and T_1 would inherit the priority of T_3 (by the PCP inheritance clause). So, T_1's priority would change from 10 to 15.

3.6   DIFFERENT TYPES OF PRIORITY INVERSIONS UNDER PCP

Tasks sharing a set of resources using PCP may undergo three important types of priority inversions: direct inversion, inheritance-related inversion, and avoidance inversion.

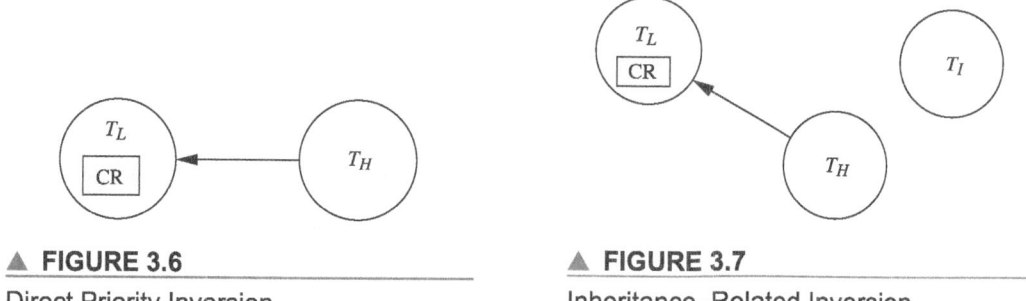

▲ **FIGURE 3.6**	▲ **FIGURE 3.7**
Direct Priority Inversion	Inheritance–Related Inversion

1. Direct Inversion: Direct inversion occurs when a higher priority task waits for a lower priority task to release a resource that it needs.

Consider the example shown in Fig. 3.6. Suppose a low priority task T_L is holding a critical resource named CR. Now if a higher priority task T_H needs this resource, then it would have to wait till T_L finishes using CR and releases it. We can see that in this type of inversion, a lower priority task directly causes a higher priority task to undergo inversion by holding the resource it needs.

2. Inheritance-Related Inversion: Consider a situation where a lower priority task is holding a resource and a higher priority task is waiting for it. Then, the priority of the lower priority task is raised to that of the waiting higher priority task by the inheritance clause of PCP. As a result, the intermediate priority tasks not needing the resource undergo inheritance-related inversion.

Inheritance-related inversion has been illustrated in Fig. 3.7. T_H is a higher priority task than T_L, and T_I has priority intermediate between T_L and T_H. T_H and T_L both need the critical resource CR, whereas T_I has no resource requirements. At some point of time in the execution, a low priority task T_L has acquired a resource CR. Therefore, CSC value is set to Ceil (CR) by the resource request clause. A little later, a high priority task T_H requests the resource CR. T_H would block on CR by the resource request clause. By the inheritance clause, T_L would inherit the priority of T_H. Now, consider the intermediate priority task T_I. Though T_I needs no resource, it can not execute due to the raised priority of T_L. In this case, the task T_I is said to undergo inheritance-related inversion.

3. Avoidance-Related Inversion: In PCP, when a task requests a resource its priority is checked against CSC. The requesting task is granted use of the resource only when its priority is greater than CSC. Therefore, even when a resource that a task is requesting is idle, the requesting task may be denied access to the resource if the requesting task's priority is less than CSC. A task whose priority is greater than the currently executing task, but greater than CSC and needs a resource that is currently not in use, is said to undergo avoidance-related inversion.

Avoidance-related inversion is also sometimes referred to as priority ceiling-related inversion, since a higher priority task is not allowed to execute, not because it requests a resource that is already locked by another task, but because its priority is less than the value of CSC. In avoidance-related inversion, a higher priority task blocks for a resource that is not being used by any of the tasks. Though this restriction might appear to be too restrictive and wasteful, a little thought would show that this restriction is necessary to prevent deadlocks. This type of inversion is, therefore, popularly called deadlock avoidance inversion, or simply avoidance inversion; the reason being that the blocking caused due to the priority ceiling rule is the cost for avoidance of deadlock among tasks.

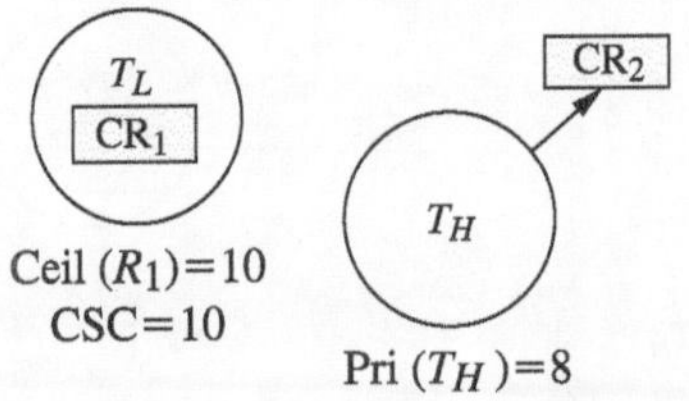

▲ FIGURE 3.8

Avoidance-Related Inversion

We now illustrate deadlock avoidance inversion using an example. Consider the example shown in Fig. 3.8. In Fig. 3.8, a low priority task (T_L) and a high priority task (T_H) both need two resources R_1 and R_2 during their computations. Assume that the low priority task T_L is presently using a critical resource CR_1. This means that when the resource was granted, CSC must have been set equal to the Ceil (CR_1). Now, when a high priority task T_H requests to use the resource CR_2, it blocks because its priority is less than CSC. As already pointed out, this provision has been incorporated in PCP in order to avoid deadlocks. Not allowing the task T_H to access R_2 precludes the possibility that T_H may later request R_1 and T_L may request R_2 leading to a deadlock. Also, note that if T_H's priority is higher than CSC, then it does mean that T_H will never need R_1 and T_H in that case can safely be allowed to access R_2. The example shows that avoidance-related inversion is the price to pay to avoid deadlocks. However, a task may be denied access to a resource even when a grant of the resource could in no way would have caused a deadlock. That is, it is possible that under PCP a task undergoes avoidance inversion, though its request for a resource in no way could have caused any deadlocks. We illustrate this aspect in the following using an example.

Consider a real-time system in which there are four tasks T_1, T_2, T_3, and T_4. Assume that the priorities of these three tasks are 2, 4, 5, and 10, respectively. Further assume that the tasks T_1 and T_4 share a critical resource CR_1 and that the tasks T_2 and T_3 share a critical resource CR_2. The ceiling priorities of the resources CR_1 and CR_2 are 10 and 5, respectively. Assume that the task T_1 first acquires the resource CR_1. Then, the CSC would be set to 10 (ceiling priority of CR_1) by the resource grant clause. If task T_2 requests CR_2 next, then it would be refused access because T_2's priority is less than CSC. In this case, T_2 would suffer avoidance inversion though there is no possibility of a deadlock even if T_2 was permitted access to CR_2.

Now, let us try to quantitatively determine the duration for which a task may undergo the different types of inversions when resources are shared under PCP. To illustrate how this can be done, we compute the task inversions due to resource sharing through the following two examples. In the analysis regarding priority inversions due to resource sharing, we have assumed that once a task releases a resource, it does not acquire any other resource. In other words, tasks execute in two phases, resource acquire phase followed by resource release phase. In the resource acquire phase, tasks keep on acquiring the resources they need (no release) and in the resource release phase they only release resources (no acquiring). Unless the tasks are enforced to follow this discipline, determination of a quantitative bound on the inversion time would become difficult.

Example 3.2

A system has four tasks: T_1, T_2, T_3, T_4. These tasks need two critical resources CR_1 and CR_2. Assume that the priorities of the four tasks are as follows: pri $(T_1) = 10$, pri $(T_2) = 7$, pri (T_3) $= 5$, pri $(T_4) = 2$. The four tasks: T_1, T_2, T_3 and T_4 have been arranged in decreasing order of their priorities. That is, pri $(T_1) >$ pri $(T_2) > \ldots >$ pri (T_4). The exact resource requirements of these tasks and the duration for which the tasks need the two resources have been shown in Fig. 3.9. Compute the different types of inversions that each task might have to undergo in the worst case.

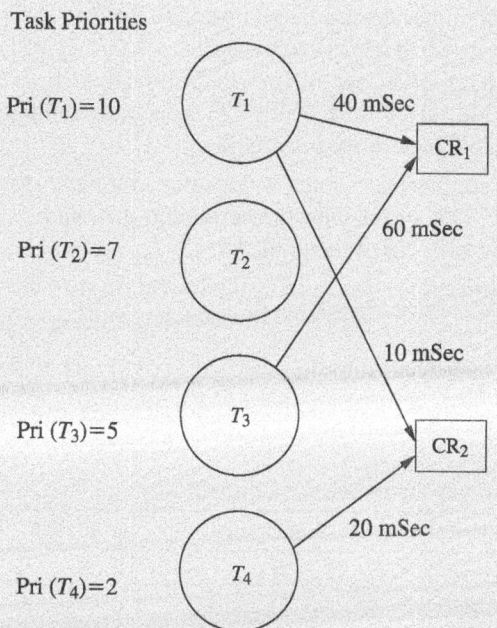

▲ **FIGURE 3.9**

Task Graph of Example 3.2

Solution. As shown in Fig. 3.9, the task T_1 would require the resource CR_1 for 40 mSec and CR_2 for 10 mSec. The task T_3 would require resource CR_1 for 60 mSec and task T_4 would require CR_2 for 20 mSec. Let us assume FCFS scheduling among equal priority tasks. Now the ceiling of any resource CR can be calculated using Expr. 3.1 as:

$$\text{Ceil (CR)} = \max \left(\{\text{pri}\{T_i\}/T_i \text{ may need CR}\} \right)$$

Using this, we get $\text{Ceil}(CR_1) = \max(\{10, 5\}) = 10$ and $\text{Ceil}(CR_2) = \max(\{10, 2\}) = 10$. Let us now determine the different types of inversions that each task might suffer, and the duration of the inversions. Considering the tasks one by one:

- Task T_1 can suffer direct inversion (due to the resource CR_1) by task T_3 or (due to the resource CR_2) by T_4. From an inspection of Fig. 3.9 it can be easily seen that T_1 can suffer direct inversion due to T_3 for 60 mSec and due to T_4 for 20 mSec. T_1 will not suffer any inheritance-related inversion, since it is the highest priority task. From a similar reasoning, it is easy to see that T_1 can not undergo deadlock avoidance inversion.

- Task T_2 will not suffer any direct inversion, since it does not need any resource for its computations. But, T_2 can suffer inheritance-related inversion due to T_3 when T_3 acquires CR_1 and T_1 waits for CR_1. It is not difficult to see from Fig. 3.9 that T_2 will suffer inheritance-related inversion on account of T_3 for 60 mSec. Similarly, due to T_4 it can undergo inheritance-related inversion for 20 mSec. Since T_2 does not require any resource, it can not suffer any deadlock avoidance-related inversion.

- T_3 will not suffer any direct inversion since it does not share any resource with a lower priority task. However, T_3 can suffer inheritance related inversion and deadlock avoidance related inversion due to T_4 for at most 20 mSec.

- T_4 will not suffer any priority inversion, as it is the lowest priority task.

We now represent the maximum duration for which each task suffers from each type of inversion in Table 3.1.

TABLE 3.1   Priority Inversions for Example 3.2

Task	Direct			Inheritance			Avoidance		
	T_2	T_3	T_4	T_2	T_3	T_4	T_2	T_3	T_4
T_1	x	60	40	x	x	x	x	x	x
T_2	x	x	x	x	60	20	x	x	x
T_3	x	x	x	x	x	20	x	x	20

Example 3.3

Let us consider a system with a set of periodic real-time tasks $T_1 \ldots T_6$. The resource and computing requirements of these tasks have been shown in Fig. 3.10. Assume that the tasks $T_1 \ldots T_6$ have been arranged in decreasing order of their priorities. Compute the different types of inversions that a task might have to undergo.

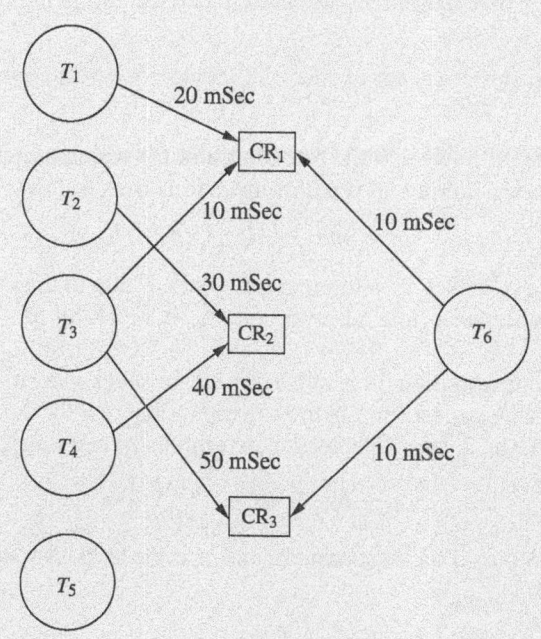

▲ FIGURE 3.10

Resource Sharing Among Tasks of Example 3.3

Solution. For each of the given tasks we have computed the maximum duration for which it might have to suffer from different types of inversions and have represented those in Table 3.2.

TABLE 3.2 Different Types of Inversions for Example 3.3

Task	Direct					Inheritance					Avoidance				
	T_2	T_3	T_4	T_5	T_6	T_2	T_3	T_4	T_5	T_6	T_2	T_3	T_4	T_5	T_6
T_1	x	10	x	x	10	x	x	x	x	x	x	x	x	x	x
T_2	x	x	40	x	x	x	10	x	x	10	x	10	x	x	10
T_3	x	x	x	x	10	x	x	40	x	10	x	x	40	x	10
T_4	x	x	x	x	x	x	x	x	x	10	x	x	x	x	10
T_5	x	x	x	x	x	x	x	x	x	10	x	x	x	x	x

Let us now examine some of the properties of an inversion table.

- Each inversion table is an upper triangular matrix. The lower triangular items of each table are all zero. This structure of the inversion tables is expected since a lower priority task can not suffer any inversions due to a higher priority task.

- The avoidance table is similar to inheritance table except for the case of a task that does not need any resource. The reason for this is again not very far to seek. The tasks not needing any resource, never request for any resource, consequently, they can not suffer avoidance inversions.

From Corollary 1 of Theorem 3.2 we already had the following result:

A task can suffer at best any one of direct, inheritance, or avoidance inversions.

From this result it follows that the total duration for which any task T_i may be blocked by lower priority tasks, considering all types of inversions is as follows:

$$bt_i = max_j^{i-1}\{(b_{idj}), (b_{iij}), (b_{iaj})\} \qquad (3.5)$$

where b_{idj} is blocking of task T_i by a lower priority task T_j due to direct inversion, b_{iij} is blocking of T_i by T_j due to inheritance-related inversion, b_{iaj} is blocking of T_i by T_j due to avoidance-related inversion.

Thus, the maximum duration for which a task can be blocked by its lower priority tasks on account of sharing of is the largest entry in the corresponding row for the task in the inversion table. We can now modify Expr. 2.16 of Chapter 2 to determine the response time of a task T_i as follows:

$$e_i + bss_i + bt_i + \sum_{j=1}^{i-1}\left[\frac{p_i}{p_j}\right] * e_j \qquad (3.6)$$

where bss_i is the delay due to self-suspensions, and bt_i is the total inversion due to resource sharing.

3.7   IMPORTANT FEATURES OF PCP

In this section, we discuss some important features of PCP. We first prove that tasks are single blocking on account of resource usage.

THEOREM 3.2   *Tasks are single blocking under PCP.*

PROOF   Consider that a task T_i needs a set of resources SR = $\{R_i\}$. Obviously, the ceiling of each resource R_i in SR must be greater than or equal to pri (T_i). Now, assume that when T_i acquires some resource R_i, another task T_j was already holding a resource R_j, and that $R_i, R_j \in$ SR. Such a situation would lead T_i to block after acquiring a resource. But, when T_j locked R_j CSC should have been set to at least pri(T_i) by the resource grant clause of PCP and T_i could not have been granted R_i. This is a contradiction with the premise. Therefore, when T_i acquires one resource all resources required by it must be free.

We can in a similar way show that once a task T_i acquires a resource, it can not undergo any inheritance-related inversion. Assume that a lower priority task T_k is holding some resource R_z and a higher priority task T_h is waiting for the resource. But, this is not possible as Ceil(R_z) must be at least as much as pri (T_h). The CSC should, therefore, have been set to a value that is at least as much as pri (T_h) and T_i would have been prevented from accessing the resource R_i in the first place. This is a contradiction with the premise we started with. Therefore, it is not possible that a task undergoes inheritance-related inversion after it acquires a resource.

Using a similar reasoning, we can show that a task can not suffer any avoidance inversion after acquiring a resource.

Thus, once a task acquires a resource it can not undergo any inversion. It is, therefore, clear that tasks under PCP are single blocking.

The following corollary easily follows from Theorem 3.2.

Corollary 1. *Under PCP a task can undergo at most one inversion during its execution.*

Priority Ceiling Protocol is free from deadlocks, unbounded priority inversions, and chain blockings. In the following, we discuss these features of PCP.

How is deadlock avoided in PCP?

Deadlocks occur only when different (more than one) tasks hold parts of each other's required resources at the same time, and then they request for the resources being held by each other. But under PCP, when one task is executing with some resources, any other task can not hold a resource that may ever be needed by this task (by Theorem 3.2). That is, when a task is granted one resource, all its required resources must be free. This prevents the possibility of any deadlock.

How is unbounded priority inversion avoided?

A higher priority task suffers unbounded priority inversion, when it is waiting for a lower priority task to release some of the resources required by it, and meanwhile intermediate priority tasks preempt the low priority task from CPU usage. But such a situation can never happen in PCP since whenever a higher priority task waits for some resources which is currently being used by a low priority task, then the executing lower priority task is made to inherit the priority of the high priority task (by Theorem 3.2). So, the intermediate priority tasks can not preempt lower priority task from CPU usage. Therefore, unbounded priority inversions can not occur under PCP.

How is chain blocking avoided?

By Theorem 3.2, resource sharing among tasks under PCP is single blocking.

3.8 SOME ISSUES IN USING A RESOURCE SHARING PROTOCOL

In this section we discuss some issues that may arise while using resource sharing protocols to develop a real-time application requiring tasks to share non-preemptable resources. The first issue that we discuss is how to use PCP in dynamic priority systems. Subsequently, we discuss the situations in which the different resource sharing protocols would be useful.

3.8.1 Using PCP in Dynamic Priority Systems

So far in all our discussions regarding usage of PCP, we had implicitly assumed that the task priorities are static. That is, a task's priority does not change for its entire lifetime—from the time it arrives to the time it completes. In dynamic priority systems, the priority of a task might change with time. As a consequence, the priority ceilings of every resource needs to be appropriately recomputed each time a task's priority changes. In addition, the value of the CSC and the inherited priority values of the tasks holding resources also need to be changed. This represents a high runtime overhead. The high runtime overhead makes use of PCP in dynamic priority systems unattractive.

3.8.2 Comparison of Resource Sharing Protocols

We have so far discussed three important resource sharing protocols for real-time tasks: priority inheritance protocol (PIP), highest locker protocol (HLP) and priority ceiling protocol (PCP). The shortcomings and advantages of these protocols are discussed below.

- Priority Inheritance Protocol (PIP): This is a simple protocol and effectively overcomes the unbounded priority inversion problem of traditional resource sharing techniques. This protocol requires the minimal support from the operating system among all the resource sharing protocols we discussed. However, under PIP tasks may suffer from chain blocking and PIP also does not prevent deadlocks.

- Highest Locker Protocol (HLP): HLP requires only moderate support from the operating system. It solves the chain blocking and deadlock problems of PIP. However, HLP can make the intermediate priority tasks undergo large inheritance-related inversions and can, therefore, cause tasks to miss their deadlines.

- Priority Ceiling Protocol (PCP): PCP overcomes the shortcomings of the basic PIP as well as HLP protocols. PCP protocol is free from deadlock and chain blocking. In PCP priority of a task is not changed until a higher priority task requests the resource. It, therefore, suffers much lower inheritance-related inversions than HLP.

From the above discussions we can infer that PCP is well-suited for use in applications having large number of tasks and many critical resources, while PIP being a very simple protocol is suitable to be used in small applications.

3.9 HANDLING TASK DEPENDENCIES

An assumption that was implicit in all the scheduling algorithms we discussed in Chapter 2 is that the tasks in an application are independent. That is, there is no constraint on the order in which the different tasks can be taken up for execution. However, this is far from true in practical situations, where one task may need results from another task, or the tasks might have to be carried out in certain order for the proper functioning of the system. When such dependencies among tasks exist, the scheduling techniques discussed in Chapter 2 turn out to be insufficient and need to be suitably modified.

We first discuss how to develop a satisfactory schedule for a set of tasks than can be used in table-driven scheduling.

Table-driven algorithm: The following are the main steps of a simple algorithm for determining a feasible schedule for a set of periodic real-time tasks whose dependencies are given:

```
1. Sort task in increasing order of their deadlines, without violating any
   precedence constraints and store the sorted tasks in a linked list.
2. Repeat
           Take up the task having largest deadline and not yet
           scheduled (i.e., scan the task list of step 1 from left).
           Schedule it as late as possible.
   until all tasks are scheduled.
3. Move the schedule of all tasks to as much left (i.e., early) as
   possible without disturbing
   their relative positions in the schedule.
```

We now illustrate the use of the above algorithm to compute a feasible schedule for a set of tasks with dependencies.

Example 3.4

Determine a feasible schedule for the real-time tasks of a task set $\{T_1, T_2, \ldots, T_5\}$ for which the precedence relations have been shown in Fig. 3.11 for use with a table-driven scheduler. The execution times of the tasks $T_1, T_2, \ldots, T_5$ are: 7, 10, 5, 6, 2 and the corresponding deadlines are 40, 50, 25, 20, 8, respectively.

Solution.   The different steps of the solution have been worked out and shown in Fig. 3.12.

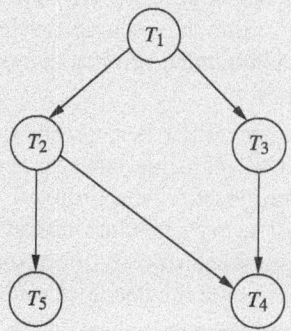

▲ **FIGURE 3.11**

Precedence Relationship Among Tasks for Example 3.4

Step 1:   Arrangement of Tasks in Ascending Order:

$T_1 \ T_3 \ T_2 \ T_5 \ T_4$

Step 2:   Schedule Tasks as Late as Possible
              without Violating Precedence Constraints:

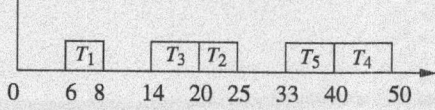

Step 3:   Move Tasks as Early as Possible
              without Altering the Schedule:

$T_1 \ T_3 \ T_2 \ T_5 \ T_4$

0   2   8   13   20   30

▲ **FIGURE 3.12**

Solution of Example 3.4

EDF and RMA-based Schedulers: Precedence constraints among tasks can be handled in both EDF and RMA through the following modification to the algorithm.

- Do not enable a task until all its predecessors complete their execution.
- Check the tasks waiting to be enabled (on account of its predecessors completing their executions) after every task completes.

We, however, must remember that the achievable schedulable utilization of tasks with dependencies would be lower compared to when the tasks are independent. Therefore, the schedulability results worked out in the last chapter would not be applicable when task dependencies exist.

SUMMARY

- In many real-life applications, real-time tasks are required to share non-preemptable resources among themselves. If traditional resource sharing techniques such as semaphores are deployed in this situation, unbounded priority inversions might occur leading to real-time tasks to miss their deadlines.

- The priority inheritance protocol (PIP) is possibly the simplest protocol for sharing critical resources among a set of real-time tasks. It requires minimal support from the underlying real-time operating system. This protocol for sharing critical resources is, therefore, supported by almost every real-time operating systems. The priority inheritance mechanism prevents unbounded priority inversions. However, it becomes the programmer's responsibility to overcome the deadlock and chain blocking problems through careful programming.

- PCP incorporates additional rules in the basic PIP and overcomes the deadlock, unbounded priority inversion, and chain blocking problems of PIP. However, under PCP tasks might still suffer moderate inversions. PCP has been widely accepted as a popular resource sharing protocol and is normally used for developing moderate and large real-time applications. PCP is supported by many modern commercial real-time operating systems.

- Task dependencies can be handled through minor alterations to the basic task scheduling algorithms. However, the achievable utilization of the schedulers drop when tasks are not independent.

EXERCISES

1. Determine whether the following statements are TRUE or FALSE. In each case justify your choice in one or two sentences.

   (a) Rate monotonic scheduling can satisfactorily be used for scheduling access of several hard real-time periodic tasks to a certain shared critical resource.

   (b) Algorithms exist which permit sharing of a set of resources in the exclusive mode among tasks of different priorities without any tasks having to incur any priority inversion.

   (c) When a set of real-time tasks are scheduled using RMA and share critical resources using the priority ceiling protocol (PCP), it is possible that a task may be denied access to a resource even when the resource is not required by any other task.

   (d) Highest locker protocol (HLP) maintains the tasks waiting for a shared non-preemptable resource in FIFO order.

(e) When a set of periodic real-time tasks scheduled using RMA share certain critical resources using priority inheritance protocol (PIP), some of the tasks might suffer unbounded priority inversions.

(f) In the highest locker protocol (HLP), for each critical resource a separate queue needs to be maintained for the tasks waiting for the resources.

(g) Using the basic priority inheritance protocol (PIP) for scheduling access of a set of real-time tasks to a set of non-preemptable resources would result in tasks incurring unbounded priority inversions.

(h) When a set of static priority periodic real-time tasks scheduled using RMA share some critical resources using the priority ceiling protocol (PCP), the time duration for which a task can undergo inheritance-related inversion is exactly the same as the duration for which it can undergo deadlock avoidance-related inversion.

(i) Suppose a task needs three non-preemptable shared resources CR1, CR2, and CR3 during its computation. Under highest locker protocol (HLP), once the task acquires one of these resources, it is guaranteed not to block for acquiring the other required resources.

(j) When highest locker protocol (HLP), is used as the protocol for sharing some critical resources among a set of real-time tasks, deadlock can not occur due to resource sharing.

(k) If traditional resource sharing mechanisms such as semaphores and monitors are used to share access of several real-time tasks to a single critical resource, neither unbounded priority inversions, nor deadlocks can occur.

(l) When a set of periodic real-time tasks scheduled using RMA share critical resources using the priority ceiling protocol (PCP), if a task can suffer inheritance blocking by another task for certain duration, then it may also suffer direct inversion due to that task for the same duration.

(m) When a set of periodic real-time tasks scheduled using RMA share certain critical resources using the priority ceiling protocol (PCP), if a task T_1 can suffer inheritance blocking by another task T_2 for certain duration, then it may also suffer deadlock avoidance inversion for the same duration due to T_2 excepting if T_1 does not need any resource.

(n) When a set of real-time tasks share certain critical resources using the priority ceiling protocol (PCP), the highest priority task does not suffer any inversions.

(o) When a set of real-time tasks share critical resources using the priority ceiling protocol (PCP), the lowest priority task does not suffer any inversions.

(p) It is possible that in a real-time system even the lowest priority task may suffer unbounded priority inversions unless a suitable resource-sharing protocol is used.

(q) When a set of real-time tasks share critical resources using the priority ceiling protocol (PCP), a task can undergo at best one of direct, inheritance, or avoidance-related inversion due to any task.

(r) The priority ceiling protocol (PCP) can be considered to be a satisfactory protocol to share a set of serially reusable preemptable resources among a set of real-time tasks.

(s) If priority ceiling protocol (PCP) is implemented in Unix operating systems, then the ceiling priority value of a critical resource would be the maximum of the priority values of all the tasks using this resource.

(t) The duration for which a lower priority task can inheritance block a higher priority task is also identical to the duration for which it can avoidance block it.

(u) Under PCP even a task which does not require any resource can undergo priority inversion for some duration.

2. Explain the problems that might arise if hard real-time tasks are made to share critical resources among themselves using traditional operating system primitives such as semaphores or monitors. Briefly explain how these problems can be overcome.

3. Explain using an appropriate example as to why a critical resource can get corrupted if the task using it is preempted, and then another task is granted use of the resource.

4. What do you understand by the term "priority inversion" in the context of real-time task scheduling? When several tasks share a set of critical resources, is it possible to avoid priority inversion altogether by using a suitable task scheduling algorithm? Explain your answer.

5. Explain the operation of priority ceiling protocol (PCP) in sharing critical resources among real-time tasks. Explain how PCP is able to avoid deadlock, unbounded priority inversions, and chain blockings.

6. Explain the different types of priority inversions that a task might suffer due to a lower priority task when the priority ceiling protocol (PCP) is used to share critical resources among a set of real-time task. Can a task suffer both inheritance-related inversion and direct inversion due to some lower priority task? If you answer in the affirmative, construct a suitable example to corroborate your answer. If you answer in the negative, explain why.

7. Define the terms *priority inversion* and *unbounded priority inversion* as used in real-time operating systems. Is it possible to devise a resource-sharing protocol which can guarantee that no task undergoes: (i) priority inversion? (ii) unbounded priority inversion? Justify your answers.

8. What do you understand by *inheritance-related inversion?* Explain how it can arise when resources are shared in exclusive mode in a real-time environment. Can inheritance-related inversion be eliminated altogether? If your answer is "yes", explain how? If your answer is "no", then explain how inheritance-related inversions can be contained?

9. Using two or three sentences explain how PCP can be used for resource sharing among a set of tasks when the tasks are scheduled using EDF. Can your solution be used in practical situations? If not, why?

10. When EDF is used for task scheduling in a real-time application, explain a scheme by which sharing of critical resources among tasks can be supported. Give an algorithm in pseudo-code notation to describe the steps to handle resource grant and release.

11. A set of hard real-time periodic tasks need to be scheduled on a uniprocessor using RMA. The following table contains the details of these periodic tasks and their use of three non-preemptable shared resources. Can the tasks T_2 and T_3 meet their respective deadlines when priority ceiling protocol (PCP) is used for resource scheduling?

Task	p_i	e_i	R_1	R_2	R_3
T_1	400	30	15	20	
T_2	200	25	—	20	10
T_3	300	40	—	—	—
T_4	250	35	10	10	10
T_5	450	50	—	—	5

p_i indicates the period of task T_i and e_i indicates its computation time. The period of each task is the same as its deadline. The entries in the R_1, R_2, and R_3 columns indicate the time duration for which a task needs the named resource in non-preemptive mode. Assume that after a task releases a resource, it does not acquire the same or any other resource.

12. While it is generally true that avoidance inversion in PCP is the price paid to avoid situations leading to deadlocks, sometimes tasks might undergo avoidance inversion when their request for a resource can in no way cause deadlocks. Illustrate this by constructing an example to show that even when

there is no chance of any deadlocks being caused, a task under PCP might still undergo avoidance in-version.

13. A set of periodic tasks need to be scheduled on a uniprocessor. The following table contains the de-tails of these periodic tasks and their use of non-preemptable shared resources R_1, R_2, and R_3. Can task T_3 meet its deadline when the tasks are scheduled under RMA and priority ceiling protocol (PCP) is used for resource scheduling?

Task	p_i	e_i	R_1	R_2	R_3	s_i
T_1	400	30	15	20		10
T_2	200	25	—	20	10	20
T_3	300	40	—	—	—	10
T_4	250	35	10	10	10	40
T_5	450	50	—	—	5	55

p_i indicates the period of task T_i and e_i indicates its computation time. The entries in the R_1, R_2, and R_3 columns indicate the time duration for which a task needs the named resource in non-preemptive mode, s_i is the self suspension time of task T_i. All time units have been specified in milliseconds.

14. A set of periodic tasks need to be scheduled on a uniprocessor. The following table contains the details of these periodic tasks and their use of non-preemptable shared resources. Can the task T_3 meet its deadline when the tasks are scheduled under RMA and the priority ceiling protocol (PCP) is used for resource scheduling?

Task	p_i	e_i	R_1	R_2	R_3
T_1	400	30	15	20	
T_2	200	25	—	20	10
T_3	300	40	—	—	—
T_4	250	35	10	10	10
T_5	450	50	—	—	5

p_i indicates the period of task T_i and e_i indicates its computation time. The entries in the R_1, R_2, and R3 columns indicate the time duration for which a task needs the named resource in non-preemptive mode. All time units have been specified in milliseconds.

15. Consider a real-time system whose task characteristics and dependencies are described in the following table. Assume that the tasks have zero phasing and repeat with a period of 90 mSec. Determine a feasible schedule which could be used by a table-driven scheduler.

Task	Computation Time (e_i) mSec	Deadline (d_i) mSec	Dependency
T_1	30	90	—
T_2	15	40	T_1, T_3
T_3	20	40	T_1
T_4	10	70	T_2

16. Consider a real-time system in which five real-time periodic tasks $T_1 \ldots T_5$ have zero phasing and repeat with a period of 150 mSec. The task characteristics and dependencies are described in the following table. Determine a feasible schedule which could be used by a table-driven scheduler.

Task	Computation Time (e_i) mSec	Deadline (d_i) mSec	Dependency
T_1	15	40	—
T_2	30	70	T_1
T_3	10	90	T_2
T_4	20	40	T_1

17. Consider a real-time system whose task characteristics and dependencies are described in the following table. These tasks repeat every 150 mSec. Determine a feasible schedule which could be used by a table-driven scheduler.

Task	Computation Time (e_i) mSec	Deadline (d_i) mSec	Dependency
T_1	10	50	—
T_2	10	80	T_1
T_3	30	60	T_1
T_4	50	150	T_3, T_2
T_5	35	140	T_2

4

Scheduling Real-Time Tasks in Multiprocessor and Distributed Systems

The use of multiprocessor and distributed systems in real-time applications is becoming popular. One reason for this popularity of multiprocessor and distributed systems is the recent drop in their prices. Now dual processor machines are available at 50 to 60,000 rupees and the prices are set to drop even further. Besides, distributed platforms such as networked PCs are common place. Another reason that attracts real-time system developers to deploy multiprocessor and distributed systems is the faster response times and fault-tolerance features of such systems. Further, distributed processing is often suitable for applications that are naturally distributed and the events of interest are generated at geographically distributed locations. An example of such an application is an automated petroleum refinery, where the plant is spread over a considerable geographic area.

As compared to scheduling real-time tasks on a uniprocessor, scheduling tasks on multiprocessor and distributed systems is much more difficult. We had seen that optimal schedulers for a set of independent real-time tasks have polynomial complexity (in the number of tasks to be scheduled). However, determining an optimal schedule for a set of real-time tasks on a multiprocessor or a distributed system is an NP-hard problem [12].

Multiprocessor systems are known as tightly coupled systems. This characteristic of a multiprocessor system denotes the existence of shared physical memory in the system. In contrast, a distributed system is called a loosely coupled system and is devoid of any shared physical memory. In a tightly coupled system, the interprocess communication (IPC) is inexpensive and can be ignored compared to task execution times. This is so because inter-task communication is achieved through reads and writes to the shared memory. However, the same is not true in the case of distributed computing systems where inter-task communication times are comparable to task execution times. Due to this, a multiprocessor system may use a centralized dispatcher/scheduler whereas a distributed system can not. A centralized scheduler would require maintaining the state of the various tasks of the system in a centralized data structure. This would require various processors in the system to update it whenever the state of a task changes and consequently, would result in high communicational overheads.

Scheduling real-time tasks on distributed and multiprocessor systems consists of two sub-problems: task allocation to processors and scheduling tasks on the individual processors. The task assignment problem is concerned with how to partition a set of tasks and then how to assign these to the processors. Task assignment can either be static or dynamic. In the static allocation scheme, the allocation of tasks to nodes is permanent and does not change with time whereas in the dynamic task assignment, tasks are assigned to nodes as they arise. Thus, in the dynamic case, different instances of a task may be allocated to different nodes. After successful task assignment to the processors, we can consider the tasks on each processor individually and, therefore, the second phase of the multiprocessor and distributed systems reduces to the scheduling problem in uniprocessors.

The task allocation to processors in multiprocessor and distributed environments is an NP-hard problem and determining an optimal solution has exponential complexity. So, most of the algorithms that are deployed in practice are heuristic algorithms. Task allocation algorithms can be classified into either static or dynamic algorithms. In static algorithms all the tasks are partitioned into subsystems and each subsystem is assigned to a separate processor. In contrast, in a dynamic system tasks ready for execution are placed in one common priority queue and dispatched to processors for execution as the processors become available. It is, therefore, possible that different instances of periodic tasks execute on different processors. Most hard real-time systems built to date are all static in nature. However, intuitively a dynamic real-time system can make more efficient utilization of the available resources.

This chapter is organized as follows. We first discuss task allocation schemes for multiprocessors. We next discuss dynamic allocation of tasks to processors. Finally, we address the clock synchronization problem in distributed systems.

4.1 MULTIPROCESSOR TASK ALLOCATION

In this section we discuss a few algorithms for statically allocating real-time tasks to the processors of a multiprocessor system. We already know that in a static task allocation algorithm, allocation is made before run time, and the allocation remains valid throughout a full run of the system. As already mentioned, the task allocation algorithms for multiprocessors do not try to minimize communication costs as interprocess communication time is low. This is because in multiprocessors, communication time is the same as memory access time, due to the availability of the shared memory. This is the reason why the task allocation algorithms that we discuss in this section may not work satisfactorily in distributed environments. The allocation algorithms that we discuss are centralized algorithms. In the following, we discuss a few important multiprocessor task allocation algorithms.

Utilization Balancing Algorithm.   This algorithm maintains the tasks in a queue in increasing order of their utilizations. It removes tasks one by one from the head of the queue and allocates them to the least utilized processor each time. The objective of selecting the least utilized processor each time is to balance utilization of the different processors. In a perfectly balanced system the utilization u_i at each processor equals the overall utilization of the processors $\bar{u}$ of the system. Here the utilization of a processor P_i is the summation of the utilization of all tasks assigned to it. If ST_i is the set of all tasks assigned to a processor P_i, then the utilization of the processor P_i is $u_i = \sum_{j \in ST_i} u_{t_j}$, where $\bar{u}_{tj}$ is the utilization due to the task T_j. If PR is the set of all processors in the systems, then $\sum_{j \in PR} u_i$. However, using this algorithm it is very difficult to achieve perfect balancing of utilizations across different processors for an arbitrary task set. That is, it is very difficult to make $u_i = \bar{u}$ for each P_i. The simple heuristic used in this algorithm gives suboptimal results. The objective of any good utilization balancing algorithm is to minimize $\sum_{i=1}^{n} |(\bar{u} - u_i)|$, where n is number of processors in the system, $\bar{u}$ is average utilization of processors, and u_i is utilization of processor i.

This algorithm is suitable when the number of processors in a multiprocessor is fixed. The utilization balancing algorithm can be used when the tasks at the individual processors are scheduled using EDF.

Next-Fit Algorithm for RMA.   In this algorithm, a task set is partitioned so that each partition is scheduled on a uniprocessor using RMA scheduling. This algorithm attempts to use as few processors as possible. Unlike the utilization balancing algorithm this algorithm does not require the number of processors of the system to be predetermined and given before hand. It classifies the different tasks into a few classes based on the utilization of the task. One or more processors are assigned exclusively to each class of tasks. The essence of this algorithm is that tasks with similar utilization values are scheduled on the same processor.

In this algorithm, tasks are classified based on their utilization according to the following policy. If the tasks are to be divided into m classes, a task T_i belongs to a class j, $0 \leq j < m$, if

$$(2^{\frac{1}{j+1}} - 1) < e_i/p_i \leq (2^{\frac{1}{j}} - 1) \tag{4.1}$$

Suppose, we wish to partition the tasks of a system into four classes. Then, by using Expr. 4.1, the different classes can be formulated depending on the utilization of the tasks as follows:

Class 1: $(2^{\frac{1}{2}} - 1) < C_1 \leq (2^{\frac{1}{1}} - 1)$

Class 2: $(2^{\frac{1}{3}} - 1) < C_2 \leq (2^{\frac{1}{2}} - 1)$

Class 3: $(2^{\frac{1}{4}} - 1) < C_3 \leq (2^{\frac{1}{3}} - 1)$

Class 4: $0 < C_4 \leq (2^{\frac{1}{4}} - 1)$

From the above, the utilization grid for the different classes can be found to be: class 1: (0.41, 1), class 2: (0, 26, 0.41), class 3: (0.19, 0.26), and class 4: (0, 0.19).

We can view Expr. 4.1 as defining grids on the utilization plot of the tasks. A task is assigned to a grid depending on its utilization. It is not difficult to observe that the size of the grids at higher task utilization values are coarser compared to that at low task utilization values. The grid size of class 1 tasks is $1 - 0.41 = 0.59$, whereas the grid size of the class 3 tasks is 0.07. Simulation studies indicate that using the next fit algorithm at most 2.34 times the optimum number of processors are required. We now illustrate the working of this task allocation method using an example.

Example 4.1

The following table shows the execution times (in milliseconds) and periods (in milliseconds) of a set of 10 periodic real-time tasks. Assume that the tasks need to run on a multiprocessor with four processors. Allocate the tasks to processors using the next fit algorithm. Assume that the individual processors are to be scheduled using RMA algorithm.

TABLE 4.1 Task Set for Example 4.1

Task	T_1	T_2	T_3	T_4	T_5	T_6	T_7	T_8	T_9	T_{10}
e_i	5	7	3	1	10	16	1	3	9	17
p_i	10	21	22	24	30	40	50	55	70	100

Now, we can determine the utilization of the different tasks and based on that we can assign the different tasks to different classes. The following table shows the computation of the utilization of each task and based on that the assignment of the tasks to different classes.

TABLE 4.2   Solution for Example 4.1

Task	T_1	T_2	T_3	T_4	T_5	T_6	T_7	T_8	T_9	T_{10}
e_i	5	7	3	1	10	16	1	3	9	17
p_i	10	21	22	24	30	40	50	55	70	100
u_i	0.5	0.33	0.14	0.04	0.33	0.4	0.02	0.05	0.13	0.17
Class	1	2	4	4	2	2	4	4	4	3

Bin Packing Algorithm for EDF.   This algorithm attempts to allocate tasks to the processors such that the tasks on the individual processors can be successfully scheduled using EDF. This means that tasks are to be assigned to processors such that the utilization at any processor does not exceed 1. Bin packing is a standard algorithmic problem. We formulate the task allocation problem as a bin packing problem in the following.

We are given n periodic real-time tasks. When the individual processors are to be scheduled using the EDF algorithm, the number bins necessary can be expressed as: $[\Sigma_{i=1}^n u_i]$. The bin packing problem is known to be NP-complete.

Several bin packing algorithms exist. The two that we discuss are the first-fit random algorithm and the first-fit decreasing algorithm. In the first fit random algorithm, tasks are selected randomly and assigned to processors in an arbitrary manner as long as the utilization of a processor does not exceed 1. In this scheme, at most 1.7 times the optimum number of processors are required.

In the first-fit decreasing algorithm, the tasks are sorted in non-increasing order of their CPU utilization in an ordered list (that is, the task with the highest utilization is assigned the first position, and so on). The tasks are selected one by one from the ordered list and assigned to the bin (processor) to which it can fit in (that is, does not cause the utilization to exceed 1). A task is assigned to the processor to which it fits first. Simulation studies involving large number of tasks and processors show that the number of processors required by this approach is 1.22 times the optimal number of processors.

4.2 DYNAMIC ALLOCATION OF TASKS

So far we had discussed static allocation of tasks to processors. However, in many applications tasks arrive sporadically at different nodes. In such a scenario, a dynamic algorithm is needed to handle the arriving tasks. Dynamic algorithms assume that any task can be executed on any processor. Many of the dynamic solutions are naturally distributed and do not assume that there is a central allocation policy running on some processor.

In the dynamic algorithms, rather than preallocating tasks to processors, the tasks are assigned to processors as and when they arise. Since the task allocation to nodes can be made on the instantaneous load position of the nodes, the achievable schedulable utilization in this case should be better than the static approaches. However, the dynamic approach incurs high run time overhead since the allocator component running at every node needs to keep track of the instantaneous load position at every other node. In contrast, in a static task allocation algorithm, tasks are permanently assigned to processors at the system initialization time and no overhead is incurred during run time. Also, if tasks are bound to a single processor or a subset of processors, dynamic allocation would be ineffective.

In this section we discuss two popular dynamic real-time task allocation algorithms.

Focussed Addressing and Bidding.   In this method, every processor maintains two tables called status table and system load table. The status table of a processor contains information about the tasks which it has committed to run, including information about the execution time and periods of the tasks. The system load table contains the latest load information of all other processors of the system. From the latest load information at the other processors, the surplus computing capacity available at the different processors can be determined.

The time axis is divided into windows, which are intervals of fixed duration. At the end of each window, each processor broadcasts to all other processors the fraction of computing power in the next window that is currently free for it—that is, the fraction of the next window for which it has no committed tasks. Every processor on receiving a broadcast from a node about the load position updates the system load table. When tasks arise at a node, the node first checks whether the task can be processed locally at the node. If it can be processed, then it updates its status table. If not, it looks out for a processor to which it can offload the task.

While looking out for a suitable processor, the processor consults its system load table to determine the least loaded processors in the system which can accommodate this task. It then sends out Request for bids (RFBs) to these processors. While looking out for a processor, an overloaded processor checks its surplus information and selects a processor (called the focussed processor). However, remember that the information (i.e., the system load table) might be out of date. Therefore, there is a likelihood that by the time the processor with excess load sends a task to a focussed processor, the focussed processor might have already changed its status and become overloaded. For this reason, a processor can not simply off-load a task to another node based on the information it has in the system load table.

The problem of obsolete information at the nodes is overcome using the following strategy. A processor sends out RFBs only if it determines that the task would complete in time, even when the time needed to get the bids from the other processors and then sending out the task to the focussed processor. The criteria for selecting a processor may be based on factors such as proximity to the processor, its exact load information, etc.

The focussed addressing and bidding strategy, however, incurs high communication overhead in maintaining the system load table at the individual processors. Window size is an important parameter determining the communication overhead incurred. If the window size is increased, then the communication overhead decreases; however, the information at various processors would be obsolete. This may lead to a scenario where none of the focussed processors bids due to status change in the window duration. If the window duration is too small then the information would be reasonably uptodate at the individual processors, but the communication overhead in maintaining the status tables would be unacceptably high.

Buddy Algorithm.   The buddy algorithm tries to overcome the high communication overhead of the focussed addressing and bidding algorithm. The buddy algorithm is very similar to focussed addressing and bidding algorithm, but differs in the manner in which the target processors are found.

In this algorithm, a processor can be in any of the following two states: underloaded and overloaded. The status of a node is underloaded if its utilization is less than some threshold value.

That is, a processor P_i is said to be underloaded if $u_i < Th$, The processor is said to be overloaded if its utilization is greater than the threshold value (i.e., $u_i \geq Th$).

Unlike focussed addressing and bidding, in the buddy algorithm broadcast does not occur periodically at the end of every window. A processor broadcasts only when the status of a processor changes either from overloaded to underloaded or vice versa. Further, whenever the status of a processor changes, it does not broadcast this information to all processors and limits it only to a subset of processors called its *buddy set*. There are several criteria on which the buddy set of a processor design is based. First, it should be neither too large nor too small. In multi-hop networks, the buddy set of a processor is typically the processors that are its immediate neighbours.

4.3 FAULT-TOLERANT SCHEDULING OF TASKS

Task scheduling techniques can be used to achieve effective fault-tolerance in real-time systems. This is an efficient technique as it requires very little redundant hardware resources. Fault-tolerance can be achieved by scheduling additional ghost copies in addition to the primary copy of a task. The ghost copies may not be identical to the primary copy but may be stripped down versions that can be executed in shorter durations than the primary, The ghost copies of different tasks can be overloaded on the same slot and in case of a success execution of a primary, the corresponding backup may be deallocated.

4.4 CLOCKS IN DISTRIBUTED REAL-TIME SYSTEMS

Besides the traditional use of clocks in a computer system, clocks in a system are useful for two main purposes: determining timeouts and time stamping. Timeouts are useful to a real-time programmer in a variety of situations, and its use includes determining the failure of a task due to the missing of a deadline. Timeouts at both the sender and receiver ends is especially convenient for communication in distributed environments. They can be used as indicators for possible transmission faults or delays, or for non-existent receivers. Time stamping is useful in several applications. But a prominent use of time stamping is in message communication among tasks. The idea is that the message sender would also include the current time along a message. Time stamps not only give the receiver some idea about the age of a message, but can also be used for ordering purposes. Time stamping relies on good real-time clock services.

A distributed system typically has one clock at each node. Different clocks in a system tend to diverge since it is almost impossible to have two clocks that run exactly at the same speed. This lack of synchrony among clocks is expressed as the *clock slew* and determines the attendant drift of the clocks with time. Lack of synchrony and drift among clocks makes the time stamping and timeout operations in a distributed real-time system meaningless. Therefore, to have meaningful timeouts and time-stamping spanning more than one node of a distributed system, the clocks need to be synchronized. This makes clock synchronization a very important issue in distributed real-time systems. The following discussions are intended to provide some basic ideas regarding clock synchronization.

4.4.1 Clock Synchronization

The goal of clock synchronization is to make all clocks in the network agree on their time values. For most distributed real-time applications, it is often sufficient to get the different clocks of a system agree on some time value which may be different from the world time standard. Many of you might know that the world time standard is called universal coordinated time (UTC). UTC is based on the international atomic time (TAI) maintained at Paris by averaging a number of atomic clocks from laboratories around the world. UTC signals can be made use of through GPS (Global Positioning System) receivers and specialized radio stations.

When the clocks of a system are synchronized with respect to one of the clocks of the system, it is called internal clock synchronization. When synchronization of a set of clocks with some external clock is performed, it is called external synchronization. There are two main approaches for internal synchronization: centralized clock synchronization and distributed clock synchronization.

4.5 CENTRALIZED CLOCK SYNCHRONIZATION

In centralized clock synchronization, one of the clocks is designated as the master clock. The other clocks of the system are called slaves and are kept in synchronization with the master clock. The master clock is also sometimes called the *time server*. The arrangement of the clocks in this scheme of clock synchronization has schematically been shown in Fig. 4.1. In Fig. 4.1, the clocks $C_1, \ldots C_n$ are the slave clocks that are to be synchronized with the master clock.

The server broadcasts its time to all other clocks for synchronization after every ΔT time interval. Once the slave clocks receive a time broadcast from the master, they set their clock as per the time at the master clock. The parameter ΔT should be carefully chosen. If ΔT is chosen to be too small, then the broadcast from the master is frequent and the slaves remain in good synchronization with the master at all times, but unnecessarily high communication overhead is incurred. If ΔT is chosen to be too large, then the clocks may drift too much apart. Let us assume that the maximum rate of drift between two individual clocks is restricted to ρ. It should be possible to determine the maximum drift rate between any two clocks, clock manufacturers usually specify this as one of the specification parameters of a clock. The parameter ρ is unit

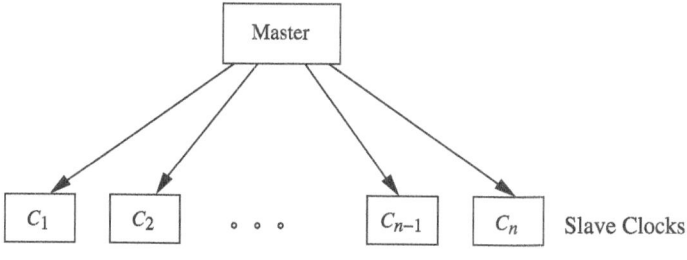

▲ FIGURE 4.1

Centralized Synchronization System

Example 4.2

Assume that the drift rate between any two clocks is restricted to $\rho = 5 \times 10^{-6}$. Suppose we want to implement a synchronized set of six distributed clocks using the central synchronization scheme so that the maximum drift between any two clocks is restricted to $\epsilon = 1mSec$ at any time, determine the period with which the clocks need to be resynchronized.

Solution.   The maximum drift rate between any two arbitrary clocks when the clocks are synchronized using a central time server with a resynchronization interval of ΔT is given by $2\rho\Delta T < \epsilon$. Therefore, the required resynchronization interval ΔT can be expressed as:

$$\Delta T < \frac{1 \times 10^{-3}}{5 \times 10^{-6} \times 2} \sec = \frac{10^{-3}}{10^{-5}} \sec = \frac{1}{10^{-2}} \sec = 100 \sec$$

Therefore, resynchronization period must be less than 100 sec.

less since it measures drift (time) per unit time. Suppose clocks are resynchronized after every ΔT interval. Then, the drift of any clock from the master clock will be bounded by $\rho\Delta T$. From this, it can be concluded that the maximum drift between any two clocks will be limited to $2\rho\Delta T$.

In the above calculations, we have ignored the communication time. That is, the time it takes for a clock time broadcast to be received at the other clocks. Similarly, we have assumed that once the clock broadcasts are received, the clocks are set to the received time instantly. However, in reality it takes a finite amount of time to set a clock. Therefore, unless the communication time and the time to set the clock are suitably taken care of, the synchronized time would become slower and slower with respect to an external clock. Though they would still remain synchronized among themselves within the specified bound. However, it is very difficult to compensate these two terms in practical systems. We leave this as an exercise to the reader to determine the rate at which a centrally synchronized clock would drift with respect to an external clock.

4.6   DISTRIBUTED CLOCK SYNCHRONIZATION

The main problem with the centralized clock synchronization scheme is that it is susceptible to single point failure. Any failure of the master clock causes breakdown of the synchronization scheme. Distributed clock synchronization overcomes this severe handicap of the centralized clock synchronization scheme. In distributed clock synchronization, there is no master clock with respect to which all slave clocks are to be set. But, all the clocks of a system are made to periodically exchange their clock readings among themselves. Based on the received time readings each clock in the system computes the synchronized time, and sets its clock accordingly (see Fig. 4.2). However, it is possible that some clocks are bad or become bad during the system operation. Bad clocks exhibit large drifts—drifts larger than the manufactured specified tolerance. Bad clocks may even stop keeping time all together. Fortunately, the bad clocks can be easily identified and taken care of during synchronization by

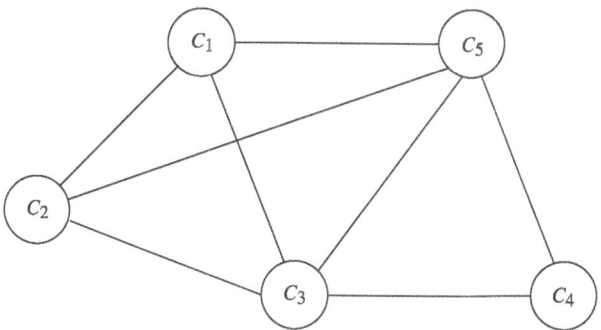

▲ **FIGURE 4.2**

Distributed Clock Synchronization

rejecting the time values of any clock which differs by any amount larger than the specified bound. A more insidious problem is posed by Byzantine clocks. A Byzantine clock is a two-faced clock. It can transmit different values to different clocks at the same time. In Fig. 4.3, C_1 is a Byzantine clock that is sending time value $t + e$ to clock C_5 and $t - e$ to clock C_2 at the same time instant.

It has been proved that if less than one-third of the clocks are bad or Byzantine (i.e., no more than one out of four are bad or Byzantine), then we can have the good clocks approximately synchronized. The following is the scheme for synchronization of the clocks. Let there be n clocks in a system. Each clock periodically broadcasts its time value at the end of certain interval. Assume that the clocks in the system are required to be synchronized within ϵ time units of each other. Therefore, if a clock receives a time broadcast that differs from its own time value by more than ϵ time units, then it can determine that the sending clock must be a bad one and safely ignore the received time values. Each clock averages out all good time values received after a broadcast step and sets its time value with this average value. This scheme has

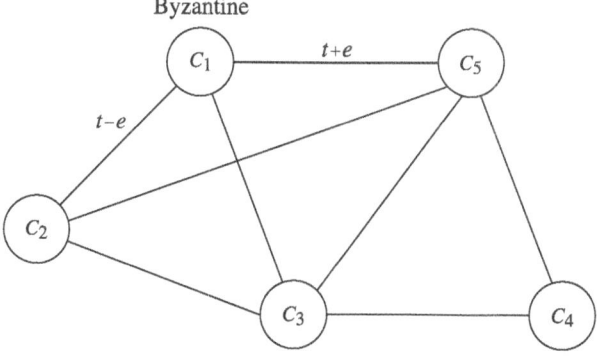

▲ **FIGURE 4.3**

Byzantine Clock is a Two Faced Clock

been presented in pseudo code form in the following. Each clock C_i carries out the following operations:

Procedure distributed clock synchronization:

```
good-clocks = n;
for(j = 1; j < n; j++){
if (||(c_i - c_j)| > ε) good-clocks--;    //Bad clock
else total-time = total-time + c_j;
c_i = total-time/good-clocks;             //set own time equal to the computed
                                            time

}
```

Note that each clock of the system independently carries out the same set of steps. If all n clocks of a distributed system carry out the above steps, and at most m clocks out of n clocks are bad, and $n > 3 * m$, then we show in the following that the good clocks will be synchronized within $\frac{3\epsilon m}{n}$ bound.

We first show in the following theorem that a Byzantine clock can make two good clocks differ in their computed average time by at most $\frac{3\epsilon}{n}$.

THEOREM 4.1   *In a distributed system with n clocks, a single Byzantine clock can make two arbitrary clocks in a system to differ by $\frac{3\epsilon}{n}$ in time value, where ϵ represents the maximum permissible drift between two clocks.*

PROOF: Let us consider three clocks C_1, C_2, C_3 of a distributed system as shown in Fig. 4.3. In Fig. 4.3, C_2 and C_3 are two good clocks and C_1 is a Byzantine clock. The clocks C_2 and C_3 are required not to differ by more than ϵ. C_3 being a Byzantine clock shows two different values to C_1 and C_2. Now, the effect of the Byzantine clock in the total time calculation is to make the two good clocks differ by at most $3 * \epsilon$ as shown in Fig. 4.4. Therefore, the effect of a single Byzantine clock can make two arbitrary clocks in a system to differ by $\frac{3\epsilon}{n}$ in time value.

So, for m Byzantine clocks can make two good clocks differ by at most $3\epsilon m$ in average computation. From this it follows that from the time computation by the individual clocks, the individual clocks will be synchronized within $\frac{3\epsilon m}{n}$.

Let the time required for two clocks to drift from $\frac{3\epsilon m}{n}$ to ϵ be ΔT.

or,

$$2\Delta T\rho \leq \frac{n\epsilon - 3\epsilon m}{n}$$

(4.2)

or,

$$\Delta T \leq \frac{n\epsilon - 3\epsilon m}{n \times 2\rho}$$

where ΔT is the time required for two good clocks to drift from $\frac{3\epsilon m}{n}$ to ϵ.

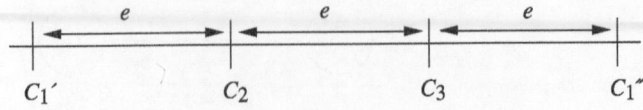

▲ **FIGURE 4.4**

Drift Between Two Clocks in Presence of Byzantine Clocks

We know that

$$\Delta T \le \frac{(3m + 1)\epsilon - 3\epsilon m}{n \times 2\rho}$$

$$\Delta T \le \frac{\epsilon}{2n\rho}$$

(4.3)

We now illustrate the computation of the synchronization period for the distributed clock synchronization algorithm using an example.

Example 4.3

Let a distributed real-time system have 10 clocks, and it is required to restrict their maximum drift to $\epsilon = 1mSec$. Let the maximum drift of the clocks per unit time (ρ) be 5×10^{-6}. Determine the required synchronization interval.

Solution.   From the derivation for distributed clock synchronization, we have

$$\Delta T = \frac{10^{-3}}{2 \times 10 \times 5 \times 10^{-6}}$$

$$\Delta T = 10 \text{ sec}$$

Thus, the required synchronization interval is 10 sec.

SUMMARY

- In this chapter we first discussed how real-time tasks can be scheduled on multiprocessor and distributed computers. Task scheduling in multiprocessor and distributed systems is a much more complex problem than the uniprocessor scheduling problem.

- We saw that the task scheduling problem in multiprocessor and distributed systems consists of two sub-problems: task allocation to individual processors and task scheduling at the individual processors. The task allocation problem is an NP-hard problem.

- In a distributed real-time system, it is vital to have all the clocks in the systems synchronized within acceptable tolerance. We examined a centralized and a distributed clock synchronization scheme.

- Centralized clock synchronization is susceptible to single point failure. On the other hand, a distributed clock synchronization scheme can keep the good clocks in a distributed system synchronized only if no more than 25% of the clocks are bad or Byzantine.

- In the centralized synchronization scheme, unless the communication time and the time to set the clock are suitably compensated, the synchronized time may progressively become slower and slower with respect to the world time (UTC).

EXERCISES

1. State whether you consider the following statements TRUE or FALSE. Justify your answer in each case.

   (a) Optimal schemes for scheduling hard real-time tasks in multiprocessor computing environments have been devised by suitably extending the EDF algorithm.

(b) Using the distributed clock synchronization scheme, it is possible to keep the good clocks of a distributed system having 12 clocks synchronized, when two of the clocks are known to be Byzantine.

(c) In a distributed hard real-time computing environment, task allocation to individual nodes using a bin packing algorithm in conjunction with task scheduling at the individual nodes using the EDF algorithm can be shown to be the most proficient.

(d) The focussed addressing and bidding algorithm used for task allocation in distributed real-time systems statically allocates tasks to nodes.

(e) The focussed addressing and bidding algorithm for task allocation can handle dynamic task arrivals and is suited for use in multiprocessor-based real-time systems.

(f) Buddy algorithms require less communication overhead compared to focussed addressing and bidding algorithms in multiprocessor real-time task scheduling.

(g) The bin-packing scheme is the optimal algorithm for allocating a set of periodic real-time tasks to the nodes of distributed system.

(h) In a distributed system when the message communication time is non-zero and significant, the simple internal synchronization scheme using a time server makes the synchronized time incrementally delayed by the average message transmission time after every synchronization interval.

2. Explain why algorithms that can be satisfactorily used to schedule real-time tasks on multiprocessors often are not satisfactory to schedule real-time tasks on distributed systems, and vice versa?

3. In a distributed system, six clocks need to be synchronized to a maximum difference of 10 mSec between any two clocks. Assume that the individual clocks have a maximum rate of drift of 2×10^{-6}. Ignore clock set-up times and communication latencies.

(a) What is the rate at which the clocks need to be synchronized using (i) a simple central time server method? (ii) simple internal synchronization (averaging) method?

(b) What is the communication overhead in each of the two schemes?

(c) Assuming the average communication latency to be 0.1 mSec, what would be the drift of the synchronized time with respect to the UTC for each of the two synchronization schemes?

4. (a) Why is the clock resolution provided to real-time programs by different commercial real-time operating systems rarely finer than few hundreds of milliseconds though giga hertz clocks are used by these systems?

(b) Can clock resolution finer than milliseconds be provided to real-time programs at all? If yes, briefly explain how.

5. Why is it necessary to synchronize the clocks in a distributed real-time system? Discuss the relative advantages and disadvantages of the centralized and distributed clock synchronization schemes.

6. Describe the *focussed addressing and bidding* and the *buddy* schemes for running a set of real-time tasks in a distributed environment. Compare these two schemes with respect to communication overhead and scheduling proficiency.

7. Suppose a distributed system has 12 clocks. Assuming that no clocks in the system are Byzantine, determine the total number of message exchanges required per hour to keep the clocks synchronized within 1 mSec of each other in the centralized and distributed schemes. Assume that the maximum drift rate of the clocks is given to be $6 * 10^{-6}$.

5 Commercial Real-Time Operating Systems

In the last three chapters we discussed the important real-time task scheduling techniques. We highlighted that timely production of results in accordance with a physical clock is vital to the satisfactory operation of a real-time system. We had also pointed out that real-time operating systems are primarily responsible for ensuring that every real-time task meets its timeliness requirements. A real-time operating system, in turn, achieves this by using appropriate task scheduling techniques. Normally, real-time operating systems provide flexibility to the programmers to select an appropriate scheduling policy among several supported policies. Deployment of an appropriate task scheduling technique out of the supported techniques is, therefore, an important concern for every real-time programmer. To be able to determine the suitability of a scheduling algorithm for a given problem, a thorough understanding of the characteristics of various real-time task scheduling algorithms is important. We, therefore, had a rather elaborate discussion on real-time task scheduling techniques and certain related issues such as sharing of critical resources and handling task dependencies.

In this chapter, we examine the important features that a real-time operating system is expected to support. Unless these features are adequately supported by an operating system, it becomes difficult to satisfactorily implement certain categories of real-time applications on this operating system. We discuss to what extent these required features are supported by the various commercially available real-time operating systems. To gain a better insight, we also investigate the internals of the operating systems to examine the exact ways in which the required features are supported.

To appreciate some of the fundamental issues affecting the design and development of a satisfactory real-time operating system, we discuss the problems that would crop up if one attempts to use a general purpose operating system such as Unix or Windows for developing real-time applications. Many real-time operating systems are at present commercially available. We analyze some popular real-time operating systems, and investigate why these popular systems can not be used across all applications. We also examine the POSIX standard for real-time operating systems and its implications.

This chapter is organized as follows. First, we discuss the important features that are usually required to be supported by a real-time operating system. We start by discussing the time service supports provided by the real-time operating systems, since accurate and high precision clocks are very important to the successful operation of any real-time application. Subsequently, we discuss the issues that arise if we attempt to use a general purpose operating system such as Unix or Windows in a real-time application. Next, we explain how some of the fundamental problems associated with traditional operating systems (as far as real-time applications are concerned) are overcome in the contemporary real-time operating systems. We then survey some of the important features of the different real-time operating systems that are being commercially used. Finally, we identify some of the important parameters on which various real-time systems can be benchmarked.

5.1   TIME SERVICES

Clocks and time services are among some of the basic facilities provided to programmers by every real-time operating system. The time services provided by an operating system are based on a software clock called the system clock. The system clock is maintained by the operating system kernel based on the interrupts received from the hardware clock. Since hard real-time systems usually have timing constraints that are of the order of a few microseconds, the system clock should have sufficiently fine resolution[1] to support the necessary time services. However, designers of real-time operating systems find it very difficult to support fine resolution system clocks. In current technology, the resolution of hardware clocks is finer than a nanosecond (contemporary processor speeds exceed 3 GHz). But, the clock resolution being made available by modern real-time operating systems to the programmers is only of the order of several milliseconds or worse. Let us first investigate why real-time operating system designers find it difficult to maintain system clocks with sufficiently fine resolution. We then examine various time services that are built based on the system clock, and made available to the real-time programmers.

The hardware clock in a computer periodically generates interrupts (often called time service interrupts). After each clock interrupt, the kernel updates the software clock and also performs certain other functions (explained in Section 5.1.1). A thread can get the current time reading of the system clock by invoking a system call supported by the operating system (such as the POSIX clock-gettime()). The finer the resolution of the clock, the more frequent need to be the time service interrupts and larger is the amount of processor time the kernel spends in responding to these interrupts. This overhead places a limitation on how fine the system clock resolution a computer can support. Another issue that caps the resolution of the system clock is that the response time of the clock-gettime() system call is not deterministic. In fact, every system call (or for that matter every function call) invocation has some associated jitter. Remember that jitter was defined as the difference between the worst-case response time and the best-case response time (see Section 2.3.1). The jitter is caused partly on account of interrupts having higher priority than system calls. When an interrupt occurs, the processing of a system call is stalled. The problem gets aggravated in such a situation. Further, the preemption time of system calls can vary because many operating systems disable interrupts while processing a system call. The variation in the response time (jitter) introduces an error in the accuracy of the time value that the calling thread gets from the kernel. In commercially available operating systems, jitters associated with system calls can be several milliseconds. This jitter introduces an error in the time readings obtained by a program. A software clock resolution finer than this error is, therefore, not meaningful.

We now examine the different activities that are carried out by a handler routine after a clock interrupt occurs. Subsequently, we discuss how sufficiently fine resolution can be provided in the presence of jitter in function calls.

---

[1]Clock resolution denotes the time granularity provided by the system clock of a computer. Thus, the resolution of a system clock corresponds to the duration of time that elapses between two successive clock ticks.

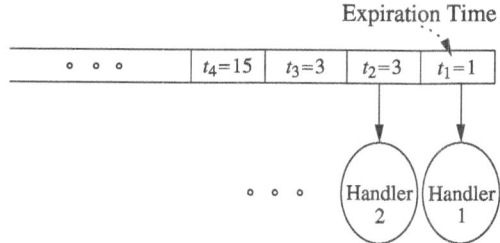

▲ **FIGURE 5.1**

Structure of a Timer Queue

5.1.1 Clock Interrupt Processing

Each time a clock interrupt occurs, besides incrementing the software clock, the handler routine carries out the following activities:

- **Process timer events:** Real-time operating systems maintain either per-process timer queues or a single system-wide timer queue. The structure of such a timer queue has been shown in Fig. 5.1. A timer queue contains all timers arranged in order of their expiration times. Each timer is associated with a handler routine. The handler routine is the function that needs to be invoked when the timer expires. At each clock interrupt, the kernel checks the timer data structures in the timer queue to see whether any timer event has occurred. If it finds that a timer event has occurred, then it queues the corresponding handler routine in the ready queue.

- **Update ready list:** Since the occurrence of the last clock event, some tasks might have arrived or become ready due to the fulfillment of certain conditions they were waiting for. Recollect from a basic course on operating system that arriving tasks and tasks waiting for some event (such as a page fetch or a semaphore event) are queued in a wait queue. The tasks in the wait queue are checked to see if any task has become ready meanwhile. The tasks which are found to have become ready, are queued in the ready queue. If a task having higher priority than the currently running task is found to have become ready, then the currently running task is preempted and the scheduler is invoked.

- **Update execution budget:** At each clock interrupt, the scheduler decrements the time slice (budget) remaining for the executing task. If the remaining budget for the task becomes zero and the task is not yet complete, then the task is preempted and the scheduler is invoked to select another task to run.

5.1.2 Providing High Clock Resolution

We had pointed out in Section 5.1 that there are two main difficulties in providing a high resolution timer. First, the overhead associated with processing the clock interrupt becomes excessive as the time service resolution gets finer. Secondly, the jitter associated with the time lookup system call (clock-gettime()) is often of the order of several milliseconds. Therefore, it is not useful to provide a clock with a resolution any finer than this. However, some real-time applications need to deal with timing constraints of the order of a few nanoseconds. For such applications, an important question is: Is it at all possible to support time measurement with nanosecond resolution? A way to provide sufficiently fine clock resolution is by mapping a hardware clock into the address space of applications. An application can then read the hardware clock directly through a normal memory read operation without having to make a system call. For example, on a Pentium processor, a user thread can be made to read the Pentium time stamp counter. This counter starts at 0 when the system is powered on and increments after each hardware clock interrupt. At today's processor speed, this means that during every nanosecond interval, the counter increments several times.

However, making the hardware clock readable by an application significantly reduces the portability of the application. For example, when an application running on a Pentium processor is ported to a different processor, the new processor may not have a high resolution counter, and certainly the memory address map and resolution would differ.

5.1.3 Timers

We had pointed out that timer service is a vital service that is provided to applications by all real-time operating systems. Real-time operating systems normally support two main types of timers: periodic timers and aperiodic (or one shot) timers.

Periodic Timers.   Periodic timers are used mainly for sampling events at regular intervals or performing some activities periodically. Once a periodic timer is set, it expires periodically. This is implemented using the timer queue as follows. Each time periodic timer expires, the corresponding handler routine is invoked, and the timer data structure is inserted back into the timer queue (see Fig. 5.1). For example, a periodic timer may be set to 100 mSec and its handler set to poll the temperature sensor after every 100 mSec interval.

Aperiodic (or One Shot) Timers.   These timers are set to expire only once. Watchdog timers are a popular example of one shot timers.

Watchdog timers are used extensively in real-time programs to detect if a task misses its deadline, and then to initiate exception handling procedures upon a deadline miss. An example use of a watchdog timer has been illustrated in Fig. 5.2. In Fig. 5.2, a watchdog timer is set at the start of a certain critical function f() through a wd_start(t1) call. The wd_start(t1) call sets the watchdog timer to expire by the specified deadline (t_1 time units) from the starting of the task.

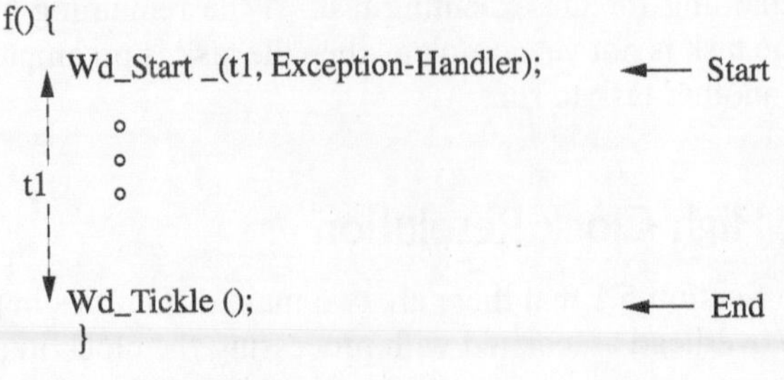

```
f() {
        Wd_Start _(t1, Exception-Handler);        ◄─── Start
              o
  t1          o
              o
        Wd_Tickle ();                              ◄─── End
     }
```

▲ **FIGURE 5.2**

Use of a Watchdog Timer

If the function f() does not complete even after t_1 time units have elapsed, then the watchdog timer expires, indicating that the task deadline is missed and the exception handling procedure is initiated. In case the task completes before the watchdog timer expires (i.e., the task completes within its deadline), then the watchdog timer is reset using a wd_tickle() call.

5.2 FEATURES OF A REAL-TIME OPERATING SYSTEM

Before discussing commercial real-time operating systems, we must clearly understand the features normally expected of a real-time operating system. This will also enable us to compare the features supported by different real-time operating systems for selecting an appropriate operating system for an application at hand. This would also let us understand the differences between a traditional operating system and a real-time operating system. In the following, we identify some important features required of a real-time operating system, and especially those that are normally absent in traditional operating systems.

Clock and Timer Support.   Clock and timer services with adequate resolution are one of the most important issues in real-time programming. Hard real-time application development often requires support of timer services with resolution of the order of a few microseconds. Still finer resolutions may be required in case of certain special applications. Clocks and timers are a vital part of every real-time operating system. On the other hand, traditional operating systems normally do not provide time services with sufficiently high resolution.

Real-Time Priority Levels.   A real-time operating system must support static priority levels. A priority level supported by an operating system is called static, when once the programmer assigns a priority value to a task, the operating system does not change it by itself. Static priority levels are also called *real-time priority levels*. We discuss in Section 5.3 that a traditional operating system dynamically changes the priority levels of tasks from programmer assigned values to maximize system throughput. Such priority levels that are changed dynamically by the operating system are obviously not static priorities.

Fast Task Preemption.   For successful operation of a real-time application, whenever a high priority critical task arrives, an executing low priority task should be made to instantly yield the CPU to it. The time duration for which a higher priority task waits before it is allowed to execute is quantitatively expressed as *task preemption time*. Contemporary real-time operating systems have task preemption times of the order of a few microseconds. However, in traditional operating systems, the worst case task preemption time is typically of the order of a second. We discuss in the next section that this significantly large latency is caused by a non-preemptive kernel. It goes without saying that a real-time operating system needs to have a preemptive kernel and should have task preemption times of the order of a few microseconds.

Predictable and Fast Interrupt Latency.   Interrupt latency is defined as the time delay between the occurrence of an interrupt and the running of the corresponding Interrupt Service Routine (ISR). In real-time operating systems, the upper bound on interrupt latency must be bounded and is expected to be less than a few microseconds. Low interrupt latency is achieved by performing bulk of the activities of ISR in a Deferred Procedure Call (DPC). A DPC is essentially a task that performs most of the ISR activity, but executes (after ISR completes) at a lower priority value. Further, support for nested interrupts are usually desired. That is, a real-time operating system should not only be preemptive while executing kernel routines, but should be preemptive during interrupt servicing as well. This is especially important for hard real-time applications with sub-microsecond timing requirements.

Support for Resource Sharing Among Real-Time Tasks.   We had already discussed in Chapter 3 that if real-time tasks are allowed to share critical resources among themselves using the traditional resource sharing techniques, then the response times of tasks can become unbounded leading to deadline misses. This is one compelling reason as to why every commercial real-time operating system should at the minimum provide the basic priority inheritance mechanism discussed in Chapter 3. Support of Priority Ceiling Protocol (PCP) is also desirable, if large and moderate sized applications are to be supported.

Requirements on Memory Management.   As far as general-purpose operating systems are concerned, it is rare to find one that does not support virtual memory and memory protection features. However, embedded real-time operating systems almost never support these features. Only those that are meant for large and complex applications do. Real-time operating systems for large and medium-sized applications are expected to provide virtual memory support, not only to meet the memory demands of the heavyweight real-time tasks of an application, but to let the memory demanding non-real-time applications such as text editors, e-mail software, etc. also run on the same platform. Virtual memory reduces the average memory access time, but degrades the worst-case memory access time. The penalty of using virtual memory is the overhead associated with storing the address translation table and performing the virtual to physical address translations. Moreover, fetching pages from the secondary memory on a page fault incurs significant latency. Therefore, operating systems supporting virtual memory must provide the real-time applications with some means of controlling paging, such as *memory locking*. Memory locking prevents a page from being swapped from memory to hard disk. In the absence of memory locking feature, memory access times of even critical real-time tasks can show large jitter, as the access time would greatly depend on whether the required page is in the physical memory or has been swapped out.

Memory protection is another important issue that needs to be carefully considered. Lack of support for memory protection among tasks leads to a single address space for all the tasks. Arguments for having only a single address space include simplicity, saving memory bits, and lightweight system calls. For small embedded applications, the overhead of a few kilobytes of memory per process can be unacceptable. However, when no memory protection is provided by the operating system, the cost of developing and testing a program without memory protection becomes very high when the complexity of the application increases. Also, maintenance cost increases as any change in one module would require retesting the entire system.

Embedded real-time operating systems usually do not support virtual memory; they create physically contiguous blocks of memory for an application upon request. However, memory fragmentation is a potential problem for a system that does not support virtual memory. Also, memory protection becomes difficult to support a non-virtual memory management system. For this reason, in many embedded systems, the kernel and the user processes execute in the same space, i.e., there is no memory protection. Hence, a system call and a function call within an application are, indistinguishable. This makes debugging applications difficult, since a run-away pointer can corrupt the operating system code, making the system 'freeze.'

Support for Asynchronous I/O.   Asynchronous I/O means non-blocking I/O. Traditional read() or write() system calls perform synchronous I/O. If a process attempts to read or write using the normal, synchronous read() or write() system calls, then it needs to wait until the hardware has completed the physical I/O. It is then informed of the success or failure of the operation, and the required data in the case of a successful read. Thus, in case of synchronous or blocking I/O execution of the process is blocked while it waits for the results of the system call.

However, if a process uses asynchronous *aio_read*() or *aio_write*() system calls (called *aioread*() and *aiowrite*() in some operating systems), then the system call will return immediately once the I/O request has been passed down to the hardware or queued in the operating system, typically before the physical I/O operation has even begun. The execution of the process is not blocked, because it does not need to wait for the results of the system call. Instead, it can continue executing and then receive the results of the I/O operation later, once they are available.

Additional Requirements for Embedded Real-Time Operating Systems.   Embedded applications usually have constraints on cost, size, and power consumption. Embedded real-time operating systems are, therefore, often required to be capable of diskless operation. This is because disks are usually too bulky to use in embedded systems; they increase power consumption, and the cost of deployment. For this reason, of late flash memory is being increasingly used for this purpose.

Embedded operating systems usually reside on either flash memory or ROM. For certain applications which require faster response, it may be necessary to run the real-time operating system on a RAM. This would result in faster execution, since the access time of a RAM is lower than that of a ROM. Irrespective of whether ROM or RAM is used, all ICs are expensive. Therefore, for real-time operating systems designed for embedded applications, it is desirable to have as small a footprint (memory usage) as possible. Since embedded products are typically manufactured on a large scale, every rupee saved on memory and other hardware requirements impacts millions of rupees in profit.

5.3 UNIX AS A REAL-TIME OPERATING SYSTEM

Unix is a popular general purpose operating system that was originally developed for the mainframe computers. However, Unix and its variants have now permeated to desktop and even handheld computers. Since Unix and its variants are inexpensive and widely available, it is worthwhile to investigate whether Unix can be used in real-time applications. This investigation would lead us to some significant findings and would give us some crucial insights into the current Unix-based real-time operating systems that are currently commercially available.

The traditional Unix operating system suffers from several shortcomings when used in real-time applications.

> The two most important problems that a real-time programmer faces while using Unix for real-time applications are non-preemptive Unix kernel and dynamically changing priorities of tasks.

5.3.1 Non-Preemptive Kernel

One of the biggest problems that real-time programmers face while using Unix for real-time application development is that Unix kernel cannot be preempted. That is, all interrupts are disabled when any operating system routine runs. To set things in proper perspective, let us elaborate this issue.

Application programs can invoke operating system services through *system calls*. Examples of system calls include the operating system services for creating a process, interprocess communication, I/O operations, etc. After a system call is invoked by an application, the arguments given by the application while invoking the system call are checked (see Fig. 5.3). Next, a special instruction called a trap (or a software interrupt) is executed. As soon as the trap instruction is executed, the handler routine changes the processor state from *user mode* to *kernel mode* (or *supervisor mode*), and the execution of the required kernel routine starts. The change of mode during a system call has schematically been depicted in Fig. 5.3.

At the risk of digressing from the focus of this discussion, let us understand an important operating systems concept. Certain operations such as handling devices, creating processes, file operations, etc. need to be done in the kernel mode only. That is, application programs are prevented from carrying out these operations, and need to request the operating system (through a system call) to carry out the required operation. This restriction enables the kernel to enforce discipline among different programs in accessing these objects. In case such operations are not performed in the kernel mode, different application programs might interfere with each other's operation. An example of an operating system where all operations were performed in user mode is the once popular operating system DOS (though DOS is nearly obsolete now). In DOS, application programs are free to carry out any operation in user mode,[2] including crashing the system by deleting the system files. The instability this can bring about is clearly unacceptable in real-time environment, and is usually considered unsatisfactory in general applications as well.

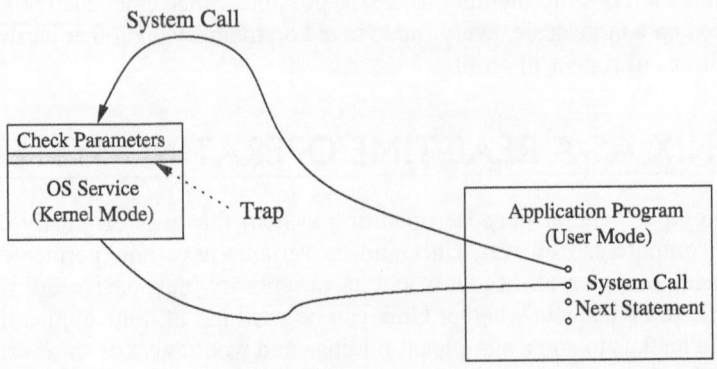

▲ **FIGURE 5.3**

Invocation of an Operating System Service through a System Call

---

[2]In fact, in DOS there is only one mode of operation, i.e., kernel and user modes are indistinguishable.

In Unix, a process running in kernel mode can not be preempted by other processes. In other words, the Unix kernel is *non-preemptive*. On the other hand, the Unix system does preempt processes running in the user mode. A consequence of this is that even when a low priority process makes a system call, the high priority processes would have to wait until the system call by the low priority process completes. For real-time applications, this causes a priority inversion. The longest system calls may take up to several hundreds of milliseconds to complete. Worst-case preemption times of several hundreds of milliseconds can easily cause high priority tasks with short deadlines of the order of a few milliseconds to miss their deadlines.

Let us now investigate why the Unix kernel was designed to be non-preemptive. In Unix when a kernel routine starts to execute, all interrupts are disabled. The interrupts are enabled only after the operating system routine completes. This was a very efficient way of preserving the integrity of the kernel data structures. It saved the overheads associated with setting and releasing of locks and resulted in lower average task preemption times. Though a non-preemptive kernel can result in worst-case task response time of up to a second, it was considered acceptable by the Unix designers. At that time, the Unix designers did not foresee usage of Unix in real-time applications. Of course, it could have been possible to ensure correctness of kernel data structures by using locks at appropriate places rather than disabling interrupts, but it would have resulted in increasing the average task preemption time. In Section 5.4.4 we investigate how modern real-time operating systems make the kernel preemptive through use of kernel-level and spin locks.

5.3.2 Dynamic Priority Levels

In traditional Unix systems, real-time tasks can not be assigned static priority values. Soon after a programmer sets a priority value for a task, the operating system keeps on altering it during the course of the execution of the task. This makes it very difficult to schedule real-time tasks using algorithms such as RMA or EDF, since both these schedulers assume that once task priorities are assigned, it should not be altered by any other part of the operating system. It is instructive to understand why Unix needs to dynamically change the priority values of tasks.

Unix uses round-robin scheduling of tasks with multilevel feedback. In this scheme, the scheduler arranges tasks in multilevel queues as shown in Fig. 5.4. At every preemption point,

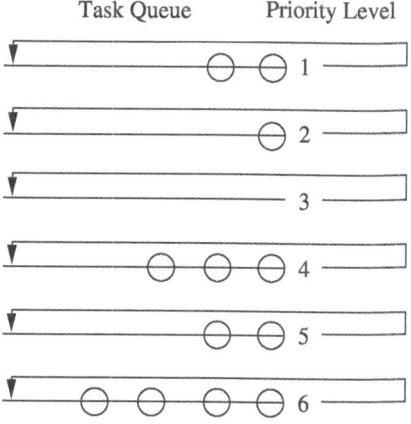

▲ **FIGURE 5.4**

Multi-Level Feedback Queues

the scheduler scans the multilevel queue from the top (highest priority) and selects the task at the head of the first non-empty queue. Each task is allowed to run for a fixed time quantum (or time slice) at a time. Unix normally uses one second time slice. That is, if the running process does not block or complete within one second of its starting execution, it is preempted and the scheduler selects the next task for dispatching. Unix system, however, allows configuring the default one second time slice during system generation. The kernel preempts a process that does not complete within its assigned time quantum, recomputes its priority, and inserts it back into one of the priority queues depending on the recomputed priority value of the task.

Unix periodically computes the priority of a task based on the type of the task and its execution history. The priority of a task (T_i) is recomputed at the end of its jth time slice using the following two expressions:

$$\text{pri}(T_i, j) = \text{Base}(T_i) + CPU(T_i, j) + \text{nice}(T_i) \tag{5.1}$$

$$CPU(T_i, j) = \frac{U(T_i, j-1)}{2} + \frac{CPU(T_i, j-1)}{2} \tag{5.2}$$

where pri(T_i, j) is the priority of the task T_i at the end of its jth time slice; $U(T_i, j)$ is the utilization of the task T_i for its jth time slice, and $CPU(T_i, j)$ is the weighted history of CPU utilization of the task T_i at the end of its jth time slice. Base(T_i) is the base priority of the task (T_i) and nice(T_i) is the nice value associated with T_i. User processes can have non-negative nice values. Thus, effectively the nice value lowers the priority value of a process (i.e., being nice to the other processes),

Expr. 5.2 has been recursively defined. Unfolding the recursion, we get:

$$CPU(T_i, j) = \frac{U(T_i, j-1)}{2} + \frac{CPU(T_i, j-2)}{4} + \cdots \tag{5.3}$$

It can be easily seen from Expr. 5.3 that in the computation of the weighted history of *CPU* utilization of a task, the activity (i.e., processing or I/O) of the task in the immediately concluded interval is given the maximum weightage. If a task uses up *CPU* for the full duration of its allotted time slice (i.e., 100% *CPU* utilization), then $CPU(T_i, j)$ is computed (by Expr. 5.3) to be a high value—indicating a lowering of the priority of the task. On the other hand, if the task immediate blocked for I/O as soon as it started computing during its allotted time slice, then $CPU(T_i, j)$ would be computed as a low value, indicating an increase of the priority of the task. Observe that the activities of the task in the preceding intervals get progressively lower weightage. It should be clear that $CPU(T_i, j)$ captures the weighted history of *CPU* utilization of the task T_i at the end of its jth time slice.

Now, substituting Expr 5.3 in Expr. 5.1, we get:

$$\text{pri}(T_i, j) = \text{Base}(T_i) + \frac{U(T_i, j-1)}{2} + \frac{U(T_i, j-2)}{4} + \cdots + \text{nice}(T_i) \tag{5.4}$$

The purpose of the base priority term (Base (T_i)) in the priority computation expression (Expr. 5.4) is to divide all tasks into a set of fixed bands of priority levels. Once a task is assigned to a priority level, it is not possible for the task to move out from its assigned band to other priority bands due to dynamic priority recomputations. The values of $U(T_i, j)$ and nice (T_i) components are deliberately restricted to be small enough to prevent a process from migrating from its assigned band. The bands have been designed to optimize I/O completion times, especially block I/O.

Dynamic recomputation of priorities was motivated by the following consideration. Unix designers observed that in any computer system, I/O transfer rate is primarily responsible for any slow response time. Processors are extremely fast compared to the transfer rates of I/O devices. Delay caused by I/O transfers, therefore, are the bottleneck in achieving faster task response times. To mitigate this problem, it is desirable to keep I/O channels as busy as possible. This can be achieved by assigning the I/O bound tasks high priorities.

As already mentioned, Unix has a set of priority bands to which different types of tasks are assigned. The different priority bands under Unix in decreasing order of priorities are: swapper, block I/O, file manipulation, character I/O and device control, and user processes. Tasks performing block I/O are assigned the highest priority band. But when are block I/O required? To give an example of block I/O, consider the I/O that occurs while handling a page fault in a virtual memory system. Block I/O uses DMA-based transfer, and hence makes efficient use of I/O channel. Character I/O includes mouse and keyboard transfers. The priority bands were designed to provide the most effective use of the I/O channels.

To keep the I/O channels busy, any task performing I/O should not be kept waiting very long for CPU. For this reason, as soon as a task blocks for I/O, its priority is increased by the priority recomputation rule given in Expr. 5.4. However, if a task makes full use of its last assigned time slice, it is determined to be computation-bound and its priority is reduced. Thus, the basic philosophy of the Unix operating system is that the interactive tasks are made to assume higher priority levels and are processed at the earliest. This gives the interactive users good response time. This technique has now become an accepted way of scheduling soft real-time tasks across almost all available general purpose operating systems, such as Microsoft's Windows operating systems.

We can state from the above observations that the overall effect of periodic recomputation of task priority values using Expr. 5.4 is as follows:

In Unix, dynamic priority computations cause I/O intensive tasks to migrate to higher and higher priority levels, whereas CPU-intensive tasks are made to seek lower priority levels.

No doubt that the approach taken by Unix is very appropriate for maximizing the average task throughput, and does indeed provide good average response time to interactive (soft real-time) tasks. In fact, almost every modern operating system does very similar dynamic recomputation of the task priorities to maximize the overall system throughput and to provide good average response time to the interactive tasks. However, for hard real-time tasks, dynamic shifting of priority values is clearly inappropriate, as it prevents tasks being constantly scheduled at high priority levels, and also prevents scheduling under popular real-time task scheduling algorithms such as EDF and RMA.

5.3.3 Other Deficiencies of Unix

We have so far discussed two glaring shortcomings of Unix in handling the requirements of real-time applications: dynamic priority recomputations and non-preemptable kernel. We now discuss a few other deficiencies of Unix that crop up while trying to use it in real-time applications.

Insufficient Device Driver Support.   In Unix (remember that we are talking or the original Unix System V), device drivers run in kernel mode. Therefore, if support for a new device is to be added, then the driver module has to be linked to the kernel modules—necessitating a system generation step. As a result, providing support for a new device in an already deployed application is cumbersome.

Lack of Real-Time File Services.   In Unix, file blocks are allocated as and when they are requested by an application. As a consequence, while a task is writing to a file, it may encounter an error when the disk runs out of space. In other words, no guarantee is given that disk space would be available when a task writes a block to a file. Traditional file writing approaches also result in slow writes because the required space has to be allocated before writing a block. Another problem with the traditional file systems is that blocks of the same file may not be contiguously located on the disk. This would result in read operations taking unpredictable times, resulting in jitter in data access. In real-time file systems significant performance improvement can be achieved by storing files contiguously on the disk. Since the file system preallocates space, the times for read and write operations are more predictable.

Inadequate Timer Services Support.   In Unix systems, real-time timer support is insufficient for many hard real-time applications. The clock resolution that is provided to applications is 10 mSec, which is too coarse for many hard real-time applications.

5.4 UNIX-BASED REAL-TIME OPERATING SYSTEMS

We have already seen in the previous section that traditional Unix systems are not suitable for use in hard real-time applications. In this section, we discuss the different approaches that have been undertaken to make Unix suitable for real-time applications.

5.4.1 Extensions to the Traditional Unix Kernel

A naive attempt made in the past to make traditional Unix suitable for real-time applications was by adding some real-time capabilities over the basic kernel. These additionally implemented capabilities included real-time timer support, a real-time task scheduler built over the Unix scheduler, etc. However, these extensions do not address the fundamental problems with the Unix system that were pointed out in the last section; namely, non-preemptive kernel and dynamic priority levels. No wonder that superficial extensions to the capabilities of the Unix kernel without addressing the fundamental deficiencies of the Unix system fell short of the requirements of hard real-time applications.

5.4.2 Host-Target Approach

Host-target operating systems are popularly being deployed in embedded applications. In this approach, the real-time application development is done on a host machine which is either a traditional Unix operating system or a Windows system. The real-time application is developed on the host and the developed application is downloaded onto a target board that is to be embedded in a real-time system. A ROM-resident small real-time kernel is used in the target board. This approach has been schematically shown in Fig. 5.5.

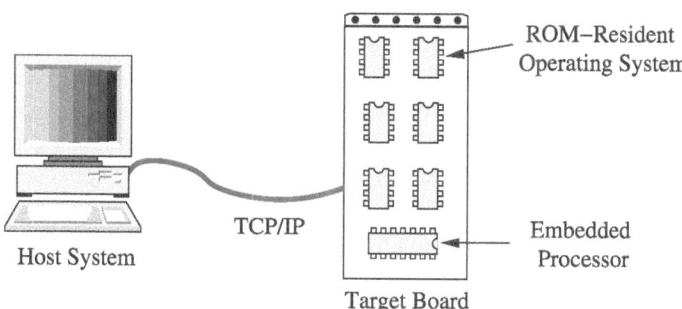

▲ **FIGURE 5.5**

Schematic Representation of a Host-Target System

The main idea behind this approach is that the real-time operating system running on the target board needs to be kept as small and simple as possible. This implies that the operating system on the target board would lack virtual memory management support, neither would it support any utilities such as compilers, program editors, etc. The processor on the target board would run the real-time operating system.

The host system is a Unix or Windows-based system supporting the program development environment, including compilers, editors, library, cross-compilers, debuggers etc. These are memory demanding applications that require virtual memory support. The host is usually connected to the target using a serial port or a TCP/IP connection (see Fig. 5.5). The real-time program is developed on the host. It is then cross-compiled to generate code for the target processor. Subsequently, the executable module is downloaded to the target board. Tasks are executed on the target board and the execution is controlled at the host side using a symbolic cross-debugger. Once the program works successfully, it is fused on a ROM or flash memory and becomes ready to be deployed in applications.

Commercial examples of host-target real-time operating systems include PSOS, VxWorks, and VRTX. We examine these commercial products in Section 5.7. We would point out that the target operating systems due to their small size, limited functionality, and optimal design achieve much better performance figures than full-fledged operating systems. For example, the task preemption times of these systems are of the order of few microseconds compared to several hundreds of milliseconds for traditional Unix systems.

5.4.3 Preemption Point Approach

We have already pointed out that one of the major shortcomings of the traditional Unix V code arises from the fact that during a system call, all interrupts are masked (disabled) for the entire duration of execution of the system call. This leads to unacceptable worst case task response times of the order of a second, making Unix-based systems unacceptable for most-hard real-time applications.

An approach that has been taken by a few vendors to improve the real-time performance of non-preemptive kernels is the introduction of preemption points in system routines. Preemption points in the execution of a system routine are the instants at which the kernel data structure is consistent. At such points, the kernel can safely be preempted to make way for any waiting higher priority real-time tasks to run without corrupting any kernel data structures. In this approach, when the execution of a system call reaches a preemption point, the kernel checks to see whether any higher priority tasks have become ready. If there is at least one, it preempts the processing of the kernel routine and dispatches the waiting highest priority task immediately. The worst-case preemption latency in this technique, therefore, becomes the longest time between two consecutive preemption points. As a result, the worst-case response times of tasks improves several folds compared to those for traditional operating systems without preemption points. This makes preemption point-based operating systems suitable for use in many categories of hard real-time applications, though it still falls short of the requirements of hard real-time applications requiring preemption latency of the order of a few microseconds or less. Another advantage of the preemption point approach is that it involves only minor changes to be made to the kernel code. Many operating systems in fact have taken the preemption point approach in the past. Prominent commercial examples of this approach include HP-UX and Windows CE.

5.4.4 Self-Host Systems

Unlike the host-target approach where application development is carried out on a separate host machine running traditional Unix, in self-host systems a real-time application is developed on the same operating system on which the real-time application would finally run. Of course, while deploying the application, the operating system modules that are not essential during task execution are excluded to minimize the size of the operating system in the embedded application. As we had pointed out earlier, minimizing the size of the operating system in an embedded application is a major requirement. This requirement is based on cost, size and power consumption considerations. Remember that in host-target approach, the target real-time operating system was a lean and efficient system that could only run the application but did not include program development facilities; program development was carried out on the host system. This made application development and debugging difficult and required cross-compiler and cross-debugger support. Self-host systems take a different approach. The real-time application is developed on the full-fledged operating system. Once the application runs satisfactorily on the host, it is fused on a ROM or flash memory on the target board along with a greatly stripped down version of the operating system.

Most of the currently available self-host operating systems are based on micro-kernel architecture.

In a micro-kernel architecture, only the core functionalities such as interrupt handling and process management are implemented as kernel routines. All other functionalities such as memory management, file management, device management, etc. are implemented as add-on modules which operate in the user mode.

The use of a micro-kernel architecture for a self-host operating system entails several advantages. The add-on modules can be easily excluded, whenever these are not required. As a result, it becomes very easy to configure the operating system, resulting in a small-sized system. Also, the micro kernel is lean and, therefore, becomes much more efficient compared to a monolithic one. Another difficulty with monolithic operating systems is that they bind most drivers, file systems, and protocol stacks to the operating system kernel and all kernel processes share the same address space. Hence, a single programming error in any of these components can cause a fatal kernel fault. In micro kernel-based operating systems, these components run in separate memory-protected address spaces. So, system crashes on this count are very rare, making micro kernel-based operating systems very reliable.

We have already discussed in Section 5.3 that in order to be useful in hard real-time applications, any Unix-based system has to overcome the following two main shortcomings of the traditional Unix kernel: non-preemptive kernel and dynamic priority values. We now examine how these problems are overcome in self-host systems.

Non-Preemptive Kernel. We had identified the genesis of the problem of non-preemptive Unix kernel in Section 5.3.2. We had remarked that in order to preserve the integrity of the kernel data structures, all interrupts are disabled as long as a system call does not complete. This was done from efficiency considerations and worked well for non-real-time and uniprocessor applications.

Masking interrupts during kernel processing makes even very small critical routines which should complete in a few milliseconds, to have worst-case response times of the order of a second. Further, this approach of masking interrupts to preserve the kernel data structures would not work in multiprocessor environments. In multiprocessor environments masking the interrupts for one processor does not help in ensuring the integrity of the kernel data structures, as the tasks running on other processors can still corrupt the kernel data structure.

It is necessary to use locks at appropriate places in the kernel code to overcome the problem. The fundamental issue surrounding locking is the need to provide synchronization in certain code segments in the kernel. These code segments are called critical sections. Without proper locking, race conditions might develop. Just to exemplify the problem, consider the case where there are two processes and each process needs to increment the value of a shared variable i. Suppose, one process reads i, and then the other. They both increment it, then they both write i back to memory. If i was originally 2, it would now be 3, instead of 4! Such problems in the kernel code can cause system crash.

It should be clear that in order to make the kernel preemptive, locks must be used at appropriate places in the kernel code. In fully preemptive Unix systems, normally two types of locks are used: kernel-level locks and spin locks.

A kernel-level lock is similar to a traditional lock. When a task waits for a kernel-level lock to be released by another task holding it, it is blocked and undergoes a context switch. It becomes ready only after the required lock is released by the holding task and becomes available. Kernel-level locks are inefficient when critical resources are required for short durations of times that are comparable to context switching times, i.e., of the order of a few milliseconds or less. In such situations, context switching overheads can increase the task response times unduly and are not acceptable. Let us elaborate this. Assume that two tasks T_i and T_j each require certain critical resources for a very small time (say 1 mSec) for some simple processing (possibly a single arithmetic operation). Assume that a context switch requires 1 mSec. Suppose a kernel-level lock is used to guard the resource. Assume T_i requests the lock and that task T_j is holding the lock at the time. In this case, T_i would be blocked and undergo a context switch. Further, it is likely that the cache contents, pages etc. corresponding to T_i may be swapped. After a short time, say 1 mSec, T_j completes its processing with the lock and releases it. Another context switch would now be incurred for T_i to run (assuming that it is the highest priority task at that time). Hence, the response time of T_i would be a little more than 3 mSec—though if it had simply 'busy waited' for the lock to be released, then the response time would have been 2 mSec. In such a situation, a spin lock would be appropriate.

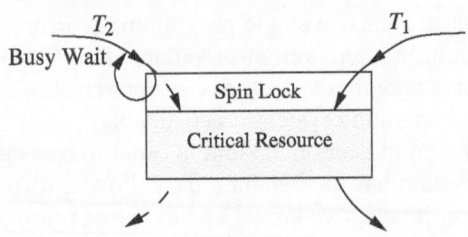

▲ FIGURE 5.6

Operation of a Spin Lock

Let us now understand the operation of a spin lock. A spin lock has schematically been shown in Fig. 5.6. In Fig. 5.6 a critical resource is required by both the tasks T_1 and T_2 for very short times (comparable to a context switching time). This resource is protected by a spin lock. Suppose, task T_1 has acquired the spin lock guarding the resource. Meanwhile, task T_2 requests the resource. Since task T_1 has locked it, T_2 can not get access to the resource, it just busy waits (shown as a loop in the figure) and does not block and suffer a context switch. T_2 gets the resource as soon as T_1 relinquishes the resource.

In a multiprocessor system, spin locks are normally implemented using the cache coherency protocol such that each processor loops on a local copy of the lock variable. The exact details of implementation of a spin lock is beyond the scope of this book and the interested reader is referred to [9]. Let us now discuss how a spin lock can be implemented on a uniprocessor system. On a uniprocessor system, when a critical resource is required for a very short time, mutual exclusion is easily accomplished by disabling interrupts. On Intel x86 systems, this is done with the "cli" instruction. Interrupts are re-enabled with "sti". Thus, spin locks on a uniprocessor get compiled in as calls to "cli" and "sti."

Real-Time Priorities. Let us now examine how self-host systems address the problem of dynamic priority levels of the traditional Unix systems. In Unix-based real-time operating systems, in addition to dynamic priorities, real-time and idle priorities are supported. Figure 5.7 schematically shows the three available priority levels.

Idle (Non-Migrating). This is the lowest priority level. The task that runs when there are no other tasks to run (the idle task), runs at this level. Idle priorities are static and are not recomputed periodically.

Dynamic. Dynamic priorities are recomputed periodically to improve the average response time of soft real-time (interactive) tasks. Dynamic recomputation of priorities ensures that I/O bound tasks migrate to higher priorities and CPU-bound tasks operate at lower priority levels. As shown in Fig. 5.7, tasks at the dynamic priority level operate at priorities higher than the idle priority, but at lower priority than the real-time priorities.

Real-Time. Real-time priorities are static priorities and are not recomputed during run time. Hard real-time tasks operate at these levels. Tasks having real-time priorities get precedence over tasks with dynamic priority levels (see Fig. 5.7).

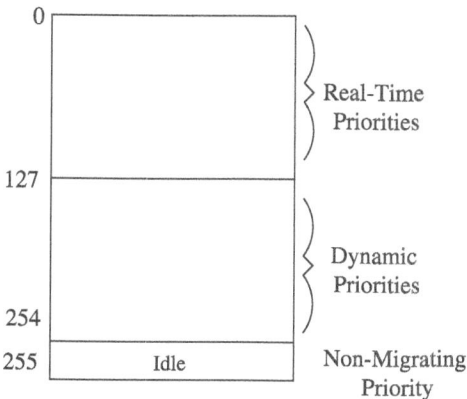

▲ **FIGURE 5.7**

Priority Levels in Self-host Unix Systems

5.5 WINDOWS AS A REAL-TIME OPERATING SYSTEM

Microsoft's Windows series of operating systems are extremely popular in desktop computers. Windows operating systems have evolved over the last 25 years from the naive Disk Operating System (DOS) that was developed by Microsoft in the early 80s. DOS was a very simple operating system that was single tasking and used a segmented memory management scheme. Microsoft kept on announcing new versions of DOS almost every year and each successive version supported new features and improved the existing features. DOS evolved to the Windows series operating systems in the late 80s. The main distinguishing feature of the Windows operating system from DOS was a graphical front-end. As several new versions of Windows kept on appearing through enhancements to the DOS code, the structure of the code degenerated to such an extent that it had become very difficult to debug and maintain the code. The Windows code was completely rewritten in 1998 to develop the Windows NT system. Since the code was completely rewritten, Windows NT system was much more stable (does not crash) than the earlier DOS-based systems. The later versions of Microsoft's operating systems were descendants of the Windows NT and the DOS-based systems were scrapped. Figure 5.8 shows the genealogy of the various operating systems from the Microsoft stable. As already mentioned, stability of ancestors of Windows NT was not satisfactory. Because stability of the operating system is a major concern in hard real-time applications, we restrict our discussions to Windows NT and its descendants and do not include the DOS line of products.

Computer systems based on Windows NT and its descendants are being extensively used in homes, offices, and industrial establishments. An organization owning Windows NT systems might be interested to use them for its real-time applications for cost saving or convenience. This is especially true in prototype application development and also when only a limited number of deployments are required. In the following, we critically analyze the suitability of Windows NT for real-time application development. First, we highlight some features of Windows NT that are very relevant and useful to a real-time application developer. In the subsequent subsection, we point out some of the lacuna of Windows NT when used in real-time application development.

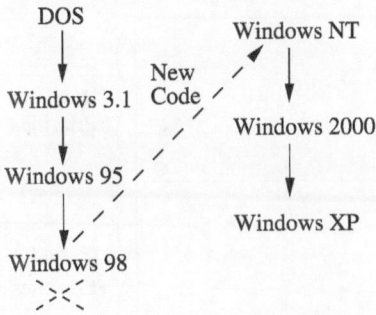

▲ **FIGURE 5.8**

Genealogy of Operating Systems from Microsoft's Stable

5.5.1 Important Features of Windows NT

Windows NT has several features which are very desirable for real-time applications, such as support for multithreading, and availability of real-time priority levels. Also, the timer and clock resolutions are sufficiently fine for most real-time applications.

Windows NT supports 32 priority levels (see Fig. 5.9). Each process belongs to one of the following priority classes: idle, normal, high, real-time. By default, the priority class at which a user task runs is normal. Both normal and high priority classes are variable type, that is, the priorities of tasks in this class are recomputed periodically by the operating system. NT lowers the priority of a task (belonging to variable type) if it used all of its last time slice. It raises the priority of a task, if it blocked for I/O and could not use its last time slice in full. However, the change of a task from its base priority is restricted to ±2. NT uses priority-driven preemptive scheduling and threads of real-time priorities have precedence over all other threads including kernel threads. Processes such as screen saver use priority class idle.

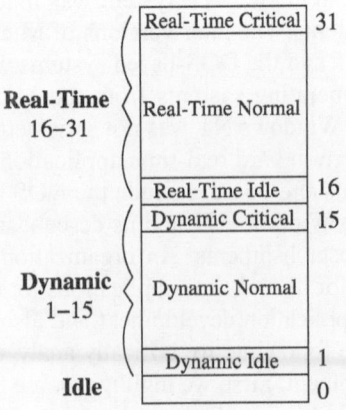

▲ **FIGURE 5.9**

Task Priorities in Windows NT

5.5.2 Shortcomings of Windows NT

In spite of the impressive support that Windows provides for real-time programming (as discussed in Section 5.1), a programmer trying to use Windows in real-time system development has to cope with several problems. Of these, the following two problems are the most troublesome.

- **Interrupt Processing.** In Windows NT, the priority level of interrupts is always higher than that of the user-level threads, including the threads of real-time class. When an interrupt occurs, the handler routine saves the machine's state and makes the system execute an Interrupt Service Routine (ISR). Only very critical processing is performed in ISR and the bulk of the processing is done later at a lower priority in the form of a Deferred Procedure Call (DPC). DPCs for various interrupts are queued in the DPC queue in a FIFO manner. While this separation of ISR and DPC has the advantage of providing quick response to further interrupts, it has the disadvantage of maintaining all DPCs at the same priority values. A DPC can not be preempted by another DPC but can be preempted by an interrupt. DPCs are executed in FIFO order at a priority lower than the hardware interrupt priority but higher than the priority of the scheduler/dispatcher. It is not possible for a user-level thread to execute at a priority higher than that of ISRs or DPCs. Therefore, even ISRs and DPCs corresponding to very low priority tasks can preempt real-time processes. As a result, the potential blocking of real-time tasks due to DPCs can be large. For example, interrupts due to page faults generated by low priority tasks would get processed faster than real-time processes. Also, ISRs and DPCs generated due to keyboard and mouse interactions would operate at higher priority levels compared to real-time tasks. Therefore, in presence of processes carrying out network or disk I/O, the effect of system-wide FIFO queues of DPCs may lead to unbounded response times even for real-time threads. This problem has been avoided in the Windows CE operating system (see Section 5.8.8) through the use of a priority inheritance mechanism.

- **Support for Resource Sharing Protocols.** We had discussed in Chapter 3 that unless appropriate resource sharing protocols are supported by an operating system, tasks of a real-time application while accessing shared resources may suffer unbounded priority inversions leading to deadline misses and even system failure. Windows NT does not provide any support (such as priority inheritance, etc.) to support real-time tasks to share critical resources among themselves. This is a major shortcoming of Windows NT when used in real-time applications. Since most real-time applications do require sharing critical resources among tasks, we outline below a few possible ways in which user-level functionalities can be added to the Windows NT system. The simplest approach to let real-time tasks share critical resources without unbounded priority inversions is by careful priority settings while acquiring and releasing locks. As soon as a task is successful in locking a non-preemptable resource, its priority can be raised to the highest priority [31]. As soon as a task releases the required resource, its priority can be restored. However, we know that this arrangement would lead to large inheritance-related inversions (see Section 3.4).

  Another possibility is to implement the Priority Ceiling Protocol (PCP). To implement this protocol, we need to restrict the real-time tasks to have even priorities (i.e., 16, 18, . . . , 30) only. The reason for this restriction is that Windows NT does not support FIFO scheduling among equal priority tasks. If the highest priority among all tasks needing a resource is $2 * n$,

TABLE 5.1   Windows NT versus Unix

Real-Time Feature	Windows NT	Unix V
DPCs	Yes	No
Real-time priorities	Yes	No
Locking virtual memory	Yes	Yes
Timer precision	1 mSec	10 mSec
Asynchronous I/O	Yes	No

then the ceiling priority of the resource is $2 * n + 1$. In Unix, FIFO option among equal priority tasks is available, therefore, all available priority levels can be used to assign to tasks.

5.5.3 Windows NT versus Unix

In this section, we compare Windows NT and Unix with respect to their suitability for deployment in real-time applications.

A comparison of the extent to which some of the the basic features required for real-time programming are provided by Windows NT and Unix V is indicated in Table 5.1. It can be seen that Windows NT supports a much finer time granularity (1 mSec) compared to Unix (10 mSec). Windows NT has many of the features desired of a real-time operating system. However, the way it executes DPCs, together with its lack of protocol support for resource sharing among equal priority tasks makes it unsuitable for use in safety-critical hard real-time applications. With careful programming, Windows NT can be successfully used for applications that can tolerate occasional deadline misses, and have deadlines of the order of hundreds of milliseconds rather than a few microseconds. Of course, to be used in such applications, the processor utilization must be kept sufficiently low and priority inversion control must be provided at the user level.

Though Windows-based systems are popular for desktop applications and provide most of the desired features required for real-time programming, Unix-based systems are overwhelmingly popular for real-time applications due to cost considerations and the 'hacker mentality' of the real-time programmers [22].

5.6 POSIX

POSIX stands for Portable Operating System Interface. The letter "X" has been suffixed to the abbreviation to make it sound Unix-like. Over the last decade, POSIX has become an important standard for operating systems, including real-time operating systems. The importance of POSIX can be gauged from the fact that nowadays it is rare to come across a commercial operating system that is not POSIX-compliant. POSIX started as an open software initiative, but has now almost become a *de facto* standard for operating systems. Since POSIX has now become overwhelmingly popular, we discuss the POSIX standard for real-time operating systems. We start with a brief introduction to the open software movement and then trace the historical events that have led to the emergence of POSIX. Subsequently, we highlight the important requirements of real-time POSIX.

5.6.1 Open Software

Before we discuss open software, let us discuss open systems, which has a much wider connotation. An *open system* is a vendor neutral environment, which allows users to intermix hardware, software, and networking solutions from different vendors. Open systems are based on open standards and are not copyrighted, saving users from expensive intellectual property right (IPR) law suits. Open system advocates standard interfaces for similar products, so that users can easily integrate their application with the products supplied by any vendor. This leads to vendor-neutral solutions. The most important goals of open systems are: interoperability and portability. Interoperability means systems from multiple vendors can exchange information among each other. A system is portable if it can be moved from one environment to another without modifications. As part of the open system initiative, open software movement has become popular.

Open software holds out tremendous advantages to both the users as well as system developers. Advantages of open software include the following: it reduces the cost of development and time to market a product. It helps increase the availability of add-on software packages, enhances ease of programming and facilitates easy integration of separately developed modules. POSIX is an off-shoot of the open software movement.

Open software standards can be divided into three categories:

- **Open Source:** Provides portability at the source code level. To run an application on a new platform would require only compilation and linking. ANSI and POSIX are important open source standards.

- **Open Object:** This standard provides portability of unlinked object modules across different platforms. To run an application in a new environment, relinking of the object modules would be required.

- **Open Binary:** This standard provides complete software portability across hardware platforms based on a common binary language structure. An open binary product can be portable at the executable code level. At the moment, no open binary standards exist.

The main goal of POSIX is application portability at the source code level. Before we discuss the RT-POSIX, let us explore the historical background under which POSIX was developed.

5.6.2 Genesis of POSIX

Unix was originally developed by AT&T Bell Labs in the early 70s. Since AT&T was primarily a telecommunication company, it felt that Unix was not commercially important for it. Therefore, it distributed Unix source code free of cost to several universities. UCB (University of California at Berkeley) was one of the earliest recipients of the Unix source code.

AT&T later got interested in computers. It realized the potential of Unix and started developing Unix further and came up with Unix V. Meanwhile, UCB had incorporated TCP/IP into Unix through a large DARPA (Defence Advanced Research Project Agency of USA) grant. UCB came up with its own version of Unix and named it Berkeley Software Distribution (BSD). At this time, the commercial importance of Unix started to grow very rapidly. As a result, many vendors implemented and extended Unix services in different ways: the prominent examples being IBM with its AIX, HP with its HP-UX, Sun with its Solaris, Digital with its Ultrix, and SCO with SCO-Unix. Since there were so many variants of Unix, portability of applications across Unix platforms became a problem. It resulted in a situation where a program written on one Unix platform would not run on another Unix platform.

The need for a standard Unix was recognized by all. The first effort towards standardization of Unix was taken by AT&T in the form of its System V Interface Definition (SVID). However, BSD and other vendors ignored this initiative. The next initiative was taken under ANSI/IEEE, which yielded POSIX.

5.6.3 Overview of POSIX

POSIX is an off-shoot of the open software movement. A major concern of POSIX is the portability of applications across different variants of Unix operating systems. However, POSIX has been so widely accepted now that even non-Unix operating systems try to become POSIX compliant.

> POSIX standard defines only interfaces to operating system services and the semantics of these services, but does not specify how exactly the services are to be implemented.

For source code-level compatibility, POSIX specifies the system calls that an operating system needs to support, the exact parameters of these system calls, and the semantics of the different system calls. Trying not to be unnecessarily restrictive, POSIX leaves the operating system vendors the freedom to implement the system calls as per their design. The standard does not specify whether the operating system kernel must be single-threaded or multithreaded or at what priority level the kernel services are to be executed, or in what programming language it must be written.

POSIX standard has several parts. The important parts of POSIX and the aspects that they deal with are the following:

- POSIX.1: system interfaces and system call parameters
- POSIX.2: shells and utilities
- POSIX.3: test methods for verifying conformance to POSIX
- POSIX.4: real-time extensions

5.6.4 Real-Time POSIX Standard

POSIX.4 deals with real-time extensions to POSIX and is also popularly known as POSIX-RT. For an operating system to be POSIX-RT compliant, it must meet the different requirements specified in the POSIX-RT standard. The main requirements of the POSIX-RT are:

- **Execution scheduling:** A POSIX-RT compliant operating system must provide support for real-time (static) priorities.
- **Performance requirements on system calls:** Worst-case execution times required for most real-time operating system services have been specified by POSIX-RT.
- **Priority levels:** The number of priority levels supported should be at least 32.
- **Timers:** Periodic and one shot timers (also called watchdog timer) should be supported. The system clock is called CLOCK_REALTIME when the system supports real-time POSIX.
- **Real-time files:** Real-time file system should be supported. A real-time file system can pre-allocate storage for files and should be able to store file blocks contiguously on the disk. This enables predictable delays in file access.

- **Memory locking:** Memory locking should be supported. POSIX-RT defines the operating system services: mlockall() to lock all pages of a process, mlock() to lock a range of pages, and mlockpage() to lock only the current page. The unlock services are munlockall(), munlock(), and munlockpage(). Memory locking services have been introduced to support deterministic memory access by a real-time program.

- **Multithreading support:** POSIX-RT mandates threading support by an operating system. Real-time threads are schedulable entities of a real-time application that can have individual timeliness constraints and may have collective timeliness constraints when belonging to a runnable set of threads.

 # 5.7 A SURVEY OF CONTEMPORARY REAL-TIME OPERATING SYSTEMS

In this section we briefly survey the important features of some of the popular real-time operating systems that are being used in commercial applications. A study of the features of the commercially available real-time operating systems can give us an idea about which real-time operating system to use in a specific real-time application.

Before we survey some of the popular commercial real-time operating systems, we need to mention that many of these operating systems come with a set of tools to facilitate the development of real-time applications. Besides the general programming tools such as editors, compilers, and debuggers, several advanced tools specifically designed to help real-time application development are included. These tools include memory analyzers, performance profilers, simulators, etc.

5.7.1 PSOS

PSOS is a popular real-time operating system that is being primarily used in embedded applications. It is available from Wind River Systems, a large player in the real-time operating system arena [22]. It is a host-target type of real-time operating system (see Section 5.4.2). PSOS is being used in several commercial embedded products. An example application of PSOS is in the base stations of cell phone systems.

PSOS-based application development has schematically been shown in Fig. 5.10. The host computer is typically a desktop that supports both Unix and Windows hosts. The target board contains the embedded processor, ROM, RAM, etc. The host computer runs the editor, cross-compiler, source-level debugger, and library routines. PSOS+ and other optional modules such as PNA+, PHILE, and PROBE are installed on a ROM on the target board. PNA+ is the network manager that provides TCP/IP communication between the host and the target over Ethernet and FDDI. It conforms to Unix 4.3 (BSD) socket syntax and is compatible with other TCP/IP-based networking standards such as ftp and NFS. Using these, PNA+ provides efficient downloading and debugging communication between the target and the host. PROBE+ is the target debugger and XRAY+ is the source-level debugger. XRAY+ invokes PROBE+ to provide a seamless debugging environment to the real-time application developer. The application development is done on the host machine and is downloaded to the target board. The application is debugged using the source debugger (XRAY+). During application development,

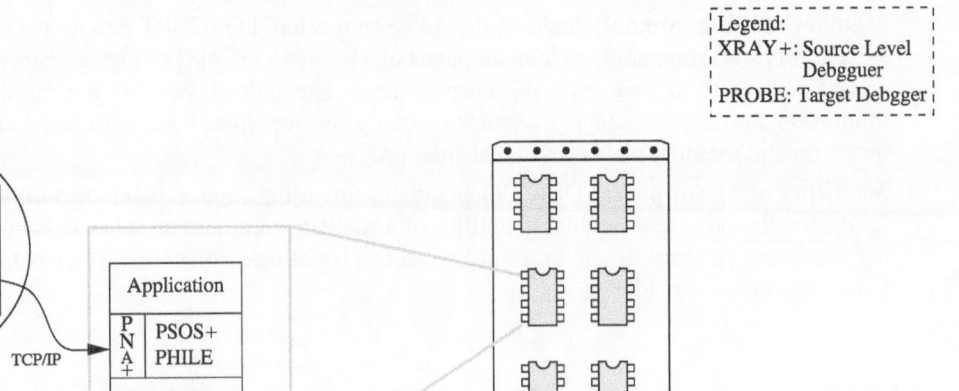

▲ FIGURE 5.10

PSOS-Based Development of Embedded Software

the application is downloaded on to a RAM on the target. Once the application runs satisfactorily, it is fused on a ROM.

We now highlight some important features of PSOS. PSOS supports 32 priority levels which can be assigned to tasks. In the minimal configuration, the footprint of the target operating system is only 12 KB. For sharing critical resources among real-time tasks, it supports priority inheritance and priority ceiling protocols, and segmented memory management but does not support virtual memory as it is intended to be used in small and moderate-sized embedded applications. PSOS defines a *memory region* to be a physically contiguous block of memory. A memory region is created by the operating system in response to a call from an application. A programmer can allocate a task to a memory region.

In most modern operating systems, the control jumps to the kernel when an interrupt occurs. PSOS takes a different approach. Device drivers are outside the kernel and can be loaded and removed at the run time. When an interrupt occurs, the processor jumps directly to the ISR (interrupt service routine) pointed to by the vector table. The intention is not only to gain speed, but also to give the application developer complete control over interrupt handling.

5.7.2 VRTX

VRTX is a POSIX-RT compliant operating system from Mentor Graphics. VRTX has been certified by the US FAA (Federal Aviation Agency) for use in mission and life-critical applications such as avionics. VRTX is available in two multitasking kernels: VRTXsa and VRTXmc.

VRTXsa is used for large and medium-sized applications. It supports virtual memory, has a POSIX-compliant library and supports priority inheritance. Its system calls complete deterministically in fixed time intervals and are fully preemptable. VRTXmc is optimized for power consumption and ROM and RAM sizes. It, therefore, has a very small footprint. The kernel typically requires only 4 to 8 KBytes of ROM and 1 kb of RAM. It does not support virtual memory. This version is targeted for use in embedded applications such as computer-based toys, cell phones and other small handheld devices.

5.7.3 VxWorks

VxWorks is a product from Wind River Systems. It is host-target type real-time operating system and the host can be either a Windows or a Unix machine. VxWorks conforms to POSIX-RT and comes with an Integrated Development Environment (IDE) called Tornado. In addition to the standard support for program development tools such as editor, cross-compiler, cross-debugger, etc., Tornado contains VxSim and WindView. VxSim simulates a VxWorks target for use as a prototyping and testing environment in the absence of the actual target board. WindView provides debugging tools for the simulator environment. VxMP is the multiprocessor version of VxWorks.

VxWorks was deployed in the Mars Pathfinder which was sent to Mars in 1997. Pathfinder landed in Mars, responded to ground commands, and started to send science and engineering data. However, a hitch was that it repeatedly reset itself. Engineers on ground remotely using trace generation, logging, and debugging tools of VxWorks, determined that the cause was unbounded priority inversion that caused real-time tasks to miss their deadlines. As a result, the exception handler reset the system each time. Although VxWorks supports priority inheritance, it was found out by using the remote debug tool to have been disabled by oversight in the configuration file. The problem was fixed by enabling it.

5.7.4 QNX

QNX is a product from QNX Software System Ltd (http://www.qnx.com). QNX is intended for use in mission-critical applications in the areas such as medical instrumentation, Internet routers, telemetric devices, process control applications, and air traffic control systems. QNX Neutrino offers POSIX-compliant APIs and is implemented using a microkernel architecture.

The microkernel architecture of QNX is shown in Fig. 5.11. Because of the fine grained scalability of the microkernel architecture, it can be configured to a very small size—a critical advantage in high volume devices, where even a 1% reduction in memory costs can return millions of dollars in profit.

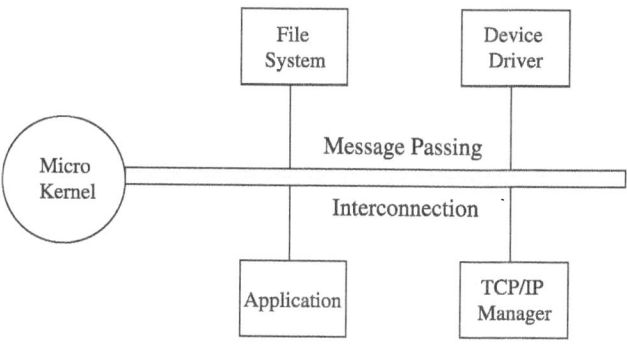

▲ **FIGURE 5.11**

Microkernel Architecture of QNX

Neutrino and its "microGUI"—called Photon, are designed to operate extremely fast on a very small memory footprint, making their inclusion in portable devices possible. In fact, QNX and Neutrino already power Web appliances, set-top boxes, MP3 players, equipment used in the industrial and medical fields. QNX Neutrino has been ported to a number of platforms and now runs on most modern CPUs that are used in the embedded market. This includes the Intel x86 family, MIPS, PowerPC, and the ARM family of processors. A version of QNX for non-commercial use can be downloaded for free from the company's web site (http://www.qnx.com).

5.7.5 μC/OS-II

μC/OS-II is available from Micrium Corporation (www.ucos-ii.com). This real-time operating system is written in ANSI C and contains a small portion of assembly code. The assembly language portion has been kept to a minimum to make it easy to port it to different processors. To date, μC/OS-II has been ported to over 100 different processor architectures ranging from 8-bit to 64-bit microprocessors, microcontrollers, and DSPs. Some important features of μC/OS-II are highlighted in the following:

- μC/OS-II was designed to let the programmers have the option of using just a few of the offered services or select the entire range of services. This allows the programmers to minimize the amount of memory needed by μC/OS-II on a per-product basis.
- μC/OS-II has a fully preemptive kernel. This means that μC/OS-II always ensures that the highest priority task that is ready would be taken up for execution.
- μC/OS-II allows up to 64 tasks to be created. Each task is required to operate at a unique priority level, among the 64 priority levels. This means that round-robin scheduling is not supported. The priority levels are used as the Process Identifier (PID) for the tasks.
- μC/OS-II uses a partitioned memory management scheme. Each memory partition consists of several fixed sized blocks. A task obtains memory blocks from the memory partition and the task must create a memory partition before it can be used. Allocation and deallocation of fixed-sized memory blocks is done in constant time and is deterministic. A task can create and use multiple memory partitions, so that it can use memory blocks of different sizes.
- μC/OS-II has been certified by Federal Aviation Administration (FAA) for use in commercial aircraft and meets the demanding requirements of its standard for software used in avionics. To meet the requirements of this standard, it was demonstrated through documentation and testing that it is robust and safe.

5.7.6 RT Linux

Linux is a free operating system. It is robust, feature-rich, and efficient. However, Linux per se is a general purpose operating system. Several real-time implementations of Linux (RTLinux) are available. In this discussion, we consider some generic features of real-time Linux systems.

RT Linux is a self-host operating system (see Fig. 5.12) that runs along with a Linux system. The real-time kernel sits between the hardware and the Linux system. To the standard Linux kernel, the RT Linux layer appears to be the actual hardware. The RT Linux kernel intercepts all

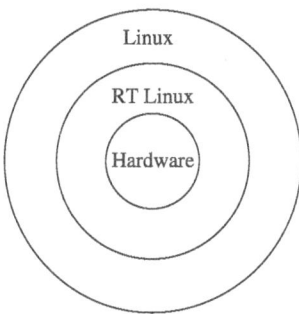

▲ **FIGURE 5.12**

Schematic Overview of the Operation of RT Linux

interrupts generated by the hardware. Hardware interrupts that are not related to real-time activities are held and then passed to the Linux kernel as software interrupts when the RT Linux kernel is idle and the standard Linux kernel runs. Figure 5.12 schematically shows this aspect. If an interrupt is to cause a real-time task to run, the real-time kernel preempts Linux, if Linux is running at that time and lets the real-time task run. Thus, in effect Linux runs as a low priority background task of RT Linux.

Real-time applications are written as loadable kernel modules. In essence, real-time applications run in the kernel space.

In the approach taken by RT Linux, there are effectively two independent kernels: real-time kernel and Linux kernel. This approach, therefore, is also known as the *dual kernel approach* as the real-time kernel is implemented outside the Linux kernel. Any task that requires deterministic scheduling is run as a real-time task. These tasks preempt Linux whenever they need to execute and yield the CPU to Linux only when no real-time task is ready to run.

Compared to the microkernel approach, the following are some of the important shortcomings of the dual-kernel approach.

- **Duplicated Coding Efforts:** Tasks running in the real-time kernel can not meaningfully use the Linux system services—file systems, networking, and so on. The reason for this is that if a real-time task invokes a Linux service, it will be subject to the same preemption problems that prohibit Linux processes from behaving deterministically. As a result, new drivers and system services must be created specifically for the real-time kernel—even when equivalent services already exist for Linux. Thus, real-time application development might entail significant duplication of coding effort. For example, when a real-time task needs to use network communications, or for that matter file accesses, appropriate drivers must be written in the real-time kernel.

- **Fragile Execution Environment:** Tasks running in the real-time kernel do not benefit from the MMU-protected environment that Linux provides to the regular non-real-time processes. Instead, they run unprotected in the kernel space. Consequently, any real-time task that contains a coding error such as a corrupt C pointer can easily cause a fatal kernel fault. This is serious problem because many embedded applications are safety-critical in nature.

- **Limited Portability:** In the dual kernel approach, the real-time tasks are not Linux processes at all; but programs written using a small subset of POSIX APIs (Application Programmer Interfaces). To aggravate the matter, different implementations of dual kernels use different APIs. As a result, real-time programs written using one vendor's RT-Linux version may not run on another.

- **Programming Difficulty:** RTLinux kernels support only a limited subset of POSIX APIs. Therefore, application development can take more effort and time.

5.7.7 Lynx

Lynx is a self-host real-time operating system and is available from www.lynuxworks.com. The currently available version of Lynx (Lynx 3.0) is a microkernel-based real-time operating system, though the earlier versions were based on monolithic design. Lynx is fully compatible with Linux. With Lynx's binary compatibility, a Linux program's binary image can be run directly on Lynx. On the other hand, for other Linux compatible operating systems such as QNX, Linux applications need to be recompiled in order to run on them. The Lynx microkernel is 28 KB in size and provides the essential services for task scheduling, interrupt dispatch, and synchronization. The other services are provided as Kernel Plug-Ins (KPIs). By adding KPIs to the microkernel, the system can be configured to support I/O, file systems, sockets, and so on. With full configuration, it can even function as a multipurpose Unix machine on which both hard and soft real-time tasks can run. Unlike many embedded real-time operating systems, Lynx supports memory protection.

5.7.8 Windows CE

Windows CE is a stripped down version of Windows operating system, and has a minimum footprint of 400 kb only. It provides 256 priority levels and to optimize performance, all threads are run in the kernel mode. The timer accuracy is 1 mSec for sleep and wait related APIs. The different functionalities of the kernel are broken down into small non-preemptive sections. As a result, during system call, preemption is turned off for only short periods of time. Also, interrupt servicing is preemptable. That is, it supports nested interrupts and uses Memory Management Unit (MMU) for virtual memory management.

Windows CE uses a priority inheritance scheme to avoid the priority inversion problem that is present in Windows NT. Normally, the kernel thread handling the page fault (i.e., DPC) runs at priority level higher than NORMAL (see Section 5.5.2). When a thread with priority level NORMAL suffers a page fault, the priority of the corresponding kernel thread handling this page fault is raised to that of the priority of the thread causing the page fault. This ensures that a thread is not blocked by any lower priority thread, even when it suffers a page fault.

5.8 BENCHMARKING REAL-TIME SYSTEMS

During design and platform evaluation stage, system developers often find it necessary to benchmark computer systems. Let us first examine how this is done for traditional computer systems. Subsequently, we shall examine this issue for real-time computers. To understand the issues involved, consider the following situation. Assume that the organization you work for entrusts you to select the "best" computer (from those available in the market) on price and performance considerations to be used to host the company's web site. It is possible that you can ask for bids from vendors and obtain their price and performance specifications. Now the question is how would you determine which among a set of computers quoted by different vendors would perform best for your application?

Of course, your evaluation would be very accurate if you actually got each of the machine for which you received the quote and then actually ran your application on each of them and evaluated various performance parameters such as response time for queries under different load conditions. However, it would be infeasible to carry this out from cost, effort, and time considerations. One possibility is that you can use two traditional metrics used by vendors to indicate the performance of their computer systems: Million Instructions Per Second (MIPS) and Floating Point Operations Per Second (FLOPS). However, an evaluation based on these metrics can often be highly misleading. The situation is so disgusting that someone even proposed that a more suitable full form of MIPS should be "Misleading Information about Processor Speed." Let us examine why this is so. To determine the MIPS rating of a computer, a program is run on it and the run time is measured. The number of instructions in the program is divided by the run time to give the MIPS rating of the computer. However, it is not specified as to what type of program needs to run. Consequently, vendors take the liberty of running programs that generate only those (machine) instructions that have very short cycle times for their processor, resulting in artificially inflated MIPS ratings. As a result, if you make your buying decisions based on the quoted MIPS and FLOPS ratings, then you are most likely to be disappointed. It is very likely that when you actually get the computer you selected based on MIPS rating and run your application, your application would not run as fast as you had expected.

Everybody soon realized that MIPS and FLOPS ratings are misleading. Vendors, therefore, started to express performance ratings of their computer systems in terms of peak MIPS and peak FLOPS to indicate that the ratings have been obtained by using their fastest instructions. However, this did not ease the problem in any way.

To overcome this problem of MIPS and FLOPS ratings in performance evaluation, synthetic benchmarks were developed. Let us understand what synthetic benchmarks are. A large number of practical problems were analyzed to determine the statistical distribution of various instructions in an average program (e.g., arithmetic instructions 20%, I/O 10%, register transfer 10%, etc.). Using this information, a benchmark program is written that has the same distribution of the different instructions. Of course, the benchmark program need not compute any meaningful results. It is simply synthesized using instructions with required statistical distributions. It is, therefore, called a synthetic benchmark. It should be clear that the performance results obtained by running the synthetic benchmark program should be very closely related to what would be expected by running an average practical program. Some examples of synthetic benchmarks are *Whetstone, Linpack and Dhrystone*. Standard Performance Evaluation Corporation (SPEC) which was formed in the late 80s is a non-profit association of computer manufacturers and academicians that develops and publicizes benchmark suites for specific applications. For example, SPECWEB is the benchmark for web applications. The SPEC benchmark programs can be downloaded from www.spec.org.

5.8.1 Rhealstone Metric

For real-time systems, *Rhealstone* metric [11] is popular for benchmarking. In the Rhealstone metric, six parameters of real-time systems are considered. These identified parameters indicate

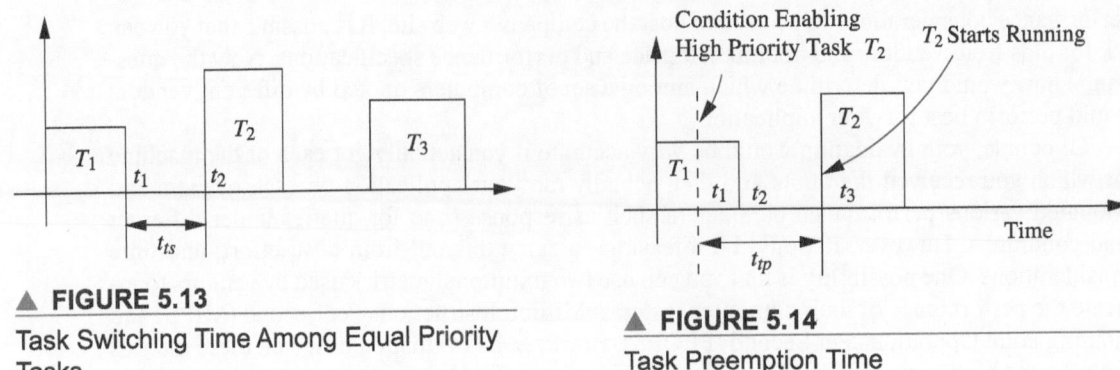

▲ FIGURE 5.13

Task Switching Time Among Equal Priority
Tasks

▲ FIGURE 5.14

Task Preemption Time

the parameters that are important in a typical real-time applications. We now briefly discuss
these parameters in the following:

1. **Task Switching Time (t_{ts}).** Task switching time is defined as the time it takes for one context switch among equal priority tasks. Consider the example shown in Fig. 5.13. Assume
   that T_1, T_2, T_3 are equal priority tasks and that round-robin option among equal priority
   tasks is supported by the scheduler. In Fig. 5.13, (t_{ts}) is the time after which T_2 starts to execute after T_1 completes its time slice, blocks, or completes ($t_{ts} = t_2 - t_1$). Task switching
   time is determined by the efficiency of the kernel data structure.

2. **Task Preemption Time (t_{tp}).** Task preemption time is defined as the time it takes to start
   execution of a higher priority task (compared to the currently running task), after the condition enabling the task occurs. Task preemption time has been illustrated in Fig. 5.14. Task
   preemption time consists of three components: task switching time t_{ts}, time to recognize the
   event enabling the higher priority, and the time to dispatch it. Clearly, task preemption time
   would be normally larger than task switching time.

3. **Interrupt Latency Time (t_{il}).** Interrupt latency time is defined as the time it takes to start
   the execution of the required ISR after an interrupt occurs. Interrupt latency time for an example has been shown in Fig. 5.15. Interrupt latency time consists of the following components: hardware delay in CPU recognizing the interrupt, time to complete the current instruction, time to save the context of the currently running task, and then to start the ISR.

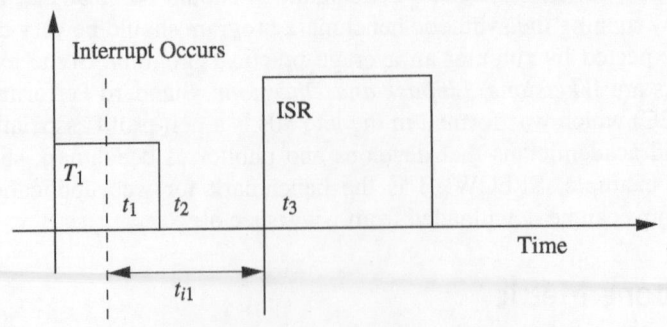

▲ FIGURE 5.15

Interrupt Latency Time

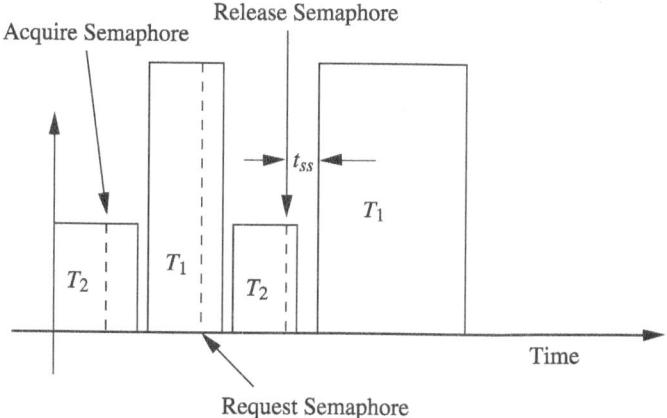

FIGURE 5.16

Semaphore Shuffling Time

4. **Semaphore Shuffling Time (t_{ss}).** Semaphore shuffling time is defined as the time that elapses between a lower priority task releasing a semaphore and a higher priority task to start running. Semaphore shuffling time has been illustrated in Fig. 5.16. In Fig. 5.16, at a certain time task T_2 holds the semaphore. The task T_1 requests for the semaphore and blocks. The interval between T_1 returning the semaphore and T_2 running is known as the semaphore shuffling time.

5. **Unbounded Priority Inversion Time (t_{up}).** As shown in Fig. 5.17, unbounded priority inversion time t_{up} is computed as the time it takes for the operating system to recognize priority inversion (t_1) and run the task holding the resource and start T_2 after T_1 completes (t_2). Symbolically, $t_{up} = t_1 + t_2$.

6. **Datagram Throughput Time (t_{dt}).** This parameter indicates the number of kilobytes of data that can be transferred between two tasks without using shared memory or pointers. This parameter measures the efficiency of the data structures handling message passing primitives.

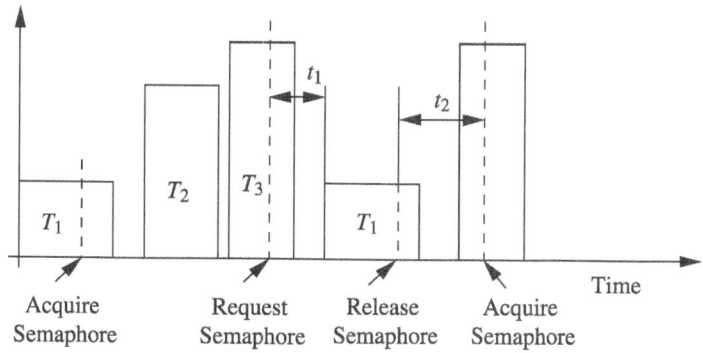

FIGURE 5.17

Unbounded Priority Inversion Time

The Rhealstone metric is computed as a weighted average of the identified parameters:

$$\text{Rhealstone Metric} = a_1 * t_{ts} + a_2 * t_{tp} + a_3 * t_{il} + a_4 * t_{ss} + a_5 * t_{up} + a_6 * t_{dt}$$

where, $a_1, \ldots, a_6$ are empirically determined constants.

Rhealstone benchmark's figure of merit characterizes the kernel-hardware combination of a system. This is, therefore, a comprehensive benchmark. However, Rhealstone has some serious drawbacks. First, the ability to meet deadlines of applications (task scheduling etc.) is not considered at all. Also, the six measurement categories are somewhat ad hoc and there is no proper justification as to why only these six measurements have been chosen.

5.8.2 Interrupt Processing Overhead

Let t_0 be the time to complete a certain task when there are no interrupts and let $t_{20,000}$ be the time to complete the same task when 20,000 interrupts occur per second. Then, the overhead due to 20,000 interrupts per second is given by:

$$I_{20,000} = \frac{t_{20,000} - t_0}{t_0}$$

Consider that $t_{20,000}$ is 1.6 sec and t_0 is 1 sec. Then, the interrupt processing overhead $I_{20,000}$ is 0.6 (or 60%) of the task execution time. The overhead considered is only for processing the immediate part of the interrupts and not the deferred parts.

5.8.3 Tridimensional Measure

Tridimensional measure considers three factors that affect the performance of a real-time system. These identified parameters are: Millions of Instructions Processed per Second (MIPS1), Millions of Interrupts Processed per Second (MIPS2), Number of I/O Operations Per Second (NIOPS). Once these three parameters have been determined, the Tridimensional Measure (TM) can be obtained by using the following expression:

$$TM = (\text{MIPS1} * \text{MIPS2} * \text{NIOPS})^{\frac{1}{3}}$$

5.8.4 Determining Kernel Preemptability

Sometimes it becomes necessary to determine the extent to which an operating system kernel is preemptable by higher priority real-time tasks. Figure 5.18 shows an experimental set up that can indicate kernel preemptability. In Fig. 5.18, the TRIANG module generates random triplets denoting three vertices of a triangle. There are n real-time tasks $RT_1, \ldots RT_n$ which read the triangle vertices and carry out certain processing and finally output the original triangle vertices to the analyzer module through message passing. TRIANG operates at a higher priority than real-time tasks. The timer first invokes TRIANG, and then invokes a system call such as process creation, and subsequently triggers a different real-time task $(RT_1, \ldots RT_n)$ each time. The analyzer compares the triangle vertices received from the TRIANG and from the real-time task. If the system kernel is not preemptable, then even before the real-time task can read the triangle value, the next set of triangle values overwrites the last generated values. The timer frequencies are varied and the analyzer results are observed. The timer frequency at which vertices get missed (as identified by the analyzer), indicates the worst-case kernel preemption time.

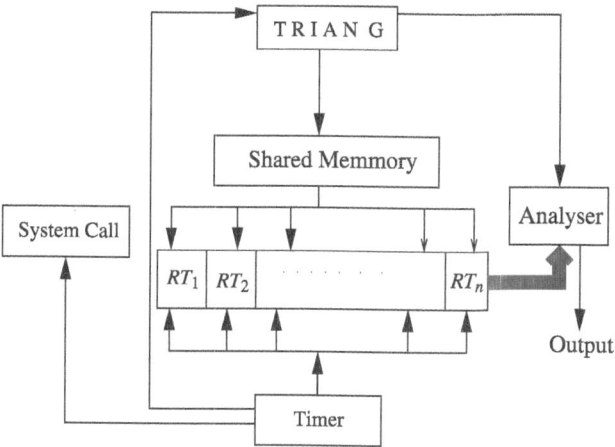

▲ **FIGURE 5.18**

Setup for TRIANG

SUMMARY

- We first discussed the basic features that any real-time operating system is required to support. Some of the important features required of a real-time operating system, if it is to be used for hard real-time applications, are: high resolution clock and timer services, static priority levels, low task preemption times (of the order of a few microseconds), low interrupt latency time, low jitter in memory access, and support for resource sharing among real-time tasks.

- We explained why traditional operating systems such as Unix and Windows are not suitable for hard real-time applications. We pointed out that the main problems that a programmer would face while developing a real-time application using Unix are dynamic priority levels and non-preemptable kernel. Though Windows NT supports many features that are required for real-time programming, the way Windows NT handles interrupts might result in unbounded response times for real-time tasks.

- We surveyed the important features of some of the commercially used real-time operating systems. We discussed why free real-time operating systems such as RTLinux, μCOS, and Lynx are gaining ground.

- We highlighted the parameters based on which the performance of real-time systems can be benchmarked.

EXERCISES

1. State whether you consider the following statements to be TRUE or FALSE. Justify your answer in each case.

   (a) In real-time Linux (RTLinux), real-time processes are scheduled at priorities higher than the kernel processes.

(b) EDF scheduling of tasks is commonly supported in commercial real-time operating systems such as PSOS and VRTX.

(c) POSIX 1003.4 (real-time standard) requires that real-time processes be scheduled at priorities higher than kernel processes.

(d) Under the Unix operating system, computation intensive tasks dynamically gravitate to higher priorities.

(e) When PCP (priority ceiling protocol) is implemented in Windows NT by an application programmer, any real-time priority levels can be assigned to tasks and ceiling values computed on these to implement PCP.

(f) Normally, task switching time is larger than task preemption time.

(g) Between segmented and virtual addressing schemes, the segmented addressing scheme would, in general, incur lower jitter in memory access compared to the virtual addressing scheme.

(h) POSIX is an attempt by ANSI/IEEE to enable executable files to be portable across different Unix machines.

(i) If FIFO scheduling among equal priority tasks is not supported by an operating system, then in an implementation of Priority Ceiling Protocol (PCP) at the user-level, only half of the available priority levels can be meaningfully assigned to the tasks.

(j) Suppose a real-time operating system does not support memory protection, then a procedure call and a system call are indistinguishable in that system.

(k) Watch dog timers are typically used to start sensor and actuator processing tasks at regular intervals.

(l) For memory of same size under segmented and virtual addressing schemes, the segmented addressing scheme would, in general, incur lower memory access jitter compared to the virtual addressing scheme.

(m) For faster response time, an embedded real-time operating system needs to be run from a ROM rather than a RAM.

2. Even though clock frequency of modern processors is of the order of several GHz, why do many modern real-time operating systems not support nanosecond or even microsecond resolution clocks? Is it at all possible for an operating system to support nanosecond resolution clocks at present? Explain how this can be achieved.

3. Give an example of a real-time application for which a simple segmented memory management support by the RTOS is preferred and another example of an application for which virtual memory management support is essential. Justify your choices.

4. Is it possible to meet the service requirements of hard real-time applications by writing additional layers over the Unix System V kernel? If your answer is no, explain why? If your answer is yes, explain what additional features would you implement in the external layer of Unix System V kernel for supporting hard real-time applications?

5. As the developer of hard real-time applications, explain the features that you consider necessary for a Real-Time Operating System (RTOS) to support.

6. Briefly indicate how Unix dynamically recomputes task priority values. Why is such recomputation of task priorities required? What are the implications of such priority recomputations on real-time application development?

7. What is the difference between synchronous I/O and asynchronous I/O? What are the implications of these two types of I/O for real-time applications?

8. Explain the pros and cons of supporting virtual memory in embedded real-time applications.

9. What do you understand by memory protection in operating system parlance? Compare the pros and cons of requiring an embedded Real-Time Operating System (RTOS) to support memory protection.

10. What is the difference between block I/O and character I/O? For each type of I/O, give an example of a task that needs to use it. Which type of I/O is accorded higher priority by Unix? Why?

11. Why is Unix V non-preemptive in kernel mode? How do fully preemptive kernels based on Unix (e.g., Linux) overcome this problem? Briefly describe an experimental set up that can be used to determine the preemptability of different operating systems by high-priority real-time tasks when a low priority task has made a system call.

12. Suppose that you have to select a suitable computer for a process control application, out of several available computers. Write four important performance parameters which you would consider in benchmarking real-time computer systems. Define these parameters and explain why they are important in real-time applications.

13. Explain the time services that a Real-Time Operating System (RTOS) is expected to support. Also, briefly highlight how timer services are implemented in a real-time operating system.

14. What is an open system? Compared to a closed system what are its advantages?

15. What is a watchdog timer? Explain the use of a watchdog timer using an example.

16. List four important features that a POSIX 1003.4 (Real-Time standard) compliant operating system must support. Is preemptability of kernel processes required by POSIX 1003.4? Can a Unix-based operating system using the preemption-point technique claim to be POSIX 1003.4 compliant? Explain your answers.

17. Suppose you are the manufacturer of small embedded components used mainly in consumer electronics goods such as automobile, MP3 players, and computer-based toys. Would you prefer to use PSOS, WinCE, or RT-Linux in your embedded component? Explain the reasons.

18. Explain how interrupts are handled in Windows NT. Explain how the interrupt processing scheme of Windows NT makes it unsuitable for hard real-time applications. How has this problem been overcome in WinCE?

19. Windows NT does not provide any support to synchronize access of tasks to critical resources. Explain how resource sharing among tasks can be supported, when the application is required to run on Windows NT.

20. Would you recommend Unix System V to be used for a few real-time tasks for running a data acquisition application? Assume that the computation time for these tasks is of the order of few hundreds of milliseconds and the deadline of these tasks is of the order of several tens of seconds. Justify your answer.

21. Explain the problems that you would encounter, if you try to develop and run a hard real-time application on the Windows NT operating system.

22. How is the integrity of the kernel data structure preserved in Unix V in the face of preemptions of the kernel by interrupts and higher priority real-time tasks? Why does this technique not work successfully in preserving the integrity of the kernel data structures in multiprocessor implementations? Very briefly explain the important approaches that have been adopted to overcome this problem of making Unix-based systems suitable for real-time application development.

23. Briefly explain why the traditional Unix kernel is not suitable to be used in a multiprocessor environment. Explain a spin lock and a kernel-level lock and discuss their use in realizing a preemptive kernel.

24. What do you understand by a microkernel-based operating system? Explain the advantages of a microkernel-based real-time operating system over a monolithic operating system in supporting real-time applications.

25. What is the difference between a microkernel-based real-time operating system and a dual kernel real-time operating system? Give an example of each. Compare the pros and cons of the two approaches to developing a real-time operating system.

26. What is a real-time file system? What additional features does a real-time file system support compared to traditional file systems? Why is use of a real-time file system essential in hard real-time applications?

27. What is the difference between a system call and a function call? What problems, if any, might arise if the system calls are indistinguishable from procedure calls?

28. Explain how a real-time operating system differs from a traditional operating system. Name a few real-time operating systems that are commercially available.

29. What is the difference between a self-host and a host-target based embedded operating system? Give at least one example of a commercial commercial operating system from each category. What problems would a real-time application developer face while using RT-Linux for developing hard real-time applications?

30. What is an open software? Does an open software mandate portability of the executable files across different platforms? Name an open software standard for real-time operating systems. What is the advantage of using an open software operating system for real-time application development?

31. What are the important features that a real-time application developer expect from a real-time operating system? Analyze to what extent these features are provided by Windows NT and Unix V.

32. What do you understand by a host-target type of real-time operating system? Give two commercial examples of host-target type of real-time operating system. Explain the architecture of such an operating system and also explain how a real-time application can be developed on a host-target type of operating system.

33. Identify at least four important advantages of using VxWorks as the operating system for large hard real-time applications compared to using Unix V.3.

34. What is an open software? What are the pros and cons of using an open software product in program development, compared to using an equivalent proprietary product?

35. What is an open source standard? How is it different from open object and open binary standards? Give some examples of popular open source software products.

36. Can multithreading result in faster response times (compared to single-threaded tasks) even in uniprocessor systems? Explain your answer and identify the reasons to support your answer.

37. Explain why traditional (non-real-time) operating systems need to dynamically change the priority levels of tasks. What is the implication of this for real-time application development using such an operating system?

6 Real-Time Communication

$\mathbf{R}$eal-time applications are increasingly being implemented on distributed platforms and there are several reasons for their popularity. One important reason is that it is often cost-effective to have a distributed solution using many pieces of cheap hardware, rather than having a centralized, sophisticated, and costly machine. Further, many real-time applications are inherently distributed with different data sources (e.g., sensors) and data receivers (e.g., actuators) of a system placed at geographically separate locations. A distributed implementation in such a situation makes good design sense. Another point going in favour of distributed implementations is fault-tolerance which is very important for safety-critical applications. It is easier to provide fault-tolerance in distributed implementations compared to centralized systems. All distributed real-time systems are based on an underlying communication network. Such networks are expected to deliver messages in a timely fashion, and are often referred to as supporting real-time communication.

> We can define real-time communication as one where an application can make specific quality of service demands such as maximum permissible delay, maximum loss rate, etc. on the underlying communication network; and once the network accepts a connection request, it guarantees the requested service quality.

Traditional network protocols such as Ethernet are designed for "best-effort" performance. A best-effort network strives to achieve good average performance, and makes no attempt to meet the individual quality of service requirements for different connections. These networks are intended for use in applications where long delays and high data loss under heavy load conditions are acceptable. Best-effort networks have very little restrictions on the quality of service they deliver, and, therefore, can use protocols that make best utilization of the network resources. It is needless to say that best-effort networks are insufficient for use in real-time applications. In real-time applications, deterministic delays and predictable performance issues take precedence over network utilization considerations.

With increasing automation of day-to-day life with a variety of gadgets and the popularity of embedded systems in industrial applications, the necessity of real-time communications has increased tremendously. This has been manifested in the proliferation of research efforts to support real-time communications. Many of the available literature address hard real-time communication. In hard real-time communication unless an absolute delay bound is met, the communication is assumed to have failed. Many of the industrial and embedded real-time applications require hard real-time communication. On the otherhand, in a firm real-time communication, if occasionally a message delayed, then the delayed message is merely discarded, without affecting the system to any great extent. Such types of communications are usually required in multimedia applications. Soft real-time communication, on the other hand, is best-effort communication. This chapter focusses on the latest techniques available in the different types of real-time communication.

In this chapter, we first discuss a few examples of applications requiring real-time communications. Next, we discuss some basic concepts concerning computer networks and real-time communication techniques. Subsequently, we consider how real-time communication can be supported in multiple access networks. Finally, we discuss how real-time communication can be supported in packet-switched networks.

6.1 EXAMPLES OF APPLICATIONS REQUIRING REAL-TIME COMMUNICATION

In this section, we discuss a few applications whose satisfactory functioning is to a great extent dependent on the underlying network's capability to support real-time communication. We should bear these applications in mind while trying to understand various issues in real-time communications discussed later in this chapter. Traditionally, real-time communication technologies were used in distributed process control applications such as computer-controlled power plants, avionics, chemical process control, and automobile. However, current advancements in communication technologies have made it possible for supporting applications requiring real-time communication in many different areas such as manufacturing automation, video broadcast and Internet applications like online banking, stock trading, e-commerce, etc.

Manufacturing Automation: There are several types of manufacturing automation, leading to different scenarios of use of real-time communication in such applications. Here we discuss an example concerning a very simple scenario of manufacturing automation. However, we must remember that very different scenarios than those discussed here are possible.

In an automated factory a set of robots carry out manufacturing activities. Here, the network spans a small geographic area in a LAN environment. The robots communicate among themselves and with the controller (typically, a powerful computer) using a real-time communication protocol implemented on a wireless medium (see Fig. 6.1). The controller coordinates the activities of the robots. The messages that the robots communicate with the controller range from non-critical and non-real-time event logging information to highly critical and hard real-time control information. These communication should be treated differently by the underlying network for satisfactory performance of the application. Naturally, the underlying real-time communication system would be called upon to support these communication requests having widely varying service quality requirements.

Automated Chemical Factory: Consider a chemical factory in which an existing LAN set up is used for controlling and monitoring the parameters of their chemical plant on a real-time basis. The sensors transmit the sampled parameter values at periodic intervals to the computer that acts as the controller. The controller computes the corrections that may be necessary based on the sensed parameter values, and transmits commands to the actuators located inside the plant to carry out certain actions as and when required. These critical activities proceed along with other non-critical activities such as logging, e-mail handling, and surveillance, etc.

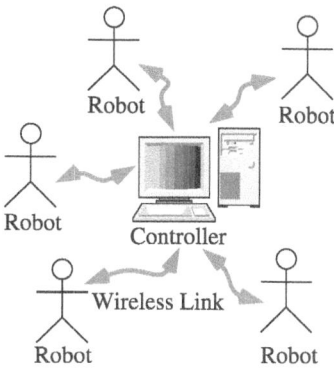

▲ **FIGURE 6.1**

Communication Among Robots in an Automated Factory

A real-time communication protocol guarantees the service quality of different categories of messages.

Internet-Based Banking Applications: In an Internet-based banking application, bank customers carry out their banking transactions using web browsers in the comfort of their homes. Though this is often considered to be very desirable, implementation of such an application requires use of sophisticated techniques and designs. For supporting such Internet banking applications, the underlying network needs to be extremely secure and reliable due to the sensitive nature of the financial transactions involved. These applications also have stringent delay requirements. Unless a transaction completes on time, the server may time-out, leading to rejection of user requests and user dissatisfaction.

Multimedia Multicast: In a multimedia multicast application, many receivers placed at various geographical locations receive multimedia information from a set of multimedia servers. The multimedia information is usually delivered in the form of streaming video and audio. Transmission and processing of such information is associated with firm real-time constraints. Another important issue that arises here is the efficient use of network resources—a multicast communication should not be implemented as a set of one-to-one (unicast) communications between the source and the different destinations.

Internet Telephony: VoIP is all set to revolutionize long-distance voice communication. VoIP stands for Voice over IP, where IP refers to the Internet Protocol that underlies all Internet communication. By using VoIP phones and technology one can make phone calls through the Internet. The benefit of this over traditional telephony is that as the actual voice traffic is carried over the Internet, VoIP communication would cost just a small fraction of what an actual telephone call costs. This would be much more expressed, especially over long distances. In a VoIP implementation, the network encrypts voice signals into data packets at the sender end, places it on the network, and decrypts it into voice signals at the receiver end. VoIP applications normally use simple microphones and computer speakers. But, use of IP telephones can provide an experience identical to normal telephoning. VoIP applications require firm real-time data transfer support.

6.2   BASIC CONCEPTS

In this section, we discuss a few basic concepts such as classification of real-time computer communication networks, quality of service parameters and traffic categorization.

6.2.1 Types of Networks

Three types of networks are mainly relevant in real-time communication: Controller Area Networks (CANs), Local Area Networks (LANs), and packet-switched networks. This classification is made on the basis of the size of the network and the communication technology deployed.

Controller Area Network: A Controller Area Network (CAN) is essentially a very small network. CANs are typically used to connect the different components of an embedded controller. The end-to-end length of a CAN is usually less than 50 meters. Since the propagation time of a CAN is very small, functionally a CAN behaves more like a local bus in a computer.

To understand the genesis of CAN and its operation, consider the present day automotive systems. The present day automotive electronics is fairly sophisticated, with automated support for several activities such as engine management, fuel injection, active suspension, braking, lighting, air-conditioning, security, and central locking. A considerable amount of information exchange among various automotive components is required when the engine is operational. The conventional method of networking the components in older models of cars was point-to-point wiring. This interconnection method was a straightforward evolution of the simple electrical systems used in cars where the different electrical components (motor, generator, light, battery, ignition system, etc.) were interconnected using point-to-point wiring. However, as the sophistication of the cars grew, use of such a simple scheme would have required several kilometers of wiring, adding to the cost of manufacturing, weight, complexity, and at the same time contributing to severely reduced reliability.

The limitations of fixed point-to-point wiring techniques in handling the demands of modern automated cars and other embedded applications gave rise to the development of CAN. A special requirement on CAN is effective handling of noise. Automotive components such as electric motors, ignition systems, and RF transmissions are heavy producers of noise. Another distinguishing feature of CAN is the 12 volt power supply that was mandated by the conventional 12 volt automotive power supply. CAN specifies only the physical and data link layers of ISO/OSI model, with higher layers left to the specific implementations.

Because of its robustness, CAN has expanded beyond its automotive origins and can now be found in diverse application areas such as industrial automation systems, trains, ships, agricultural machinery, household appliances, office automation systems, and elevators. Now CAN is an international standard under ISO11898 and ISO11519-2.

Local Area Network: A Local Area Network (LAN) is typically deployed in a building or a campus and is usually privately owned. For example, a LAN can be used to connect a number of computers within an organization to share data and other resources such as a files, printers, FAX services, etc. LANs typically operate at data rates exceeding 10 mbps and many present-day LANs (gigabit Ethernets) operate at 1 gbps. We provide a brief overview of LANs in Section 3.1. The available literature on LANs and their protocols is large, and the reader is referred to [27] for a comprehensive treatment of the subject.

Packet Switched Networks: Packet-switching refers to protocols in which messages are divided into relatively small units of data called packets before they are sent over the network. Each packet is then transmitted individually and a packet can even follow a route different from that taken by other packets to reach its destination. The individual packets are routed through a network based on the destination address contained within each packet. Once all the packets forming a message arrive at the destination, they are recompiled into the original message. Breaking down communication into packets allows the same data path to be shared among several users in the network. This type of communication between sender and receiver is known as connectionless and is in sharp contrast to the dedicated connections realized in connection-oriented networks. Packet-switched networks are usually wide area networks. A prominent example of a packet-switched network is the Internet.

The Internet, sometimes simply called "the Net," is a worldwide system of computer networks—a network of networks in which users at any one computer can, if they have permission, get information from any other computer using protocols such as ftp, http, etc; the user can even talk directly to users at other computers using VoIP. We must, however, be aware of the following two distinctions: the internet is any collection of separate physical networks, interconnected by a common protocol, to form a single logical network while the Internet is the worldwide collection of interconnected networks, which grew out of the ARPANET project [27]. It uses Internet Protocol (IP) to link various physical networks into a single logical network. The Internet began in 1962 as an attempt towards a resilient computer network for the US military and over time has grown into a global communication tool of more than a million computers connected to several tens of thousands of computer networks that share a common addressing scheme.

6.2.2 Quality of Service (QoS)

We had already pointed out that for their satisfactory operation, real-time applications need guarantees regarding the service quality from the underlying network. The service quality expected by an application from the underlying network is often expressed in terms of certain Quality of Service (QoS) parameters. Real-time applications usually have stringent requirements on the following QoS parameters: bandwidth, maximum transmission delay, delay jitter, loss rate, and blocking probability.

Delay: A successful delivery of a packet by a communication network in a real-time application not only depends on the intact receipt of the packet at the receiver end, but what also matters is the time at which it is received. If the time the network takes to deliver a packet exceeds the specified delay bound, then the application times out and can result in a failure in case of a hard real-time application. In a firm real-time application, the data received after the expiry of the specified delay bound would be discarded by the receiver. In case of a soft real-time application, exceeding the delay bound in delivery of messages would result in a degradation of the performance of the application.

Packet delay consists of three parts: propagation, transmission, and queuing delays. Propagation delay depends on the distance the packet travels and the medium in which it travels. Approximately, it is 5μ seconds per kilometer for the commonly used media. The per-hop transmission delay is given by packet size divided by the link bandwidth. The queuing delay is determined by the time that a packet waits in a queue before being transmitted. During network congestion, queuing delay is far greater than the other delay components.

Delay Jitter: Jitter is defined as the maximum variation in delay experienced by messages or packets in a single session. In other words, it is the difference between the maximum and minimum delays that messages might encounter. In a packet-switched network, for example, if the minimum end-to-end delay that a packet may experience during a call is 1 mSec, and the maximum delay is 10 mSec, then the delay jitter of the call is 9 mSec.

In a LAN using a collision-based protocol, jitter may be caused when there are variations in the network load. At high loads, jitter can considerably increase. On the other hand, in a packet-switched network, jitter may arise due to the fact that as packets travel in the network, they may suffer different amounts of queuing delays at different nodes. Also, packets may travel in different paths having different number of hops, resulting in jitter. Jitter is unacceptable in many applications. In many hard real-time applications, presence of jitter exceeding the specified bound can make the system fail. Jitter is very undesirable in many firm real-time applications as well. For example, in a video conferencing application, jitter can show up as a picture frame remaining still for a certain time.

Buffers at the receiver-end can be used to control jitter in many cases. In a packet switched network for example, removing jitter might involve collecting packets in a buffer at the receiver end, and holding them long enough to allow the slowest packets to arrive in time to be processed in correct sequence. The amount of buffer space required at a receiver can be determined from the peak rate of the arriving messages and the delay jitter. The size of the buffer required at the receiver-end would in fact be given by *peak rate × delay jitter*.

Example 6.1

Consider a single video source transmitting 30 frames per second to a certain receiver. Each frame contains 2 mb of data. The jitter in the network is known to be 1 sec. Compute the amount of buffer space required at the receiver to compensate for the jitter.

Solution.   The required buffer size at the receiver is given by (peak rate * jitter) = 2 mb * 30 = 60 mb.

From the above example, it can be easily seen that a tight delay jitter bound can help reduce the buffering requirement at the receiver end.

Bandwidth: This parameter indicates the rate at which a connection would be serviced by the network. Bandwidth determines an application's maximum throughput, and in some cases determines the bounds on the end-to-end delay. Sufficient bandwidth is required to sustain the required throughput for an application. In a CAN or LAN environment, the delay experienced by a message is inversely proportional to the bandwidth at which it would be served. That is, the higher the allocated bandwidth, the lower is the delay. However, in a packet switched network such as the Internet, this is only partly true—the transmission delay in Internet due to finite available bandwidth is often insignificant compared to the queuing delays that packets undergo at the switches.

Loss Rate: Loss rate denotes the percentage of all transmitted packets that may be lost during transmission. Packets in a connection may be treated as lost due to a variety of reasons such as delay-bound violation, delay jitter-bound violation, buffer overflow, and data corruption. Data corruption depends to a large extent on the type of the media being used. Data corruption is insignificant in fibre optic media and can be ignored, whereas data corruption is considerably large in wireless media. Different applications are sensitive to loss rate to different extents. Process control applications typically require zero loss rate, while applications such as multimedia can tolerate a certain amount of data loss.

Blocking Probability: Blocking probability is the probability of a new connection being rejected by the admission control mechanism of a network. A call may be rejected under heavy load situations or want of resources such as bandwidth.

The requirements of different real-time applications with respect to the above QoS parameters may be very different. For example, certain applications such as non-interactive television and audio broadcasting require stringent bounds on jitter but are rather insensitive to delay. On the other hand, sensor data processing in a fly-by-wire aircraft is very sensitive to delay—often only sub-millisecond delays in receipt of sensor signals by the controller is acceptable. In contrast, traditional computer communication applications such as file transfer, electronic mail, and remote login are non-real-time applications. The QoS parameters for such applications are very different from what we discussed for real-time applications. For non-real-time applications, bounds on average packet delay and average throughput are important, and such as worst-case packet delay, jitter, or worst-case throughput are not. Non-real-time applications, however, have strict reliability requirements, since any corruption of parts of a document can make the entire document unusable. Indeed, much of the complexity of the traditional network protocols arises from the need for loss-free communication between non-real-time applications.

Multimedia applications are not affected so much by delay as jitter and loss rate. For example, video transmissions are very sensitive to packet losses since these show up as flickers or glitches on the display screen. In voice applications, the quality of the voice degrades rapidly with loss rate and jitter. Voice data packet sizes are, therefore, deliberately kept small to minimize the packetization delays and to limit the effect of packet losses. The standard 48-byte cell size for ATM network, for example, was chosen primarily for the benefit of the voice applications.

6.2.3 Traffic Categorization

It is important to categorize a traffic source based on its traffic generation characteristics. Such categorization becomes necessary, since a network can guarantee the required quality of service only when these traffic characteristics are specified. The traffic generated by a source can be categorized based on the rate at which data are generated by the source for transmission on a network. The following are three important categories of traffic that are commonly encountered.

CBR Traffic: CBR traffic arises due to Constant Bit Rate data generation by a source. Data generation and transmission involved in hard real-time applications are often CBR traffic. For example, periodic data generated by sensors are CBR type of traffic. In this case, fixed sized messages are transmitted over fixed intervals.

VBR Traffic: VBR traffic, as the name suggests, consists of different rates of data transmission at different times. VBR sources can be of several types. A common type of VBR traffic generated by a data source alternates between a period in which fixed sized packets are generated with deterministic spacing and an idle period. An example of such VBR traffic is the compressed audio signals generated by speech signals. Typically, in compressed speech signals, to reduce the size of voice traffic, no data is generated during periods of silence. This results in on-off sources where fixed sized data is generated during on periods and no data is generated during idle periods. While silence suppression can produce significant reductions in the bandwidth requirements, this can only be achieved at the cost of having to reconstruct the original traffic at the receiver. Another example of VBR traffic is compressed video signals where variable sized data is generated periodically. Redundancy in digitized video data is usually very high. It, therefore, is often compressed using algorithms such as MPEG, before being transmitted over a network. In such types of VBR traffic, the source periodically submits variable sized packets to the network. It should be clear that variable bit rate transmission is intended to make better use of available bandwidth in applications requiring transmission of video or audio signals.

Sporadic Traffic: Sporadic traffic consists of a special type of variable sized packet transmissions. In sporadic traffic, the packets are generated in bursts followed by long periods of silence. Sporadic traffic is thus a special type of VBR traffic which occurs under very special circumstances. For example, the traffic consisting of certain command, control, and alarm messages generated in response to some exception conditions belong to this category. Consider a fire alarm. When a fire condition is detected, a large number of alarm, command and response messages are generated. The sudden peak load due to alarms is usually called an *alarm avalanche*.

6.3 REAL-TIME COMMUNICATION IN A LAN

Many hard real-time applications span small geographical areas. Examples of such applications include automated manufacturing systems, industrial process control applications, high-speed data acquisition systems. In such applications, Local Area Networks (LANs) usually turn out to be the preferred choice for networking. In these situations, networks such as dedicated point-to-point links or circuit-switching among the different nodes (computers) in the system turn out to be very inefficient and costly. A circuit-switched network simply sets aside a fixed portion of the network bandwidth according to the estimated peak bandwidth requirement of each application. However, such a technique does not work well for those real-time traffic that are inherently bursty in nature. In fact, many categories of real-time traffic are bursty in nature. For such traffic, unless the idle times can be filled by non-real-time traffic, circuit-switching would lead to very low effective bandwidth utilization. As a result, point-to-point or circuit switched networks are not very popular in many real-time applications.

In a LAN, there is a single shared channel and only one node can transmit at any time. The exact time when a node can transmit on the channel is determined by the access arbitration policy of the network. The transmission control policy determines how long a node can transmit. These two policies together are called the access control technique and form the Media Access Control (MAC) layer protocol. In other words, the MAC protocol in a LAN consists of two parts: an access arbitration part that determines when a node can use the channel and a transmission control part that determines for how long a node can continue to use the channel once it starts using it. Before we discuss how real-time communication can be achieved in a LAN, let us first review some basic aspects of LANs that are crucial to understanding our subsequent discussions.

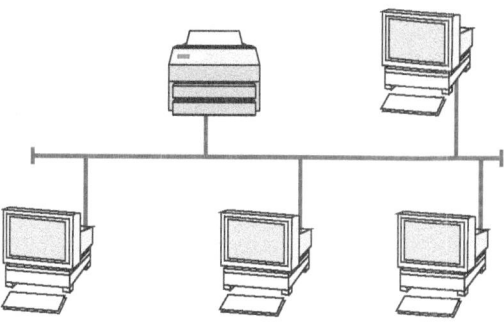

▲ **FIGURE 6.2**

A Bus Interconnection Network

6.3.1 LAN Architectures

Two major LAN architectures are being used: the bus and the ring architectures [13, 27]. These two architectures use different access control techniques. We first briefly discuss these two LAN architectures, and then discuss the associated access control techniques.

Bus Architectures: In bus-based architectures, nodes are connected to the network cable using T-shaped network interface connectors as shown in Fig. 6.2. Terminating points are placed at each end of the network cable. There is a single shared channel (bus) for which the transmitting nodes contend. In a bus architecture, nodes communicate using broadcasting. The most commonly used protocol for access control in traditional bus networks is the Carrier Sense Multiple Access with Collision Detection (CSMA/CD) [27]. CSMA/CD networks are also called multiple access networks. In CSMA/CD networks, when two or more nodes transmit packets simultaneously, the transmissions overlap in time and the resulting signal gets garbled. Such an event is called a collision. A collision entails retransmission of the corrupted data.

In CSMA/CD networks, any node can at any time sense the channel to determine whether the channel is idle. A node transmits a packet only if it senses the channel to be idle. But, this does not guarantee that there will be no collisions. Several nodes might sense the channel to be idle at the same time instant and start transmitting simultaneously, resulting in a collision. The transmitting nodes can detect a collision when it occurs. Therefore, while transmitting a packet, a node would check for a collision and would immediately stop transmitting, if it detects one. It should, therefore, be clear that larger the propagation delay of a network, larger is the probability of collisions of packets.

Ethernet is a LAN standard based on CSMA/CD access control. CSMA/CD protocol does not define a collision resolution protocol on its own. Ethernet uses Binary Exponential Back-Off (BEB) algorithm for collision resolution. Due to its ubiquity, high speed, simplicity and low cost, Ethernet has over the years emerged as one of the most preferred LAN protocols. It is, therefore, not surprising that many attempts have been made in the past to develop protocols based on Ethernet to support real-time communication. However, as far as real-time communications are concerned, the logical ring architecture possesses significant advantages over Ethernet due to its inherent deterministic access arbitration mechanism in contrast to the collision based mechanism

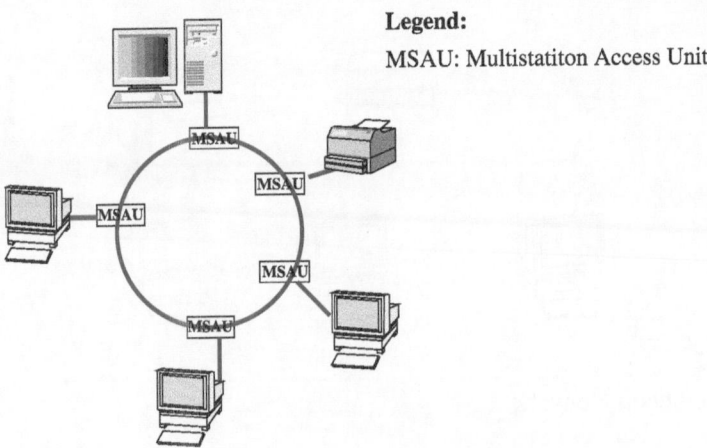

Legend:

MSAU: Multistatiton Access Unit

▲ **FIGURE 6.3**

A Ring Network

of Ethernet. In a collision-based network, under high load situations the number of collisions per unit time would increase very rapidly with load, leading to increased retransmissions rapid drop in throughput and rise in delay. As a result, in Ethernet the delay in message transmission increases rapidly as the traffic increases. This puts Ethernet-based networks at a disadvantageous position as far as real-time applications are concerned.

Ring Architectures: A ring architecture has schematically been shown in Fig. 6.3. Nodes in Fig. 6.3 have been shown to be connected to the network using MSAUs. An Multistation Access Unit (MSAU) is a hub or concentrator that connects a group of computers ("nodes" in network terminology) to the ring. The nodes are placed along the ring. The nodes transmit in turn. Each node usually transmits for a certain predetermined period of time. Therefore, packet transmission delays become predictable and can be made sufficiently small as per requirement. As a result, ring-based architectures are often preferred in real-time applications.

However, the ring architecture suffers from a few important problems. First, any break in the ring can bring the whole network down. This makes reliability of ring networks a major concern. Further, ring is a poor fit to the linear topology normally found in most assembly lines and other applications. This made researchers to look for alternative technologies which can have the advantages of both the bus and ring architectures. This led to the development of the token bus architecture. A token bus is a bus-based architecture (see Fig. 6.4), where the stations on the bus are logically arranged in a ring with each station knowing the address of the station to its "left" and "right."

When the logical ring is initialized, the highest numbered station gets a chance to start its transmission. After transmitting for a predetermined duration, the station passes the transmission permission to its immediate neighbour (left or right as per the convention adopted) by sending a special control frame called a *token*. The token propagates around the logical ring. At any time, only the token holder is permitted to transmit packets. Since only one station at a time holds the token in a ring network, collisions can not occur. An important point that must be kept in mind is that the physical order in which the stations are connected to the cable need not be the same as the

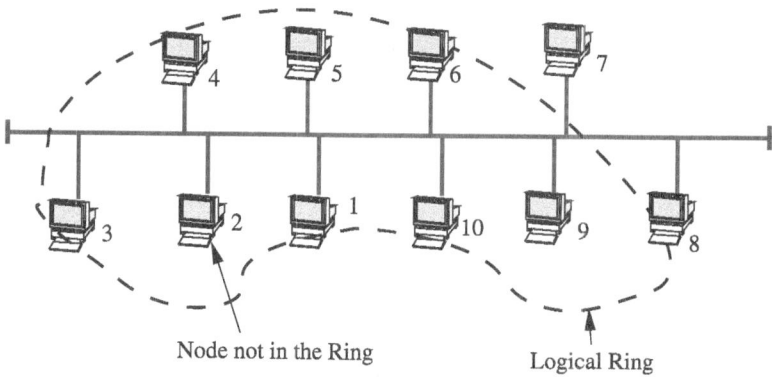

Node not in the Ring   Logical Ring

▲ FIGURE 6.4

A Logical Ring in a Token Bus

---

order of the stations in the logical ring. This is because a cable is inherently a broadcast medium. Each station would receive every frame transmitted, and discard those that are not addressed to it. After a node exhausts its assigned time slot for transmission, it hands over the token to its logical neighbour. For this, it transmits a special token, specifically addressed to its logical neighbour in the ring, irrespective of whether that station is physically adjacent to the concerned node or not. It is also worth noting that many stations on the network may not be in the ring. For example, the stations 2, 5, 7, and 9 in the Fig. 6.4 are not on the ring at all. The MAC protocol in a token ring network should support adding stations to, and removing stations from the logical ring [27].

6.4 SOFT REAL-TIME COMMUNICATION IN A LAN

Soft real-time communication networks are not expected to provide any absolute QoS guarantees to the applications. They only ensure prioritized treatment for real-time messages, so that the message deadline miss ratio (for real-time messages) can be kept to a minimum and the soft real-time messages can be provided statistical guarantees on delay bounds.

Soft real-time protocols usually assume that both soft real-time and non real-time messages would be transmitted over the network. Soft real-time traffic is assumed to be generated by CBR and VBR sources. Soft real-time message rates are assumed to be very low compared to the channel capacity. Non-real-time messages and certain soft real-time messages may arrive aperiodically in bursts. In presence of bursts, it becomes very difficult to sustain the guarantees to the real-time traffic unless specific arrangements are made. Therefore, the bursts need to be smoothened out for meeting the statistical guarantees on deadline bounds for real-time messages. In the following, we discuss a few important techniques available for this purpose.

A Fixed-Rate Traffic Smoothing Algorithm: Kweon and Shin developed a fixed-rate traffic-smoothing algorithm [15] that is based on the considerations of limits on the transmission capacity of a network. From the limits on the transmission capacity, the input limit for each node in the system is derived. The traffic smoother, which is placed between the MAC layer and TCP/IP layer, smooths a non-real-time stream so that guarantees to real-time messages would not be violated. The traffic-smoothing technique used is a leaky bucket algorithm called Credit

Bucket Depth (CBD). It has two important parameters: CBD and Refresh Period (RP). These two parameters are fixed statically. CBD is the maximum number of credits that are added to the bucket at every refresh. It is also the maximum number of credits that a bucket can hold. RP is the refresh period with which the bucket is replenished with new credits. The ratio CBD/RP is the average guaranteed throughput for non-real-time messages. The number of credits present in the bucket at any time is denoted as the Current Network Share (CNS). A waiting message is taken up for transmission, if the message size is smaller than CNS. When the number of available credits (CNS) is positive, but is smaller than the the size of a message to be transmitted, credits are allowed to be borrowed. So, it is possible that the balance of credits can become negative at times. The CNS may become negative, if credits have been borrowed. At every refresh, the number of credits in the bucket (CNS) is updated as follows: CNS = min(CNS + CBD, CBD). That is, CBD amount of credits are replenished, subject to the limit that CNS does not exceed CBD. When a non-real-time message arrives at a node for transmission, the smoothing mechanism carries out the following steps:

```
if (CNS > 0){
        CNS = CNS - message.number of Bytes;
        /*  message.number of Bytes is the size of the message */
        send message for transmission;}
else    {
        hold message in buffer until CNS > 0;}
```

The disadvantage of the fixed-rate traffic smoothing technique is that it is not very flexible as once the delay requirements of the real-time messages are known, the network-wide input limit is fixed. The transmission rate of the non-real-time sources is, therefore, limited and gets reduced as the number of nodes increases on the LAN. Consequently, an increase in the number of stations, leads to a decrease in traffic generations limits of the stations. This shows up as a corresponding decrease in throughput of non-real-time traffic. This technique is also very pessimistic since it is based on worst-case calculations on the total real-time traffic arrival rates in the system.

Adaptive Traffic Smoothing: Kweon and Shin have proposed an adaptive traffic smoother that addresses some of the shortcomings of the CBD algorithm [14]. The main idea behind adaptive traffic smoothing is that in order to provide a reasonable throughput for non-real-time messages, in the presence of VBR real-time traffic sources, the non-real-time traffic transmission rate can be allowed to adapt itself to the load conditions of the underlying network. That is, the nodes are allowed to increase their transmission limits, if the utilization of the network is low. On the other hand, when the utilization of the network becomes high, the nodes transmitting non-real-time messages are made to decrease their transmission limits. In order to implement such a rate adaptive traffic smoother, which would meet the delay requirements of real-time packets and at the same time provide improved average throughput for non-real-time packets, the following two problems must be resolved:

- How to detect a change in network utilization?
- How to adapt the transmission limits to a detected change in network utilization?

The solution that has been proposed is that the number of collisions per unit time can be used as a measure of network utilization. This proposal is based on the observation that at higher network utilizations, more collisions can be expected. This is a simple and approximate way to determine network utilization at any time. In the event of a collision, the credit bucket is immediately emptied causing suspension of non-real-time packets, except for the packets that are already under transmission. This increases the chance to deliver the real-time packets generated from other nodes within the specified delay bounds, and prevents delays caused by bursts of non-real-time packets generated from this node. For this reason, packet collision is used as a trigger to decrease the throughput as well as to deplete the current credits.

The station input limit CBD/RP can be adapted by either changing the CBD or the RP parameter. The station input limit is increased periodically by decreasing RP periodically by a fixed number, if no collisions have been observed recently. Of course, the lower bound of RP is fixed by some predefined value RP_{min}. When a collision is detected, all credit buckets are depleted and RP is doubled. The upper bound of RP is fixed by a certain predefined value RP_{max}.

Experimental results have shown that by using the adaptive traffic smoothing scheme, message deadline miss ratios (for real-time messages) can be kept well within an acceptable range, for arbitrary arrival rates for non-real-time messages. It should, however, be remembered that this technique though efficient, fails to provide deterministic real-time communication. It is, therefore, suitable only for soft real-time systems and can not be satisfactorily used to support hard real-time communications.

6.5 HARD REAL-TIME COMMUNICATION IN A LAN

We had discussed several example applications in Section 6.1, for which hard real-time communication in a LAN environment becomes necessary. Hard real-time applications often involve transmission of CBR traffic such as periodic sensor signals. In hard real-time applications, the network utilization is deliberately kept low since predictability of network delay takes precedence over network utilization aspects. However, to improve the network utilization, soft and non-real-time traffic are usually allowed to be transmitted in the intervals during which hard real-time messages are not present.

In a LAN, hard real-time communications are normally supported using any of the following three classes [16, 19] of protocols: global priority-based, calendar-based, and bounded-access protocols. We first discuss some important features of these three classes of hard real-time communication protocols. Subsequently, we discuss a few important protocols belonging to these three classes.

Global Priority Protocols: In a global priority protocol, each message in the network is assigned a priority value. This MAC layer protocol tries to ensure that at any time the channel is serving to the highest priority message in the network. This opens up the possibility of using RMA or EDF for scheduling messages in a network deploying a global priority-based protocol. As discussed in Chapter 2, RMA and EDF are optimal static and dynamic priority task scheduling protocols, respectively, and are very popular with real-time application developers. However, the following two problems arise while trying to implement RMA or EDF-based message scheduling algorithms in a network using a global priority-based scheduling protocol:

- After the transmission of a packet starts, it can not be stopped halfway and the remaining bits of the packets transmitted at a later time. In other words, unlike the way tasks could be preempted from CPU usage, packet transmissions can not be meaningfully preempted from channel usage.

- A global priority protocol can not instantaneously determine the message that has the highest priority. Since messages originate at different nodes, a centralized knowledge of messages that are currently eligible to be transmitted is absent. As we shall see in our subsequent discussions, what can be obtained in practice would have to be based on somewhat outdated information.

Both these problems cause violation of some of the basic premises that were made for RMA (and EDF) to optimally schedule tasks. Therefore, if RMA (or for that matter EDF) is used to schedule messages on a network deploying a global priority protocol—the two above mentioned problems would restrict the achievable schedulable utilization of the channel to very low values.

Bounded Access Scheduling: In bounded access scheduling, messages are provided real-time guarantees by bounding the access times of every node to the channel. This ensures that the time for which a packet may have to wait before being transmitted is bounded. Bounded access scheduling protocols fix the time for which a node is permitted to transmit its messages. The individual nodes use a local scheduling algorithm to determine the order in which packets queued up at the local node are taken up for transmission.

Calendar-based Scheduling: A calendar-based protocol, as the name suggests, maintains a calendar that indicates which node is permitted to transmit during which time period. A copy of the calendar is maintained by every node. Traffic sources can reserve time interval for packet transmission by broadcasting. When a node needs to transmit a message for which no reservation was made, it finds a free slot by consulting its local copy of the calendar and reserves the required time interval by broadcasting the reservation information to all nodes. A calendar-based protocol is simple, efficient, and works very well when all messages in the system are periodic and predictable.

In the following, we discuss some important protocols from each of these three categories of protocols.

6.5.1 Global Priority-Based Scheduling

A few important global priority arbitration based protocols are discussed in the following.

Countdown Protocol: In this protocol, the time line is divided into fixed sized intervals called slots. At the start of every slot, priority arbitration is carried out to determine the highest priority message in the network. As soon as priority arbitration is complete, the node having the highest priority message is allowed to transmit. In other words, this scheme involves periodic priority arbitration followed by message transmission as shown in Fig. 6.5.

Priority arbitration is achieved as follows. Over each slot, every node that has a pending message, transmits the priority value of its highest priority pending message with msb first as shown in Fig. 6.6. Since simultaneous transmission follows *or* logic, a node that transmits a 0 and receives a 1, knows that there is at least one node that is having a higher priority pending message, and drops out of the contention. The node that transmits last without any collision, can conclude that no nodes have any higher priority messages, and can begin its transmissions.

An important parameter in the efficient working of this protocol is the slot size, Therefore, the slot size needs to be carefully selected. Each slot duration is usually made equal to

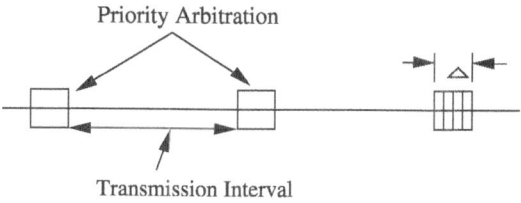

▲ **FIGURE 6.5**

Priority Arbitration and Transmission Intervals

the end-to-end propagation delay of the medium. If the slot size is made any smaller than this, then the priority arbitration scheme would not work since even when a collision occurs, it would not be detected. A slot size larger than this would lead to an increase in channel idle time during every slot.

To illustrate the working of this protocol, transmission of bits by different nodes in an arbitration example has schematically been shown in the Fig. 6.6. In Fig. 6.6, three nodes N_1, N_2, and N_3 are participating in the arbitration process. The priorities of messages at the nodes N_1, N_2, and N_3 are 10, 16, and 20, respectively. As shown, node N_1 drops out after transmitting the first bit as it transmits a 0 but listens a 1. Similarly, the node N_2 drops out after transmitting the third bit when it transmits a 0 and listens to a 1. Finally, after transmitting the last bit, node N_3 concludes that it has the highest priority message and begins its transmission.

Virtual Time Protocol: In this protocol, a node uses the state of the channel to reason about the pending packets residing at other nodes. Each node with a packet to send waits for an interval of time that is inversely proportional to the priority of the highest priority message it has. This protocol assigns priority to nodes. The priority of a node is equal to the highest priority message that it has. That is, the lower the priority of the highest priority message that a node has, the longer it waits. At the expiration of the waiting time of a node, it senses the status of the channel. If the channel is busy, then this would imply that a higher priority message is being transmitted and it would need to wait until an idle period. Otherwise, it starts to transmit.

What should be the difference in wait times of two nodes which have messages whose priorities differ by one? Because of the propagation delay in the network, a node can not

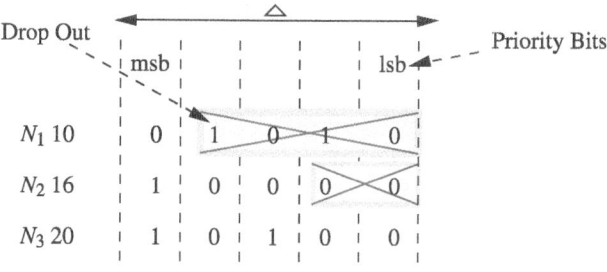

▲ **FIGURE 6.6**

Priority Arbitration Example

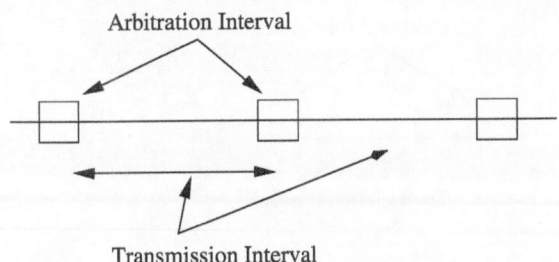

▲ FIGURE 6.7

Priority Arbitration in Virtual Time Protocol

instantaneously detect when another node starts to transmit during arbitration. As a result, unless the wait times of two nodes differ by at least as much as the propagation time, the following problem would occur. Assume that two nodes N_1 and N_2 have their priorities differing by one. After N_1 starts transmitting, if N_2 waits for any time shorter than the propagation time, then it can not detect the transmission of N_1 and would start transmitting. This would lead to a collision and result in incorrect priority arbitration. Thus, propagation time effectively bounds the difference between the wait times of two nodes that have consecutive priorities (see Fig. 6.7). However, a wait time much larger than the propagation time would lead to channel idle times and underutilization of the channel.

IEEE 802.5:   IEEE 802.5 is a priority-based token ring protocol. In this protocol, the header of the token contains two fields: a reservation field and a mode field (see Fig. 6.8). The token alternates between two modes: a reservation mode and a free mode. A node can at any time determine the mode of the token by examining the mode bit in the header of the token. The messages to be transmitted are split into frames. The token may contain a frame as a payload as shown in Fig. 6.8.

To be able to support different classes of network traffic, IEEE 802.5 supports assigning priorities to messages. The priority of the message that is being transmitted is recorded in the reservation field of the header.

Packet transmissions occur in the reservation mode. The priority of a message that is being transmitted at any time is registered in the reservation field of the header of the token as shown in Fig. 6.8. As the token passes through the ring, every node with pending messages inspects the reservation field in the token header. A node having a higher priority message than that is being transmitted, registers its priority in the priority field of the header. When the token returns to the

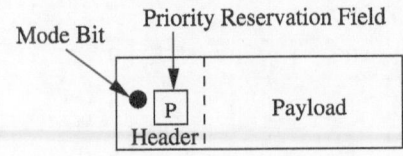

▲ FIGURE 6.8

Structure of a Token in IEEE 802.5

sending node, it observes the reservation made by another node, puts the token in free mode and releases it. As the free mode token passes through the ring, the node that made the reservation seizes the token, puts it into the reservation mode, and starts transmitting.

Two important results about this protocol are presented in the following two theorems.

THEOREM 6.1 *The minimum time required to complete transmission of a frame using IEEE 802.5 protocol is max(F, θ), where F is the frame transmission time and θ is the propagation time.*

PROOF A node does not start transmitting the next frame until:

- It has completed transmission of the last bit of the frame.
- It has received the header of the transmitted token back.

The first activity takes F time units, which is the frame transmission time. The second activity takes $θ$ time units, which is the propagation time. Therefore, the transmission time is the higher of the two values, which is $max(F, θ)$.

Theorem 6.1 indicates that when a packet is being transmitted, the minimum time before which transmission of the next packet can not start is bounded by $max(F, θ)$.

THEOREM 6.2 *A higher priority packet might undergo inversion for at most 2 × max(F, θ) time units.*

PROOF: A higher priority message undergoes inversion, until:

- The reservation mode completes.
- The node receives the token in free mode.

Each of the above step takes $max(F, θ)$ time units to complete (by Theorem 6.1). Therefore, the total time a higher priority packet may have to wait before being transmitted is given by $2 × max(F, θ)$.

Window-Based Protocol: This is also a global priority-based protocol. In this protocol, the time line is divided into frames as shown in Fig. 6.9. Every node maintains the current transmission window defined by priority values (*low*, *high*). A node that has a message in the window, i.e., a message whose priority is within the range defined by the *low* and *high* values can start to transmit. However, at the start of a frame it is possible that more than one node may find that they have a message that is eligible for transmission and start transmitting it. This

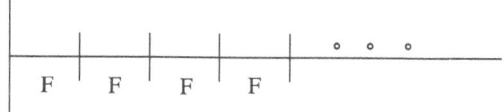

▲ **FIGURE 6.9**

Frames in the Window-Based Protocol

would result in a collision. On a collision, every node increments the value of low (i.e., makes *low* + +) and on a free frame every node decrements the value of low (i.e., makes *low* − −).

6.5.2 Calendar-Based Protocol

An example of calendar-based scheduling protocol is the dynamic reservation technique. In this protocol, each node maintains a calendar data structure where information about the access time reservations of the guaranteed messages of all nodes are maintained. When a message for which no reservation has yet been made arrives at a node, the node first determines a free slot by consulting its local calendar data structure. It then attempts to reserve a suitable free future time interval by broadcasting a *control message* to all nodes. Every node on receipt of a control message, updates its calendar accordingly. This protocol can efficiently handle deterministic periodic messages, and unlike the global priority-based protocols there is no overhead in priority arbitration. However, it becomes very difficult to handle aperiodic and sporadic messages in this protocol. Therefore, this protocol is used only in very simple networks such as CANs.

6.6   BOUNDED ACCESS PROTOCOLS FOR LANs

IEEE 802.4 and RETHER are two popular examples of bounded access protocols that can support real-time communication in a LAN.

6.6.1   IEEE 802.4

IEEE 802.4 protocol can be used in token ring and token bus networks. This protocol is often referred to as the *timed token protocol*. In this protocol, a node can transmit, when it holds the token. Real-time guarantees to messages are provided by bounding the amount of time each node holds the token. This protocol has been incorporated in Fibre Distributed Data Interface (FDDI).

In IEEE 802.4, Target Token Rotation Time (TTRT) is used as a design parameter. TTRT is defined as the expected time between two consecutive visits of the token to a node. At the network initialization time, TTRT is specified by the network administrator depending on the characteristics of the messages that would be transmitted over the network.

The real-time messages of a node are assumed to be periodic in nature and are termed synchronous messages, and the non-real-time messages are termed asynchronous messages. Individual nodes are allocated a portion of TTRT, known as the node's *synchronous bandwidth*. This allotment is made according to the timing characteristics of the synchronous messages originating at all the nodes taken together.

Let the synchronous bandwidth of a node N_i be H_i time units. We have already mentioned that TTRT is distributed among the nodes such that each time the token visits a node N_i, it can transmit its synchronous messages for at most H_i duration. Let SN be the set of all nodes in the network. Then, TTRT can be represented as: $TTRT = \theta + \Sigma_{N_i \in SN} H_i$, where θ is the propagation time and H_i is the token holding time at node N_i. When a node receives the token, it first transmits its synchronous traffic for a time bounded by its synchronous bandwidth. After transmitting all its synchronous traffic, it may transmit its asynchronous traffic, only the token had arrived early at the node. That is, it transmits asynchronous traffic only if the time since the previous departure of the token from the same node is less than TTRT.

A node can transmit non-real-time messages only when the token arrives at the node earlier than expected. The time for which asynchronous frames are transmitted is called *asynchronous overrun*. Asynchronous overrun reduces the effective bandwidth available to transmit synchronous messages and delays the time between consecutive arrival of the token at a node. In the absence of any asynchronous overrun, the expected interval of successive visits of the token to a node is TTRT. Due to asynchronous overrun, the worst case time between two successive visits of the token to a node is $2 \times$ TTRT. Suppose, no node has either any synchronous or asynchronous message to transmit. In this situation, assume that the token arrives at node N_{i+1} TTRT time units early. Now, suppose node N_i transmits asynchronous messages for TTRT time units and the node N_i and all subsequent nodes make full use of their assigned time slots for transmitting synchronous messages. Then, the token would arrive at node i after $2 * $ TTRT time units since its last visit. Therefore, a network that uses only synchronous mode, time between consecutive token arrivals would be limited by TTRT.

Suppose, among all messages that can originate at the different nodes, let the node N_i have the message having the smallest deadline Δ. That is, Δ is the shortest deadline among all messages in the network. Since, the worst case time between two successive visits of the token to a node is $2 \times$ TTRT, unless TTRT is set to a value smaller than $\Delta/2$ during the network initialization time, the deadline for the shortest deadline message would not be met. On the other hand, a TTRT value much smaller than $\Delta/2$ would lead to increase in larger overhead and would result in low network capacity utilization If TTRT is set to be larger than $\Delta/2$, then real-time messages would miss their deadlines.

Token holding time of an individual node is the synchronous bandwidth alloted to the node. As soon as a node N_i receives the token, it starts a timer set to its synchronous bandwidth (H_i), and releases the token upon expiry of the timer. The synchronous bandwidth allocated to a node N_i is given by the following expression:

$$H_i = (\text{TTRT} - \theta) * \frac{C_i/T_i}{\Sigma C_i/T_i} \tag{6.1}$$

where C_i is the size of the message (in bits) that node N_i requires to transmit over T_i interval, and $\frac{C_i}{T_i}$ is the channel utilization due to the node N_i.

Example 6.1

Suppose a network designed using IEEE 802.4 protocol has three nodes. Node N_1 needs to transmit 1 mb of data every 300 mSec. Node N_2 needs to transmit 1.2 mb of data every 500 mSec. Node N_3 needs to transmit 1.2 mb of data every 500 mSec. Select a suitable TTRT for the network and compute the token holding time for each node. Ignore the propagation time.

Solution. From an examination of the messages, it can be seen that the shortest deadline among all messages is 200 mSec. Therefore, we can select $TTRT = \frac{200}{2} = 100$ mSec. The channel utilization due to the different nodes would be:

$$\frac{C_1}{T_1} = \frac{1 \times 8}{300} \text{ mb/mSec}$$

$$\frac{C_2}{T_2} = \frac{1.2 \times 8}{500} \text{ mb/mSec}$$

$$\frac{C_3}{T_3} = \frac{2 \times 8}{200} \text{ mb/mSec}$$

$$\frac{C_1}{T_1} + \frac{C_2}{T_2} + \frac{C_3}{T_3} = \frac{1 \times 8}{300} + \frac{1.2 \times 8}{500} + \frac{2 \times 8}{200} = \frac{377.6}{3000} \text{ mb/mSec}$$

Using Expr. 6.1, the token holding times (H_i) of the different nodes can be determined as follows:

$$H_1 = 100 \times \frac{8}{300} \times \frac{3000}{377.6} = 21.18 \text{ mSec}$$

$$H_2 = 100 \times \frac{9.6}{500} \times \frac{3000}{377.6} = 15.25 \text{ mSec}$$

$$H_3 = 100 \times \frac{16}{200} \times \frac{3000}{377.6} = 63.56 \text{ mSec}$$

6.6.2 RETHER

RETHER stands for Real-time ETHERnet. RETHER enhances TCP/IP to provide real-time performance guarantees to real-time applications, without modifying the existing Ethernet hardware [28]. In RETHER, network transmissions can occur in two modes: CSMA/CD mode or RETHER mode. The network switches transparently to RETHER-mode when there are real-time sessions and transits back to CSMA/CD-mode when all real-time sessions terminate. Protocol switching is done to minimize the performance impacts on non-real-time traffic when there are no real-time sessions. In RETHER mode, a token passing scheme is used.

Protocol Description: In the absence of any real-time messages at the nodes, nodes compete for the channel using the usual CSMA/CD protocol. When a node receives a real-time request from a local application, it broadcasts a Switch-to-RETHER message, if the network is not already in RETHER mode. Every node that receives this message responds by setting the mode of its protocol to RETHER mode and acknowledges back to the initiator. The transmitting node waits for the ongoing packet transmission to complete. It then sends an acknowledgment back to the initiator, indicating its willingness to switch to RETHER mode and that there is no data left in the back-off phase of CSMA/CD protocol. After receiving all the acknowledgments, the initiating node creates a token and begins circulating it. This completes a successful switch to RETHER mode.

If more than one initiator tries to initiate RETHER-mode at the same time, each node acknowledges its switch message to the initiator with the smallest ID among the initiating nodes. An initiator only sends an acknowledgment to another initiator, if its node ID is smaller than its own. In case of loss of the acknowledgment, or when some node does not receive the Switch-to-RETHER broadcast, or when some nodes are dead, then the initiator times out due to non-receipt of all the acknowledgments. After a fixed number of retries, it concludes that the nodes that did not acknowledge are dead, and conveys this to all other live nodes.

The RETHER mode uses a timed token scheme (see Section 6.6.1) to provide bandwidth guarantees. At any time, there can be only one real-time request per node and each real-time request specifies the required transmission bandwidth in terms of the amount of data it needs to send during a fixed interval of time called Targetted Token Rotation Time (TTRT). The maximum token holding time is calculated for each node based on this information (amount of data and TTRT). Based on this information, bandwidth is reserved for each session.

We now discuss the behaviour of the nodes on receipt of the token. The control token circulates among two sets of nodes, the Real-Time Set (RTS) and the Non-Real-Time Set (NRTS). Only nodes that have made a bandwidth reservation belong to RTS. All other nodes belong to NRTS. During each token rotation, the token visits all nodes in the real-time set in order. When a node in real-time set receives the token, it sends its real-time data and passes the token to its next neighbour in the real-time set. The last node in the RTS passes the token to the NRTS, if there are no reservations. Let TTRT be the mean token rotation time and let $MTHT_i$ be the mean token holding time for node N_i. The token is then tagged with a Time-ToDeadline field computed as:

$$TimeToDeadline = TTRT - \sum_{i \in RTS} MTHT_i$$

A positive value of TimeToDeadline would indicate that some NRT messages can be transmitted even after transmitting all real-time messages. When an NRT node receives the token, it determines whether there is sufficient time to send a packet without negatively affecting the real-time messages at any of the nodes. If sufficient time exists, it sends a packet, and decrements TimeToDeadline accordingly. It then passes the token to the next node in NRTS. If there is no time to send a packet, it informs the last node in the real-time set that it should be the first node to get the token among NRTS nodes during the next round, and it passes the token to the first node in the RTS.

Every new real-time request goes through an admission control procedure that determines if it is possible to accept the request. Admission control is performed locally on each node: A real-time request is admitted, only if

$$\sum_{i \in RTS} MTHT_i + MTHT_{new} + TBNRT \leq TTRT$$

where TBNRT is the bandwidth reserved for the NRT set. $MTHT_{new}$ is the bandwidth required by the new node in the RT set. When a real-time node wants to terminate its real-time connection, it merely removes itself from the RTS information on the token.

6.6.3 Switched Real-Time Ethernet

Modern Ethernet networks are more and more being built using switches instead of hubs or coaxial cables. Use of hubs and switches creates a star-like network (see Fig. 6.10). The difference between switches and hubs is intelligence. Hubs simply pass on incoming traffic from any port to all other ports. On the other hand, switches selectively send the traffic through a specific port based on their knowledge of the network topology. In the star-like network topology that is

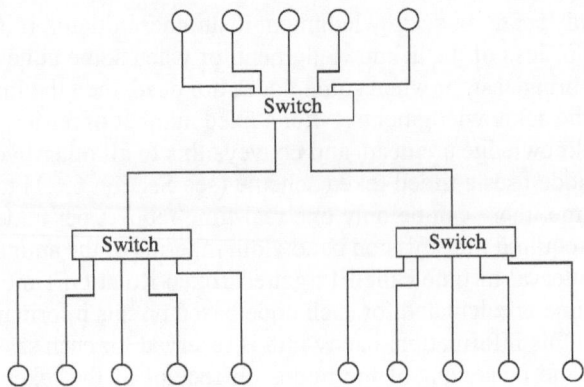

▲ **FIGURE 6.10**

Switched Real-Time Ethernet

realized, there is a dedicated cable in each direction. Therefore, collisions can not occur on any network cable. The switches do not provide any guarantees as to which one will be sent first. A switch deploying bandwidth reservation can solve this problem.

6.7 PERFORMANCE COMPARISON

In this section, we compare the effectiveness of the different protocols discussed for providing QoS guarantees to real-time applications. We focus our attention only on the bounded access protocol (IEEE 802.4) and a priority-based protocol (IEEE 802.5).

At the design time, a detailed knowledge of the message set that would be transmitted is often unavailable. However, the designers of a real-time network usually have an estimate of the traffic generated by the different real-time sources in terms of the respective channel utilizations. Therefore, a utilization-based metric is appropriate for being used during the network design stage.

We first discuss an intuitive classification of the various types of message sets that may be used in an application. We then discuss two metrics that are based on channel utilization on account of the different message sets. Each network needs to cater to a certain number of real-time messages, called a message set. Of course, there can be a large number of message sets that may arise in practice for different applications. The entire population of real-time message sets can be divided into three classes depending on the schedulability offered by a network as shown in Fig. 6.11. These three classes of messages sets are:

Unsaturated Schedulable: The message sets in this class are schedulable, and remain schedulable even when the size of any message in a message set is slightly increased. These message sets typically result in low channel utilization.

Saturated Schedulable: The message sets in this class are schedulable, but any increase in the size of a message, would make the corresponding message set unschedulable, and messages would miss their respective deadlines.

Unschedulable: The unschedulable set refers to those message sets for which deadlines of at least some messages would be missed.

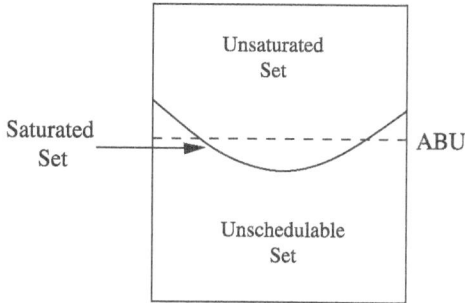

▲ **FIGURE 6.11**

Schematic Representation of All Message Sets

We now discuss two utilization-centered metrics based on the above classification of real-time message sets.

- **Absolute Breakdown Utilization (ABU):** This metric indicates the expected value of utilization of a message set S, at which messages start to miss their respective deadlines. It is the average of the utilization of all messages in the saturated set. This metric can more formally be defined as follows. Let $U(S)$ be the utilization of the channel due to a certain message set S. $U(S)$ can be expressed as follows.

$$U(S) = \sum_{i \in S} \frac{C_i}{T_i}$$

where C_i is the size of message $i \in S$, and T_i is its period. ABU can now be defined as:

$$\text{ABU} = \frac{\sum_{S \in \text{Sat}} U(S)}{|\text{Sat}|}$$

where Sat is the set of all saturated message sets. We can informally view this metric to indicate how much traffic a network can accommodate on the average case, without any message having to miss its deadline.

- **Guarantee Probability (GP(U)):** GP(U) is the guarantee probability at channel utilization U, (GP(U)) indicates the probability that all deadlines of a message set with utilization U would be met.

We can expect GP(U) to be close to 1 for utilization lower than ABU, and approach 0 as utilization increases beyond ABU.

In a performance study of the priority-based protocols and bounded access protocols against the above two metrics it was observed that in low bandwidth networks, priority-based protocols work better, whereas at higher bandwidths, the bounded access protocols work better [10]. Results of experimental studies have been shown in Figs. 6.12 and 6.13. The results indicate the the performance of the bounded access protocol improves monotonically with bandwidth. However, the performance of the priority-driven protocol initially improves as the bandwidth is increased, but starts to drop off beyond a certain point. This is against the intuition that the performance of a protocol should improve as the bandwidth is increased. Let us now analyze this anomalous behaviour.

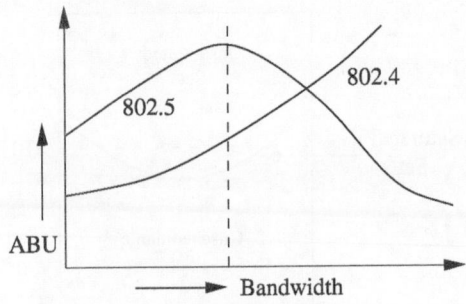

▲ **FIGURE 6.12**

Absolute Breakdown Utilization versus Bandwidth

When the bandwidth is increased beyond a certain value, in case of the priority-based protocol (IEEE 802.5) the decrease in transmission time causes the frame transmission time F to be less than the token rotation time θ. In this case, before releasing a new token, the transmitting node has to wait for the token to return, even after it has completed the transmission of a frame. Thus, the effective frame transmission time in this case is θ and the fraction of the wasted bandwidth is $(\theta - F)/F$. The propagation time (θ) is independent of the bandwidth and hence can be considered as a constant. The token transmission time decreases with increasing bandwidth. Therefore, the percentage of wasted bandwidth increases with increase in bandwidth. This leads to deterioration of performance with increase in bandwidth after a certain bandwidth at which $\theta = F$. The timed token protocol does not exhibit this anomaly, because a node is permitted to transmit continuously during the time it holds the token.

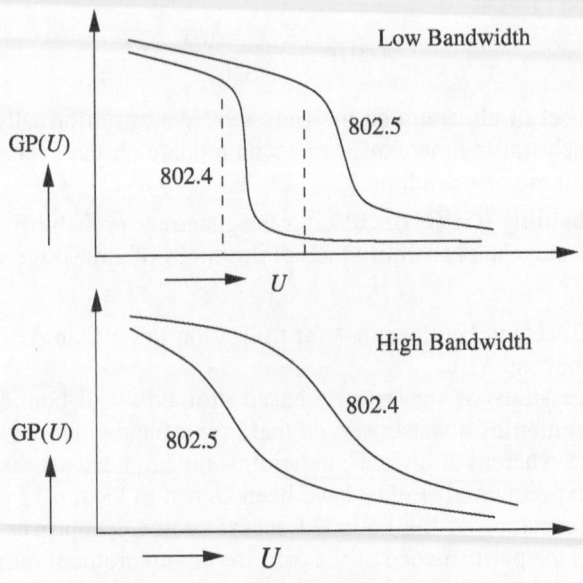

▲ **FIGURE 6.13**

GP(U) versus Utilization at Low and High Bandwidths

From Fig. 6.12 it can be seen that in all cases, the guarantee probability remains close to 1 as long as the utilization is less than ABU. There is a sharp drop in the guarantee probability at utilization values close to ABU. This demonstrates that ABU is a robust measure of average performance of real-time networks. Now, we can summarize our observations as follows. At low network bandwidth, the priority inversions caused by the round-robin scheduling approach of the bounded access protocol tends to adversely impact messages with short deadlines. Thus, at low bandwidths, priority-driven protocol is better suited than the timed token protocol for real-time applications. However, at high bandwidth, priority-driven protocol leads to low channel utilization due to priority arbitration overheads.

6.8 REAL-TIME COMMUNICATION OVER PACKET SWITCHED NETWORKS

Packet switching is popularly deployed in wide area networks. A prominent example of a packet switched network is the Internet. From a modest beginning made a little over a decade ago, Internet has become a vast repository of information, and enabler of several new applications such as e-commerce. Internet provides *best-effort* service to applications, that is, traffic is processed as quickly as possible. However, there is no guarantee of timeliness or actual delivery. With the increasing commercial usage of Internet, there is now a need to support soft and firm real-time applications. In this section, we first provide some basic concepts about Internet. Subsequently, we discuss how QoS guarantees can be provided on the Internet. In particular, we discuss QoS routing, resource reservation, traffic shaping and policing—some of the key techniques that are being used to provide QoS guarantees to applications.

6.8.1 A Basic Model of Internet

The basic Internet service model has been schematically shown in Fig. 6.14. As shown in the figure, the receiver and the sender are connected to each other through several (possibly thousands of) routers and links. The routers are of two basic types: edge routers and core routers. The core routers are typically located at the ISP[1] and the edge routers are connected to the nodes at the periphery of the network. The edge routers can either be ingress or egress type. The egress routers are attached at the receiver-end, whereas an ingress router is attached at the sender's end. An ingress router is the first interface to the data sent by a sender host. As shown in Fig. 6.14, the different hosts and routers are interconnected using links. The type of physical media used at a link can be as varying as a twisted pair cable, a fiber optic cable, or even a wireless medium. The data generated by various users are routed by the ingress routers to the routers at the ISP. The routers at the ISP are termed core routers. The density of these routers is very high at the ISP end, since huge amount of data and links typically converge at the ISP. From the core routers, data is forwarded through the egress routers (at the receiver end) to the corresponding receivers.

Real-time communication can be supported on the Internet by providing preferential treatment to data of certain senders that have entered into a contract with the ISP. But for that to happen, data packets must have been classified before transmission. At the connection set-up time, the sender provides the ISP with two parameters: the traffic specification and the QoS specification.

---

[1]ISP stands for Internet Service Provider. It is the institution that provides access to the users to the Internet.

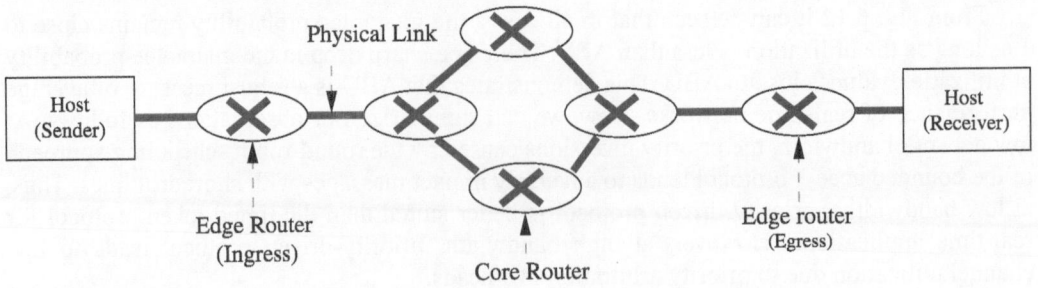

▲ FIGURE 6.14

A Simple Model of the Internet

The ISP uses this to determine whether it can accept or has to refuse the client request. It checks for the availability of resources on the possible routes on which it can forward the data packets. Alternatively, we can say that it tries to find a path (unicast or multicast routing) having the necessary resources to satisfy the required QoS for the specified traffic pattern to be generated by the source.

When the network accepts a connection request, it guarantees that the required QoS will be met. However, the given guarantee remains valid only if the client-generated traffic remains within the specified traffic bounds. If the client traffic violates the prespecified traffic bounds, then the network may drop packets and/or reshape the traffic. Policing is the term used to indicate dropping of the packets of misbehaving traffic sources. Note that the network needs to meet the given performance bounds as long as the client traffic remains within the traffic specification, irrespective of the behaviour of other clients. However, this performance can not be guaranteed, if the connections are not protected from the misbehaving (or malicious) real-time and non real-time sources. To avoid violating the guarantees made to real-time connections, the network must either explicitly control the input rates on a per-connection basis (shaping and policing) or adopt scheduling algorithms at the switches. Several popular scheduling algorithms such as Fair Queuing, Weighted Fair Queuing, etc. exist. These techniques are a part of the modern QoS architectures for the Internet such as IntServ and DiffServ. We elaborate these topics, as well as how QoS guarantees can be provided to the real-time traffic in the following sections.

6.8.2 Traffic Characterization

As already mentioned, while requesting for a real-time connection, the source has to specify the traffic characteristics and the required QoS. The network, in turn, uses the two to check whether it has adequate resources to meet the required QoS. This is part of an admission control procedure. Traffic characterization is essentially a model of the characteristics of the data generated by a source to be transmitted over a network. Normally, traffic is characterized by bounding the volume of data it can generate per unit time. An accurate bound on the volume of the traffic can help to bound the amount of network resources that may have to be reserved to provide the required quality of services. During connection establishment, traffic sources are required to specify their traffic characteristics. Network resources are reserved based on the traffic characterization and the service requirements. Many models have been proposed for traffic characterization. In the following, we discuss a few important ones.

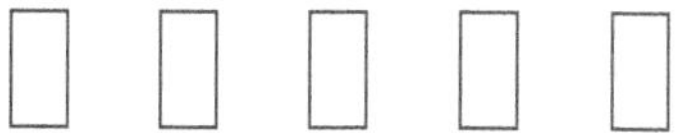

▲ **FIGURE 6.15**

Constant Bit-Rate Traffic

(X_{min}, S_{max}) model: The (X_{min}, S_{max}) model bounds a traffic source with a peak rate. A connection satisfies (X_{min}, S_{max}) model, if the inter-arrival times between two packets is always less than X_{min}, and size of the largest packet does not exceed S_{max}. Both the peak and average rates of traffic in this model are identical, and is given by $\frac{S_{max}}{X_{min}}$.

A CBR traffic has been shown in Fig. 6.15. It can be observed from Fig. 6.15 that for CBR traffic both the worst case and the average packet arrival times are indeed the same. Therefore, this model provides a tight bound for CBR traffic. However, this model can not accurately specify bursty traffic and models the worst-case traffic in this case. If bursty traffic is specified using this model, then it leads to very conservative resource reservation, resulting in low utilization of the reserved resources and inefficient functioning of the network.

(r, T) model: In this model, the time axis is divided into intervals of length T each. Each such interval is called a frame. A source satisfies (r, T) model, if it generates no more than $r . T$ bits of traffic in any interval T. In this model, r is the upper bound on the average rate at which traffic is generated over the averaging interval T. This model is in many ways similar to the (X_{min}, S_{max}) model. It also provides a tight bound for CBR traffic. However, for bursty traffic it leads to very conservative resource reservation, leading to low utilization of the reserved resources.

$(X_{min}, X_{avg}, S_{max}, I)$ model: In this model, X_{min} specifies the minimum inter-arrival time between two packets. S_{max} specifies the maximum packet size and I is an interval over which the observations are valid. X_{ave} is the average inter-arrival time of packets over an interval of size I. A connection would satisfy $(X_{min}, X_{avg}, S_{max}, I)$ model, if it satisfies (X_{min}, S_{max}) model, and additionally, during any interval of length I the average inter-arrival time of packets is X_{ave}. In this model, the peak and the average rates of the traffic are given by S_{max}/X_{min} and S_{max}/X_{ave}, respectively. Note that this model bounds both peak and average rates of the traffic. Therefore, this model provides a more accurate characterization of VBR traffic compared to either (X_{min}, S_{max}) model or (r, T) model.

(σ, ρ) model: In this model, σ is the maximum burst size and ρ is the long term average rate of the traffic source. Average traffic ρ is calculated by observing the number of packets generated over a sufficiently large duration and dividing this by the size of the duration. A connection would satisfy (σ, ρ) model, if during any interval of length t, the number of bits generated by the connection in that interval is less than $\sigma + \rho \times t$. This model can satisfactorily be used to model bursty traffic sources.

Multiple rate bounding: Bursty traffic sources can be characterized sufficiently accurately by bounding the traffic over multiple averaging intervals. A traffic would satisfy $\{(r_1, T_1)$ $(r_2, T_2) \ldots\}$, if $T_1 < T_2 < T_3 \ldots$, and over any interval I the number of bits generated is bounded by $r_i \times T_i$, if $T_{i-1} < I < T_i$. As the averaging T_i interval gets longer, a source is bounded by a rate lower than its peak rate, and closer to its long term average rate.

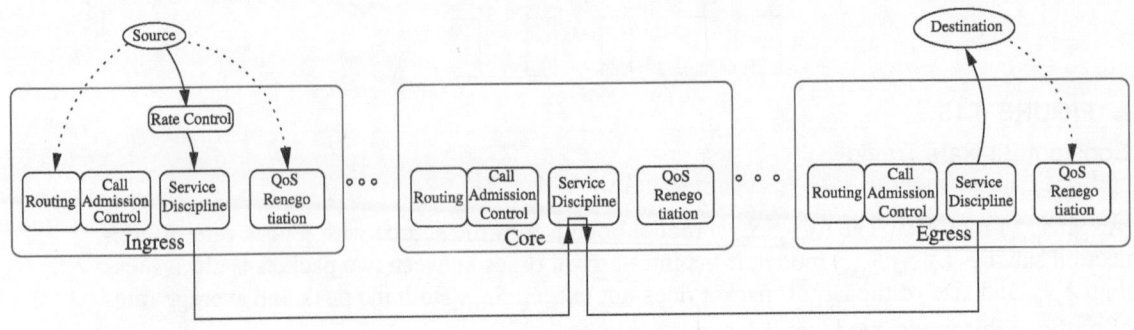

FIGURE 6.16

QoS Framework

6.9 QoS FRAMEWORK

There are several components that work to provide QoS support to a connection request. These components can be viewed as the elements of a QoS framework to be set up by a network. This QoS framework has been shown in Fig. 6.16. The different elements of this framework are briefly discussed in the following. In the subsequent sections we provide a more elaborate treatment of these elements.

Call Admission Control: Call admission control tests whether the required resources are available. Then the required resources are reserved during call establishment, so that traffic can flow according to QoS specification. When the life time of a call is over, the call is torn down; this should involve releasing the resources reserved for the call.

Rate Control: Rate control ensures that the source does not violate the traffic (rate) contract, to which it has agreed. A source might violate its prespecified traffic (rate) due to malicious users or inexact traffic characterization.

Service Discipline: Service discipline allocates resources to connections during data transfer, adhering to the reservations made during channel establishment. Three types of resources allocated by a service discipline, namely, bandwidth, processing time (for deciding the time of service), and buffer space.

QoS Renegotiation: A renegotiation request can come either from the user who wants to change his own QoS requirement, or from the network due to overload and congestion.

6.10 ROUTING

As described in the previous section, packet routing is an important element that can be effectively leveraged to provide QoS guarantees to applications. Once a traffic source has specified its traffic characteristics and its QoS requirements to the network, it waits for the network to accept the request before it can start its transmissions. The network, on its part, checks whether adequate resources are available along any path from source to destination to meet the request.

If no route with required resources are available, then the request is rejected. Route selection for a session takes place during the connection establishment phase in both unicast and multicast connections.

Traditional Internet protocols use routing algorithms such as the shortest path routing in which the routing can be optimized for some metric without taking into account whether the required resource is actually available. Consequently, the flows might finally be routed over paths that are unable to support the necessary resource requirements while other paths might exist which could have easily satisfied the specified requirements. Such a situation might lead to a breach of committed QoS guarantees to connections. Researchers have now proposed *QoS routing* or *constraint-based routing* which can overcome these problems. The primary goals of QoS routing are:

- To select routes that can meet the QoS requirements of a connection.
- To increase the utilization of the network.

While determining a route, QoS routing schemes not only consider the topology of a network, but also the requirements of the flow, the resource availability at the links, etc. Therefore, QoS routing would be able to find a longer and lightly-loaded path rather than the shortest path that may be heavily loaded. QoS routing schemes are, therefore, expected to be more successful than the traditional routing schemes in meeting QoS guarantees requested by the connection.

6.10.1 Routing Algorithms

The complexity of a QoS routing algorithm depends on the chosen QoS constraints such as hop count, bandwidth, delay, delay-jitter etc. Let us now analyze the QoS constraints, as they have a major impact on the complexity of a QoS routing algorithm.

The QoS constraints can be divided into three broad classes [30]. Let $d(i, j)$ denote a chosen constraint for the link (i, j). For any path $P = (i, j, k, \ldots l, m)$, a constraint d would be termed *additive*, if $d(P) = d(i, j) + d(j, k) + \cdots + d(l, m)$. That is, the constraint for a path is the sum of the constraints of the individual links making up the path. For example, end-to-end delay is an additive constraint and is equal to the sum of the delay of the individual links in the path. Jitter, cost, and hop count are a few more important additive constraints.

A constraint is termed *multiplicative*, if $d(P) = d(i, j) \times d(j, k) \times \cdots \times d(l, m)$. For example, reliability constraint is multiplicative. The reliability of a path is given by the product of the reliability of the individual links in the path.

A constraint is termed *concave*, if $d(P) = \min\{d(i, j), d(j, k), \ldots, d(l, m)\}$. That is, for a concave constraint, the constraint of a path is the minimum of all the constraints of the individual links making up the path. An example of a concave constraint is bandwidth. Bandwidth on a path is equal to the minimum bandwidth of a link on that path. Wang and Crowcroft proved that the problem of finding a path subject to two or more additive and/or multiplicative constraints in any possible combination is NP-complete [31]. However, the proof of NP-completeness is based on the assumptions that: 1) all the considered constraints are independent; and 2) the delay and jitter of every link are known a priori. Although the first assumption is normally true for circuit-switched networks; bandwidth, delay, and jitter are not independent parameters in case of packet-switched networks. In spite of this, it is true that determining a route subject to the path constraints is a computationally expensive problem. As a result, polynomial algorithms like Bellman-Ford and the extended Dijkstra's algorithm [27] exist for computing routes with hop count, delay, and jitter constraints. Interestingly, bandwidth and hop count constraints are more important than the delay or jitter constraints, since these two are to a large extent determined by the bandwidth and hop count constraints. Most real-time services require bandwidth as an essential constraint, while the hop count constraint determines effective resource utilization.

In the last two decades, several algorithms have been proposed to address the various problems associated with unicast and multicast routing. Comprehensive reviews of unicast and multicast algorithms for QoS routing are available in [3, 21]. Multimedia applications, which require multicast QoS routing, are becoming very important and are being widely used. In the following, we discuss some issues relevant to multicast QoS routing.

6.10.2 Multicast Routing

Internet is increasingly being used for many firm real-time applications. Video-on-demand and VoIP have already become common place. Besides, many distributed applications require multicast communication. Giving each source an independent point-to-point connection to each destination is an unacceptable approach because of the potential wastage of resources. An approach that is commonly being used is to construct a multicast tree connection which connects each source to all the receivers. Each vertex on a multicast tree would represent either a router or a host.

When there are many sources transmitting to several receivers—during multicast routing, considerable savings of resources can be achieved by having the sources share resources whenever possible. This is because all the sources are not active all the time. For example, in an audio conference, only one (or at best a few) people speak at any time. Therefore, several audio conference connections can share resources to optimally use the resources. In this case, the total resources for all the connections taken together can be significantly smaller than the sum total of the resources required for individual point-to-point connections, and yet meeting the necessary QoS requirements. In such a scenario, we can define a *multicast group* as one in which traffic from a set of sources traverse some common routers and transmission links.

The QoS routing function in a multicast application involves finding a tree rooted at a source and covering all the receivers, with every path from the sender to the receivers satisfying the QoS requirement. There are essentially two basic types of tree construction algorithms: source-based and core-based. In a source-based algorithm, the construction of the multicast tree is achieved by initiating the tree construction from each of the sources, whereas in a core-based algorithm a core is formed first, each receiver then joins the core.

6.11   RESOURCE RESERVATION

A network can provide QoS guarantees to connections only if it can successfully reserve appropriate resources along the identified routes. Merely finding a route that has sufficient resources may not automatically solve the problem of providing QoS guarantees. If no reservation scheme is undertaken, then the traffic being dynamic, can increase and congest the system that, in turn, will hurt the QoS guarantees badly. So, definite allocation of resources helps in safeguarding the QoS guarantees to the individual connections. In this section we discuss a popular and widely used protocol named Resource reSerVation Protocol (RSVP) [32, 35]. RSVP attempts to reduce the bandwidth and buffer space reserved for a multicast group at the routers and links traversed by more than one multicast tree by considering the aggregate requirement of the multicast group as a whole. Further, the reservation is dynamic in nature, that is, a receiver needs to periodically send messages to the routers to maintain its resources. This results in efficient resource usage in the Internet environment, since in the Internet environment receivers may not formally tear down connections when they do not require a connection any more.

6.11.1 Resource reSerVation Protocol (RSVP)

RSVP was designed in 1993 at Xerox Palo Alto Research Center. The idea was to design a resource reservation protocol that can scale to multicast communication and can incorporate heterogeneous receivers. It is important to remember that RSVP is solely a resource reservation protocol, it does not construct any routes. It assumes that the multicast tree has been set up by the routers of the network. Admission of a new multicast connection is handled by the admission control module in a lower layer.

RSVP establishes and maintains a *sink tree* for each destination and uses it to send control messages from each destination. A sink tree is a spanning tree that is rooted at the destination and connects all the sources in a multicast group. It is obtained by tracing in the reverse direction from the destination to every source along the paths in a multicast tree.

Each router used by a multicast group maintains two types of information: *path state* and *reservation state*. The path state of each router consists of the path used by the multicast group. RSVP uses this information to maintain the sink trees of the destination. The reservation state of each router is concerned with resources set aside for different destinations to support the required QoS. The name of the destination (reserver) and the amount reserved are among the information provided by the reservation table.

Protocol Operation: RSVP is a receiver-oriented protocol. That is, the receiver of a data flow initiates and maintains the resource reservation used for that flow. Each router may receive reservation messages from each of the downstream links in the multicast tree, but it sends only one reservation message to its upstream link.

A path message is a control message sent by a source and forwarded by the routers in a multicast tree. Each source sends its first path message before it commences transmission and sends subsequent path messages periodically. Among the information carried in each path message of a source is the flow specification of its message stream. A router updates the *path state* upon receiving the path message from a source.

Each destination sends reservation request messages (resv messages, for short) which are forwarded along the sink tree of the destination. Among the information contained in each reservation message is the flow specification giving the QoS requirement of the receiver.

It is clear that the amount of bandwidth that a router reserves should not exceed the link's capacity. Towards this, whenever the router receives a new reservation message, it determines if its downstream links on the multicast tree can provide the required reservation. If the admission test fails, the router rejects the reservation and returns an error message to the appropriate receiver(s). RSVP does not define any specific admission test, but it assumes that the router performs such a test and that the RSVP can request for such a test to be performed.

The destination sends its first reservation message when it receives a path message from a source whose message stream it wishes to receive. Afterwards it sends reservation messages periodically to maintain reservation. The maintenance of reservation through periodic messages is what sets RSVP apart from most of the other resource reservation protocols. This is called *soft state* and is the preferred design choice for applications that are dynamic in nature. However, the need for each host to periodically transmit messages for the purpose of refreshing the states maintained by routers leads to a higher protocol overhead. This overhead is somewhat lessened by the fact that control messages require lower overhead than data messages. Merging of control messages from all hosts and forwarding whenever there is no new state information, the protocol overhead can further be reduced.

Another concept associated with RSVP is that of a filter. A filter is a list of the names of sources whose message streams can use the resources reserved for the destination. A destination that wants a filter, includes the filter in its reservation message. When no filter is applied, all sources in the multicast group can use the resources reserved for it.

6.12 RATE CONTROL

In a resource sharing packet-switched network, the admission control and service disciplines by themselves are not sufficient to provide performance guarantees. This is so because users may, inadvertently or otherwise, attempt to exceed the rates specified at the time of channel establishment. Rate control is the key mechanism used to prevent the greedy or malicious real-time and non real-time sources from negatively affecting the QoS guarantees given to other connections. Rate control can be achieved using either traffic shaping or policing. Table 6.1 summarizes the main differences between shaping and policing. The choice between which one to use depends on the type of application and its specific QoS requirements.

Several traffic shaping and policing techniques are available. In the following, we discuss an important traffic shaping and policing technique called *token bucket with leaky rate control*.

Token Bucket with Leaky Rate Control: A popular technique used in shaping and policing is token bucket with leaky rate control [27]. The leaky bucket algorithm is a linear bounded arrival process. This technique has schematically been shown in Fig. 6.17. As shown in Fig. 6.17, a bucket can hold up to certain prespecified number of tokens. Assume that a certain token bucket can hold up to b tokens. Tokens are added to this bucket as follows: new tokens that might be added to the bucket are generated at a rate of r tokens per second. If the bucket contains less then b tokens when a token is generated, the newly generated token is added to the bucket, otherwise the newly generated token is ignored, and the token bucket remains full with b tokens.

TABLE. 6.1   Traffic Shaping versus Policing

	Shaping	Policing
Objective	Buffers the packets that are above the committed rates.	Drops the excess packets over the committed rates. Does not buffer.
Handling Bursts	Uses a leaky bucket to delay traffic, achieving a smoothing effect.	Propagates bursts. Does no smoothing.
Advantage	Avoids retransmission due to dropped packets.	Avoids delay due to queuing.
Disadvantages	Can introduce delays due to queuing.	Can reduce throughput of affected streams.

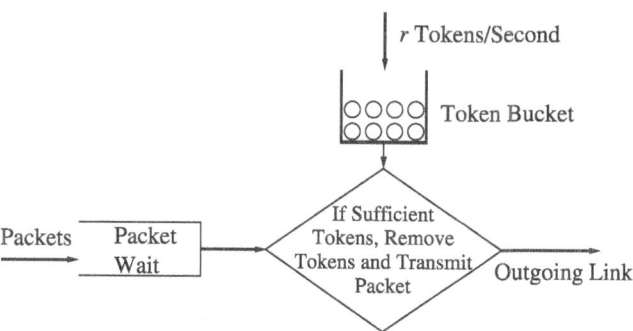

▲ **FIGURE 6.17**

Token Bucket with Leaky Rate Control

In leaky rate control, a waiting packet is taken for transmission only if there is at least one token in the bucket. If enough tokens are not available in the bucket, then the packet waits until the bucket has enough tokens in case of a shaper. However, in case of a policer, the packet is discarded. If transmission of the packet takes place, then the token is removed. Because there can be at most b tokens in the bucket, the maximum burst size of a leaky-bucket-policed flow is b packets. Furthermore, because the token generation rate is r, the maximum number of packets that can enter the network of any interval of time of length t is $rt + b$. Thus, the token generation rate, r, serves to limit the long-term average rate at which the packet can enter the network. This technique can also be used to police the peak rate along with long-term average rate.

6.12.1 Service Discipline

A simple model of an Internet is a collection of sending and receiving nodes and network switches. At every switch, there may be many incoming and many outgoing communication links as shown in Fig. 6.18. Depending upon the destination of a packet, it is queued in the buffer

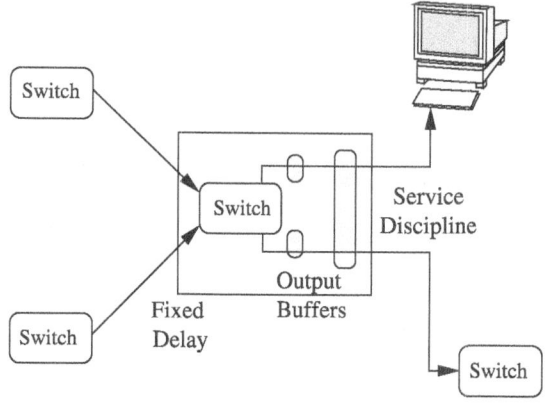

▲ **FIGURE 6.18**

A Model of a Packet Switched Network

of the particular outgoing link. A scheduler selects packets to be transmitted from the buffer at the output link based on some scheduling policy. A service discipline is the terminology used to denote the mechanism used to schedule incoming packets for transmission. For real-time connections, rate-based service disciplines are used to protect the guarantees given to connections from network load fluctuations. This guarantees a minimum service rate to individual connections regardless of the traffic generated by other connections.

A service discipline helps isolate well-behaved guaranteed traffic sources from ill-behaved sources, network load fluctuation and best-effort traffic. An ill-behaving user or a malfunctioning equipment may send packets to the switch at a higher rate than declared. Even when the source is well-behaved, network load fluctuations may cause higher instantaneous arrival rate even from the source, though the traffic satisfied the specified rate at the entrance of the network. That is, a traffic may lose its original rate characteristics as it progresses through the network.

> Unless special care is taken, traffic gets burstier and burstier after it passes through each switch, and it may no longer satisfy its source characterization. This is because the queuing at each switch has a bunching effect on the packets of a session.

For example, if a connection satisfies (σ, ρ) model at the source, then its worst case traffic characterization just before the ith switch becomes $(\sigma + \Delta\sigma, \rho)$, where $\Delta\sigma = \Sigma_{j=1}^{i-1} \rho \cdot d_j^{max}$ and d_j^{max} is the local delay bound for the connection at the jth switch.

In the case of best-effort traffic, since the traffic is not constrained they can very well cause congestion and disrupt the service to the well-behaved guaranteed traffic sources. The service discipline at any time decides output buffers from which packets would be taken up for transmission next. The switch/router does the switching of the data packets from its input port to the desired output port, so that it reaches the destination address. Every switch/router can be modelled as a queue, where packets from different flows compete for the switching processing time and output link. There may be many incoming links to a switch, and a number of virtual connections for each link, and there may be a number of packets in each connection to be served. These packets may compete for the same output link. The manner in which the queued packets are selected for transmission on the link is known as the scheduling discipline. The scheduling discipline at each switch selects which packet to transmit next by discriminating packets based on their QoS requirements.

6.12.2 Traffic Distortion and Its Control

The role of the traffic distortion handling is to modify the input traffic either by reconstructing it to its original source characteristics or by deriving the new traffic characterization at the entrance to the switch assuming the worst case multiplexing. Another way to handle the traffic pattern distortion is to control it at every switch by reconstructing the traffic of a connection to its source characterization. All non-work-conserving disciplines proposed in the literature use this technique. They separate the service discipline into two components:

1. **A rate controller:** It controls the distortion on each connection using regulators and allocates bandwidth to them.
2. **A scheduler:** It orders transmission of packets from different connections, and provides per-connection delay bounds.

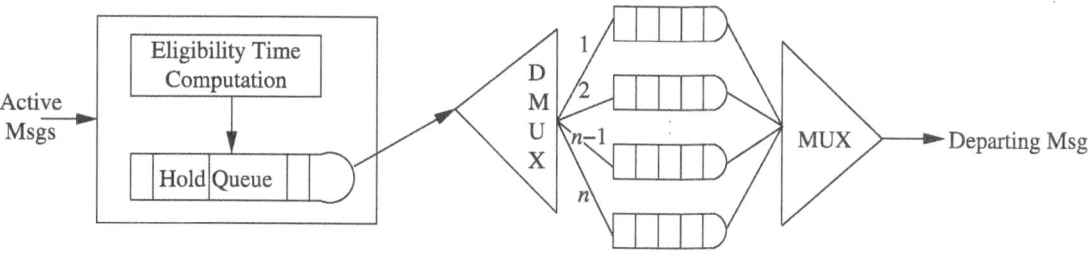

Processing in a Non-Work Conserving Service Discipline

6.12.3 Types of Service Disciplines

There are essentially two types of service disciplines:

- **Work Conserving Discipline:** In work conserving scheduling schemes, the server is never idle if there is a packet to be sent. Thus, a work conserving service discipline forwards an incoming packet on a required outgoing link, as long as the outgoing link is idle. It queues the packet, if the required outgoing link is busy. Thus, work conserving service discipline does not help in achieving traffic shaping. A few of the well-known work-conserving service disciplines are: WFQ, multi-level FCFS queue, and Delay-EDD.

- **Non-Work Conserving Discipline:** In a non-work conserving discipline, each packet is assigned, either explicitly, or implicitly, an eligibility time, a time after which a packet becomes eligible to be serviced (see Fig. 6.19). An outgoing link idles when no packets are eligible for transmission. For supporting best-effort service, conventional service disciplines such as FCFS or round-robin services are sufficient. However, per connection performance guarantees need more elaborate service disciplines. A server is allowed to send only the packets which are eligible and it is never idle as long as there are eligible packets to send. A few of the well-known non-work-conserving disciplines are Jitter-EDD, Stop-and-Go, HRR, and RCSP.

   The type of service discipline being deployed (i.e., work conserving or non-work conserving) affects buffer requirements, delay and delay jitter. Work conserving disciplines need less buffer and cause shorter delay but can not bound delay jitter tightly. The opposite is true for non-work conserving disciplines: they need a larger buffer, cause longer delay, but can bound delay jitter tightly. A comprehensive analysis of various traffic disciplines (both work conserving and non-work conserving) and their relative comparison can be found in [33].

   In the following, we first discuss a few work conserving disciplines, and subsequently, discuss a few non-work-conserving service disciplines.

6.12.4 Work Conserving Discipline

In this subsection, we discuss a few important work-conserving service disciplines.

Multi-level FCFS Queue: It is used to implement static priority schedulers. Each level of a FCFS queue corresponds to a different priority level. Each connection is assigned a priority and all packets from that connection are inserted into the FCFS queue of that priority level. Multiple connections can be assigned to the same priority level. Packets are scheduled in FCFS order from the highest-priority non-empty queue for transmission. The only restriction in using multi-level FCFS queue for static priority schedulers is that the number of different delay bound values that can be provided to the connections are bounded by the number of priority levels of the system.

Weighted Fair Queuing (WFQ):   WFQ [6] has evolved from Fluid Fair Queuing (FFQ), also known as Packet Generalized Processor Sharing (PGPS). In FFQ there is a separate FIFO queue for each connection sharing the same link. During any time interval when there are exactly N non-empty queues, the server serves the N packets at the head of the queues simultaneously, each at the rate of $1/N$th of the link speed. FFQ allows different connections to have different service shares. An FFQ is characterized by N positive real numbers $\phi_1, \phi_2 \cdots \phi_N$, each corresponding to one queue. At any time, the service rate for a non-empty queue i is exactly $(\phi_i / \Sigma_{j \in B(\tau)} \phi_j) * C$ where $B(\tau)$ is the set of non-empty queues and C is the link speed. Therefore, FFQ serves packets in non-empty queues according to their service shares. FFQ is impractical as it assumes that the server can serve all connections with non-empty queues simultaneously and that the traffic is infinitely divisible. In a more realistic packet system, only one connection can receive service at a time and an entire packet must be served before another packet can be served.

6.12.5 Non-Work Conserving Disciplines

In the following, we discuss a few important non-work-conserving service disciplines.

Jitter-Earliest Due Date: Jitter-Earliest Due Date (Jitter-EDD) [29] provides delay-jitter bounds. After a packet has been served at a server, a field in its header is stamped with the difference between its deadline and the actual finishing time. A regulator at the entrance of the next server holds the packet for this period before it is made eligible to be scheduled.

Jitter-EDD is illustrated in Fig. 6.20, which shows the progress of a packet through two adjacent switches i and $i + 1$. As shown in Fig. 6.20, in the first server at switch $i - 1$, the packet got served PreAhead seconds before its deadline. So, in the next server (switch i), it is made eligible to be sent only after PreAhead seconds. Since there is a constant delay between the eligibility times of the packet at two adjacent servers, the packet stream can be provided a delay

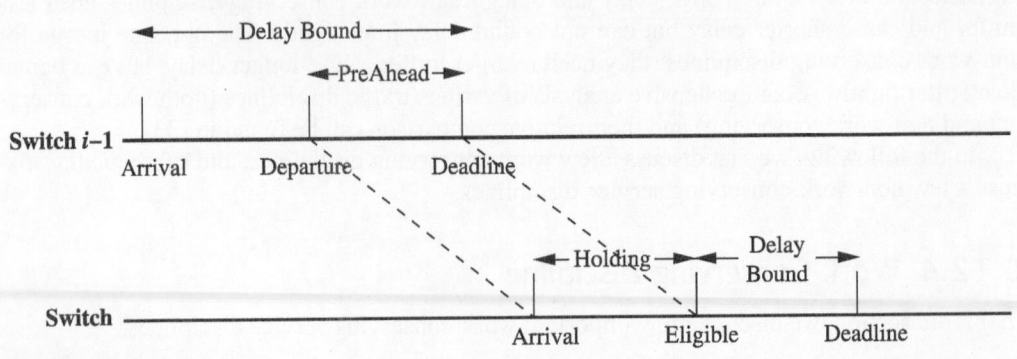

▲ **FIGURE 6.20**

Packet Service in Jitter-EDD

jitter bound. Assuming that there is no regulator at the destination host, the end-to-end delay jitter bound is the same as the local delay bound at the last server.

Stop-and-Go: Stop-and-Go discipline [7] is based on multi-level framing strategy. First, we describe this discipline using one-level framing, and then we extend it to multi-level framing. Let us consider one-level framing first. In one-level framing, at each node, the local time axis is divided into intervals of fixed size T, called a frame. Although convenient, frames of different nodes need not be synchronized. Bandwidth is allocated to each connection as a certain fraction of the frame time, which bounds the average rate of the traffic of a connection, where the averaging interval is T. Stop-and-Go defines departing and arriving frames for each link. At each switch, the arriving frame of each incoming link is mapped to the departing frame of the output link by introducing a constant delay θ, where $0 \leq \theta < T$. According to the Stop-and-Go discipline, the transmission of a packet that has arrived on any link l during a frame f should always be postponed until the beginning of the next frame. Thus, the server remains idle until then, even if there are packets queued for transmission.

The framing strategy introduces the problem of coupling between delay bound and bandwidth allocation granularity. The delay of any packet at a single switch is bounded by two frame times. To reduce the delay, a smaller T is desired. However, since T is also used to specify traffic it is tied to bandwidth allocation granularity. Assuming a fixed packet size P, the minimum granularity of bandwidth allocation is P/T. To have more flexibility in allocating bandwidth, or smaller bandwidth allocation granularity, a larger T is preferred. It is clear that low delay bound and fine granularity of bandwidth allocation can not be achieved simultaneously in a framing strategy like Stop-and-Go.

Multi-level framing is used to get around this coupling problem. In this, the time axis is divided into a hierarchical framing structure shown in Fig. 6.21. For a n level framing with frame sizes $T_1, \ldots, T_n$, and $T_m + 1 = K_m.T_m$ for $m = 1, \ldots, n - 1$, packets on a level p connection need to observe the Stop-and-Go rule with frame size T_p. That is, level p packets which arrived at an output link during a T_p frame will not become eligible for transmission until the start of next T_p frame.

Rate-Controlled Static-Priority: The previously discussed service-disciplines were either based on sorted priority queue mechanism (e.g., WFQ) or framing strategy (e.g., Stop-and-Go). Sorted priority service-disciplines are complex and difficult to implement and framing strategy suffer from the dependencies between queuing delay and granularity of bandwidth. To get around these problems, Zhang and Ferrari [34], proposed Rate-Controlled Static-Priority wherein the function of rate control has been decoupled from delay control.

As shown in Fig. 6.22, an RCSP server has two components: a rate-controller and a static priority scheduler. Conceptually, a rate controller consists of a set of regulators corresponding to each connection; each regulator is responsible for shaping the input traffic of the corresponding connection into the desired traffic pattern. Upon arrival of each packet, its eligibility time is calculated by the regulator and this time is assigned to the packet. The packet is held at the

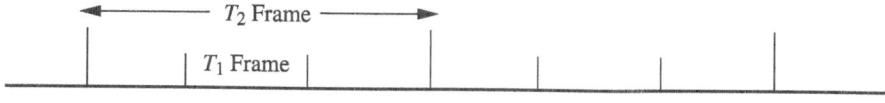

▲ **FIGURE 6.21**

Two-Level Framing with $T_2 = 3 \times T_1$

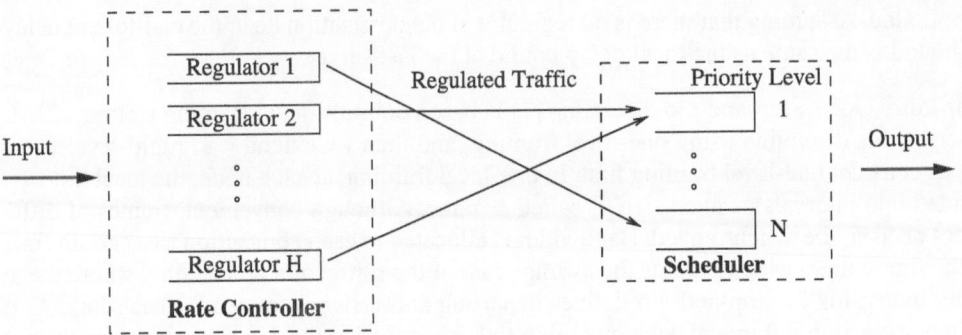

▲ **FIGURE 6.22**

Rate Controlled Static Priority

regulator till its assigned eligibility time expires, after which it is handed to the scheduler for scheduling and transmission. The scheduler is implemented by a multi-level FCFS queue, which serves the packets in order of their priorities, i.e., the first packet is chosen from the highest priority non-empty queue. There are two types of regulators:

- Rate-jitter (RJ) regulator, which controls rate-jitter by partially reconstructing the traffic.
- Delay-jitter (DJ) regulator, which controls delay-jitter by fully reconstructing the traffic. We assume that the RCSP satisfy the (X_{min}, X_{ave}, I) characterization. The (X_{min}, X_{ave}, I) RJ regulator ensures that the output of the regulator satisfy the (X_{min}, X_{ave}, I) traffic model, while the DJ regulator ensures that the output traffic of the regulator is exactly the same as the output traffic of the regulator at the previous server. Thus, if the traffic satisfies the (X_{min}, X_{ave}, I) characterization at network entrance, both types of regulators will ensure that the output of the regulator, which is the input to the scheduler, will satisfy the same traffic characterization.

In an RCSP server the scheduler uses a non-preemptive static priority policy; it always selects the packet at the head of highest priority queue that is not empty. The SP scheduler has a number of priority levels with each priority level corresponding to a delay bound. Each connection is assigned to a priority level during connection establishment time. Multiple connections can be assigned to the same priority level, and all packets on the connections associated with a priority level are appended to the end of the queue for that priority level.

6.13 QoS MODELS

Internet Engineering Task Force (IETF)[2] proposed several models for providing QoS assurances to Internet-based applications. These models are called *QoS models* or *QoS architectures*. The models require that the connections requesting QoS must follow certain procedures to avail QoS guarantees. There are three major QoS models that have been proposed: Integrated Services (IntServ), Differentiated Services (DiffServ) and lastly Multi-Protocol Label Switching

---

[2]The Internet Engineering Task Force (IETF) is a large open international community of network designers, operators, vendors, and researchers concerned with the evolution of the Internet architecture and the smooth operation of the Internet.

(MPLS). DiffServ is an improvement on IntServ, while MPLS is a packet-forwarding scheme having the advantages of both IntServ and DiffServ. In the following, we discuss IntServ and DiffServ service models.

6.13.1 Integrated Services

The Internet has emerged as a common platform for both real-time and non-real-time traffic and thus precludes the need to design a parallel infrastructure for real-time traffic. Use of existing Internet-layer protocol (e.g., IP) for real-time data is proposed so that economy of communication and interoperability between IntServ and non-IntServ networks can be realized. Integrated Services (IntServ) Model [2] includes two types of services targeted towards real-time traffic: guaranteed and predictive services. It integrates these two types of services, and it is designed to work well with multicast as well as unicast traffic. IntServ requires explicit resource reservation to be done, which, in turn, requires flow-specific states to be maintained in the routers.

IntServ is a per-flow based QoS framework with dynamic resource reservation. Routers reserve resources for specific traffic flows using RSVP [32, 35].

As stated earlier, IntServ has been designed to provide two types of services:

- **Guaranteed Service:**Guaranteed service provides an upper bound on end-to-end queuing delay. This service model is aimed to support applications with hard real-time requirements.

- **Predictive Service:**Predictive service can provide only statistical guarantees.

By using per-flow resource reservation, IntServ can provide per flow QoS guarantees. However, introduction of flow-specific states in routers represents a fundamental change to the Internet architecture. Another fact that makes an IntServ difficult to implement is that in the Internet backbone, where thousands of flows may be present, the router may find it impractical to maintain soft states for each flow. The important limitations of IntServ that deter its widespread use can be summarized as follows:

- The amount of state information increases proportionally with the number of flows. This places a huge storage and processing overhead on the routers. Therefore, this architecture does not scale well in the Internet core;

- The routers incur considerable processing overhead. All routers must implement RSVP, admission control, packet classification and packet scheduling techniques;

- Ubiquitous deployment of IntServ is required for guaranteed service. Incremental deployment of IntServ is difficult.

6.13.2 Differentiated Services

To overcome the limitations of IntServ, IETF proposed Differentiated Services (DiffServ) [1], which is simpler and more scalable. DiffServ redefines the Type of Service (TOS) field in the header of IPv4 or IPv6 traffic class byte as Differentiated Service (DS) field. The first six bits of the field are called DS Code Point (DSCP). The different markings of DSCP indicates the behaviour (known as per-hop behaviour or PHB) each router is required to apply to individual packets.

The information required by the buffer management and scheduling mechanisms is carried within the packet. Therefore, differentiated services do not require special signalling protocols to control the mechanisms that are used to select different treatments for the individual packets. Consequently, the amount of state information, which is required to be maintained per node, is proportional to the number of service classes and not proportional to the number of application flows. This is a major improvement over IntServ.

Before a packet enters a DiffServ domain, its DSCP field is marked by the sending-host or the ingress router according to the QoS the packet is entitled to have. Within a DiffServ domain, each router only needs to examine the DSCP field to decide the proper treatment for the packet.

DiffServ is based on an important design principle. It tries to push complex processings associated with QoS provisioning to the network boundary. The network boundary refers to the application hosts, and the edge routers. Since a network boundary handles only a small number of flows, it can efficiently perform tasks such as packet classification and traffic conditioning. In contrast, core routers usually deal with very large number of flows, and should, therefore, only perform simple operations. This differentiation of the network boundary and the core routers is a vital part of the scalability of DiffServ.

Currently, DiffServ provides two service models besides the best-effort model: premium service model and assured service model. Premium service is a guaranteed peak rate service, which is optimized for regular traffic patterns and incurs almost no queuing delays. This model can provide absolute QoS guarantees. An example application of this service class, is a virtual leased line. A virtual leased line can eliminate the cost of having to maintain a separate network for an organization. Assured service class provides statistical guarantees to applications.

SUMMARY

- Real-time communication is different from traditional computer communication because the latter provides best-effort service, where as real-time communication networks can support the Quality of Service (QoS) requirements of applications.

- The QoS parameters that are usually considered by real-time communication networks include delay, jitter, loss rate, and bandwidth (throughput) requirements.

- Real-time communication protocols allow both non-real-time and real-time messages to be handled in the same framework.

- Controller Area Networks (CANs) are small networks spanning a few meters and use simple protocols such as a calendar-based protocol to guarantee the QoS requirements of applications.

- Real-time LANs are useful in industrial and automated home and office environments. The protocols used for supporting QoS guarantees are usually based on Ethernet or token ring protocols. For hard real-time communications, token ring protocols have natural advantages over Ethernet-based protocols.

- In the Internet environment, QoS requirements can be provided by using the techniques of QoS routing, resource reservation, traffic shaping and policing.

- IntServ and DiffServ are two important QoS models for use in the Internet domain.

EXERCISES

1. State whether you consider the following statements to be TRUE or FALSE. Justify your answer in each case.

   (a) Streaming compressed video transmission is an example of real-time VBR (variable bit rate) traffic.

(b) In a logical ring, the order of nodes in the ring must be the same as their order in the physical network.

(c) The virtual time protocol is an example of a bounded access type of scheduling in a multiple access network.

(d) In a bounded access token ring protocol using either the proportional or the local transmission time allocation schemes, the sums of the synchronous bandwidths ΣHi equals 1.

(e) Under normal real-time traffic conditions, the maximum delay suffered by the highest priority packets at a switch when a multi-level FIFO queue-based service discipline is deployed would be lower compared to the case when a framing-based service discipline is deployed.

(f) Real-time computer communication is essentially communication at high data rates.

(g) Under normal traffic conditions, a priority queue-based service discipline would incur less processing overheads at a switch compared to a multi-level FIFO queue-based one.

(h) In the virtual-time protocol, suppose the highest priority packet that a node needs to transmit at some instant of time is m. Then, for efficient working of the protocol, during priority arbitration interval the node should wait for $2 * \delta * m$ time units before starting transmission. (δ is the propagation delay in the network.)

(i) The countdown protocol should work successfully irrespective of whether the priority arbitration transmissions start with either the msb or lsb end of the priority value, as long as all nodes agree on the convention.

(j) Even when a global priority-based message transmission is supported by a real-time communication network, Rate Monotonic Algorithm (RMA) scheduling of real-time messages is ineffective.

(k) For transmitting VBR real-time traffic among tasks over a LAN, a calendar-based reservation protocol would yield higher GP(U) than either a global priority-based, or a bounded access type of protocol. (GP(U) is the guarantee probability at utilization U)

(l) In multiple bounding average rate characterization of bursty traffic, the larger the averaging interval the lower is the rate with which the source is bound.

(m) The (X_{min}, S_{max}) model for real-time traffic can be satisfactorily used for resource reservation to provide QoS guarantee for compressed audio and video signals.
   (In the (X_{min}, S_{max}) model the minimum interarrival time between packets is bounded below by X_{min} and the largest packet size is bounded above by S_{max})

(n) Propagation delay primarily determines the end-to-end delay that a message might suffer while being transferred over a network.

(o) The maximum delay suffered by packets under a multi-level FCFS queue-based service discipline would be lower than that in a framing-based service discipline under similar traffic conditions.

(p) In any practical real-time communication protocol, we can expect that the guarantee probability (GP) to be close to 0 for utilization lower than the Average Breakdown Utilization (ABU) and GP would approach 1 as the utilization increases beyond ABU.

(q) If a certain token-passing network has a channel capacity of 100 mbps, then the IEEE 802.5 (priority-based protocol) would provide higher guarantee probability compared to IEEE 802.4 (timed token protocol) at very low channel utilizations.

(r) The countdown real-time global priority communication protocol should work successfully irrespective of whether the priority arbitration transmissions start with either the msb or lsb end of the priority value, as long as all nodes agree on the convention.

(s) Even when a global priority-based message transmission is supported by a real-time communication network, Rate Monotonic Algorithm (RMA) scheduling of real-time messages is not very effective.

2. Dynamic changes to the reserved resources is an important distinguishing characteristic of the RSVP protocol. Using four or five sentences explain how RSVP protocol is capable of dynamically changing the reservation status of a connection during the life time of the connection.

3. What do you understand by the term "hard real-time communication support by a network?" Give two example applications where hard real-time communication support from the underlying communication network is required. Give an overview of how hard real-time communication can be supported by a network.

4. What do you understand by the term "firm real-time communication support by a network?" Give two example applications where firm real-time communication support from the underlying communication network is required. Give an overview of how firm real-time communication can be supported by a network.

5. In an IEEE 802.4 network, if δ is the shortest deadline of all messages required to be transmitted over the network, identify the pros and cons of making TTRT equal to

    (a) δ (b) $\dfrac{\delta}{10}$ (c) $\dfrac{\delta}{2}$ (d) $2 \times \delta$

6. Answer the following in the context of a chemical manufacturing company that wishes to automate its process control application:

    (a) What problems might arise if an attempt is made to implement the chemical plant control software using the Ethernet LAN available in the factory?

    (b) How can a global priority protocol be supported in a LAN with collision-based access?

    (c) If RMA scheduling of packets is to be supported, what is the maximum channel utilization that can be achieved?

    (d) What are the main obstacles to efficiently implement RMA in this set up?

7. Consider the use of timed token protocol (IEEE 802.4) in the following situation. We have four nodes in the system. The real-time requirement is that node N_i be able to transmit up to b_i kilobytes over each period of duration P_i milliseconds, where b_i and P_i are given in the table below. Assume that the propagation time is negligible compared to TTRT and that the network bandwidth is 1 mbps.

Node	b_i	P_i
$n1$	100 kb	10 mSec
$n2$	200 kb	15 mSec
$n3$	500 kb	100 mSec

    (a) Choose suitable Target Token Rotation Time (TTRT).

    (b) What is the maximum time for which a real-time message may suffer inversion?

    (c) Obtain suitable values of f_i (total number of bits that can be transmitted by the nodes n_1, n_2, and n_3 over every cycle) under proportional and local allocation schemes.

    (d) Determine the worst case times by which n_1 completes transmitting 100 kb of real-time message under each of the two bandwidth allocation schemes.

    (e) Determine the worst case time by which n_1 completes transmitting 100 kb of non-real-time message under each of the two bandwidth allocation schemes.

8. Consider a calendar-based reservation protocol to transmit real-time messages over a collision-based network such as a Controller Area Network (CAN):

    (a) Explain how transmission of asynchronous messages by nodes can be handled. (Asynchronous messages have probabilistic arrival times and do not have any specified time bounds).

    (b) Explain with proper reasoning the types of traffic for which a calendar-based protocol would perform satisfactorily and the types for which it will not.

9. The bandwidth of a priority-based token ring network (IEEE 802.5) is 100 mbps. Assume that the propagation time of the network is 10 mSec. Determine the fraction of bandwidth wasted during every frame transmission, when the frame size is 2 kbps (kilobytes per second) Under what conditions would the wasted bandwidth be zero?

10. Explain two traffic specification models that can be satisfactorily used to specify bursty traffic.

11. Identify the factors which contribute to delay jitter in real-time communications in packet-switched networks. Assume that a certain real-time application receives data at the rate of 10 mbps. The QoS guarantee to the application permits a delay jitter of 20 mSec. Compute the buffer requirement at the receiver.

12. Consider the use of timed token protocol (IEEE 802.4) in the following situation. We have four nodes in the system. The real-time requirement is that node N_i be able to transmit up to b_i bits over each period of duration P_i milliseconds, where b_i and P_i are given in the table below.

Node	b_i	P_i
N_1	1 K	10,000
N_2	4 K	50,000
N_3	16 K	90,000
N_4	16 K	90,000

Choose suitable Target Token Rotation Time (TTRT) and obtain suitable values of f_i (total number of bits that can be transmitted by node N_i over every cycle). Assume that the propagation time is negligible compared to TTRT and that the system bandwidth is 1 mbps.

13. If you are constrained to use an existing Ethernet LAN for a factory automation application, what are the different protocols that you can use to support communicating real-time tasks? Which of the alternatives that you have identified would work best? Give your reason.

14. Consider a 10 mbps token-ring network operating under the priority-based protocol (IEEE 802.5). For this network, the walk time is 2 mSec and the frame length is 1024 bytes. Determine the fraction of wasted bandwidth due to the wait time required for the token to return to the transmitting node after transmission of a frame is complete. At the given bandwidth would a bounded access protocol perform better? Explain your answer.

15. Consider a 10 mbps token ring network. The walk time is 1 mSec and the frame size is 512 bytes. Determine the maximum time for which a message may undergo priority inversion under IEEE 802.4 and IEEE 802.5 protocols.

16. (a) Identify at least two factors which contribute to delay jitter in real-time communications and explain how they cause jitter.

    (b) What is the difference between execution time and response time of a task? In what circumstances can they be different?

17. Consider the use of timed token protocol (IEEE 802.4) in the following situation. We have four nodes in the system. The real-time requirement is that node N_i be able to transmit up to b_i bits over each period of duration P_i milliseconds, where b_i and P_i are given in the table below.

Node	b_i in kilobytes	P_i in milliseconds
N_1	4	10
N_2	10	50
N_3	10	90
N_4	20	100

Choose suitable Target Token Rotation Time (TTRT) and obtain suitable values of f_i (total number of bits that can be transmitted by node N_i over every cycle). Assume that the propagation time is 1 mSec and that the bandwidth of the network is 10 mbps.

18. A (σ, ρ) traffic characterization of a certain packet switched real-time traffic is characterized by a peak traffic (σ) of 100 packets and average traffic rate (ρ) of 10 packets per second. The packet size is 512 bytes. Assuming that the packets undergo a maximum queuing delay of 50 mSec at each of the switches, what would be the traffic characterization after the 10th switch on the route?

19. Consider a 10 mbps token-ring network operating under the priority-based protocol (IEEE 802.5). For this network, the walk time is 2 mSec and the frame length is 1024 bytes. Determine the fraction of wasted bandwidth due to the wait time required for the token to return to the transmitting node after transmission of a frame is complete. At the given bandwidth would a bounded access protocol perform better? Explain.

20. Consider a 10 mbps token ring network. The walk time is 1 mSec. The frame size is 512 bytes. Determine the maximum time for which a message may undergo priority inversion under IEEE 802.4 and IEEE 802.5 protocols.

21. Consider the use of timed token protocol (IEEE 802.4) in the following situation. We have four nodes in the system. The real-time requirement is that node N_i be able to transmit up to b_i bits over each period of duration P_i milliseconds, where b_i and P_i are given in the table below.

Node	b_i in kilobytes	P_i in milliseconds
N_1	4	10
N_2	10	50
N_3	10	90
N_4	20	100

Choose suitable Target Token Rotation Time (TTRT) and obtain suitable values of f_i (total number of bits that can be transmitted by node N_i over every cycler). Assume that the propagation time is 1 mSec and that the bandwidth of the network is 10 mbps.

22. Would it be advisable to use an Ethernet LAN in a hard real-time application such as factory automation? Justify your answer. Evaluate the pros and cons of using an Ethernet-based protocol in such an application.

23. Suggest a scheme that can help handle aperiodic and sporadic messages in a reservation (calendar-based) protocol without making major changes to the protocol.

24. Identify the factors which contribute to delay jitter in real-time communications. Assume that a certain real-time application receives data at the rate of 10 mbps. The QoS guarantee to the application permits a delay jitter of 20 mSec. Compute the buffer requirement at the receiver.

25. In a real-time packet-switched network, explain the roles of a traffic policer and a traffic shaper. Explain one popular traffic shaping and one traffic policing technique.

26. Explain why traffic gets distorted in a packet-switched network and how traffic reshaping is achieved for providing QoS guarantee.

27. Compare the performance of IEEE 802.4 protocol with IEEE 802.5 protocol for real-time applications at high, medium, and low bandwidths.

28. Explain using four or five sentences, how global priority arbitration is achieved using virtual time protocol. At which ISO layer would such a protocol operate?

29. Suppose we have three periodic messages m_1, m_2, and m_3 to be transmitted from three stations S_1, S_2, and S_3, respectively, on an FDDI network. Let the Token Rotation Time (TTRT) be 10 mSec and the walk time be 1 mSec . The transmission time (C_i mSec) and the period of the messages (T_i) are as fol-

lows: $(C_1 = 9$ mSec, $T_1 = 110$ mSec); $(C_2 = 12$ mSec, $T_2 = 150$ mSec); $(C_3 = 15$ mSec, $T_3 = 160$ mSec). Determine the synchronous bandwidth that needs to be allocated to each station for successful transmission of the messages.

30. Explain the important shortcomings of the IntServ architecture in supporting real-time communication. How does DiffServ overcome it?

31. Compare the advantages and disadvantages of using a ring network versus a collision-based network for real-time communication.

32. What is the difference between a work conserving and a non-work-conserving service discipline? Explain how a non-work-conserving service discipline can help in controlling traffic distortion.

33. What do you understand by QoS routing. Explain the different types of QoS routing algorithms.

34. Explain what are the different QoS constraints that are considered during QoS routing. Explain the features of these constraints based on which the constraints can be classified. What are the implications of these features on the routing algorithms?

35. What do you understand by QoS routing? Give some examples of additive, multiplicative, and concave constraints that are normally considered in QoS routing schemes. Explain how these features are considered in QoS routing protocols.

36. Explain the difference between traffic shaping and policing. Name a traffic shaping and policing protocol and briefly describe its operation.

37. What is a Controller Area Network (CAN)? Name a few applications that are based on CAN. Explain a real-time communication protocol that can be used in a CAN.

38. Explain how soft real-time communication with statistical delay guarantees can be provided in an Ethernet LAN environment using rate-adaptive traffic smoothing technique.

39. Explain the different elements that play a role in provisioning QoS guarantees to applications in the Internet.

7 Real-Time Databases

Many real-time applications need to store large amounts of data and process these data for their successful operation. Such storing requirements occur when a controlling system needs to maintain an up-to-date state of the controlled system. A few examples of such systems include a network management system, an industrial control system, and an autopilot system. Whenever storing and processing large amounts of data is required, a database management system is used. The need for a database management system for storage and processing of large volumes of data and the basic issues in Relational Database Management Systems (RDBMS) have been profusely discussed in standard database literature such as [5, 20, 25] and we assume that the reader is already familiar with these issues. The focus of this chapter is Real-Time Database Management Systems (RTDBMS) that are used in data intensive real-time applications, such as network management systems, industrial control systems, autopilot systems, etc.

As traditional database systems do, real-time database systems also serve as repositories of large volumes of data and provide efficient storage, retrieval, and manipulation of data. However, there are a few important differences between traditional and real-time databases.

> The main differences between a conventional database and a real-time database lie in the temporal characteristics of the stored data, timing constraints imposed on the database operations, and the performance goals.

We elaborate these issues in this chapter. It would become clear that these issues make design and development of a satisfactory real-time database application much more difficult and complicated compared to traditional database application.

This chapter has been organized as follows. First, we briefly examine a few applications needing support of a real-time database. Next, we review some of the basic concepts in traditional database technique that are relevant to the discussions in this chapter. Subsequently, we elaborate implications of the temporal characteristics of data in a real-time database. Finally, we discuss some concurrency control protocols that can be used in real-time databases.

7.1 EXAMPLE APPLICATIONS OF REAL-TIME DATABASES

In this section we review a few sample applications that need to use real-time databases. These applications are the representatives of a cross-section of applications having stringent timing requirements. An understanding of these applications would let us view the issues addressed in the subsequent sections in a proper perspective.

Process Control. As already discussed in Example 1.1 of Section 1.1, industrial control systems are usually attached to sensors and actuators. The sensors monitor the state of some real-world processes, and the controllers manipulate the valves. Control decisions are made based on the input data and controller configuration parameters. Input data are generated from field devices such as sensors, transmitters, and switches that are connected to the controller's data acquisition interfaces, and also from other controllers via inter-controller connections. The input data and the controller configuration parameters run into several megabytes of information even for moderately large systems. For successful operation of a typical process control application, the valve control has to be achieved with the accuracy of a few milliseconds. Therefore, the database transactions have to be completed within a few milliseconds, even under worst-case load on the system.

Internet Service Management. Internet traffic has grown phenomenally in the last few years. Also, advanced network services are increasingly becoming available as the Internet Service Providers (ISPs) vie to maintain their edge over each other. Towards this end, service providers are increasingly deploying Service Management Systems (SMS). An SMS lets an ISP create and provide IP services such as e-mail, VPN, LDAP directory services, etc. It also streamlines allocation of resources to subscribers, resource management, and controlling all the relevant network components at a single centralized point in the network. An SMS needs to use a real-time database for performing authorization, authentication, and accounting for the Internet users. The SMS must manage such data as session status as well as information about the network, subscriber, and policies—in the face of the number of subscribers running into millions. Real-time database management systems are used to maintain these data.

Spacecraft Control System. In a spacecraft, a control system is responsible for the successful overall operation of the spacecraft. It is also responsible for receiving command and control information from the ground computer. A spacecraft control system maintains contact with the ground control using antennae, receivers, and transmitters. The control system monitors several parameters relevant to the successful operation of the spacecraft through several sensors mounted on and within the spacecraft. In addition to controlling the regular operation of the spacecraft, the controller also monitors the "health" of the spacecraft (power, telemetry, etc.). The reliability requirements for such systems dictate redundancy in all hardware and software components—increasing the volume of data and adding to the complexity of data management. The controlling information maintained by the controller include the track information. The volume of data maintained by this kind of applications is relatively small and restricted to a few megabytes of information, but the timing and performance attributes are very stringent.

Network Management System. A network management system for modern networks can be quite complex. The network management system stores and deals with large amounts of data pertaining to network topology, configuration, equipment settings, etc. In addition, switches create large amounts of data pertaining to network traffic and faults. The network control, management, and administration operations lead to several real-time transactions on the database for storing and accessing the relevant data.

The database requirements for the above example applications vary in their timing requirements, from microseconds to make routing decisions in a network management system, to milliseconds for opening and closing of valves in an industrial process control application, and seconds for materials movement on a factory floor. However, irrespective of the magnitude of the timing constraint, what is more important is that unless the transaction timing constraints are met, the system would fail.

7.2 REVIEW OF BASIC DATABASE CONCEPTS

In this section we review a few relevant database concepts. However, as already remarked these topics are widely covered in standard database literature such as [5, 20, 25], and the review in this section is by no means intended to be comprehensive. A relational database consists of a set of fact tables. Each fact table consists of several records. In many applications, it is required that the database records are prevented from assuming certain values or certain combination of values. Assertions about the values that the records can assume are called *consistency constraints*.

Database applications are normally structured into transactions. A transaction is a sequence of reads and writes on the database to achieve some high-level function of the application. A database transaction transforms a database from one consistent state to another. Normally, different transactions on a database operate in an interleaved manner. Interleaving the access of different transactions to the database can remarkably improve the throughput and resource utilization of the database. Therefore, one important aim in the design of database systems is to maximize the number of transactions that can be active at a time. A particular sequencing of actions of different transactions is called a *database schedule*. However, concurrent execution of transactions can lead to some database schedules that violate the integrity of the database. Due to the possibility of violation of integrity, databases normally restrict concurrent execution of transactions through the use of *concurrency control protocols*.

Concurrency control protocols maintain the integrity of the data by requiring the transactions to satisfy four important properties known as ACID properties.

Atomicity: Either all or none of the operations of a transaction are performed. That is, all the operations of a transaction are together treated as a single indivisible unit.

Consistency: A transaction needs to maintain the integrity constraints on the database.

Isolation: Transactions are executed concurrently as long as they do not interfere in each other's computations.

Durability: All changes made by a committed transaction become permanent in the database, surviving any subsequent failures.

Let us now examine how ACID properties are ensured in a database in the presence of interleaved execution of transactions. While each transaction preserves consistency of the database at its boundaries, a transaction that fails to complete might cause the integrity of the database to be violated. Rollback protocols are used to ensure atomicity and durability properties when a transaction fails to complete. Isolation can be ensured through the use of locking and rollback protocols.

Let us examine how a rollback protocol works. If a transaction t_j reads a value that was written by an aborted transaction t_i, then t_j must be aborted to enforce the atomicity property. In other words, a transaction might need to be rolled back and restarted because it had read a value that was produced by some other transaction which got aborted. However, it must be remembered that roll backs can lead to cascaded aborts. In this context, rollbacks have important implications for real-time applications—rollbacks often imply undoing significant amounts of accomplished work—the resultant delay in redoing the work could make a transaction miss its deadline.

To ensure the durability property, once a transaction commits, it can not be aborted, neither its effects changed due to cascading aborts. Cascadeless aborts can be achieved by ensuring that every transaction reads only data values written by committed transactions.

7.3 REAL-TIME DATABASES

Before we understand the various issues associated with real-time databases, we must understand how a real-time database differs from a traditional database. There are three main counts on which these two types of databases differ. First, unlike traditional databases, timing constraints are associated with the different operations carried out on real-time databases. Second, real-time databases have to deal with temporal data compared to static data as in the case of traditional databases. Third, the performance metrics that are meaningful to the transactions of these two types of databases are very different. We now elaborate these three issues.

Temporal Data: Data whose validity is lost after the elapse of some prespecified time interval are called temporal data or perishable data. Examples of such data include the following.

- Consider the periodic data generated by a temperature sensor. The temperature sensor transmits sampled temperature data periodically to the controller, say every 100 mSec. As new temperature readings become available, the old temperature data become stale and are reduced to archival data.

- Consider stock market price quotations. As new price quotations come in, data pertaining to previous quotations becomes obsolete.

- Consider the controller of a fly-by-wire aircraft. The fly-by-wire aircraft is expected to travel along a predetermined path. Every few milliseconds, the controller receives the current altitude, velocity, and acceleration data from various sensors mounted on the aircraft. From the received data and the last computed position of the aircraft, it computes the current position of the aircraft and the deviation of the aircraft from the predetermined path. Here, the current position, altitude, velocity, and acceleration values are temporal data, whereas the data representing the predetermined path is a traditional non-temporal data. This example application shows that a real-time database would have to deal with both temporal as well as archival data. In such a system, a database operation might compute results by combining the values of several temporal as well as archival data items.

Timing Constraints on Database Operations: Tasks and transactions are similar abstractions in the sense that both are units of work as well as scheduling. However, unlike real-time tasks, a transaction execution might require many data records in exclusive mode. Also, while the execution times of tasks can reasonably be assumed to be deterministic, the transaction execution times are much more unpredictable, especially if disk accesses are required.

Performance Metric: The most common performance metric for all databases—real-time or not—is transaction response time. For traditional database systems, this characteristic boils down to the number of transactions completed per unit time. This measurement, therefore, is used heavily in optimizing the average response time for traditional (non-real-time) applications. For real-time databases, on the other hand, the typical metric of interest is the number of transactions missing their deadlines per unit time.

7.3.1 Real-Time Database Application Design Issues

Design of a real-time database application is much more intricate than design of databases for non-real-time applications. Let us investigate the reasons behind this. Irrespective of whether real-time or not, database transactions have extensive data requirements. Therefore, in case of real-time databases, if the data is stored in a secondary storage, the delay in accessing the data can make a transaction miss its deadline. Also, it becomes almost impossible to predict the response time for transactions due to the intricate protocols such as concurrency control protocols, commit protocols, and recovery protocols used to maintain the consistency of the database. Secondly, roll backs can have cascading effects and can introduce unpredictable amounts of delay.

In the face of the above mentioned problems, it might appear that use of databases is impractical in hard real-time applications. However, there are several advantages. First, use of an in-memory database can solve the identified problems. Further, it must be remembered that in real-time applications, the set of transactions are simple and are known before hand (e.g., periodic sensor update). These transactions are fixed in the sense that they use the same amount and types of data each time. Therefore, plans for effective resource usage can be made to achieve deterministic transaction executions.

7.4 CHARACTERISTICS OF TEMPORAL DATA

A typical real-time system consists of a controlled system (environment) and a controlling system (computer). In other words, the controlling system maintains an image of the environment through periodic polling of sensor data. On the other hand, the environment is dynamic in nature and keeps changing its state unpredictably. The data representing the current state of the environment is an example of temporal data and is highly perishable. As an example, consider an anti-missile system. In this, the controller maintains accurate information about the state of the missile given by its position, velocity, and acceleration data. The trajectory of an incoming missile is unpredictable and the anti-missile system must maintain the state of the missile given by its current position, velocity, and acceleration values at any time. The current information maintained by the controller should be consistent with the actual state of the environment. This leads to the notion of temporal consistency. The need to maintain consistency between actual data of the environment, and that perceived by the controlling system necessitates the notion of *temporal consistency*.

Since the values of a set of parameters of the environment are recorded in a database table again and again, temporal attributes of these data must be stored. In Subsection 7.4.1, we elaborate how temporal data can be represented in a database. In addition to temporal data, a real-time database may also contain archival data such as the desirable environment state (e.g., robot path). Therefore, real-time databases should be able to handle both temporal as well as archival data. Many transactions might have to combine several temporal data and possibly some archival data to derive new data. For example, in a rocket, the sampled velocity, acceleration, and position values can be used with the pre-stored desired path data to track the path error.

7.4.1 Temporal Consistency

Temporal consistency of data requires the actual state of the environment and the state represented by the database be very close and remain case within the limits required by the application. Temporal consistency of data has the following two main requirements:

Absolute Validity: This is the notion of consistency between the environment and its reflection in the database given by the data collected by the system about the environment.

Relative Consistency: This is the notion of consistency among the data that are used to derive new data.

Before we examine these notions in more detail, let us examine how data items can be represented in a real-time database and the notion of a relative consistency set.

How to Represent Data Items in a Real-Time Database? A data item d can be represented as a triplet d: (value,avi,timestamp). The three components of a data item d are denoted as d_{value}, d_{avi}, and $d_{timestamp}$; where $d_{timestamp}$ denotes the time when measurement of d took place; d_{avi} is the absolute validity interval for the data item d and represents time interval following the $d_{timestamp}$ during which the data item d is considered to have absolute validity; d_{value} represents the value recorded for d. For example, a data item $d = (120, 5 \text{ mSec}, 100 \text{ mSec})$ represents the value of the data item to be 120, recorded at 100 mSec, with an absolute validity interval of 5 mSec.

Relative Consistency Set. Consider a situation where a set of data items is used to derive a new data. For the derived data items to be correct, the set of data items on which it is based must be relatively consistent with each other. For example, in an anti-missile system, the current velocity and position of a missile can be used to predict its new position. In this case, it would be incorrect to use an earlier sampled position with the velocity value to determine the new position of the missile. In other words, relative consistency ensures that only contemporary data items are used to derive new data. The set of data items that are relatively consistent with each other, form a relative consistency set R. Each R is associated with a relative validity interval (rvi), denoted by R_{rvi}. The relative consistency of the data items in the relative consistency set can be determined by using R_{rvi} as explained below.

Based on the above discussions, we can now define the conditions for absolute and relative validity as follows:

Condition for Absolute Validity: A data item d is absolutely valid, if (*Current time* $- d_{timestamp}) \leq d_{avi}$

Condition for Relative Consistency: A set R of data items is relatively consistent, if $d_{timestamp} - d_{timestamp}| \leq R_{rvi}$

Example 7.1

Given a temporal data item $d = (10,2500 \text{ mSec}, 100 \text{ mSec})$ and the value of current time as 2700 mSec. Is the given data item absolutely valid?

Solution.   It has been given that $d_{avi} = 100$. So, d is valid during the interval between 2500 and 2600. Hence, the given data item d is not absolutely valid at the time instant 2700 mSec.

Example 7.2

Let a relative consistency set R be {temperature, pressure} and lat R_{rvi} be 2.

(a) Are temperature = {347°C, 5 mSec, 95 mSec} and pressure = {50 bar, 10 mSec, 97 mSec} relatively consistent?
(b) Are temperature = {347°C, 5 mSec, 95 mSec} and pressure = {50 bar, 10 mSec, 92 mSec} relatively consistent?

Solution.

(a) Temperature = {347°C, 5 mSec, 95 mSec} and pressure = {50 bar, 10 mSec, 97 mSec} are relatively consistent.
(b) Temperature = {347°C, 5 mSec, 95 mSec} and pressure = {50 bar, 10 mSec, 92 mSec} are not relatively consistent.

Example 7.3

Given that a relative consistency set R = {position, velocity, acceleration} and $R_{rvi} = 100$ mSec and following data items: Position = (25 m, 2500 mSec, 200 mSec), Velocity = (300 m/s, 2550 mSec, 300 mSec), Acceleration = (20 m/s^2, 2425 mSec, 200 mSec), Current time = 2600 mSec. Are the given data items absolutely valid? Also, are they relatively consistent?

Solution

Position is absolutely valid as $(2600 - 2500) < 200$
Velocity is also absolutely valid as $(2600 - 2550) < 300$
Acceleration is also absolutely valid as $(2600 - 2425) < 200$
For relative consistency, we have to check whether the different data items are pair-wise consistent. It can be easily checked that the given set of data is not relatively consistent, since for velocity and acceleration: $(2550 - 2425) \nless 100$.

7.5   CONCURRENCY CONTROL IN REAL-TIME DATABASES

Each database transaction usually involves access to several data items, using which it carries out the necessary processing. Each access to data items takes considerable time, especially if disk accesses are involved. This contributes to making transactions of longer duration than a typical task execution in a non-database application. For improved throughput, it is a good idea to start the execution of a transaction as soon as the transaction becomes ready (that is, concurrently along with other transactions already under execution), rather than executing them one after the other. Concurrent transactions at any time are those which are active (i.e., started but not yet complete). The concurrent transactions can operate either in an interleaved or in a "truly concurrent" manner—it does not really matter. What is important for a set of transactions to be concurrent is that they are active at the same time. It is very unlikely to find a commercial database that does not execute its transactions concurrently. However, unless the concurrent transactions are properly controlled, they may produce incorrect results by violating some ACID properties, e.g., result recorded by one transaction is immediately overwritten by another. ACID properties were discussed in Section 7.2. The main idea behind *concurrency control* is to ensure non-interference (isolation and atomicity) among different transactions.

Concurrency control schemes normally ensure non-interference among transactions by restricting concurrent transactions to be *serializable*. A concurrent execution of a set of transactions is said to be serializable, if the database operations carried out by them is equivalent to some serial execution of these transactions. In other words, concurrency control protocols allow several transactions to access a database concurrently, but leave the database consistent by enforcing serializability.

Concurrency control protocols usually adopt any of the following two types of approaches: by disallowing certain types of transactions from progressing, or by allowing all transactions to progress without any restrictions imposed on them, and then pruning some of the transactions. These two types of concurrency control protocols correspond to pessimistic and optimistic protocols. In a pessimistic protocol, permission must be obtained by a transaction, before it performs any operation on a database object. Permissions to transactions to access data items is restricted normally through the use of some locking scheme. Optimistic schemes neglect such permission controls and allow the transactions to freely access any data item they require. However, at transaction commitment, a validation test is conducted to verify that all database accesses maintain serializability. In the following, we first discuss a traditional locking-based concurrency control protocol called 2PL that is being popularly used in commercial non-real-time database management systems. We then discuss how this protocol has been extended for real-time applications. Subsequently, we examine a few optimistic concurrency control protocols designed for real-time applications.

7.5.1 Locking-Based Concurrency Control

First, we discuss 2PL, a popular pessimistic concurrency control protocol and then examine how this protocol has been extended for real-time applications.

2PL: It is a pessimistic protocol that restricts the degree of concurrency in a database. In this scheme, the execution of a transaction consists of two phases: a growing phase and a shrinking phase. In the growing phase, locks are acquired by a transaction on the desired data items. Locks are released in the shrinking phase. Once a lock is released by a transaction, its shrinking phase starts, and no further locks can be acquired by the transaction.

A strict 2PL is the most common protocol implemented in commercial databases. This protocol imposes an additional restriction on 2PL in that a transaction can not release any lock until after it terminates (i.e., commits or aborts). That is, all acquired locks are returned by a transaction only after the transaction terminates or commits. Though, this simplifies implementation of the protocol, a strict 2PL is too "strict" and prevents concurrent executions which could have easily been allowed without causing any violation of consistency of the database. A strict 2PL, therefore, introduces extra delays.

The conventional 2PL is unsatisfactory for real-time applications for several reasons: possibility of priority inversions, long blocking delays, lack of consideration for timing information, and deadlock. A priority inversion can occur, when a low priority transaction is holding a lock on a data item, and a high priority transaction needing the data item waits until the low priority transaction releases the lock. A transaction might undergo long blocking delays, since any other other transaction which might have acquired the data before it would hold it till its completion, and most transactions are usually of long duration types.

Using an example we illustrate how deadlocks can occur in 2PL. Consider the following sequence of actions by two transactions T_1 and T_2 which need access to two data items d_1 and d_2.

T_1: Lock d_1, Lock d_2, Unlock d_2, Unlock d_1
T_2: Lock d_2, Lock d_1, Unlock d_1, Unlock d_2

Assume that T_1 has higher priority than T_2. T_2 starts running first and locks data item d_2. After some time, T_1 locks d_1 and then tries to lock d_2 which is being held by T_2. As a consequence T_1 blocks, and T_2 needs to lock the data item d_1 being held by T_1. Now, the transactions T_1 and T_2 are both deadlocked.

2PL-WP: 2PL-WP (wait promote) is a scheme proposed to over-come some of the shortcomings of the pure 2PL protocol. This scheme can be written in pseudo code form as:

```
                        /* pri(T) denotes priority of transaction
                        T*/
if(pri(TR) > Pri(TH)) then /* TH holds the lock requested by TR */
           TR waits;
           TH inherits priority of TR;
else
           TR waits;
endif
```

It can be observed from the pseudo code that when a data item requested by a high priority transaction is being held by a lower priority transaction, then the low priority transaction inherits the priority of the high priority transaction. 2PL-WP, therefore, deploys a priority inheritance scheme. However, in 2PL-WP, unlike a pure priority inheritance scheme, if a higher priority transaction is aborted while it is being blocked, the elevated priority transaction retains the elevated priority until its termination. This can lead to the following undesirable situation. Under high data contention situations, 2PL-WP would result in most of the transactions in the system executing at the same priority. In this situation, the behaviour of a database deploying 2PL-WP would reduce to that of a conventional database using 2PL. However, under low load situations, 2PL-WP should perform better than 2PL.

2PL-HP: 2PL-HP (high priority) overcomes some of the problems with 2PL-WP. In 2PL-HP, when a transaction requests a lock on a data object held by a lower priority transaction in a conflicting mode, the lock holding lower priority transaction is aborted. This protocol is also known as priority abort (PA) protocol. This protocol can be expressed in the form of the following pseudo code:

```
if (no conflict) then TR accesses D/* TR is the requesting transaction */
    else                            /* transaction TH is holding the data
                                       item, */
                                    /* resolve the conflict as follows. */
if (Pri(TR) > Pri(TH)) then abort TH
    else TR waits for the lock;    /* TR blocks */
```

2PL-HP in addition to being free from priority inversion, is also free from deadlocks.

Experimental results show that real-time concurrency control protocols based on 2PL-HP outperform protocols based on either 2PL or 2PL-WP. This result might appear to be unexpected, since under 2PL-HP work is wasted due to transaction abortions occurring whenever a higher priority task requires a resource locked by a lower priority transaction. However, the result can be justified from the following consideration. Unlike tasks sharing resources intermittently, transactions under 2PL once they acquire data, hold them until their completion or abortion. Thus, the data holding time of a transaction is comparable to the life time of the transaction which is usually quite long. Transactions with resource contention, therefore, undergo serial execution under 2PL rather than serializable execution. This implies that chances of deadline misses by higher priority transactions under 2PL may be more than that in 2PL-HP. In 2PL though the chances of cascaded roll backs are less, but the average transaction execution times have been reported to be longer.

Priority Ceiling Protocol: Let us now discuss Priority Ceiling Protocol (PCP) for databases. Unlike PCP for resource sharing among tasks, PCP in database concurrency control does not make use of any priority inheritance. The main concept involved in this protocol is the establishment of a total priority ordering among all transactions. This protocol associates the following three values with every data object.

Read Ceiling: This value indicates the priority value of the highest priority transaction that may write to the data object.

Absolute Ceiling: This is the highest priority transaction that may read or write the data object.

Read-Write Ceiling: This value is defined dynamically at run time. When a transaction writes to a data object, the read-write ceiling is set equal to the absolute ceiling. However, read-write ceiling is set equal to the read ceiling for a read operation.

The priority ceiling rule is the following.

> A transaction requesting access to a data object is granted the same, if and only if the priority of the transaction requesting the data object is higher than the read-write ceiling of all data objects.

It can be shown that PCP is deadlock free and single blocking. Recollect that single blocking means that once a transaction starts executing after being blocked, it may not block again.

Let us analyze a few interesting properties of this protocol. A property of this protocol is that transactions with priorities that are lower than or equal to the read ceiling are not allowed to read the data objects even in a compatible mode. Such a pessimistic measure has been taken to ensure that a future high priority transaction will not block on low priority writers. Also, after a transaction writes a data item, no other transaction is permitted to either read or write to that data item until the original writer terminates.

Example 7.4

Assume that the read ceiling for a data item d is 20 and the absolute ceiling is 40. This means that highest priority among all the transactions that might read d is 20. After any transaction reads d, the read-write ceiling is set to 20. This prevents any transaction which needs to read d from accessing d.

7.5.2 Optimistic Concurrency Control Protocols

Optimistic Concurrency Control (OCC) protocol, as the name suggests, does not in any way prevent any transaction from accessing any data items it requires. However, a transaction is validated at the time of its commitment and any conflicting transactions are aborted.

> The concept of *validation* (also known as *certification*) is central to all OCC protocols.

If there is little contention and interference among transactions, most transactions would be successfully validated. Under heavy load conditions, however, there can be a large number of transactions that fail the validation test and are aborted. This might lead to severe reduction in throughput and sharp increase in deadline misses. Thus, the performance of OCC protocols can show a marked drop at high loads. We now discuss a few important optimistic concurrency control protocols.

Forward OCC: In this protocol, transactions read and update data items freely, storing their updates into a private work place. These updates are made public only at transaction commit time. Before a transaction is allowed to commit, it has to pass a validation test. The validation test checks whether there is any conflict between the validating transaction and other transactions that have committed since the validating transaction started executing. A transaction is aborted, if it does not pass the validation test. This guarantees the atomicity and durability properties. Since writes occur only at commit time, the serialization order in OCC is the order in which the transactions commit.

OCC Broadcast Commit: In OCC Broadcast Commit (OCC-BC) protocol, when a transaction commits, it notifies its intention to all other currently running transactions. Each of these running transactions carries out a test to check whether it has any conflicts with the committing transaction. If any conflicts are detected, then the transaction carrying out the check immediately aborts itself and restarts.

Note that there is no need for a committing transaction to check for conflicts with already committed transactions, because if it were in conflict with any of the committed transactions, it would have already been aborted. Thus, in OCC-BC once a transaction reaches its validating phase, it is guaranteed commitment. Compared to OCC-forward, it encounters earlier restarts and less wasted computations. Therefore, this protocol should perform better than the OCC-forward protocol in meeting task deadlines. However, a problem with this protocol is that it does not consider the priorities of transactions. On the other hand, it may be possible to achieve better performance by explicitly considering the priorities of the transactions.

OCC-Sacrifice: This protocol explicitly considers the priorities of transactions. Also, this protocol introduces the concept of a *conflict set*. A conflict set is the set of currently running transactions that conflict with the validating transaction. A transaction once reaches its validation stage, checks for conflicts with the currently executing transactions. If conflicts are detected and one or more of the transactions in the conflict set has higher priority than the validating transaction, then the validating transaction is aborted and restarted. Otherwise, all transactions in the conflict set are aborted and restarted. However, this protocol suffers from the problem that a transaction may be sacrificed on behalf of another transaction that is sacrificed later, and so on—leading to wasted computations and deadline misses.

7.5.3 Speculative Concurrency Control

Speculative Concurrency Control (SCC) protocol tries to overcome a major weakness of the OCC protocols. Recollect that OCC protocols ignore the occurrence of conflict between two transactions until the validation phase of one of them. At this time, it may already have become too late to correct the problem by restarting one of the transactions, especially if the transactions have tight deadlines. To overcome this problem, in SCC, conflicts are checked at every read and write operations. Whenever a conflict is detected, a new version (called the shadow version) of each of the conflicting transactions is initiated. The primary version executes as any transaction would execute under an OCC protocol, ignoring the conflicts that develop. Meanwhile, the shadow version executes as any transaction would do under a pessimistic protocol—subjected to locking and restarts. The idea is to always keep a clean version (a version without any conflicts) in case it is ever needed. This should help in meeting the deadlines of tasks with tight deadlines. When a shadow reaches a point of conflict, it blocks any transaction under a pessimistic protocol. When the primary version commits, any shadow associated with it is discarded. In addition, any shadow whose serializability depends on the discarded shadows is also discarded. However, when the primary transaction aborts, the shadow starts off executing under OCC as the new primary.

As in the OCC protocols, in SCC protocol also all updates made by a transaction are made on local copies and, therefore, are not visible until the transaction commits.

7.5.4 Comparison of Concurrency Control Protocols

Before we discuss the relative performance of the different categories of protocols, we highlight some aspects of concurrency control protocols that have significant bearings on their performance. This would help us understand the results obtained from experiments in proper perspective. Locking-based algorithms tend to reduce the degree of concurrent execution of transactions, as they construct serializable schedules. On the other hand, optimistic approaches attempt to increase parallelism to its maximum, but they prune some of the transactions in order to satisfy serializability. In 2PL-HP, a transaction could be restarted by, or wait for another transaction that will be aborted later. Such restarts and/or waits cause performance degradation.

Unlike 2PL-HP, in optimistic approaches when incorporating broadcast commit schemes (OCC-BC), only validating transactions can cause restart of other transactions. Since all validating transactions are guaranteed commitment at completion, all restarts generated by such optimistic protocols are useful [26]. Further, the OCC protocols have the advantage of being non-blocking and free from deadlocks—a very desirable feature in real-time applications.

Performance study results for the different categories of concurrency control protocols are shown in Fig. 7.1. As can be intuitively expected, at zero contention, all the three types of protocols

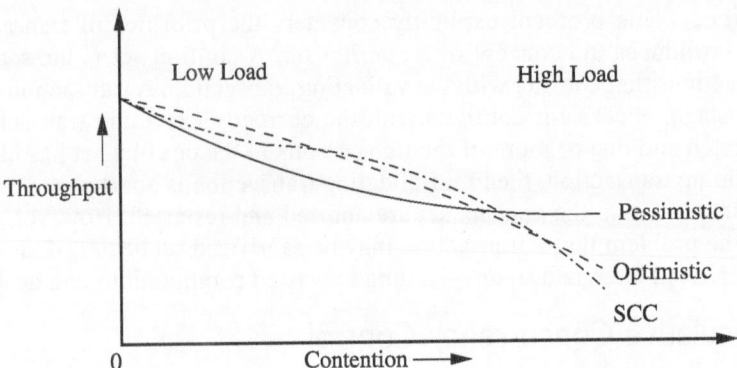

▲ FIGURE 7.1

Performance of Different Categories of Concurrency Control Protocols

result in identical performance. From Fig. 7.1 it can be seen that at low conflicts OCC outperforms pessimistic protocols. However, pessimistic protocols perform better as the load (and, therefore, the conflicts) become higher. On the other hand, SCC performs better compared to both OCC and pessimistic protocols, when transactions have tight deadlines and the load is moderate.

7.6 COMMERCIAL REAL-TIME DATABASES

A commercial real-time database needs to avoid using anything that can introduce unpredictable latencies. Thus, a commercial real-time database needs to avoid using disk I/O operations, message passing or garbage collection. Real-time databases, therefore, tend to be designed as in-memory database systems. In-memory databases do away with disk I/O entirely, and their simplified design (compared to conventional databases) minimizes message passing. Similar to non-real-time disk-based databases, in-memory databases provide database integrity through the use of conventional disks for logging and periodic checkpoints. To meet the high availability demands of applications, some in-memory databases offer data replication.

An example of a commercial real-time database is McObject's eXtremeDB (http://www.mcobject.com). eXremeDb has successfully been used in applications such as telecommunication, factory automation, process control, consumer electronic devices, and medical equipment. eXtremeDB provides applications with direct access to data that is, the database is mapped directly into the application's address space, eliminating expensive buffer managements. The eXtremeDB runtime component is directly linked to the application, eliminating the need for remote procedure calls from execution path. To provide performance and predictability, eXtremeDB uses its own memory manager for allocations and deallocations made by the database runtime. Not relying on the operating system's memory management also enables eXtremeDB to remove the bottleneck of paging data in and out during I/O operations. For supporting transaction deadline management, eXtremeDB supports five priority levels that can be assigned to transactions.

SUMMARY

- A transaction is a unit of execution in a database application, and is a concept similar to a task in a non-database application.

- Major differences between a task and a transaction include high data usage by transactions. Further, it is very difficult to predict transaction response times due to issues such as I/O scheduling (disk access), buffering, concurrency control, commit and recovery protocols used, etc. As a consequence, real-time databases used in hard real-time applications are rarely disk-based.

- Use of an appropriate concurrency protocol is important to meet transaction deadlines. The standard 2PL protocol when used in real-time databases results in many problems: long and unpredictable delays, unbounded priority inversions, and deadlocks.

- For real-time applications, an improvement of 2PL is 2PL-WP, but it behaves as badly when number of transactions and resource sharing are large. 2PL-HP overcomes some of the problems of 2PL-WP, but may result in wastage of large amounts of completed work.

- Optimistic concurrency control (OCC) protocols allow unrestricted data usage by transactions. However, they subject a committing transaction to a validation test at the time of commitment. These protocols work the best under low resource constraints and low load situations.

EXERCISES

1. State whether you consider the following statements to be TRUE or FALSE. Justify your answer in each case.

   (a) For temporal data used in a real-time application, a set of data that is absolutely consistent, is guaranteed to be relatively consistent.

   (b) The performance of the 2PL-WP protocol is better than the basic 2PL protocol when the data contention among transactions is low, but the performance becomes worse than the basic 2PL protocol under high data contention among transactions.

   (c) 2PL-WP protocol used in concurrency control in real-time databases is free from deadlocks.

   (d) 2PL-HP protocol used in concurrency control in real-time databases, is free from priority inversion and deadlocks.

   (e) Under the OCC-BC protocol used in concurrency control in real-time databases, once a transaction reaches the validation phase, it is guaranteed commitment.

   (f) In a real-time database management system, an optimistic concurrency control (OCC) protocol should be used if the choice is based purely on performance (percentage of tasks meeting their deadlines) considerations.

   (g) OCC-BC protocol requires a committing transaction to check for possible conflicts with already committed transactions before it can commit.

   (h) The serialization order under a pessimistic concurrency control protocol is the same as the committing order of the transactions.

   (i) Real-time databases typically use RAID disks for data storage during system operation.

   (j) Optimistic Concurrency Control (OCC) protocols used for concurrency control in real-time databases are free from deadlocks.

   (k) All OCC protocols essentially perform forward validations just before their commitment, i.e., a transaction validates itself with already completed transactions.

2. Explain how a real-time database differs from a conventional database.

3. Explain a few practical applications requiring the use of a real-time database.

4. What do you understand by *temporal data*? How are temporal data different from traditional data? Give some examples of temporal data.

5. Suppose, temporal data are denoted using triplets of the form {value, avi, timestamp} and that the different components of the temporal data have their usual meanings. Assume that the relative consistency set R={pressure,temperature} and R_{rvi} = 2 mSec. Suppose the temperature and pressure samples taken at some time instant are given by 223°C, 5 mSec, 112 mSec and 77°C, 10 mSec, 114 mSec} respectively. At the time instant 120 mSec, determine whether the temperature and pressure samples are i) absolutely consistent, ii) relatively consistent.

6. What is the role of a *concurrency control protocol* in a database? Why is selection of an appropriate concurrency control protocol important to meet the timeliness requirements for transactions? Explain the different categories of concurrency control protocols that can be used in real-time databases. Also, explain which category of protocol is best suited under what circumstances.

7. Traditional 2 phase locking (2PL) based concurrency control protocol may not be suitable for use in real-time databases. Why? Explain how the traditional 2PL protocol can be extended to make it suitable for use in real-time database applications.

8. For real-time applications, rank 2PL, SCC, and OCC protocols in terms of the percentage of transactions meeting their deadlines. Consider low and high degrees of conflicts among transactions, and tight and lax transaction deadlines. Explain briefly.

Glossary

AD converter An analog-to-digital converter (ADC) is used to sample an analog signal and convert the sampled value to a digital value. It is typically used to help represent an analogue signal to a computer.

avionics It is the on-board electronics used to help pilot an aircraft. Important components of an avionic system include communications subsystem, navigation subsystem, autopilot subsystem and electronic flight management subsystem.

base station A base station consists of a Base Station Controller (BSC) and a Base Transceiver Station (BTS). The BSC controls the radio signals of a cell site, and performs functions such as frequency assignment and hand-off. A BTS consists of an antenna and other radio equipment used for providing wireless service in an area.

cable modem This is a type of modem that allows people to access Internet services via their cable television network from their home computers (or network of home computers).

CAT Computerized axial tomography (CAT) is a method of examining body organs by scanning them with X-rays and using a computer to construct a series of cross-sectional scans along an axis—popularly known as a CAT scan.

cellular system It is a hand-held mobile radio telephone system. It can be used over a geographic area of several square kilometres. The area is divided into small sections called cells and each cell has its own base station.

CNC equipment A Computerized Numerical Control (CNC) equipment uses a stored program to automatically fabricate a design. For example, a CNC lathe can be fed a fabrication model in the form of a program. It can then carry this out on many work products to generate a required shape. Similarly, a CNC drilling machine can carry out automatic drilling on several work products based on a stored program.

distributed system A distributed system consists of multiple independent computers spread over a geographic area, and connected to each other over a communication network. The individual computers in a distributed system do not have any shared memory. Therefore, these are also called *loosely-coupled systems*.

DSP Digital signal processing (DSP) refers to using computers to process signals such as sound, video, and other analogue signals which have been converted to digital form. Some uses of DSP are to decode modulated signals from modems, to process sound, video and images in various ways, and to understand data from sonar, radar and seismological readings. A digital signal processor is a specialized CPU used for digital signal processing.

ethernet It is a widely used local area protocol. It implements the IEEE 802.3 standard and is based on the CSMA/CD protocol.

FDDI Fibre Distributed Data Interface (FDDI) is a standard for data transmission in a local area network that can extend in range up to 200 km (124 miles). The FDDI protocol is based on the token ring protocol. An FDDI local area network can support thousands of users. The underlying medium is usually optical fibre. However, it can be copper cable as well, in which case it is called Copper Distributed Data Interface (CDDI). An FDDI network contains two token rings, in which tokens rotate in opposite directions. One of the rings is normally used for possible backup in case the primary ring fails. The topology of FDDI is, therefore, a dual-attached, counter-rotating token ring. The primary ring offers up to 100 Mbit/s capacity. If the secondary ring is not needed for backup, it can also carry data, extending capacity of the network to 200 Mbit/s. FDDI is a product of American National Standards Institute (ANSI) and conforms to the open system interconnect (OSI) model of functional layering. FDDI has been largely made redundant by the availability of fast Ethernet and more recently gigabit Ethernet, on cost and speed considerations.

flash memory Flash memory is a type of Electrically Erasable and Programmable Read-Only Memory (EEPROM). Flash memory differs from EEPROM in that EEPROM erases its contents one byte at a time. This makes it slow to update. Flash memory, on the other hand, erases its data in entire blocks, making it a preferable technology for applications that require frequent updating of large amounts of data as in the case of a memory stick. Memory sticks are popularly used in digital cameras and several other embedded applications. However, there is a bound of the order of a million updates that a flash memory can sustain.

Of late, flash memory is being used as pen drives. Pen drives are available in capacities exceeding 1GB and can even be used as a hard drive. Flash memory can be used as a hard drive when the number of memory updates required is not very large as in Apple Computer's iPod. In this case, it has many advantages over a traditional hard drive. It is non-volatile, does not have any moving parts; it is silent, much smaller than a hard drive, weighs much less and consumes much less power than a hard drive, and has a much faster access time. However, the advantages of a traditional hard drive include more competitive price and much higher capacity. However, the prices of flash memory are falling very rapidly (about 50% every year) and the capacities are rising.

flight simulation Flight simulation is based on a simulator that tries to simulate (that is, replicate) the experience of flying an airplane as closely and as realistically as possible. The different types of flight simulators that are now available range from video games, to full-sized cockpit replicas mounted on hydraulic platforms, controlled by state of the art computer technology to give a realistic feel of flying.

GPS A global positioning system (GPS) consists of a constellation of satellites which orbits the earth, transmitting precise time and position information. A GPS receiver on earth can compute the difference in time that signals from different satellites take to reach the receiver, and from this it can determine the precise latitude and longitude of its current position.

hub A hub (sometimes referred to as a concentrator) is a common connection point for nodes in a network. Hubs are commonly used to connect the different segments of a LAN. A hub contains multiple ports. When a packet arrives at one port, it is copied to the other ports, so that all segments of the LAN can see all packets being transmitted.

In its simplest form, a hub works by duplicating the data packets received via one port and making it available on all ports, therefore, allowing data sharing among all devices connected to the hub. On the other hand, a *manageable* (or intelligent) hub allows the data transfer to be monitored and the ports to be configured individually. Another type of hub, called a switching hub, reads the destination address of each packet and then forwards the packet to the correct port.

internet routers It is a special-purpose computer (or software package) that handles the connection between two or more packet-switched networks. Routers spend all their time looking at the source and destination addresses of the packets passing through them and deciding which route to send them on.

internet telephony Internet telephony is used to transport telephone calls over the Internet.

IP address This is a dot-decimal notation that is used to identify computers on a network.

LDAP Lightweight Directory Access Protocol (LDAP) is a software protocol for enabling anyone to locate organizations, individuals and other resources such as files and devices in a network, whether on the public Internet or on a corporate intranet. LDAP is a 'lightweight' (small amount of code) version of Directory Access Protocol (DAP), which is a part of X.500, a standard for directory services in a network. LDAP is lighter because in its initial version it did not include security features. Because it is a simpler version of X.500, LDAP is sometimes called X.500-lite. Because LDAP is an open protocol, applications need not worry about the type of server hosting the directory.

On TCP/IP networks (including the Internet), the domain name system (DNS) is the directory system used to relate the domain name to a specific network address (a unique location on the network). However, you may not know the domain name. LDAP allows you to search for an individual without knowing where they are located. LDAP can assist in this search.

An LDAP directory is organized in a simple 'tree' hierarchy consisting of the following levels:

- The root directory (the starting place or the source of the tree), which branches out to;
- Countries, each of which branches out to;
- Organizations, which branch out to;
- Organizational units (divisions, departments and so forth), which branches out to (includes an entry for);
- Individuals (which includes people, files and shared resources such as printers).

LDAP originated at the University of Michigan and has been endorsed by at least 40 companies. Netscape includes it in its latest Communicator suite of products. Microsoft includes it as a part of what it calls Active Directory in a number of products including Outlook Express. Novell's NetWare Directory Services interoperates with LDAP. Cisco also supports it in its networking products.

MPEG MPEG is a standard set by the Moving Picture Experts Group (MPEG) for the compression and encoding of sound and video images. The Moving Picture Experts Group is a working group of ISO/IEC charged with the development of video and audio encoding standards. MPEG uses lossy data compression. In a lossy transform, samples of picture or sound are taken, chopped into small segments, transformed into a frequency space, and quantized. The resulting quantized values are then entropy coded. MPEG also adds extra steps to predict the picture content from past reconstructed images, and only the extra information needed to perform the prediction, are coded. This results in better compression.

MRI scanner An Magnetic Resonance Imaging (MRI) scan is a radiology technique which uses magnetism, radio waves and a computer to produce images of body structures. The magnetism in an MRI scanner is produced by a giant circular magnet surrounding a tube that acts as the platform.

multimedia multicast Multimedia applications include a synchronized set of flows of different media, such as data, voice and video. In multicast transmissions, any host can transmit to several receivers called a *multicast group*. Any host can join a multicast group and receive data. Multimedia multicast can efficiently use available network bandwidth for continuous media communications.

multiprocessor In a multiprocessor system, multiple processors share a centralized memory. Therefore, a multiprocessor is also called a *shared memory system*. A multiprocessor system is also known as a tightly coupled system.

packet switching It is a method of sending messages over a network, after fragmenting messages into packets. Each packet has a size less than a maximum limit defined by the network. Packet switching does not require any end-to-end connection to be established between the sender and the receiver.

piezoelectricity Piezoelectricity denotes the electricity produced by mechanical pressure (from Greek word piezein) on certain crystals, notably quartz or Rochelle salt. In a piezoelectric material, application of pressure or stress results in development of charge on the surface of the material. Conversely, application of charge to the same material can result in a change in mechanical dimensions leading to development of strain.

photo-voltaic cell A photo-voltaic cell (also known as a solar cell) is a semiconductor device consisting of a large-area p–n junction diode, which, in the presence of sunlight is capable of generating electrical energy. This conversion is called the *photo-voltaic effect*.

PSTN A public switched telephone network (PSTN) is a collection of interconnected telephone systems operated by various telephone companies (Telcos) and administrations around the world.

satellite tracking system It is a system for tracking positions on the Earth's surface by comparing radio signals received from several orbiting satellites. An example of a satellite tracking system is a global positioning system (GPS).

set-top box The term set-top box refers to an electronic device that sits on top of a television set and is the interface between the home television and some communication channels such as telephone, ISDN, optical fibre or cable.

streaming audio/video A technique for transferring data such that it can be processed as a steady and continuous stream. Streaming technologies are becoming increasingly important with the growth of the Internet because most users do not have fast enough access to download large multimedia files quickly. With streaming, the client browser or plug-in can start displaying the data before the entire file has been transmitted.

For streaming to work, the client side receiving the data must be able to collect the data and send it as a steady stream to the application that is processing the data and converting it to sound or pictures. This means that if the streaming client receives the data more quickly than required, it needs to save the excess data in a buffer. If the data does not come quickly enough, however, the presentation of the data will not be smooth. For audio data on the Internet, Progressive Network's RealAudio is being widely used.

switches A switch is a computer networking device that connects several local area network (LAN) segments. Looked from a different perspective, a switch effectively splits a large network into small segments, decreasing the number of nodes that share the network resources, resulting in higher transmission capacity.

symbolic debugger A conventional debugger works by examining the binary image of the program. In contrast, a symbolic debugger enables a programmer to display the lines of the original source code file, and the values of variables by referencing the variable name. It is called a symbolic debugger because variables and functions are accessed by using the symbolic names given to them in the source code file, rather than by interpreting Hex code.

system call All operating systems provide services to the user to perform low-level operations. For example, as a user you can write down a command such as mkdir at the command prompt to create a directory. However, as a programmer if you want to avail an operating system service from within a program code, you have to invoke the corresponding system call (posix system call for creating a directory has the following synopsis: *int mkdir (const char *path, mode_t mode);*).

system generation It is a utility that enables an operating system to properly configure and setup hardware and software configurations. It often requires relinking the object modules of the operating system.

TCP/IP TCP/IP stands for Transmission Control Protocol/Internet Protocol. It is a protocol suite for communication between computers. It is used as a standard for transmitting data over networks and is the basis for the immensely popular Internet. Internet Protocol is a connectionless protocol responsible for packet routing. The Transmission Control Protocol (TCP) is layered above the Internet Protocol (IP). These protocols were developed by DARPA to enable communication between different types of computers and computer networks. TCP is connection-oriented and provides reliable communication and multiplexing.

thermocouple A thermocouple is often used to measure temperature. A thermocouple consists of two wires of different metals joined at both ends. One junction is maintained at the temperature to be measured and the other is held at a fixed lower temperature. The current generated in the circuit is proportional to the temperature difference between the two joints.

transformer-coupled circuit When two electrical circuits are transformer-coupled, no direct current flows between them and they are said to be electrically isolated.

URL A uniform resource locator (URL) is an address of a web page (or web site) on the world wide web (WWW). To visit a certain web page, one needs to type in the respective URL to a browser.

VPN A virtual private network (VPN) is a network that uses a public telecommunication infrastructure, such as the Internet, to provide remote offices or individual users with secure access to their organization's network. A virtual private network can be contrasted with an expensive system of owned or leased lines that can only be used by one organization. The goal of a VPN is to provide the organization with the same capabilities, but at a much lower cost. A VPN works by using the shared public infrastructure while maintaining privacy through security procedures and tunneling protocols such as the Layer Two Tunneling Protocol (L2TP). In effect, the protocols, by encrypting data at the sending end and decrypting it at the receiving end, send the data through a 'tunnel' that cannot be 'entered' by data that is not properly encrypted. An additional level of security involves encrypting not only the data, but also the originating and receiving network addresses.

Bibliography

[1] D. Blake, S. Black and M. Carlson. An architecture for differentiated services. *RFC 2475*, Dec. 1998.

[2] D. Braden, R. Clark and S. Shenker. Integrated services in the Internet architecture: An overview. *Internet RFC 1633*, Jun. 1994.

[3] S. Chen and K. Nahrstedt. An overview of quality-of-service routing for the next generation high-speed networks: Problems and solutions. *IEEE Network: Special Issue on Transmission and Distribution of Digital Video*, Nov./Dec. 1998.

[4] B. Dasarathy. Timing constraints of real-time systems: Constructs for expressing them, methods for validating them. *IEEE Transactions on Software Engineering*, Vol. 11(1): 80–86, Jan. 1985.

[5] C.J. Date. *Database in Depth*. O'Reily, 2005.

[6] S. Demers, A. Keshav and S. Shenker. Analysis and simulation of a fair queuing algorithm. *Proceedings of ACM SIGCOMM '89, Austin TX*, pp. 1–12, Sep. 1989.

[7] S.J. Golestani. A stop-and-go queuing framework for congestion management. *SIGCOMM'90 Symposium, Communications Architecture and Protocol, Philadelphia, PA*, pp. 8–18, Sep. 1990.

[8] S. Heath. *Embedded Systems Design*. Elsevier, 2003.

[9] J.L. Hennessy and D.A. Patterson. *Computer Architecture—A Quantitative Approach*. Morgan Kaufmann, 2003.

[10] S. Kamat, N. Malcolm and W. Zhao. Performance evaluation of a bandwidth allocation scheme. *Proceedings of IEEE Real-Time Systems Symposium*, pp. 34–43, Dec. 1993.

[11] R.P. Kar and K. Porter. Rhealstone—A real-time benchmarking proposal. *Dr. Dobb's Journal*, Feb. 1989.

[12] C.M. Krishna and Shin K.G. *Real-Time Systems*. Tata McGraw-Hill, 1997.

[13] J.F. Kurose and K.W. Ross. *Computer Networking—A Top down Approach*. Pearson Education Asia, 2002.

[14] S.K. Kweon, K.G. Shin and G. Workman. Achieving real-time communication over ethernet with adaptive traffic smoothing. *Proceedings of 6th IEEE Real-Time Technology and Applications Symposium (RTAS'2000), Washington D.C., USA*, pp. 90–100, 31 May–2 Jun. 2000.

[15] S.K. Kweon, K.G. Shin, and Q. Zheng. Statistical real-time communication over ethernet for manufacturing automation systems. *Proceedings of IEEE Real-Time Technology and Applications Symposium*, pp. 192–202, 1999.

[16] A. Cilingiroglu, S. Lee and A. Agarwala. Real-time Communication. *University of Maryland Institute for Advanced Computer Studies. Department of Computer Science, University of Maryland*, Jan. 1997.

[17] John L. Lehoczky and Lui Sha. The rate-monotonic scheduling algorithm: Exact characterization and average case behaviour. *Proceedings of Real-Time Systems Symposium*, pp. 166–171, Dec. 1989.

[18] C. Liu and J.W. Layland. Scheduling algorithms for multiprogramming in hard real-time environment. *Journal of ACM*, Vol. 20(1):46–61, 1973.

[19] N. Malcolm and W. Zhao. Hard real-time communication in multiple access networks. *Journal of Real-Time Systems*, Vol. 9:75–107, 1995.

[20] Ramakrishnan Raghu. *Database Management Systems*. McGraw-Hill, 2002.

[21] D. Salama, H. Reeves and I. Viniotis. Comparison of multicast routing algorithms for high-speed networks. *IBM Technical Report, IBM-TR29.1930*, 1994.

[22] Brian Santo. Embedded battle royale. *IEEE Spectrum,* pp. 36–42, Dec. 2001.

[23] L. Sha and R. Rajkumar. Mode change protocols for priority-driven preemptive scheduling. *Real-Time Systems,* Vol. 1(3):243–265, Dec. 1989.

[24] L. Sha, R. Rajkumar and J.P. Lehoczky. Priority inheritance protocols: An approach to real-time synchronization. *IEEE Transactions on Computers,* Vol. 39:1175–1185, 1990.

[25] H.F. Silbershatz, A. Korth and S. Sudarshan. *Database System Concepts.* McGraw-Hill, 2005.

[26] X. Song and W.S. Liu . Maintaining temporal consistency: Pessimistic vs. optimistic concurrency control. *IEEE Transactions on Knowledge and Data Engineering,* Vol. 7(5):786–796, Oct. 1995.

[27] A.S. Tanenbaum. *Computer Networks, 3rd edition,* Prentice Hall of India, 1997.

[28] C. Venkatramani and T.S. Chiueh. Supporting real-time traffic on ethernet. *Proceedings of 15th IEEE Real-Time Systems Symposium,* pp. 282–286, 1994.

[29] H. Verma, D. Zhang and D. Ferrari. Guaranteeing delay jitter bounds in packet switching networks. *Proceedings of Tricomm'91, Chapel Hill, North Carolina,* pp. 35–46, Apr. 1991.

[30] B. Wang and Chao-Ju Hou. A survey on multicast routing and its qos extension: Problems, algorithms and protocols. *IEEE Network Magazine,* Vol. 14(1), Feb. 2000.

[31] Z. Wang and J. Crowcroft. Qos routing for supporting resource reservation. *IEEE Journal of Special Areas of Communication,* Sep. 1996.

[32] P.P. White. Rsvp and integrated services in the internet: A tutorial. *IEEE Communications,* May 1997.

[33] H. Zhang. Service disciplines For guaranteed performance service in packet switching networks. *Proceedings of the IEEE,* Vol. 85(10), Oct. 1995.

[34] H. Zhang and D. Ferrari. Rate-control static-priority queuing. *Proceedings of IEEE INFOCOM'93, San Francisco, CA,* pp. 227–236, 1993.

[35] S. Zhang, L. Deerling and D. Estrin. Rsvp: A new resource reservation protocol. *IEEE Network Magazine,* Sep. 1993.

Index